Visions of the Lamb of God

# Visions of the Lamb of God

A Commentary on the Book of Revelation

Andrew Scott Brake

WIPF & STOCK · Eugene, Oregon

VISIONS OF THE LAMB OF GOD
A Commentary on the Book of Revelation

Wipf & Stock
An Imprint of Wipf and Stock Publishers
199 W. 8th Ave., Suite 3
Eugene, OR 97401

www.wipfandstock.com

PAPERBACK ISBN: 978-1-5326-8940-6
HARDCOVER ISBN: 978-1-5326-8941-3
EBOOK ISBN: 978-1-5326-8942-0

Manufactured in the U.S.A.

This book is dedicated to several women in my life. To my mother, whose love for Jesus, the Lamb of God, was passed down to me. And to the female writers I have around me and far off in other parts of the world: my daughter-in-law, Emma, who brilliantly produces blogging accounts of daily life as a mother and wife (particularly of interest to me are the stories of my grandchildren); to my oldest daughter, Hannie, whose artistic imagination has led to inventive ideas for still-to-come children's books and poetry; to my second daughter, Abbie, who edited this work, and whose own writing will one day require me to play a secondary character in the miniseries based on her novel; and, most lovingly, to my wife Lora, whose intelligence and integrity continue to inspire and encourage me to deeper communion with Jesus. Keep writing, Lora!

# Contents

*Preface* | ix

*Acknowledgments* | xi

Introduction | 1

Revelation 1:1–8: The Revelation of Jesus Christ | 12

Revelation 1:9–20: Opening Vision of Jesus, the Lamb of God | 21

Revelation 2:1–7: Jesus' Message to the Church in Ephesus | 30

Revelation 2:8–11: Jesus' Message to the Church in Smyrna | 38

Revelation 2:12–17: Jesus' Message to the Church in Pergamum | 42

Revelation 2:18–29: Jesus' Message to the Church in Thyatira | 47

Revelation 3:1–6: Jesus' Message to the Church in Sardis | 53

Revelation 3:7–13: Jesus' Message to the Church in Philadelphia | 58

Revelation 3:14–22: Jesus' Message to the Church in Laodicea | 64

Revelation 4:1–11: The Vision of the Throne of God | 71

Revelation 5:1–14: The Lamb is Worthy to Open the Scroll | 80

Revelation 6:1–17: The Opening of Seals 1–6 | 89

Revelation 7:1–17: First Interlude (A Picture of the End) | 99

Revelation 8:1–13: The Opening of Seal 7 and Trumpets 1–4 | 108

Revelation 9:1–21: Trumpets 5–6 (The First Two Woes) | 115

Revelation 10:1–11: Second Interlude (The Little Scroll) | 124

Revelation 11:1–19: Third Interlude (The Two Witnesses) and Trumpet 7
    (A Picture of the End) | 132

Revelation 12:1–18: The Vision of the Woman and the Dragon | 143

Revelation 13:1–18: The Two Beasts Oppose the Servants of
    the Lamb | 155

Revelation 14:1–20: The Lamb, the Angels, and the Harvest | 164

Revelation 15:1—16:21: The Seven Bowls of Wrath | 174

Revelation 17:1–18: The Vision of the Prostitute and the Scarlet Beast | 184

Revelation 18:1–24: The Fall of Babylon | 193

Revelation 19:1–21: The Consummation of the Lamb's Victory | 201

Revelation 20:1–15: The Millennial Kingdom and the Final Doom
                    of Satan | 212

Revelation 21:1–27: A New Heaven and a New Earth | 223

Revelation 22:1–21: We Want to See Jesus, the Lamb | 234

*Bibliography* | 245

*Subject Index* | 247

*Scripture Index* | 289

# Preface

M Y INTEREST IN THE "revelation of Jesus Christ," the first words of the book of Revelation and the subject of this commentary, began when I was a child. I have a vivid memory, at six years old, of singing a song in my church about the second coming of Jesus. "Ten and nine, eight and seven, six and five and four; the countdown's getting closer every day. Three and two coming through . . ." I don't remember the rest of the song, but it began a years-long search for answers that lasted into high school, trying to make sense of the charts hanging on the walls and the occasional prophesy conferences. Like many other churches in the 1970s, my church was thoroughly dispensational, and so was I.

That is, until I was a sophomore at Wheaton College, sitting in Dr. Alan Johnson's class on Revelation. Dr. Johnson was asking us a question about the background to a particular passage in the book. When no one could answer, he graciously and properly rebuked us all for not having the adequate knowledge of the Old Testament that was required for understanding Revelation. That class opened my eyes. I realized there were other interpretations besides those I'd been taught in my church back home (several of which are noted in the introduction that follows.) I also realized how instrumental understanding the Old Testament is for interpreting the New Testament correctly.

My fascination with and growing love for the last book of the New Testament grew even more deeply when I started to focus on the central character of the text. No, I'm not talking about the charts, predictions, or symbols, though there are many.

The central character of the text, and indeed the central character of all of life, is the Lamb of God who sits on his throne. The Lamb of God himself became the important interpretive key for me, not only as I preached through a series during my ministry as a senior pastor in Ohio, but throughout my own personal and devotional study as well.

In 2016, I taught a course at Jaffray Bible Seminary in Makassar, Indonesia, called Apocalyptic Literature: Daniel and Revelation, as part of our

MA in Biblical Studies. There were about seven students in the class. I spent the bulk of the year before preparing myself to teach and to handle any questions that students might have. I had been teaching a class on ecclesiology and eschatology for about six years, so the subjects of the millennium, the timing of the second coming of Christ, and the important role of the Lamb of God were fresh in my mind.

What started out as rough English notes for an Indonesian group of students became a rough draft for a commentary at their insistence. This is the fruit of that study, but not just of that year; rather, this work is a culmination of my adoration of the Lamb of God, who takes center stage in Revelation. My hope is that the reader will see the Lamb too, in all his glory, honor, power, and might, and that the church is drawn deeper into a holy expectation of the Lamb's glorious return.

# Acknowledgments

I AM VERY THANKFUL FOR the students in my Revelation and Daniel class in Makassar, Indonesia, who encouraged me to develop my class notes into book form. I am especially grateful for Hanny Frederick, a graduate from our Biblical studies program and my pastor, whose critical thinking in that class helped both me and his fellow students to take the truth of the book of Revelation seriously as Scripture, God's word.

I also acknowledge the grace given to me by the leader at the school, Peniel Maiaweng, who allowed me to have the office time to research and write. Given the demands of mentoring and teaching on campus, it is a special blessing to be able to capture and capitalize upon those hours to study and write in peace. Thank you also to my fellow colleagues, especially Christopher Luthy. You have all helped sharpen my thinking with regard to apocalyptic literature.

Thank you to my wife, Lora, who was usually sitting at the other end of the kitchen table, listening, as I gave exhortations from Revelation and ranted about strange theories or fanciful ideas influenced by the sways of church culture.

I particularly would like to acknowledge Abigail Pettit, my daughter, for the heavy lifting of manuscript editing. Busy with the revision of her own novel, her willingness to take on this task is very much appreciated. It is a great gift to have a daughter so talented!

# Introduction

## Nature of the Book

R EVELATION IS ONE OF the most intriguing books of the New Testament. It has long been my favorite for its exalted picture of Christ, its view of heaven, and the hope it gives to the church around the world. It has also, unfortunately, been a much-abused book by those who seek to know the timing of Christ's second coming. Many have used Revelation as a guidebook for their own theories and, in doing so, have missed its exalted Christology and hope. The purpose of this commentary is to present a straightforward interpretation of Revelation that focuses on the Lamb, explaining its rich Old Testament background and symbolic nature.[1]

I take John, the apostle of Jesus, to be the most likely author (more on this below). John was a prophet, an apocalyptist, a pastor, and an apostle. Wrap all these concerns and genres together, and you get Revelation, a letter to the church in the midst of great trial. John wants to encourage the church to persevere and be faithful to Jesus to the end, both in light of what was happening at the time and also in light of what was to come.

John Christopher Thomas and Frank D. Macchia call Revelation the "most sensual document in the New Testament, filled with references to things, seen, heard, smelled, touched, and even tasted!"[2] The book was meant to be heard while it was read aloud by its audiences, the congregations in Asia Minor and beyond. G.K. Beale calls Revelation, quoting D.A. Carson, Douglas J. Moo, and Leon Morris, "a prophesy cast in an apocalyptic mold and written down in a letter form in order to motivate the audience to change their behavior in light of the transcendent reality of the book's message."[3]

1. See Osborne, *Revelation*, 12. Osborne believes that Revelation has three genres: apocalyptic, prophetic, and epistolary. It must be understood that the book is not just a casebook for identifying future events and setting up prophesy conferences, but a theological work addressing the churches in their present contexts through prophesies of the future.

2. Thomas and Macchia, *Revelation*, 2.

3. Beale, *The Book of Revelation*, 39.

Revelation leans into the Old Testament as a source text in both material and form. It takes much of its cues from Isaiah, Ezekiel, Zechariah, and
Daniel, adhering more closely to the tradition of Old Testament apocalyptic
literature rather than Jewish first-century works.

Grant Osborne argues that John is faithful, on the whole, in his interpretation of the Old Testament context, but that he transforms it deliberately
by applying it to his contention that the nations of the earth are analogous
to the nation of Israel in Zechariah.[4] Beale's concept of John's position in
relation to the Old Testament as both servant and guide is a helpful picture.
For John, the cross and the resurrection are key to understanding the Old
Testament, and reflection on the Old Testament leads to further compre-
hension of the passion event in light of the present and the future. In this
way, symbiotically, the New Testament interprets the Old, and the Old Testament interprets the New.[5]

Symbols are everywhere in Revelation, and each symbol would have
been understandable to the first-century reader. We should not play guess-
ing games trying to figure out what the symbols could mean in our context
(example: interpreting the locusts mentioned in Revelation 9 as helicop-
ters), but consider what they meant in their own. There are four main numbers that carry symbolic meaning: four, seven, ten, and twelve. Usually, the
meaning is associated with completeness. Four carries the meaning of the
four corners of the earth, or the whole world.[6]

Examples include the four corners (7:1; 20:8), the four winds (7:1),
and the fourfold division of creation (8:7–8; 14:7; 16:2–3). "The one who
lives forever and ever" is mentioned four times (4:9–10; 19:6; 15:7). As to
the number seven, John includes seven spirits, sevenfold doxologies, seven
seals, trumpets, and bowls of wrath, and seven beatitudes. Several titles of
God (e.g., Lord God Almighty, the one who sits on the throne) are mentioned seven times; Christ is mentioned seven times, Jesus fourteen times.
Jesus is called a "witness" seven times. John speaks of Christ's "coming"
seven times. The "Lamb" is referenced twenty-eight times. These cannot
all be coincidences.[7]

Beale suggests there are four levels of communication in Revelation:
1) a linguistic level, the record of the text itself to be read and heard; 2) a
visionary level, John's actual sensory experience; 3) a referential level, the
particular historical identification of the objects seen in the vision; and 4) a

---

4. Osborne, *Revelation*, 26.

5. Beale, *The Book of Revelation*, 97.

6. See Osborne, *Revelation*, 17, and Bauckham, *New Testament Theology*, 29–37.

7. Osborne, *Revelation*, 17.

symbolic level, what the symbols in the vision mean about their historical reference.[8] Beale notes, "Symbols have a parabolic function and are intended to encourage and exhort the audience. They portray a transcendent new creation that has penetrated the present old world through the death and resurrection of Christ and the sending of the Spirit at Pentecost."[9]

## Author

John, the apostle of Jesus and the brother of James, the writer of the gospel of John, is the most probable author of Revelation. As for internal evidence, the author mentions his own name in Revelation 1:1, 1:4, 1:9, and 22:8. He calls himself a "servant" (1:1) and a prophet (1:3; 22:9). There have been several suggestions as to the identity of this John: 1) as mentioned, John the apostle; 2) the elder John; 3) John Mark; 4) John the Baptist; 5) another John; 6) Cerinthus (a gnostic); 7) someone using the name of John as a pseudonym.[10] David Aune argues there are very few features that suggest that the author of Revelation was part of a Johannine community in any meaningful sense.[11] But Aune is predisposed to accept the truth of source criticism and believes that large sections of Revelation are the work of an editor. I do not see this as readily. The genre John is using is quite different from the genre of gospel writing, which accounts for the differences of style, grammar, and vocabulary that Aune and others interpret as evidence for two different authors.

The use of Greek is one of the biggest differences between the book of John and Revelation. The grammar in Revelation is unique, sometimes strange, and frequently Hebraic. But many of the solecisms (using grammar in a seemingly inappropriate way) appear deliberate, perhaps for theological purposes or influenced by the visionary experience that must have been so difficult to describe. At times, John wants his readers to make associations with Old Testament texts and uses the Hebraic form of the Greek to alert the reader to the connection.

Some scholars believe there are differences in theology. But these can be explained by the different context and genre. Is there only a God of love in the gospel of John and only a God of wrath in Revelation? This is a false contrast, and to say this shows a lack of understanding of the character of God. In fact, only in John and Revelation is Jesus called *logos* in the New

8. Beale, *The Book of Revelation*, 52–53.

9. Beale, *The Book of Revelation*, 59.

10. Osborne, *Revelation*, 2.

11. Aune, *Revelation 1–5*, lvi.

Testament. Some scholars also argue that the realized eschatology of the gospel is not compatible with the final eschatology of Revelation. But it has long been accepted that the eschatology of the gospel of John is inaugurated. The different emphases of each book mean a different perspective, but from the same author. There is, instead, a similar overall message in both John's gospel and Revelation: God seeks to bring the world to repentance. Zechariah 12:10 is quoted in John 19:37 and Revelation 1:7, using the same Greek word (*ekkenteo*), which is not used by the Septuagint and is not found elsewhere in the New Testament.[12]

Osborne notes that Justin Martyr (*Dialogue with Trypho* 81.4), Irenaeus (*Against Heresies* 4.20.11), Tertullian (*Against Marcion* 3.14.3), Clement of Alexandria (*Paedagogus* 2.108), and Origen (*De Principalis* 1.2.10) all believed John the apostle was the author. Marcion was the first to reject John's authorship. Dionysius doubted it, as well as Eusebius, Cyril of Jerusalem, and Chrysostom. Dionysius thought "another unknown John" wrote it; Eusebius believed there were two Johns at Ephesus, with the apostle John writing the gospel and the Elder John writing Revelation. It is uncertain whether using a pseudonym was practiced in the early church, which seems to limit the field of likely candidates.[13] William D. Mounce holds that the strong external evidence points to John the apostle's authorship.[14] Beale feels it is possible that John the apostle wrote the book, but that another John could have written it. He does not see the issue as important but is sure that the author at least identified himself as a prophet (1:1–3; 10:19; 4:1–2; 17:1–3; 21:9–10; 22:6–7).[15]

Given the strength of both the internal and external evidence, as I stated, I do think John the apostle is the author. For purposes of simplification and clarity, I've referred and will continue to refer to the author as "John" throughout this book.

## Date

There are two major theories regarding the dating of the book: the time of the emperor Nero or the time of the emperor Domitian. Beale provides a helpful list of arguments for both a late date (95, Domitian) and an early date (pre-70, Nero).[16]

12. See Revelation 5–6; Mounce, *The Book of Revelation*, 14.
13. Osborne, *Revelation*, 2–4.
14. Mounce, *The Book of Revelation*, 31.
15. Beale, *The Book of Revelation*, 35–36.
16. See fuller discussion in Beale, *The Book of Revelation*, 5–20.

## Evidence for a Later Date

In Revelation, John makes frequent mention of the rituals of the imperial cult and persecution against the church. People began to worship emperors prior to the time of Domitian (see 13:4–8, 15–16; 14:9–11; 15:2; 16:2; 19:20; 20:4). Hard evidence of the persecution of Christians because they resisted imperial worship comes in 113 AD during the reign of Trajan in a letter written by Pliny to Trajan. Pliny mentions people who had apostatized "many years earlier [. . .] a few as much as twenty-five years ago"[17]; in other words, during Domitian's reign. If Domitian's only motive was to purge aristocrats, using Christianity as an excuse to charge some of them, Christians would still have viewed this as persecution, especially those that were charged. Beale notes further that later Christian tradition supports the idea that Domitian's persecution may have focused on Christians in the higher classes. Eusebius writes that members of Jesus' family were brought before Domitian because "they were reported as being of the family of David"[18] and because they were identified with the movement of Christians. This also shows that Christianity, as a sub-set of Judaism and acknowledged as a religion in the Roman Empire, was beginning to be set apart.

Clement, writing in 96 AD, alludes to "the sudden and successive calamitous events which have happened to ourselves"[19]. What is clear is that from both secular and religious sources, there is some evidence of a hardening of Roman policy and persecution toward Christians who chose not to participate in the political and religious life of Greco-Roman society—in particular, the imperial cult. There is no evidence that the Neronian persecution in Rome extended to Asia Minor, the location of the seven churches in Revelation. This was a local persecution of the Christians in Rome that did affect other Christians in the empire, but not extensively in Asia Minor. And though emperor worship could have been an issue in Nero's time, it fits more closely with what was happening during the reign of Domitian. In Ephesus, for example, a giant statue of Domitian was erected that may be what Revelation 13 references, where believers are put to death for not worshipping the "image of the beast" (13:15). This kind of local evidence in Asia Minor of imperial cult pressure does not exist for the pre-70 AD date.

---

17. See Pliny the Younger, *Epistles 10.96-97*, as footnoted in Beale, *The Book of Revelation*, 5.

18. Beale, *The Book of Revelation*, 7, referencing Eusebius, *History of Eusebius* 3.20.

19. Clement in the *First Epistle of Clement to the Corinthians* 1.1, in *The Church Fathers. The Complete Ante-Nicene & Nicene and Post-Nicene Church Fathers Collection*, Kindle edition, Loc. 1880.

The conditions of the churches in Asia Minor also point to a later date. The spiritual condition of Ephesus, Sardis, and Laodicea was low. The Laodicean church, for instance, is described as quite wealthy. But the city experienced a devastating earthquake in 60–61 AD, and the city and church would have needed time to recover from this economic loss. The "synagogue of Satan" (2:9; 3:9) best fits a Domitian context. And the church of Smyrna may not have been established yet in the sixties.[20]

If it is true that 13:3–4, 17:8, and 17:11 refer to the myth of the reappearance of Nero (*Nero redivivus*), which speaks of the demise of the beast and his later revival, only a later date makes sense. Nero died in 68 AD. Surely two years would not have been enough time for the myth to take hold.

The reoccurring "Babylon" theme in Revelation is another date indicator. In Jewish literature, Babylon refers to Rome after 70 AD because the Roman armies destroyed Jerusalem and the temple, just as Babylon had done in the sixth century BC.

The earliest testimonies of church leaders date Revelation at the time of Domitian as well. These include Irenaeus, Victorinus of Pettau, Eusebius, and possibly Clement of Alexandria and Origen.[21]

Aune also notes that the use of the phrase "the twelve apostles" in Revelation 21:14 is not attested before 80 AD.[22]

## Evidence for an Earlier Date

Beale's list of arguments for an early date (pre-70) are not as convincing.[23] Yes, the temple seems to be still standing in Revelation 11:1–2. But this assumes a literal reading of the text, referring to the first-century Herodian temple. Like the rest of Revelation, chapter 11 is rich with symbolism based on Ezekiel 40–48. Some in favor of an early date have identified the seven hills in 17:9–10 that are described as kings as specifically Roman emperors, the last being Nero. But I don't think John is referring to seven literal kings of the Roman empire. For a further discussion, see my exegesis of chapter 17.

Some suggest that, together, the name values of Nero and Caesar in Hebrew letters add up to 666, which, in conjunction with 13:18, would mean an earlier date. But should we be playing number games? Was John that familiar with *gematria* (giving numerical value to letters) that he would

20. See also Osborne, *Revelation*, 9.

21. The fact that these church leaders were chronologically close to the later date gives more credence to their testimony.

22  Aune, *Revelation 1–5*, lxx.

23. Beale, *The Book of Revelation*, 21–26.

hide the meaning of who 666 is? (I include more on this in my discussion of chapter 13.)

## Final Thoughts on the Date

According to Thomas and Macchia, John seems to be intentionally concealing the date he was writing. If this is so, they say, it is in keeping with the spirit of the text to respect John's intentional ambiguity and look more closely at the intention within the text.[24] I don't see a compelling reason why John would purposefully want to conceal the time of his writing. I think it's clear that the evidence points to a later date, written by John when he was quite old. If he was a teenager when he joined Jesus as a disciple, that would put him in his eighties or so in 95 AD.

## Recipient

The list of churches in chapters 2–3 helps us to know the audience. It seems like the letter was meant to be read and then circulated to each church. Beale believes the "focus of the book is exhortation to the church community to witness to Christ in the midst of a compromising, idolatrous church and world."[25] I think Beale is mostly right. He emphasizes the apostate believers too frequently as the recipients of some of the rebukes and warnings. But there is definitely a presence in the churches of those who have fallen away or have compromised.

## Methods of Interpretation

Osborne provides a helpful summary of some of the historical methods of interpreting Revelation. I will explain them below, and then explain the position of this commentary.[26]

1. Historicist: This is the classic dispensational view, that the seven churches represent different periods of history. The historicist view is also associated with the prophesy movement that sees every detail of Revelation fulfilled in current events. This view was held by Joachim of Fiore (twelfth century). Franciscans followed him. The Reformers

---

24. Thomas and Macchia, *Revelation*, 34.
25. Beale, *The Book of Revelation*, 33.
26. For a fuller description of different methods, see Osborne, *Revelation*, 18–22.

(Martin Luther, John Calvin) saw the Pope as the antichrist in the sixteenth century.

2. Preterist: In this view, the details of the book relate to the present situation in which John lived, rather than a future period. Three main options of interpretation fall in this category: 1) those who say the situation related to the Roman Empire and the book is written about Roman oppression and the fall of the Roman Empire (R.H. Charles, Leonard Sweet, Jurgen Roloff); 2) those who say that the persecution was a perceived crisis rather than a real one, but the church was still called to follow God. The problem of the book is compromise, and the solution is true worship of Christ (Adela Yarbro Collins, John L. Thompson, Gerhard Krodel, James Barr); 3) those who think the book was written before 70 AD and prophesies the fall of Jerusalem as God's judgment upon wicked Israel for rejecting the Messiah and persecuting the church (Kenneth Gentry, D. C. Chilton), and that the beast is Rome, and the kings of the east are Roman generals.

3. Idealist: In this view, the symbols do not relate to historical events but to timeless spiritual truths. The millennium is not a future event, but more conceptual. This view is part of the amillennial position. The final cycle of the book encourages the church to carry on (William Hendriksen, Anthony Hoekema, and Philip Hughes are Idealists).

4. Futurist: In this view, chapters 4–22 refer primarily to events in the future that will take place at the end of history and usher in the end times and the return of Christ. There are two branches to a futurist view: dispensationalism, the belief that there are seven dispensations (or periods in history), and we are currently in the sixth (the church age). Revelation, according to dispensationalism, describes the seventh age, where the church is taken out before the travail of the last days, and Israel is reinstated. The second branch is classic premillennialism, which holds that there is only one return of Christ and the church must endure and be faithful through suffering and persecution before Christ's return.

5. Eclectic: This view combines more than one of the views above, avoiding the weaknesses of particular views. (Leon Morris, George Ladd, George Beasley-Murray, J. Ramsey Michaels, Alan Johnson, H. Giesen, Mounce, and Beale all subscribe to this view). I lean towards the eclectic view as well, with the proviso that we acknowledge Revelation was written in a definite context to seven specific churches while also

looking ahead to the future final conflict between the forces of Satan and the people of Christ.

## Themes

The following themes stand out in the book of Revelation:

1.  God: the one who was and is and is to come (1:4, 8; 4:8; 11:17; 16:5). He holds the world in his sovereign control. He is the Alpha and Omega, the beginning and the end. (1:8; 1:17; 22:13; 21:6; 22:13). This title is also used of Christ (1:17; 22:13). Jesus receives worship along with God. And Jesus and God seem to sit side-by-side and to share the throne and the right of judgment. This parallels Jesus' teaching in John 5–7. Another title used for God is the Lord Almighty (1:8; 4:8; 11:17; 15:3; 16:7, 14; 19:6, 15; 21:22), a title which contextually carries the implication of omnipotence and God's rightful place as master and creator. The divine passive is used frequently (6:2, 4, 8, 11; 7:2; 8:2, 3; 9:1, 3, 5; 11:1, 2; 12:14; 13:7, 14, 15; 16:8). Nothing happens outside the sovereign plan of God.

2.  Jesus, the Lamb (Revelation 5:6–6:17; 19; 22)

3.  Jesus, the warrior (Revelation 1:9–20; 7; 12; 19). As Jesus overcame through his death and resurrection, so also the saints can overcome (Revelation 6; 12; 13; 19–20).

4.  The church must be patient and endure and, in doing so, overcome trial (Revelation 2–3; 19–21).

5.  Satan's defeat (12:9; 20:2, 8, 10). The false trinity will fight the church of God but will ultimately be defeated (13:16–17; 17–18; 19–20).

6.  Theodicy: a defense of God's character and judgment[27]

7.  God's judgment reveals his righteous character (6:16–17; 11:18; 14:10, 19; 15:1, 7; 16:1, 19; 19:15).

8.  Christ comes as judge (1:16; 2:12, 16; 19:15, 21).

9.  God's judgments come because of the depravity and rejection of those on the earth. The evil of the nations is emphasized, and it is that guilt that is the basis for their judgment. God's judgments execute his righteous judgment as sin turns against itself, and God's judgments are proven through his vindication of the saints (6:10; 17:14; 18:24; 15:2; 20:4).

---

27. See Osborne, *Revelation,* 38–40.

## Outline

1:1–8 Prologue

    1:1–3 Who is the author?

    1:4 Who is the recipient?

    1:5–8 Who is the focus of the book?

1:9–20 Vision of Jesus

2:1–3:20 Jesus' message to the churches of Asia Minor

    2:1–5 To Ephesus

    2:6–11 To Smyrna

    2:12–17 To Pergamum

    2:18–29 To Thyatira

    3:1–6 To Sardis

    3:7–13 To Philadelphia

    3:14–20 To Laodicea

4:1–5:14 Vision of the throne-room

    4:1–8 The throne of God and the song of the four living creatures

    4:9–11 The song of the twenty-four elders

    5:1–5 The call for someone worthy to open the seals of the scroll

    5:6–10 The Lion/Lamb of God and the song of the creatures/elders

    5:11–12 The song of all the angels

    5:13–14 The song of every creature

6:1–17 Seals 1–6 are opened

7:1–17 First Interlude (a picture of the end)

    7:1–8 The 144,000

    7:9–117 The number beyond count

8:1–5 The seventh seal is opened

8:6–13 Trumpets 1–4

9:1–21 Trumpets 5–6

10:1–11 Second Interlude (the little scroll)

11:1–14 Third Interlude (the two witnesses)

11:15–19 Trumpet 7 (a picture of the end)

12:1–17 The sign of the woman and the dragon

13:1–18 The two beasts

13:1–10 The beast from the sea

13:11–18 The beast from the earth

14:1–20 The Lamb and the angels

14:1–5 The Lamb and the 144,000

14:6–7 The first angel

14:8 The second angel

14:9–16 The third angel and the "one like a son of man"

15:1–8 The vision of the seven angels/plagues

15:1–4 The justice and righteousness of God

15:5–8 The opening of the sanctuary

16:1–21 The seven bowls of wrath

17:1–18 The sign of the prostitute and the beast

18:1–24 The fall of Babylon

19:1–21 The consummation of the Lamb's victory

19:1–8   The wedding supper of the Lamb

19:9–21 The final victory of the Lamb

20:1–15 The millennial kingdom and the final doom of Satan

20:1–3   Satan is bound

20:4–6   The millennial reign

20:7–10 The final defeat of Satan

20:11–15 The final judgment

21:1–22:5 A new heaven and new earth

21:1–8 The vision of a new heaven and earth

21:9–27 A new Jerusalem

22:1–5 A new Eden

22:6–21 Epilogue

# Revelation 1:1–8

The Revelation of Jesus Christ

## Introduction

THERE ARE A LOT of books in bookstores, on our devices, and on the internet. Too many to read. There are science books, comic books, cooking books, classic books, history books, math books, political books, how-to books, how-not-to books. There are books published every day, every hour, every minute. There are books I would never want to read, books I would be interested in reading, and books that I know are must-reads.

There are reference books, manuals, and coffee-table books. You know, the kind that you put out so people who come to your house will think you read them when they're just for display, even though everybody else does the same thing so, in some sense, you're not fooling anyone.

Then there are those books that are indispensable. These are the kinds of books we try to get everyone to read. Of course, there are no books more valuable to read than the Bible. And within the sixty-six books of the Bible, there is no other book in the Bible that claims for itself the promise of blessings for those who read it like the book of Revelation does. Certainly, blessing comes when we read any part of the Bible. After all, in Matthew 24:35, Jesus says, "Heaven and earth will pass away, but my words will not pass away."

But Revelation is the only book that includes blessing as a direct result of reading, provided reading is accompanied by action. We see in this first section of Revelation, the prologue to the rest of the letter/vision, that this is a book about Jesus and a book given by him. No wonder there is a blessing attached to its reading!

## Exposition

From the start of Revelation, we get a lot of information. First, John tells us this is a "revelation." Our word "revelation" comes from the Greek word *apokalupsis*, which is transliterated "apocalypse" in English. This word could place John in line with the Jewish apocalyptic literature of the day, but, according to Ladd, John is different for several reasons. John names himself as the recipient of the vision, while Jewish apocalyptic literature is often written with a pseudonym. John's vision is written from the perspective of the present about the future, not placed, like Jewish literature, back in time and speaking of current events. And John's vision is a positive understanding of God's control, whereas Jewish literature is typically very pessimistic.[1]

As we read the apocalypse of John, we have to remember that this is apocalyptic imagery. What must soon take place may be couched in very symbolic terms, hard for the twenty-first century reader to understand. In other words, first-century readers would have more readily picked up the symbols and Old Testament allusions from which Revelation borrows much of its imagery.

But even Old Testament prophets did not understand everything they wrote. 1 Peter 1:10–11 says, "Concerning this salvation, the prophets who prophesied about the grace that was to be yours searched and inquired carefully, inquiring what person or time the Spirit of Christ in them was indicating when he predicted the sufferings of Christ and the subsequent glories."

Our experience of Revelation in contrast to a first-century reader's experience of Revelation is similar to how someone from the fifteenth century might feel if an American talked about a yellow penalty flag in football. Most Americans instantly recognize what a yellow flag symbolizes, but a fifteenth-century person would be mystified without the right contextual knowledge. In studying the book of Revelation, we must be diligent in our study of the Old Testament and, even so, realize there are some things we just may not understand fully yet.

This is a "revelation *of* Jesus Christ" (Revelation 1:1, emphasis mine). This could either be interpreted as a subjective genitive (a revelation given *by* Jesus Christ), or an objective genitive (a revelation *about* Jesus Christ). Mounce, among others, takes the subjective genitive view, saying, "Christ is the revealer, not in the sense that he accompanies John on his visionary experiences (angels play this role), but in that he alone is worthy to open the scroll of destiny (Revelation 5:5, 7) and disclose its contents"[2] (Revelation

---

1. Ladd, *A Commentary on the Revelation of John*, 20.

2. Mounce, *The Book of Revelation*, 64. See also Aune, *Revelation 1–5*, 12 and Osborne, *Revelation*, 52.

6:3, 3, 5, 7, 9, 12; 8:1). Both Beale[3] and Thomas[4], however, believe the text can be read either way, as do I.

The reader's takeaway should be that this book is about Jesus Christ and his victory *and* a book given by Jesus Christ to the church—both the first-century churches in Asia Minor and to all churches past and present. That is the beauty of the book of Revelation. Revelation has always been applicable at all times, and at all times it is focused on Jesus Christ, who is the same yesterday, today, and forever.

There is an urgency to John's writing. When I was a kid and heard my mother yelling from the house, "Andy, you come here right now!", her specific emphasis of words told me how fast I should get back to the house. If she said, "Andy, come here right now" with no emphasis, I would jog home. But if she said, "Come here right *now*!", I'd run fast. Revelation is a "Come here right *now*" kind of book.

This revelation is about things that must soon take place. The time is near, John declares. The world was at a critical point, the signs and circumstances of the times indicating that Jesus would come soon. Modern-day readers may be confused by the language of imminence. Have we seen these events yet or have we not? Are we still waiting? How long must we wait, and what does "soon" mean to John or to Jesus? We must understand the importance of the little Greek word δεῖ (*dei*), which means "must" or "necessary." The sovereignty of God underpins all of this. These things must take place because God's will must be accomplished. God's sovereignty is a common theme running through Revelation. Osborne notes that in John's writings δεῖ refers to God's will and way (see John 3:30; 4:20, 24).[5]

But what about the timing? If it is necessary that these things take place under the sovereign plan of God, how are we to understand the phrase "soon"? Mounce writes, "History is not a haphazard sequence of unrelated events, but a divinely decreed ordering of that which must come to pass. It is a logical necessity arising from the nature of God and the revelation of his purpose in creation and redemption."[6] In light of this, we may understand "soon" in a straightforward sense. From the perspective of the prophet, the end is always imminent. The church in every age has lived with the expectancy of the end of all things in its day. Imminence describes an event possible any day and impossible no day.[7] Contrary to this perspective, Beale thinks

---

3. Beale, *The Book of Revelation*, 183.
4. Thomas and Macchia, *Revelation*,73.
5. Osborne, *Revelation*, 54.
6. Mounce, *The Book of Revelation*, 64–65.
7. Johnson, *Hebrews through Revelation*, 417.

that "soon" refers to the "definite, imminent time of fulfillment, which likely has already begun in the present."[8] He bases this on Daniel's understanding of "soon" as not the rapid manner of the fulfillment of the prophesy but its temporal fulfillment. The activities of the revelation would begin in John's generation and had already taken place. The beginning of the fulfillment, and not the final fulfillment, is the focus of Revelation. The events described have already begun to take place.[9] There is a "now" and "not yet" aspect to the prophesies of Revelation, just as in the prophesies of the Old Testament, upon which Revelation heavily relies.

There is a defined order of dissemination in Revelation. We see it in chapter 1, and later we will see it in chapter 22. The revelation about Jesus is revealed by Jesus to an angel who then reveals it to John. Beale sees the chain even more completely from God to Jesus to an angel to John to Christian "servants."[10]

John bears witness to the word of God and the testimony of Jesus Christ, the subjective genitive mentioned earlier, the testimony that is witnessed to by Christ.[11] John is shown these things. The word for "shown" is the Greek word ἐσήμανεν (esemanen). This word, which has a sense of symbolic or analogical communication, is nicely suited to this book and should warn us not to expect literal descriptions of what John sees, but a symbolic portrayal of the things to come.[12]

Blessing is promised to all who read, hear, and keep the words of the prophesy. Those who read and hear the word of this prophesy in the context of what will be described will be able to stand firm and be resolute in their faith, even in the midst of suffering, because the time is near. The suffering of the saints is limited. Revelation should not only be considered a handbook for future things, but a call to moral and ethical faithfulness. John puts his writing on par with the Old Testament prophets, expecting obedience from believers. We will see this again in Revelation 22.[13] Osborne points out that

8. Beale, *The Book of Revelation*, 185.

9. Beale, *The Book of Revelation*, 181–82. See also Ladd (Ladd, *A Commentary on the Revelation of John*, 22), who says that there is no problem in literally interpreting the "end is near" when we remember that the prophets of the Scriptures did not think chronologically (*kronos*) but rather were event-oriented (*Kairos*). The end *was* near from the perspective that the end had already begun in the death and resurrection of Christ. From the perspective of the throne of God, the end is near and has been near since Jesus rose. We are in the end, and have been since that time.

10. Beale, *The Book of Revelation*, 183.

11. Ladd, *A Commentary on the Revelation of John*, 23.

12. Mounce, *The Book of Revelation*, 65.

13. Mounce, *The Book of Revelation*, 66 and Ladd, *A Commentary on the Revelation of John*, 24.

the idea of hearing and obeying are common themes in John's writing in his gospel (John 1:37, 40; 4:42; 5:25, 28–29; 8:38, 47; 10:3–4, 27; 12:47; 14:23–24) as well as in Revelation (1:2, 9; 6:9; 17:17; 19:9, 13; 20:4).[14] We cannot be content with simply knowing what the book of Revelation says. Taking our cues from its warnings and encouragements, we must be faithful to deepen our understanding and commitment to Jesus Christ who is coming soon. Whatever it means specifically, the end *is* near, near enough that our obedience is required *now*. The death and resurrection of Christ inaugurated a new ethical code as well as the long-awaited kingdom of the end times, which the Old Testament (Daniel, for example) had predicted, a kingdom that will continue to exist through the church age.[15]

True to its form as a letter, John begins his address to the churches in Asia Minor with the common greeting of first-century letter writers, offering them grace and peace. We see Paul use the same formula in his letters. John is writing to seven specific churches in Asia Minor. These churches may be literal churches, or they may be representative churches of all the churches that were in Asia Minor at the end of the first century. In other words, the letter was sent to Ephesus first, but the congregation of Ephesus could have been a hub or representative congregation for others around it. Although there is a specific character to the warnings from Jesus to each congregation, setting the letter in a specific time period to a specific people, there is a universal character as well.[16] John is giving these seven churches more than just a perfunctory greeting. He was earnestly praying that the grace of God be given to his readers. And this God John describes next.

The phrase "him who is and who was and who is to come" (Revelation 1:4) is important. If the letter of Revelation is given about the times that will soon take place, this phrase assures the reader that all is held in the hands of God—all past, present, and future. This threefold identity of God is probably a nod to Exodus 3:14, where God tells Moses, "I am who I am." What appears to be incorrect grammar in John's Greek rendering (there is no noun for God, but the pronoun is used), is actually kept in the nominative

14. Osborne, *Revelation*, 58.

15. Beale, *The Book of Revelation*, 185.

16. Beale believes that the concept of seven in Revelation is both literal and figurative. Here, in 1:4, it is literal, but elsewhere it could also be a case of synecdoche, a figure of speech in which the part represents the whole. The seven churches in Asia represent the universal church. Thus, Revelation would be a universal message (Beale, *Revelation*, 186–7). Aune disagrees. He believes that the concept of seven churches refers to the divine origin and authority of the message of John, not the universality of its recipients (Aune, *Revelation 1–5*, 29). However, we need to agree that there *were* seven historical churches in Asia Minor who actually received this letter. These are not symbolic creations in the mind of John.

case on purpose to highlight the Exodus 3:14 connection. The phrase may have also been a common, well-known title for God in Judaism.[17] Likewise, Aune notes that John is the first Christian author to use this pronoun as the divine name for God. (See Jeremiah 1:6; 4:10; 14:13; and 39:17 in the Septuagint.) Like Moses, John is authenticating the authority of his prophesy by appealing to the divine I am of Exodus 3:14.[18]

Part of a clear trinitarian formula appears with the next connecting phrase, "the seven spirits who are before his throne." I see the Holy Spirit as the most obvious choice for the seven spirits. Beale does as well, denying that the seven spirits could be seven angels or archangels of Jewish writings (see 1 Enoch 20:1–8).[19] Mounce disagrees. Although admitting it's difficult to determine the meaning of the sevenfold spirits, he writes, "It would seem that they are perhaps part of a heavenly entourage that has a special ministry in connection with the Lamb."[20] I think it is safer and more consistent with John's use of the number seven and the connection of the sevenfold spirit with the throne to see this as a reference to the fullness of the Holy Spirit and his perfection rather than as seven different spirits.

John identifies Jesus, the third member of the Trinity mentioned, with several significant titles: "faithful witness, the firstborn of the dead, and the ruler of kings on earth" (1:5) (see Philippians 2:5–11; Hebrews 12; Matthew 4:8–10—Jesus won the kingdoms of the earth through his death on the cross, not as a gift from the devil), "him who loves us and has freed us from our sins by his blood and made us a kingdom, priests to his God and Father" (1:5–6).

These titles become important themes throughout the book of Revelation. Jesus, as the faithful witness, gave his life as the first-fruits of the sacrifice presented to God. This is a witness and sacrifice that will be asked of his followers as well. Jesus was faithful to God's call on him and his mission to come to the world and willingly give up his life for the salvation of the world. He was a witness of God. He was God in human form, a testimony or witness to the character of God.

---

17. Beale, *The Book of Revelation*, 188.

18. Aune, *Revelation 1–5*, 31.

19. Beale, *The Book of Revelation*, 189. See also Osborne, *Revelation*, 61; Thomas and Macchia, *Revelation*, 76; Ladd, *A Commentary on the Revelation of John*, 25; and Johnson, *Hebrews through Revelation*, 420–21.

20. Mounce, *The Book of Revelation*, 70. See also Aune, who considers the seven spirits as "the seven principle angels of God" (Aune, *Revelation 1–5*, 34–35), although he does admit that in Jewish literature it is rare to find a "spirit" reference to angels. It more often refers to the demonic.

The second title, "the firstborn of the dead," is connected to two ideas in Revelation. First, Christ has taken control of death and will destroy it (firstborn in the sense of Psalm 89:27[21], as the exalted Messiah—see also Colossians 1:15 and Hebrews 1:6), and second, Christ's work on our behalf as the firstborn through his resurrection, in other words, the firstborn from among the dead.[22] Jesus is firstborn not chronologically, but firstborn in the sense of sovereignty.[23] We can also confess that Jesus was the firstborn out of the tomb, the first to be risen to glory, the forerunner of those who will be raised at the last day. This is the hope of final salvation that we have and a common theme in Revelation.[24]

This sovereign King, because of his love for us, freed us from our sins by his blood, and made us to be a kingdom and priests (1:5–6). A textual variant in verse 6 should be read as *lusanti*, not *lousanti*. The variant was probably caused by an incorrect hearing. The first, the correct reading, means "loosed" or "freed." The second means "washed." The phrase "freed us from our sins" is only found here in the New Testament. The idea of being freed from sins is based on Isaiah 40:2 ("her iniquity is pardoned [. . .] she has received from the LORD's hand double for all her sins"), as well as the redemptive language of Exodus 19:6, which reads, "and you shall be to me a kingdom of priests and a holy nation." This was God's promise to Israel after freeing them from the slavery of Egypt via the blood of the slain lamb on their doorposts. Now kings and priests, the believers' role is something that is done, accomplished, and/or administered in the present because of what Jesus has done in the past. (See Peter's use of this idea in 1 Peter 2:5–11.)[25] Ladd also makes the good point that the idea of people in the church as priests unifies the church and Old Testament Israel "in a bond of continuity. The church is the new and true Israel, inheriting the spiritual privileges of the Old Testament people of God."[26] Revelation explores this idea further, that we are in fact sealed by God, marked with his name. Because of that mark, God will keep us from spiritual destruction, for we belong to him and are his people. People like to read books that tell them how wonderful they

---

21. Psalm 89:27 reads, "And I will make him the firstborn, the highest of the kings of the earth." Beale writes, "John views Jesus as the ideal Davidic king on the escalated eschatological level, whose death and resurrection have resulted in his eternal kingship of his 'beloved' children (cf. v.5b), and this idea is developed in v.6." Beale, *The Book of Revelation*, 191.

22. Osborne, *Revelation*, 63.

23. Ladd, *A Commentary on the Revelation of John*, 25.

24. See 1 Thessalonians 4 and 1 Corinthians 15.

25. Beale, *The Book of Revelation*, 194–5.

26. Ladd, *A Commentary on the Revelation of John*, 27. See Isaiah 61:6.

are. But this is a book that tells us how wonderful the One who calls us is and makes us worth so much more because we belong to him.

Jesus is given the doxology in the second half of 1:6, where it reads: "to him be glory and dominion forever and ever." This reminds the reader and the hearer that Jesus alone, *not* Caesar, is worthy of praise and devotion as the Lord of all, for redemption comes only through him and because of him.[27] We must never lose the place of worship in the book of Revelation. Much of the vision that John receives, he receives in the presence of the One on the throne in the atmosphere of heaven itself. There are experiences of worship unlike he had ever seen or heard or felt. Revelation is a message of worship, giving us a picture of the glory of God, and of Christ, and a picture of his ultimate victory.

This is worship clearly ascribed to Jesus. There are plenty of passages in the Old Testament where worship was only given to God and only allowed to God and to no other. John attributing glory and worship to Jesus shows his understanding of Jesus as part of the Trinity on equal par with God the Father as one with the Father and the Spirit. This is a stark contrast to the cults that were calling Jesus a lesser deity or an angel.

No, John contends, Jesus is worthy of worship, and Revelation gives us many reasons why. We are so woefully inadequate in our worship because we don't see Jesus for who he really is. Revelation allows us to get a more complete picture of the Lord in all his glory. The greater our vision of Jesus, the more real our worship will become.

And to this Jesus we look for a return "with the clouds" (1:7). Two passages give background to verse 7. In Daniel 7:13, one like a son of man is coming on the clouds of heaven. He is given authority and power on the throne. Verse 14 says, "And to him was given dominion and glory and a kingdom, that all peoples, nations, and languages should serve him; his dominion is an everlasting dominion, which shall not pass away, and his kingdom one that shall not be destroyed." Another background passage is Zechariah 12:10: "[. . .] when they look on me, on him whom they have pierced, they shall mourn for him, as one mourns for an only child, and weep bitterly over him, as one weeps over a firstborn." The One who is coming back is the One who was crucified. The peoples of the earth will mourn over his return because they crucified him.

The ones who crucified Jesus will realize that he is alive and real and coming as the judge. They will realize it is too late, that they mocked him when they should have worshipped him, denying him the glory that was

27. Osborne, *Revelation*, 72.

only his to have. They persecuted his messengers instead of repenting. They will feel anguished sorrow at their unbelief.

But no anguish for those who know the truth and have chosen to follow Jesus. We have hope. Revelation gives us hope. We know Jesus will come. We also know that there are several things that must happen first, "soon." We know the most important thing: Jesus wins!

As a reiteration of the truth of him who is and who was and who is to come, the Lord God declares himself the Alpha and the Omega in verse 8. These are the first and last letters of the Greek alphabet. God is all in all. There is no other before him or after him. God is in control of all history because he is before history and he is after history. This becomes an important theme for the churches mentioned in Revelation, especially those churches who are suffering. Interestingly, we will see this designation (Alpha and Omega) again, associated with the Lamb of God, Jesus the conquering one. He also, as well as God the Father, is the Alpha and Omega. This is the mystery of the Trinity, the Three in One.

## Conclusion

Even in the midst of difficult circumstances in our lives and around the world, we can take comfort in knowing that Jesus is in control. In repenting of our sins, we are called to a more intimate relationship with Jesus. We can be encouraged that though this world is evil, and though we may suffer persecution and pain, we know that Jesus will win and bring us with him. We are encouraged by the hope of heaven, Jesus' return, and the promise that the world of evil will one day end.

This encouragement should compel us to obey him, to trust and submit to his promises. For there is no one else who deserves our lives as much as the one who freed us. We receive blessing when we give over the control of our lives to Jesus, the central focus of John's message.

# Revelation 1:9–20

Opening Vision of Jesus, the Lamb of God

## Introduction

A NATIONAL GEOGRAPHIC PHOTOGRAPHER TOLD a story of when he was asked to get photos of a forest fire in California. The editors needed the photos fast, so they sent him immediately. He got to the airport, jumped into the plane, and told the pilot to take off. After a while in the air, he told the pilot, "Just fly close to the forest fire and do a couple of circles around it." The pilot asked, "Why would I want to do that?" The photographer said, "I'm a photographer, and I need to you get close so I can get good pictures." The pilot said, "So you are *not* the instructor?"[1]

Have you ever felt like you were in a plane flown by someone who didn't really know how to fly the plane either? Or have you felt like you didn't know what plane to get into in the first place? If we were entrusting our lives to a pilot, at 37,000 feet in the air, we would certainly want to make sure he was an expert pilot, capable of dealing with turbulence and unexpected problems.

It's sad to think about how many people entrust their spiritual lives to a pilot who doesn't know what to do. Maybe some of us have entrusted our lives to Jesus, allowing him to be the spiritual pilot of our lives, but we still don't really know that much about him. As we grow in our understanding of Jesus, our confidence in his ability to handle the difficult situations of our lives will grow. We will increase in our willingness to rest in his care and control because we see him as he really is.

I believe most people are desperate for a reliable pilot right now. The world only seems to be getting scarier, and it would be nice to know there's someone at the helm of our lives who can take us the right direction. People all around us may be looking for someone other than themselves to pilot their lives, because the turbulence is too strong.

---

1. A version of this story appears in "Go Global: The Great Commission", My Bible.

Revelation 1:9–20 provides us with a picture of Jesus that should reassure us even in the most uncertain times. John was writing in the midst of the turbulence of persecution. He calls himself a "brother and partner in the tribulation and the kingdom and the patient endurance that are in Jesus" (1:9). He was writing from the island of Patmos, where he'd probably been exiled. Patmos was a penal settlement, about forty miles west-southwest of Miletus, where Roman authorities sent offenders.[2] It was like an island prison. But in the middle of this persecution and trial, John heard the voice of Jesus and came face to face with images of Jesus that seared his mind. These images were so powerful and awe-inspiring, he could only think of material and physical analogies to describe the glory of what he saw.

## Exposition

John writes that he was on Patmos "on account of the word of God and the testimony of Jesus" (1:9). This doublet in Revelation typically refers to persecution or suffering that precedes it, so it's likely that John was exiled because of his witness, just as Jesus died because of the word of God and his testimony, and just as the faithful will be martyred because of the word of God and their testimony (see the two witnesses of chapter 11). Also, the fact that John calls himself a partner in tribulation assumes that he was currently being persecuted, just as many in the recipient churches were.

Ladd thinks that the language indicates that John was no longer on Patmos when he composed Revelation.[3] But Aune makes the good point that, although this is a possibility, the use of the aorist tense itself does not prove that John was no longer on the island.[4] Why was John exiled rather than simply executed by the Roman government? Only nobility and priests were given the luxury of exile, so this may speak to John's social position.[5] But it could also speak to the honor and respect John had as an older person with recognized status in the Christian community. According to Irenaeus (*Against Heresies* 2.22.5), John was released from Patmos and lived on until the reign of Trajan.[6]

John called himself a partner in three things (all agree in the dative case): the tribulation, the kingdom, and the patient endurance in Jesus. The word for "partner" in the Greek is similar to the word for *koinonia*,

---

2. Mounce, *The Book of Revelation*, 75.

3. Ladd, *A Commentary on the Revelation of John*, 30.

4. Aune, *Revelation 1–5*, 77.

5. Thomas and Macchia, *Revelation*, 80.

6. Osborne, *Revelation*, 82.

or fellowship. There was a commonality between John and the readers. Why are tribulation, the kingdom, and patient endurance listed together? According to Osborne, all three are related and should not be understood individually. Persecution and patient endurance are a part of the believer's share in the kingdom.[7] Mounce believes the order is important. The present is a time of tribulation and the kingdom a period of future blessedness. So, in the interim period, patient endurance is required.[8] It is probably best not to think too much in terms of timing when we think about the kingdom. Revelation is a both/and kind of book. The kingdom is coming, and we dwell in the inaugurated age of the kingdom. Through our patient endurance in Jesus in the midst of trials, we will overcome (a common theme in Revelation) and inherit the kingdom of God of which we are already a part. Beale writes, "Believers are not mere subjects in Christ's kingdom. They are actively involved in enduring tribulation, and in reigning in the midst of tribulation."[9] This threefold description of believers mirrors the threefold description of Christ in 1:5a. There is a corporate identity.

John writes that he was "in the Spirit." What does ἐν πνεύματι (*en pneumati*) mean? Was he in some ecstatic state? Was he in prayer? Was he like Paul in 2 Corinthians 12:1–4? The phrase is important in Revelation, because it is the Spirit who empowered John and opened his eyes to see the heavenly visions. Though Aune writes that there is no reason to understand the phrase as referring to the Spirit of God because it could be taken as an idiom that refers to the fact that John received these revelations not "in the body" but in a trance-like visionary experience.[10] I side with Osborne[11] who takes John's words more literally here, particularly because of the important role the Holy Spirit has in the rest of John's visions. Bauckham provides other examples in the Old Testament where the divine Spirit is "the agent of visionary experience."[12] See Ezekiel 3:12, 14; 8:3; 11:1, 24; 37:1; 43:5.

John was in the Spirit "on the Lord's day" (Revelation 1:10). This means Sunday, as that day took on this special designation because it was the day of Jesus' resurrection. It does not refer to the day of the LORD, as some have proposed.[13] From the second century on, the idea of "the Lord's day" was

7. Osborne, *Revelation*, 80.

8. Mounce, *The Book of Revelation*, 75.

9. Beale, *Revelation: A Shorter Commentary*, 45

10. Aune, *Revelation 1–5*, 83.

11. Osborne, *Revelation*, 83.

12. Bauckham, *New Testament Theology*, 116.

13. See, for example, Thomas and Macchia, *Revelation*, 81.

taken to mean Sunday[14], so it should not be surprising that this was the idea in the first century as well. On Sunday, while in prayer "in the Spirit" John heard a loud voice like a trumpet. When Moses was on Mount Sinai, something similar happened. Exodus 19:16 says, "On the morning of the third day there were thunders and lightnings and a thick cloud on the mountain and a very loud trumpet blast, so that all the people in the camp trembled." If John was literarily making a reference to this trumpet blast as he heard the new trumpet sound off, he may have been placing his revelation on par with Moses' revelation on Mount Sinai, i.e., that his vision of Jesus was as legitimate as Moses' reception of the Law. Osborne mentions three other uses of the trumpet in the Old Testament: 1) to signal warfare (Judges 3:27; 6:34; Ezekiel 7:14; 2) as heralds for a king, especially in coronation (2 Samuel 6:15; Nehemiah 12:35–36); and 3) with sacrificial offerings (2 Chronicles 29:27:28).[15] Given John's richness in language and his reliance on the Old Testament, we can consider his intention a combination of these. He heard the voice like a trumpet because the final war is about to begin between the dragon and his forces against the Lamb. The trumpet is sounding forth because of the coming of the King of kings, which will signal the end of all things. And the trumpet accompanies the sacrifice of the Lamb and of those who follow the Lamb who do not love their lives as much as they love the Lamb, and so do not shrink from death.

The voice commands John to write about what he *sees*, not what he *hears*. This reminds us of the nature of Revelation. It was a vision to be passed on, penned down, for the strengthening and encouragement of the churches. The prophets of the Old Testament were also told to write for the sake of the people of God. The LORD tells Moses in Exodus 17:14, "Write this as a memorial in a book and recite it in the ears of Joshua." The LORD commands Isaiah similarly in Isaiah 30:8, "And now, go, write it before them on a tablet and inscribe it in a book, that it may be for the time to come as a witness forever." And Jeremiah was told, "Take a scroll and write on it all the words that I have spoken to you against Israel and Judah and all the nations."[16] John is part of a long tradition of prophets who are given the word of God's judgments to the nations and hope for those God has redeemed.

Revelation was to be sent to the seven churches of Asia Minor, both literally seven churches and symbolically for the church universal, represented by those seven churches. The order of the churches followed the circular path of the messenger delivering the letter to these churches, in

14. Beale, *The Book of Revelation*, 203.

15. Osborne, *Revelation*, 84.

16. Beale, *The Book of Revelation*, 203, quoting Jeremiah 36:2.

geographical order. These churches can be understood, then, both as literal churches in a literal location with real problems in the first century and as examples for other churches throughout the ages. The number seven here again stands for completion or perfection.[17]

In the middle of this trial and persecution and exile, John hears the voice of Jesus and sees images that, it's clear from the text, bewilder and overpower him. We may think it strange that John writes that he "turned to see the voice" (1:12). How do you see a voice? This may be a simple metonymy, the voice representing the person speaking, thus emphasizing the "voice as expressing an authoritative utterance."[18]

Before John sees the owner of this powerful voice, he sees "seven golden lampstands" (1:12). Lampstands appear in the Old Testament in Exodus 25:31–40 and Zechariah 4:1–6. In Exodus 25, God describes how the lampstands of the tabernacle were to be crafted. The original lampstand of Israel's sacrificial system was in the holy place. It had seven lamps and was made with gold, as is the lampstand in John's vision. In Zechariah 4:1–6, the lampstand represents the presence of the Spirit (Zechariah 4:6, "Not by might, nor by power, but by my Spirit, says the LORD of hosts.") Whereas Zechariah's lampstand was one lampstand with seven lamps, John sees seven lampstands, one for each of the seven churches and maintaining the idea of perfection. The lampstand in Zechariah stood for faithful Israel. The lampstands in Revelation are for the faithful people of God from all nations.

Jesus is standing "in the midst of the lampstands" (1:13). Described as "one like a son of man, clothed with a long robe and with a golden sash around his chest" (1:13), this is the same "one like a son of man" from Daniel 7, who "came to the Ancient of Days and was presented before him" (Daniel 7:13). The long robe and golden sash are signs of kingly authority and power. In Isaiah 6, Isaiah describes seeing the "train of [the Lord's] robe fill[ing] the temple" (Isaiah 6:1). From Exodus 28:4, we know that a robe and a sash were a part of priestly attire (see also Exodus 28:31; 29:5; 35:8; Zechariah 3:5).[19]

What does this picture of Jesus mean for us? Jesus is with us now. Jesus is not some statue or ornament or philosophy. He is real, and he is present. Since he is present with us now, he sees our deeds and knows what we are doing for him, how we are serving him. He also knows what we are *not* doing for him. We see this in his addresses to the churches when he says, "I

---

17. See discussion from chapter 1:1–8.

18. Beale, *The Book of Revelation*, 207.

19. See Beale, *The Book of Revelation*, 209; Mounce, *The Book of Revelation*, 78; and Osborne, *Revelation*, 89, who say that the robe should be interpreted more generally as that worn by dignitaries and rulers indicating Jesus' kingship. The aristocrat wore the sash around the chest, not the waist, to indicate high rank.

know your works" (Revelation 3:15). Since he is present with us, he also sees our hurts and sorrows and fears and loneliness. This is why we can trust the Bible when 1 Peter 5:7 tells us to, "[cast] all [our] anxieties on him, because he cares for [us]." He cares enough to be with us, actually to dwell with us, "taking the form of a servant [and] [. . .] humbl[ing] himself by becoming obedient to the point of death" (Philippians 2:7–8).

We live as Jesus' church with a King in our midst. People around us are looking for meaning and a real relationship with God. Even if they're not looking, this is the very thing they need, the only thing that will fill the emptiness inside. Jesus is present with his people. And as the great High Priest, this takes on even more significance. Jesus is the High Priest in that he is our mediator. He is our go-between. He represents us before God's throne, and he represents God to us. We are a kingdom and priests only by virtue of our relationship with Jesus. First Timothy 2:5 says, "For there is one God, and there is one mediator between God and men, the man Christ Jesus, who gave himself as a ransom for all."

In verse 14, John sees Jesus' hair as "white, like white wool, like snow." White hair most likely is another reference to the Ancient of Days from Daniel 7. John's vision of Christ is a reflection of the glory of God because he *is* the glory of God. His head represents his wisdom and purity, beauty and ancient knowledge. James 1:5 advises, "If any of you lacks wisdom, let him ask God." Jesus is the source of wisdom and glory. He is both the guide and the path to real holiness. Remember the pilot of a plane. We want to make sure that the pilot understands the instrument panel and has the wisdom about which direction to fly the plane. A plane from where we live in Makassar, Indonesia to Jakarta, a major city on another Indonesian island, will cross over the sea south of Kalimantan. A foolish pilot would fly it over Australia first, the wrong direction.

As the Son of Man with the Ancient of Days, Jesus is also the divine Judge. His blazing eyes can pierce all. They are flames of fire. He sees. Indeed, he is omniscient. He knows all. The flames of fire remind us also of the pillar of fire in the book of Exodus, the abiding presence of God and his protective power over his people. Daniel saw a similar vision of this in Daniel 10:6. That figure also had eyes like flaming torches, and a face like lightning.

Jesus is the Judge. We are not just trying to sneak an extra piece of cake away from the table and hoping our moms don't see us. Jesus sees the thoughts of the mind and the motivations of the heart. This is a picture of Jesus that is lost in our society. We don't serve a tame Jesus or one who is tiptoeing through the churches, making sure he doesn't disturb anybody. He comes to awaken and expose. No one can escape his eyes of judgment. We must be attentive to accurately portraying this image of our Lord to a people around us who have grown complacent in their sin and their attitude toward God. Jesus walks among the churches with the penetrating gaze of fires fully aflame.

Jesus' "feet were like burnished bronze, refined in a furnace" (1:15). This is similar to what Daniel saw in Daniel 10 and what Ezekiel saw in Ezekiel 1 when he saw the Lord on the throne. This is glory and purity and majesty. "His voice [. . .] like the roar of many waters" (1:15) is similar to the thunder of Ezekiel 1 and the thunder later heard by John in Revelation. Ezekiel 43:2 says, "And behold, the glory of the God of Israel was coming from the east. And the sound of his coming was like the sound of many waters, and the earth shone with his glory."

It is hard for us to imagine what John must have seen and heard. If you have ever stood beside a mighty waterfall, like Niagara Falls, you may have an inkling of an understanding of what the voice of Jesus must have sounded like to John. When you stand next to Niagara Falls, you not only hear the falls, but you feel the power of the water as it sprays you in the face, and you feel the wind from the falls whipping your hair and ears. Now, imagine standing in the presence of One whose voice does the same thing. This is power!

Along with this image of power, Jesus is characterized as the protector. John saw Jesus with the seven stars in his right hand. From verse 20, we know that these seven stars are seven angels/messengers for the seven churches. He holds their future in his hands. He has ultimate sovereignty. He has the final voice and decision.

When our children were small, many years ago, I brought a dog home to our house. She was only six weeks old. She was scared and cold. It was February. She had left her mother and her siblings. The home that she left was dirty (urine stains all over the carpet of the house), disorganized, and probably abusive. But this little dog didn't know me yet. She was afraid. That night, I had to sleep next to the dog on the family room floor because she was so afraid. She needed to know I was her protection, and in spite of her fears, I was going to give her a better home. We often feel that our lives would be better and more secure if we figured them out on our own. But Jesus has us in his hands. He knows better than we do, and he wants to give us a better home. To prove that, he came to live with us. He came to our level to show us the extent of God's love and protection.

Not only do we see Jesus' sovereign power and protection, we also see, through John, evidence of Jesus' authority and right to declare the truth. And the truth has the irresistible power of divine judgment. Johnson's comment is worth quoting here: "The sword is both a weapon and a symbol of war, oppression, anguish, and political authority. But John seems to intend a startling difference in the function of this sword, since it proceeds from the mouth of Christ rather than being wielded in his hand."[20] Christ conquers the world through his death and resurrection, and the sword is his word and the faithful witness of his followers.

Isaiah 11:4 says of the Branch that will come from the stump of Jesse, "he shall strike the earth with the rod of his mouth, and with the breath of his lips he shall kill the wicked." Also, of the servant of the Lord, we read in Isaiah 49:2, "He made my mouth like a sharp sword." The authoritative word of Jesus is to be understood and received and believed over and against the false demands of the religions of the world and the fraudulent promises that the world offers. The word of Christ will ultimately prevail and only Jesus has the truth. Only Jesus *is* the truth. In a world that does not know truth anymore, this is a significant part of the picture of Jesus that we need to communicate. Jesus' glorified face is a reinforcement of this truth. Like the brilliance of the sun, Jesus' face is the glory of God. Jesus was revealed like this also during the transfiguration, a good example of Jesus' declaration as the true Son of God.

John's reaction to the vision of Jesus is like the reaction of many prophets of the past when confronted with the glory of God (see Joshua 5:14; Ezekiel 1:28; Daniel 8:17; 10:15; Matthew 17:6; Acts 26:14). They fall facedown in great fear. John fell down "as though dead" (1:17) because he was probably immovable. Jesus' comforting touch, not just voice, lifted John up and encouraged him not to fear. Again, just as Daniel was touched. What is the reason John must not fear? Jesus is the first and the last, just as God declared in Revelation 1:8. Mounce writes, "The laying on of the right hand communicated power and blessing. It is a commissioning hand which restores John's confidence and prepares him to hear the words of consolation and command."[21] John puts into Jesus' mouth the familiar ἐγώ εἰμι (*ego eimi*; It is I) of the gospel of John. Combined with the truth of being the first and the last, this must be another reference to Exodus 3:14. Jesus' reassurance is not only in his touch, but in his exalted self-identity.

Part of the essential identity of Jesus is then revealed in that truth that he died, and is now living, and is alive forevermore. Because of his death and resurrection, Jesus holds the keys of Death and Hades. This is a sign of authority and ownership. To hold the keys means Jesus has the say-so of who goes into Hades. To emphasize this truth Jesus used the word, "behold"

---

20. Johnson, *Hebrews through Revelation*, 428.
21. Mounce, *The Book of Revelation*, 80.

to show John the drastic contrast. *I did die. But look! Hello! I am alive now. Death didn't hold me.*[22]

John is commanded to write about two things: what he has seen and what will take place after this. Revelation is a prophetic disclosure of what is—the current state of affairs for the church and what will come, that is, what the church will have to face. The three phrases (what you have seen, what is, and what is to come) parallel the title for God in verse 4, and "relate to the eschatological perspective of the book as a whole."[23] Jesus again confirms in John's mind and heart that this is a message for churches and that the lampstand, the presence of God, will continue shining amidst the faithful.

## Conclusion

When presented this picture of Jesus, what is our response? Like John, I think if we saw Jesus in person, we would fall to our faces in fear. But we would also be recipients of his touch. When Jesus walked the earth, this is the picture of Jesus that demons saw. They were able to see the supernatural world. They saw not only the common-looking man that Jesus was on the exterior, but also the supernatural Jesus that John saw. What was their response? "What have you to do with us, Jesus of Nazareth? Have you come to destroy us? I know who you are—the Holy One of God" (Luke 4:34). They were terrified.

Our world is in desperate need of an accurate picture of Jesus. What kind of picture are we portraying by our words and deeds? We want to make sure we lead people to the right plane with the right pilot. We can't force them to get in. But we can at least try our best to present the correct picture of him. I believe that if people are truly seeking God (Proverbs 8:17), then this picture will be irresistible.

22. According to Jewish literature, power over the keys of death and Hades belong to God alone (Jerusalem Targum. On Genesis 30:2; Sanh.113a) (Mounce, *The Book of Revelation*, 81).

23. Osborne, *Revelation*, 97.

# Revelation 2:1–7

Jesus' Message to the Church in Ephesus

## Introduction

C AN YOU IMAGINE TAKING a test on your spouse one day? You answer
every question right. If I took a test on my wife Lora, I would answer:
Color of eyes: light brown; Color of hair: light brown; Height: 5 feet and 7
inches; Weight: next question; Personality: pleasant, serious and faithful;
Hobbies: gardening, reading Victorian novels; Favorite food: Indonesian
gado-gado; Favorite color: yellow. If I answered all these questions correctly, would it be true that I know everything there is to know about my
wife? Even if I did, what if I knew all that and still didn't love her? What if I
didn't treat her right, and ignored her needs? Would people notice more my
knowledge of my wife, or my lack of love for her?

Love legitimizes knowledge. Our love for our spouses makes what we
know about them meaningful. If we do not show love, then our understanding of them does not matter. The same is true for the follower of Jesus in
reference to our relationship with God. Love legitimizes doctrine. I just referenced Luke 4, and how the demons recognized Jesus. They knew exactly who
he was, but they did not love him. Our love for God and for the people of the
church and for the people of the world proves that we know God. This is the
message of Revelation 2:1–7, the message to the church in Ephesus.

## Exposition

With chapter two, we see a shift in the nature of Revelation. John is delivering to the seven churches in Asia Minor a message from Jesus himself.
Aune writes that the form of the letters can be seen as a mixed genre created by John. The primary literary genre is that of a royal or imperial edict.
The secondary genre or mode is that of prophetic speech, or "parenetic

salvation-judgment oracle."[1] In other words, John is creating a new kind of epistle here, with the nature of an edict from a king combined with a prophetic word of either encouragement or rebuke.

The model of Jesus' letter to the churches follows this pattern: There is the addressee, "to the angel of the church in . . ." (2:1); followed by a description of the speaker, "The words of him . . ." (2:1). The description of the speaker reveals a close relationship between the seven messages of chapters 2 and 3 and the vision of Jesus in chapter 1. Following this, we see the knowledge of the Speaker, "I know . . ." (2:2). (Sometimes this is positive and sometimes this is negative). This is followed by the verdict: "[. . .] you have abandoned the love you had at first" (2:4); in this case, the command or the exhortation, "He who has an ear, let him hear" (2:7), followed by a promise of "the tree of life" (2:7) to those who are faithful.

What is the nature of these seven letters? All the letters deal with the issue of witnessing for Christ in the midst of a pagan culture. The churches with problems must repent. The churches with no problems must persevere in their faithful witness.[2] Mounce wants to see these letters as "a vital part of the Apocalypse as a whole and are intended for the exhortation and edification of the church universal." This is not a survey of the church throughout history (as in the Dispensational view), but the sequential pattern was used by John "to impress upon the church universal the necessity of patient endurance in the period of impending persecution."[3] Why these seven churches? All seven were within one hundred miles of Ephesus in the Roman proconsular province of Asia and might have formed an established circular rout that functioned as a postal route. Johns seems to have been familiar with each church's situation.[4]

The church in Ephesus was planted by the Apostle Paul. We can read that story in Acts 19. Ephesus was the first church in the order of delivery of the vision of John. As a city of trade, Ephesus was the commercial center of Asia Minor. There was an important port (except for large ships), and it became a connecting city between Syria and Egypt in the East and Italy in the West. Ephesus was considered "the first and greatest metropolis of Asia." The population was between about 200,000 and 250,000 people. Only Rome and Alexandria were bigger at the time.[5] The city of Ephesus was believed to

---

1. Aune, *Revelation 1–5*, 110. Beale calls the letters "prophetic messages" rather than epistles—Beale, *The Book of Revelation*, 225.

2. Beale, *The Book of Revelation*, 227.

3. Mounce, *The Book of Revelation*, 84.

4. Aune, *Revelation 1–5*, 131.

5. Hoehner, *Ephesians: An Exegetical Commentary*, 2002–2223.

have been protected by Artemis. For the faithful, Artemis was supposed to help and bless. She was the child of Leto and Zeus, the goddess of pregnancy and considered very powerful, the "Queen of heaven," "Lord", and "Savior." But Artemis was not the only god/goddess worshipped in Ephesus. There were about fifty others, including Aphrodite, Sybil, Demeter, Isis (Egypt), and Zeus, Apollo, and others.[6]

Jesus is described with images from the vision of John in Revelation 1, the one "who holds the seven stars in his right hand, who walks among the seven golden lampstands" (2:1). The stars are the angels of the seven churches and the seven golden lampstands are the seven churches (see 1:20). Jesus is present in the church through the sevenfold Spirit, the Holy Spirit. The stars in his right hand communicate sovereignty, control, and protection. Beale interestingly notes that a formula introducing the word from the Lord is used here, similar to that used of God (twenty-one times in the Minor Prophets), and "Thus says the Lord" (about sixty-five times in Ezekiel, thirty times in Jeremiah, and eight times in Amos). Essentially, Jesus is here assuming the role of Yahweh.[7] As the speaking Lord, and as One who is "walking" among the golden lampstands rather than simply standing, the text implies that he is one who knows the churches and is active among them.[8] Regardless of how beautiful the temple of Artemis in Ephesus, Jesus is the One who is present with his church. He is not a cold stone, gold, and jeweled building. He is the Living One who is present in our midst and is aware of our activities.

Because Jesus is the One with eyes of flames of fire, he knows the deeds of the churches, and he justly brings judgment or praise to them, depending upon their works. The congregation in Ephesus was a congregation that worked hard and persevered like John in 1:9. The same word is used for "faithful endurance." This was a congregation that did not tolerate wickedness or false teaching, that is, false prophets. They upheld the truth. Apparently, there were in the church at the time, people who would rise up and declare themselves on par with the apostles, with apostolic authority, the same as what Paul encountered in Corinth (2 Corinthians 11:13–15). Maybe their fancy words and careful rhetoric won over audiences, but the Ephesian church tested them and found them not to be genuine. They were false teachers.[9]

6. See Arnold, *Ephesians (Zondervan Exegetical Commentary on the New Testament Series,* 483–493.

7. Beale, *The Book of Revelation,* 229.

8. Thomas and Macchia, *Revelation,* 87.

9. For examining false teachers,, see 1 Thessalonians 5:19–21 and 1 John 4:1–3. Paul warned the Ephesian church of wolves that would rise among them (Acts 20:29;

Doctrinal truth is still important today, especially in light of the fact that so many churches and denominations are giving up on important matters of the faith, like the exclusive claims of Christ, the Trinity, the atonement, the role of the Holy Spirit, and the nature of judgment at the end of time. When doctrine is compromised, a door is opened to any teaching and behavior in the church. Teaching fuels behavior. We can claim that we can live holy lives, but if we do not have a correct understanding of Jesus' sacrifice for us, and the role of the Holy Spirit, our lives will be powerless.

The Ephesian church endured faithfully in what they had. The truth? The Faith? Proper teaching? The gospel? Whichever it was, and it was probably a combination of these, they had endured for the sake of the name of Jesus. They did not grow weary. This was not a casual rejection of false teaching but a persistent vigilance.

The church in Ephesus has remained faithful to sound doctrine. Their problem was that they had forsaken the heart part of their relationship. Jesus had commended them for their endurance to the truth and their stance against false teaching and false prophesy, but his complaint against them was that they had forsaken their first love. What was their first love? Jesus spoke of two commandments: vertical love for God and horizontal love for one another. Had they grown cold in their commitment to loving God and loving one another in their stressing of the truth? ἀφῆκες (*aphekes*) has the idea of forsaking, not just forgetting. They had forsaken their mission and the highest command of Jesus.

There are quite a few perspectives of what this first love actually was. Beale believes that "lost their first love" means that they had forsaken their witness to the world.[10] Thomas thinks that first love is primarily referencing Jesus. Love has an important place in Johannine literature (see John 13:34–35). The first work is love for one another, and this is reflective of our love for Jesus.[11] Mounce believes that the losing of their first love refers mainly to their love for one another.[12] Thomas is on the right track. Loss of love was caused by their struggle with false teachers and their hatred of heretical teachings, which led to harsh attitudes toward one another. This led to a lessoning of love among the brothers. We cannot separate a love for Jesus and a love for the brothers. This is clear from 1 John. If we say we love Jesus and do not love our brothers, we are lying. So, a loss of first love would include both a loss of love for the brothers as well as a loss of

cf. Matthew 7:15).

10. Beale, *The Book of Revelation*, 230. See a parallel in Matthew 24:12–14.

11. Thomas and Macchia, *Revelation*, 90.

12. Mounce, *The Book of Revelation*, 88. See also Jeremiah 2:2.

love for Christ. They go together. They had become like the older brother in the parable of the prodigal son, doing the right things out of duty, but not from a motivation of love.

Christianity is not just a matter of the mind, it is a matter of the heart, of the affections. The Ephesian church was great about their commitment to doctrinal truth, but they were lacking in their commitment to genuine love. The command from Jesus is to "remember." Remember what? Remember the place from where they had fallen. They were also to repent from this forsaking of their first love and do the works they did at first. They must continue to persevere in the truth, but without forsaking the love of Christ. "Remember" is in the present imperative, which stands in contrast with "repent" in the aorist imperative. They must keep calling to mind the love from which they had fallen, and then make a clean break from that attitude.[13]

Jesus' threat is serious. He threatened that if they did not repent, he would come and remove the lampstand from its place, that is, the light and presence of the Holy Spirit would be taken away. The glory would be removed just as the glory of God left the temple in the days of Ezekiel. Aune reiterates, this is "nothing less than a threat to obliterate the Ephesian congregation as an empirical Christian community."[14] Is this an imminent threat or an eschatological threat? I believe it should be both/and, but it was more of an imminent threat given the presence of Jesus among the churches, walking among the lampstands.

How is our commitment to genuine love both in the church and out of it? Sometimes it is easy to get caught up in right doctrine and protecting our interests as a church body, that we forget that not only are we supposed to be ministering and loving one another, but also those outside the church. This begins with a genuine love for Jesus, not only a doctrinal love, but a love that impacts our actions, a love that is real and relational. Christianity is not just a set of dos and don'ts or a series of rituals and creeds. Christianity, as the name suggests, is at the core about a relationship with Christ.

There are too many people who can quote Bible verses and give out statements of faith, but who have no love or compassion in their lives. One theologian has said (I don't remember who), "The glum, sour faces of many Christians . . . They give the impression that, instead of coming from the Father's joyful banquet, they have just come from the Sheriff who has auctioned off their sins and now are sorry they can't get them back again." In Philemon, Paul reminds us that our good doctrine of Jesus can actually be encouraged by our right love for others. He says to Philemon, "I thank my

13. Mounce, *The Book of Revelation*, 88.
14. Aune, *Revelation 1–5*, 147.

God always when I remember you in my prayers, because I hear of your love and of the faith that you have toward the Lord Jesus and for all the saints, and I pray that the sharing of your faith may become effective for the full knowledge of every good thing that is in us for the sake of Christ" (Philemon 4–6). The love we have for one another and for the world will instruct our understanding of Jesus.

Without love, a congregation ceases to be the church, and so Jesus warned against the removal of the lampstand. *I'm going to close you down if you don't start loving me and loving one another*, he's saying. In Hot Springs, Arkansas, there's a place called Morris Antique Mall. Nothing on the inside distinguishes this antique store from dozens like it in Hot Springs. There is a musty smell and dusty relics of years gone by. But if you look closely at the outside of the Morris Antique Mall, you'll see something that makes it distinct: before it was an antique store, it was a church building. Like the church that became the Morris Antique Mall is no longer there, neither is the congregation in Ephesus.

Jesus shifted the rebuke back to a closing word of encouragement for this congregation. The opening phrase of verse 6, ἀλλὰ τοῦτο ἔχεις (*alla touto ekseis*), is a way of saying, "But this you have that you are doing well." The Ephesian church could not tolerate the works of the Nicolaitans. They hated their works, just as Jesus did. The Nicolaitans allowed for compromise and went beyond what was allowed in the apostolic letter to the Gentile churches from Acts 15:29. They taught that some degree of pagan temple participation was acceptable, even compromising with the prohibition of burning incense to the image of the emperor.[15]

What would Jesus say of the modern church concerning moral purity? Are we not taking part in the practices of groups similar to the Nicolaitans? We would be quick to say that we have nothing to do with those kinds of groups. But what of the world have we allowed to creep into our homes and into our churches? If there is, at times, no statistical difference between the people outside of the church and the people inside of the church in regards to ethical standards and moral purity, that speaks a lot to our moral condition and how much we have allowed ourselves to offer sacrifices at our modern-day altars of the emperor, the materialism and self-absorption and obsession with achievement.

Our problem in evangelical churches is not so much that we don't teach the right things (though this is becoming an increasingly disturbing issue), but that we don't live out that which we teach. Parents must be willing to take strong stands on these issues. And their children must

15. Beale, *The Book of Revelation*, 233.

be willing to accept them. We must remember that Jesus is the one who walks among us. He holds his churches in his right hand. He knows our deeds. We must, therefore, put off the practices of the Nicolaitans of our generation and refuse to be influenced by them. Jesus hates their deeds. We must also hate their deeds.

In our churches today, there must be a combination of doctrine, love, and purity. Only these three combined will make an impact in our world. People will not be able to call into question our message, because the purity of our lives will prove our message is true. But our message needs to be acted out in love. "By this all men will know that you are my disciples, that you have love for one another." 2 Corinthians 5:14 says, "For the love of Christ controls us, because we have concluded this: that one has died for all, therefore all have died." If there is no doctrine but love and purity, you come across as a liberal philanthropist who believes that many roads lead to God and thus denies the glory that is only due Jesus (see 1:9–20).

If there is no love, but doctrine and purity, like in the Ephesian church, you come across as cold and uncompassionate with no heart relationship with God. There are many religious people in the world (like ascetics) who may be teaching the right things but have no relationship with Jesus.

If there is no purity, but love and doctrine, then your life denies the words that come from your mouth (see 1 Timothy 4:12–16). The Apostle Paul said to Timothy that these kinds of people have a "form of godliness but deny its power." We can talk about the power of Jesus all we want, but if it is not displayed in changing our lives, then our message is like smoke. It burns for a while, but then fades away.

## Conclusion

Jesus closes this admonition to the church in Ephesus with a promise to those who overcome or obey the words of Jesus, as he does in each case of each letter to the churches. To the church in Ephesus, he promises that they would be given the opportunity to eat from the tree of life in God's paradise. The word for "paradise" in Greek is transliterated as "paradise" in English. This was originally a Persian word, describing an enclosed garden or park that took on religious connotations. It is God's paradise here, pointing to the new heavens and the new earth of 21:1–22:5 and establishing a contrast with the temple of Artemis that promised an earthly paradise, but didn't last.[16] A paradise prepared by God, owned by God (possessive genitive), and a paradise where God dwells.

16. Osborne, *Revelation*, 124.

In this paradise is the tree of life. The tree of life recalls the tree in the Garden of Eden, which was placed in the middle. Adam and Eve were barred from the tree because of their sin. The faithful who overcome (in their perseverance against false prophets and in their remembrance of love) will be given the privilege to eat from this tree. Ladd aptly writes, "Love and loyalty to Christ will conquer fear of suffering and death."[17] No longer distant from the tree of life, the faithful will have continued access to it.

And for those who have the ears to hear, they will hear the admonitions of Jesus. This phrase was used by Jesus in the synoptic gospels (see Matthew 13:9–17, 43; see also Ezekiel 3:27; 12:2). It is Jesus who speaks, and it is the Spirit who speaks. There is no contradiction here. The Spirit is the Spirit of Christ who interprets the voice of Christ. Throughout Revelation, there is an intimate association between the Spirit of Christ and Christ, as in the rest of the New Testament.[18]

---

17. Ladd, *A Commentary on the Revelation of John*, 41.

18. Ladd, *A Commentary on the Revelation of John*, 40. Consider Isaiah 6:9–11, where those who have ears did not hear and as a result were rejected as part of God's people.

# Revelation 2:8–11

Jesus' Message to the Church in Smyrna

## Introduction

THERE ARE MANY EXAMPLES of comeback wins in the world of sports. I am a fan of the Chicago Cubs. After 108 years of frustration, they finally won the World Series in 2016. In the last game of the series, with the teams tied after winning three games each, the Cubs lost the lead in the late innings, only to win later in extra innings. It was quite dramatic, and I may never forget where I was (in Thailand) when they won.

More significant than any set-back (like the Cubs' ninth inning in game 7) in a sports contest is the loss that veterans of wars understand in light of the victories that they set out to achieve. The losses are real, and they hurt, but the victory, if it is a cause worth dying for, outweighs the losses.

And more significant still than even the losses of men in battle for a great cause, are the losses we as believers, soldiers of the Lord, face every day of our lives, the kind of losses that even take lives in some instances, as our brothers and sisters in Christ are dying every day for the sake of Jesus—some tortured, some losing home and family, some losing limbs, and some losing their own lives.

But these losses, and all others, pale in comparison to the ultimate victory. This is the message that Jesus wants to communicate to the church in Smyrna, and it is a message that we need to hear as well. We may not have seen intense persecution, and may not see it in our lifetime, but many believers around the world have endured these kinds of trials. We can take comfort in the truth that the victory is sweeter than the losses along the way. And even though our sufferings may not at times be related to persecution, the joys that we have waiting for us far outshine the hard times of our lives.

## Exposition

Jesus knows the situations we face. We remember that he is the One who walks among the golden lampstands. He knows the activities of the evil one, and he is not thwarted by them. Knowing that our Savior knows the suffering we face not only helps us get through them but compels us, just like a son playing harder when his father is watching. We endure through the pain because we know that Jesus is watching.

Jesus knew what was happening to his church in Smyrna. Smyrna is one of two churches about which Jesus had only positive things to say. This was a church that was enduring intense persecution. It seems that often during times of persecution in the church, that the church is more attuned to following God. They have less time to sin and feel more compelled to pray.

Smyrna is the only city of the seven still in existence, modern Izmir. It was located 35 miles north of Ephesus on the east shore of the Aegean Sea. It was an export city, second only to Ephesus with a population of about 200,000. It boasted a beautiful road called "The Street of God" that curved around Mount Pagus with a temple on either end: one to Cybele and the other to Zeus.[1]

Smyrna was a patriotic city, loyal to Rome, and had built more than one temple in honor of the Roman cult.[2] A certain expectation of emperor worship must have been present. The Jews would have been quick to distance themselves from the Christians and to turn them into the authorities for not also participating. Probably nowhere else was life more dangerous for the Christian at this time than at Smyrna. About 156 A.D. Polycarp, the saintly bishop of Smyrna, was burned alive at the age of 86. His words as he burned were, "86 years have I served Christ, and he has never done me wrong. How can I blaspheme my King who saved me?"

Why is Jesus described as the "First and the Last, the one who was dead and is now alive?" Because of the suffering that must have been experienced by the church in Smyrna. They needed to be reminded of the sovereignty of God. And also of the witness of Jesus who also suffered (see 1 Peter 2:21). He died and came to life again. They will suffer but will not be hurt by the second death (v.11). To a congregation threatened with imprisonment and death, it would be comforting to know that the Lord of Creation went through the same thing and he has their reward in his hands.

Jesus knew the affliction they were experiencing, and their poverty. Were they poor because of their faith in Jesus? Was this an economic affliction

---

1. Mounce, *The Book of Revelation*, 91.
2. Beale, *The Book of Revelation*, 240.

of persecution? There is good reason to believe it was. In Jesus' estimation they were not poor, but rich. They were rich because of the promise of the kingdom, and the promise of release from the second death. They were rich because they endured great hardship for their faith.[3]

Jesus knew who was persecuting them. There was a group claiming to be Jews but were really blasphemers. They were really a synagogue of Satan. Who were these people? Were these actual Jews who were trying to impose their Judaism on the church in Smyrna? These Jews who persecuted the Christian believers were not "real Jews" in the covenantal sense. They had been cut off from the tree (see Romans 9–11). To Jesus, these were not really Jews at all, in the same sense that he accused the Pharisees of not belonging to the family of Abraham, but rather were children of the devil. Notice the harsh words Jesus used again in Revelation 2. They were a synagogue of Satan.

Jesus knows what is happening to his church around the world. Smyrna can be paralleled to so many of our churches around the world, those undergoing intense persecution. Jesus knows their situations. He promises us that if we want to live a godly life in Christ Jesus, we will be persecuted (2 Tim.3:12). How much wealthier these churches are than those around the world that have the fancy, stained glass windows, the gold covered columns, and the marble entrances! It is the church that suffers in the fire of tribulation, in the crucible of testimony for the cause of Christ, that is the church that is wealthy according to Jesus.

We can be encouraged by this that Jesus does see the pain that we endure. He knows. He is not just a moral meter, taking notes on how we are doing throughout the day. He is a companion and, though he promised that the church would be persecuted, he aches when it is. He knows what it is like to be unfairly treated because of righteousness. And he knows the struggles we face, for as Hebrews says, he faced trials of many kinds, just like us.

Jesus told the church in Smyrna to not fear the coming πάσχειν (*pascheiv*) that they were expected to experience. They would be tested in prison. Tested for what? Tested by whom? The enemy would throw them into prison to see if any of them would cave into the suffering. Ten days could be an allusion to Daniel 1:12–15 and the ten days of testing of Daniel and his friends.[4] Or it could be a symbolic time period indicating a limited duration of suffering.[5] Whatever the time period, probably a short, limited period of suffering, Jesus told them to be faithful even unto death, just as he was.

---

3. Thomas and Macchia, *Revelation*, 95.

4. See Beale, *The Book of Revelation*, 242.

5. Thomas and Macchia, *Revelation*, 97. Ladd suggests that John is anticipating a localized persecution in Smyrna of short duration—Ladd, *A Commentary on the Revelation of John*, 44.

If they proved faithful, they would be given the crown of life. The Greek word for crown is the same word for the name Stephen. Are they thus reminded of Stephen's victory when he testified faithfully and was killed at the hands of the Jews? He was faithful even unto death. He saw Jesus standing in heaven to witness his sufferings. Jesus would witness the sufferings of the believers in Smyrna as well.

Death for the people was a real possibility. But those who overcame would not be injured from the second death. This is the final judgment about which John writes in Revelation 20. It is the Lake of Fire, into which the devil and the beast, and all the ungodly will be cast at the end of time. Jesus is so insistent about this that he used the double negative in the Greek, "You will no way go into the second death!"[6] To him who overcomes go the spoils. And to the believer that remains faithful during times of persecution, the crown of life will be given, and he will be spared from judgment.

## Conclusion

Life is difficult. Life is filled with trials. But the ultimate victory to come far outweighs any struggle, any trial we face. A student of mine asked me after class several years ago, "If a man holds a knife to my neck and asks me if I am a follower of Jesus, can I say "no" while still saying "yes" in my heart?" I answered him, "If you say 'no' that man will go away thinking your faith is weak and your Jesus is weak, and you will live regretting that denial. But if you say, 'yes,' and the man takes your life, you will go straight to your reward, and that man will leave you with the impression that the confession of Jesus is worth giving your life." This student smiled, knowing what the right response should be, even though it is difficult.

But the power of this perspective, Jesus' perspective, not only allows us to endure the pain and suffering of today. It also impacts those who are watching us. Our wounds, our suffering, fulfills or completes the suffering of Christ in the eyes of the world.

6. See Matthew 10:28; Luke 12:4–5.

# Revelation 2:12–17

Jesus' Message to the Church in Pergamum

## Introduction

FOR AN AMERICAN, AND probably for many in Europe, there are not many smells as pleasing to the olfactory senses as the smell of fresh baked bread. The smell is so appealing that some realtors advise their customers to bake some bread while they are showing their home. The unsuspecting home buyer is subconsciously taken in by the hominess of the home and its smell. I love to go into a bakery and smell the fresh baked loaves, cakes, and muffins. Contrast this to the smell of a garbage dump—rotting fish, decaying fruit, old cheese and curdled milk. These smells are enough to make us sick. And they certainly are not smells we seek.

It is interesting then, to wonder why we often are attracted spiritually to that which spiritually stinks, and we so often avoid the Heavenly Bread that is so much better for us. Jesus is the Bread of Life, as we read in John 6, and he offers himself to us. His fragrance is a pleasing aroma. But there are competing foods in the world that try to attract our attention. These foods are spoiled and rotten. They smell to God and should be distasteful to the people of God. We see an example of the difference between the rotten and healthy in Jesus' message to the church in Pergamum.

## Exposition

Pergamum was a city located forty miles along the coast north of Smyrna and then ten miles inland east from the Aegean Sea. It was built on a cone-shaped hill about 1,000 feet high. The name Pergamum means "citadel." It had a library with 200,000 volumes in it.[1] Jesus is pictured as the One who has a sharp, double-edged sword coming out of his mouth. The sword throughout the book of Revelation is a symbol of divine judgment. As he came to the

---

1. Mounce, *The Book of Revelation*, 95.

church in Pergamum as the Divine Judge, so he comes to us in our churches around the world. Jesus is the judge of the church but also of those who persecute the church. He will be, at the end of the ages, the One who judges the living and the dead. In 20:11–15 we see that the books will be opened at the final judgment. And we will be judged according to whether our names appear in the book of life. If they appear, there is no fear. If they do not appear, there is the eternal judgment of the lake of fire.

Jesus knew the situation of Pergamum, that they lived in a tough situation. They lived in a city where evil was very active. He even called it the place where Satan has his throne. The mention of Satan's throne is a way of saying that this city is a center of Roman government and pagan religions. It was the first city in Asia Minor to build a temple to a Roman emperor, Augustus. The image of Satan's throne may also come from a throne-like altar to Zeus on the hill behind Pergamum. It was also the host of several temples dedicated to Athene, Demeter, and Dionysius. There was also the cult of Asclepius, the god of healing.[2] Mounce and Ladd both emphasis the prominence of Pergamum as the official cult center of emperor worship in Asia.[3]

In the midst of the satanic setting, the church members held fast to the name of Jesus. Or, in keeping with the opening illustration, they remained true in the midst of the garbage heap in which they lived. Jesus even named one as someone who died in his witness for Jesus. We are not sure who Antipas was other than a follower of Jesus who was a faithful witness even until death. His faithful witness is perhaps a reminder of Isaiah 43:10–12 where God declared, "You are my witnesses, declares the Lord." In verse 13 Jesus says, "my faithful witness."[4] Antipas, and other faithful believers like him in Pergamum, chose to eat the good food of Christ rather than the garbage food of the world.

There were some in the church, however, who began to eat the garbage heap of rotten food, called sexual immorality and impurity. First, reference is made to Balaam, who in Numbers could not curse the Israelites but helped Balak gain an advantage over them by encouraging their people to inter-marry with the Israelites, thus leading them into adultery (see

2. Beale, *The Book of Revelation*, 246. Aune also lists possible meanings for Satan's throne as the judge's bench or tribunal where the proconsul sat to judge or Satan's throne as the center of Christian persecution, though he leans toward the latter—Aune, *Revelation 1–5*, 182–84.

3. Mounce, *The Book of Revelation*, 96; Ladd, *A Commentary on the Revelation of John*, 46. See also Johnson, *Hebrews through Revelation*, 440.

4. τὴν πίστιν μου is the objective genitive, which could be translated "faith in me" (Beale, *The Book of Revelation*, 246). This suggests something of the church's solidarity with the faithfulness of Jesus (Thomas and Macchia, *Revelation*, 100), though Thomas calls it a possessive genitive, as it would refer to Jesus' faithfulness.

Numbers 22:5–25:3; 31:8, 16). Numbers 25:2–3 says, "The people ate and bowed down to their gods. So Israel yoked himself to Baal of Peor: And the anger of the Lord was kindled against Israel." The sins of the people were eating food that had been sacrificed to idols and sexual immorality.[5] Sexual immorality was not only spiritual (with other gods away from their marriage to God), but also fleshly. It would have been very prevalent in Pergamum, as it would have been common in other larger Roman cities with open baths and places of temple prostitution.[6]

The practice of the Nicolaitans was also a problem in Pergamum as it was for the Ephesian church. These were people who also encouraged compromise with the rotten food of the society around them. A little compromise here, a little compromise there, and soon the church looked no different than the world. This group of Nicolaitans could have been the same group as those who followed the teachings of Balaam. Etymologically the meanings of the names are similar, "to overcome or consume the people."[7] Both compromised with the world and ate the rotten food of the society.

What is rotten food around us today? In our societies, we also face the danger of compromise. Whenever we desire the rotten food of the world rather than the Bread of Life, we compromise. There is the rotten food of sexual perversion, a sin we oftentimes do not take seriously anymore. There is the rotten food of greed and materialism. Jesus said, "You cannot serve God and money." There is the rotten food of bitterness and revenge. Jesus said, "It is mine to avenge. I will repay." He said, "Love your enemies and pray for those who persecute you." He said, "If you are offering your gift at the altar and there remember that your brother has something against you, leave you gift there before the altar and go. First be reconciled to your brother, and then come and offer your gift." There is also the rotten food of pride and selfishness.

How can we avoid this rotten food? Jesus commanded the church in Pergamum to repent. If not, Jesus would come soon to make war[8] against them. This is similar to the breath of his mouth in 2 Thessalonians with

---

5. From the word πορνεῦσαι, where we get the English word "pornography".

6. Ladd, *A Commentary on the Revelation of John*, 48. See also Osborne, *Revelation*, 145 who writes that it is probable that literal promiscuity is in view, similar to the libertinism of 1 John.

7. Beale, *The Book of Revelation*, 251.

8. The Greek word for "make war," (πολεμήσω), is the word "polemic." Beale sees an interesting parallel between the threat Balaam faced of being killed by the sword of the angel of the Lord (Numbers 22:23, 31) and his actual death when he did not heed the warning, and the threat to the church to be killed with the sword if they did not repent of his teachings—Beale, *The Book of Revelation*, 250.

which the antichrist and false prophet will be defeated. The judgment of Jesus from the witness of his word and voice is final.

Rotten food is easy to smell, especially when we know the real thing and how pleasant it is. We must seek, therefore, to know the real thing. We must study the word and spend time with Jesus. The more we know the Bread of Life, the quicker we will be at sniffing out the rotten food of the world. Rotten food must be thrown out immediately or it will spoil what is good. Ephesians 5:3 says, "But sexual immorality and all impurity or covetousness must not even be named among you, as is proper among saints."

I learned an Arabic word when I was with my mother in Florida several years ago. The word is *samek* and it refers to an awful smell. My mother and my Aunt smelled something bad in the refrigerator and they looked and looked to find out where the bad smell was coming from. I think Arabs have a more acute smell, because I really couldn't smell anything. They looked a long time, over several days (every time they opened the refrigerator, they would complain of *samek)*. They never did find it! But the effort they went to in order to rid the refrigerator of that bad smell is the same kind of effort we need to rid our lives of the rotten food of the world.

Jesus said in Matthew 6:33, "But seek first the kingdom of God and his righteousness and all these other things will be added to you." He said again in Matthew 7:7–8, "Ask and it will be given to you; seek and you will find; knock and it will be opened to you. For everyone who asks receives, and the one who seeks finds, and to the one who knocks it will be opened." And again, in response to Satan's temptation to turn the stones into bread in Matthew 4, Jesus said, "Man shall not live by bread alone, but by every word that comes from the mouth of God." We must seek the Living bread, the Bread of Life, to be our daily sustenance and our focus, our priority and our vision.

Jesus promised the church in Pergamum, "To the one who conquers I will give some of the hidden manna." Hidden manna is a reference to the Exodus story and the manna from heaven. It could also be a reference to Jesus, the Bread of Life, the Manna sent from God in John 6. The manna is contrasted with the idolatrous food. The Israelites should have trusted in God's provision at the time of Balaam and not partaken in the idolatrous feast. So also, the church in Pergamum.[9] Why is the manna called "hidden" manna? It is possible that this is a reference to the story in 2 Maccabees 2:4–7 when Jeremiah took the pot of manna that was placed in the ark as a memorial for future generations and hid it underground in Mt. Nebo before the destruction of the temple. This was an apocryphal story. But a story that may have been familiar to the church in the first century.

9. Beale, *The Book of Revelation*, 252.

Jesus must continue to be our provider, our supplier, our sustainer, and our satisfaction from heaven.

Jesus also promised a white stone to the overcoming church. White stones were given to those who were especially invited to a feast, like a wedding invitation (see Revelation 19 and the wedding supper of the Lamb). The "new name" on the white stone is a mark of genuine membership in the community, an identity deeper still than our new name/status in Christ, without which we could not enter into the kingdom of God.[10] Isaiah 62:2 says, "The nations shall see your righteousness, and all the kings your glory, and you shall be called by a new name that the mouth of the Lord will give." This stone was white because of the righteousness of the saints who refused to participate in the Balaam cult of idolatry and sexual immorality.

## Conclusion

Seeking Jesus means seeking him in prayer (alone and with others), seeking him in fellowship with other believers, seeking him as we communicate the message of the gospel and the testimony of our changed lives to neighbors, family, and friends, seeking him Sunday through Sunday, and guarding our ears and our hearts and our eyes against the unholy, rotten food of the world. We will then not fear the sword in his mouth. We will stand before him as one accepted and righteous.

Jesus said in John 6:27, "Do not work for the food that perishes, but for the food that endures to eternal life, which the Son of Man will give to you. For on him God the Father has set his seal." The people asked Jesus, "What must we do, to be doing the works of God?" Jesus simply said, "This is the work of God, that you believe in him whom he has sent." It is those who believe in the Bread from Heaven and seek him that will be given a new name—this secret name known only to God and to us when we get to Heaven. When we seek the Bread of Life for our forgiveness and salvation, we are presented the stone of invitation to the wedding banquet. We are free to enter before God because of Jesus.

---

10. Beale, *The Book of Revelation*, 253–55. See also Osborne, *Revelation*, 149, who writes, "The manna and white stone are both eschatological symbols related to the messianic feast at the eschaton but also teaching the spiritual food and new name that God gives to the believer in the present as well."

# Revelation 2:18–29

Jesus' Message to the Church in Thyatira

## Introduction

WHEN OUR YOUNGEST SON, Josiah, was little, the movie Toy Story came out. Josiah really liked Buzz Lightyear. He had a Buzz Lightyear toy that made cool sounds. One week, as Lora was praying for the kids before they went to school, she prayed that God would protect them. Josiah had asked her beforehand to pray that Buzz Lightyear would protect them. When Lora had finished praying and had not mentioned Buzz Lightyear, Josiah said, "You didn't pray that Buzz Lightyear would protect us." Lora said, "That's because Jesus is able to protect you." Josiah said, "But Jesus does not have lasers!" How about eyes of flames of fire and feet like burnished bronze!

Jesus has power. Jesus has authority. He is the One we want in our corner. But he is not the One we want to be on the wrong side of. Of the many things lacking in our cultures, one of the bigger ones is the lack of good authority figures in people's lives. Our authority figures have often proved disappointing. They lack integrity, or they don't have the kind of leadership we need. Maybe our parents have been bad examples of authority figures. Politicians we know certainly have been bad examples of authority figures. Even policemen, and sometimes teachers, have been bad examples.

With a lack of authority, there is an increasing sense of lost-ness or the feeling of chaos around us. "Who is in control anyway?" This is an especially crucial question in light of events that are happening around the world. In the book series, *The Lord of the Rings*, which was made into a motion picture, there is a time during the story where the four hobbits are walking through the old forest alone. There is no one to lead them. Their leader and teacher, Gandalf, had been detained by the once wise man who had succumbed to growing shadows of darkness. They were afraid, unaware of the dangers around them, and yet knowing that dangers were everywhere. Is this not an accurate picture of many we know? They are wandering this world with no leadership, and thus no direction, no purpose, and no hope; only fear and lost-ness and uncertainty.

The good news is that Jesus is in control! Jesus has authority. It is an authority He had before He came to the earth, and an authority He won again when He came to the earth to give up his life, so that the Father could honor him with the rule and kingdom that would last forever. It is this authority we see very clearly demonstrated in the message to the church in Thyatira. What do we know about Thyatira? It is one of the least known cities, but we do know it was situated about 40 miles east/southeast of Pergamum, along the Lycus River in fertile valleys. It was a Roman colony with many trade associations (guilds), and a religion dedicated to Apollo. It was a wealthy city. And I'm sure they had many who claimed a certain kind of authority. But the little persecuted church in this wealthy city needed a reminder of the true and real authority, Jesus alone.

## Exposition

Jesus identifies himself as the Son of God, whose eyes are flames of fire and feet like burnished bronze. These are reminders of the vision of Ezekiel, the omniscience and majesty of Jesus in all his glory. Also see Daniel 10:6. This glory is Jesus' glory as the Son of God. In Thyatira, both Apollo and the emperor, to whom local trade gilds were dedicated, were believed to be sons of Zeus. But the church in Thyatira must give heed to the real Son of God. Jewish literature of the time often combined the identity of the Son of God from Psalm 2 with the Son of Man individual in Daniel 7.[1] The Son of Man who received power and authority from the Ancient of Days is the eternal Son of God who holds the iron scepter in his hand.

Jesus commended the church in Thyatira for their deeds. Unlike Ephesus, the deeds of Thyatira got better. Their latest deeds were better than the first. They understood Jesus more. They gave more. They loved more. They served more. Jesus saw the growth. He saw the improvement when others did not. Growth is always the most imperceptible by the ones who are growing. Children rarely see that they are growing unless family members who haven't seen them for a while say, "My, how you have grown!" Believers, especially new believers, may not perceive their growth in the Lord. But Jesus sees it.

There is a four-fold commendation from Jesus to this church, evidence that they had grown. They had love, probably love for God and love for one another. Many of our acts of kindness or love that we extend to others, or

---

1. Beale, *The Book of Revelation*, 259.

sacrifices we make because of our love for God, while may not be seen by others, are seen by God. We may not get our pictures in the paper, or in the latest blog news post. But Jesus does not allow any acts of love that we give to him or to others to be overlooked. The church in Thyatira also had faith. What some may assume is foolishness or superstition on our part (believing in a God we cannot see and holding to the truth of a book written thousands of years ago), Jesus sees that faith and is pleased. He knows that with that faith, mountains can be moved, and his church can grow. Jesus also commended the church for their service. The word for service, τὴν διακονίαν (ten diakonian), is closely associated with Jesus' death in John 12:2, 26. Disciples are also to be willing to follow Jesus even unto death, loving service manifested in one's faithfulness to death,[2] accented by Jesus' forth commendation of the church's commitment to patient endurance.

It is nice to be noticed by Jesus when we are living our lives in love, faith, service, and patient endurance, similar to the church in Thessalonica. I experienced many times when I was playing baseball as a young person, when I came up to bat at the plate, connected on a solid, run-scoring double, only to look to the stands, deflated that no member of my family was there to see it happen. Well, Jesus is always "in the stands" to see when we hit a double for his kingdom. He always sees. Hebrews 12:1–2 reminds us, "Therefore, since we are surrounded by such a great cloud of witnesses (those who have gone before us), let us throw off the sin that so easily entangles us, and let us run with perseverance the race marked out for us. Let us fix our eyes on Jesus." Why? Because his eyes of blazing fire are fixed on us.

Jesus knows the good, but He also knows when his church or those in the church are not following him. The problem in the church in Thyatira was that they tolerated a woman named Jezebel who called herself a prophetess. She taught and seduced the servants of Christ to do the same that Balaam had done when he seduced the Israelites at the time of Balak. They committed sexual immorality and ate food sacrificed to idols. There was compromise in the church to the local pagan celebrations, most likely with the hope that they would not be ostracized from the local trade guild.[3]

The church tolerated this false prophet rather than take active steps to remove her from the congregation. There was a church in my district when I was a pastor in Ohio where the music leader of the church for fifteen years was carrying on an extra marital affair while still leading worship. No pastor did anything about it until a new pastor came to the church. The new pastor,

2. Thomas and Macchia, *Revelation*, 105.

3. Beale, *The Book of Revelation*, 261–62, sees a parallel between the sins of those in the church in Thyatira to the sins of Babylon listed in chapter 18. In the Old Testament, Jezebel was a worshipper of Baal and a persecutor of God's people.

when he found out, lovingly yet firmly removed him from ministry in the church. This infuriated the worship pastor and he left, taking some with him. Was the church better off? They had less members, and a music program with less quality, but Jesus saw them and was pleased with what He saw.

Jesus had given the false prophetess time to repent, but she was unwilling. So, the punishment from Jesus was harsh and complete. Consider the harsh words used by Jesus and it reminds us how seriously He takes this sin. He would "cast her on a bed of suffering," she would "suffer intensely, unless they repent," "strike her children dead," "I will repay each of you." The Greek word, κλίνην (klinen), translated "bed of suffering" in the ESV and NIV, is a Hebraism that means "to become ill,"[4] meaning that she would suffer a physical sickness, or plague of some kind, because of her wickedness. And if those who participated in her activities did not repent, they would suffer the "great tribulation" of suffering as well.

Jesus is Lord and King of his church. He will not have these kinds of behaviors muddying up the clothing of his bride and splashing dirt on her wedding gown. Can you imagine, as the groom, standing up at the altar waiting for your bride to come down the aisle? And while she approached the front, people in the pews stood up and threw waste on her, mud from the sewers, spit, and caked cow manure on her freshly made-up hair? Would you allow that? Of course not! You would go to the middle of the aisle and cast those offenders onto the streets. They had no place at the wedding. Jesus is protective of his bride. And anyone who chooses to muddy the bride will be cast out, because Jesus has the authority to do so.

Jesus will go after "her children" as well, meaning those who follower her teachings and become enamored by her idolatry. The judgment of death[5] against the children can be linked to Ezekiel 33:27–31. Verse 27 says, "As I live, surely those who are in the waste places shall fall by the sword, and whoever is in the open field I will give to the beasts to be devoured, and those who are in strongholds and in caves shall die by pestilence." When the judgment of Jesus comes, it will vindicate his person as the One who knows the minds and hearts of others. This fits with the concept of his eyes as flames of fire, the eyes of judgment and discernment. In Jeremiah 17:10, the Lord says, "I the Lord search the heart and test the mind, to give every man according to his ways,

---

4. Beale, *The Book of Revelation*, 263.

5. Mounce, *The Book of Revelation*, 105, citing James Moffat, *The Revelation of St. John the Divine*, 361 believes that this phrase, "to kill with death," is a Hebraism that means "to slay utterly." Aune does not agree (Aune, *Revelation 1–5*, 198), but does see the connection with Ezekiel 33. Also see the description of the dead in chapter 19, after Jesus comes back again.

according to the fruit of his deeds." What is clear to Jesus will be clear to all the churches as well ("all the churches will know").

Jesus knew and judged those in the church who had compromised, but he also promised reward to those in the church who refused to succumb to the false teaching. The Scripture tells us to be wise about what is good, but innocent about what is evil. The followers of Jezebel apparently thought by knowing the ways of the devil they would be able to understand the spiritual world more fully. This "freed" them from the sin of sexual immorality and idolatry even though they participated in these things. But Jesus reminded the church that the "so-called deep secrets" of Satan are just that. Satanic knowledge. This is John's ironic way of saying this in reality was what Jezebel's teaching led to, rather than to the deep things of God.[6]

The faithful were called to hold fast, or persevere, until the coming of Jesus. Authority over the nations is the reward for the overcomer, just as Jesus now has authority over the nations because of his faithfulness to the witness of the word of God, and his faithfulness as the Son of God. They will rule with a rod of iron (see Psalm 2) just as Jesus.[7] Jesus said to his disciples in Matthew 28:18–19, before he ascended, "All authority in heaven and on earth has been given to me. Go therefore and make disciples of all nations." We can continue the mission of Jesus because of the authority he has given us. And as long as we remain faithful, we will be able to go on in the authority of our Lord.

The faithful are also promised the authority of the morning star. The morning star is the prophetic image of the Messiah, as is the rod of iron. Jesus promises this to the faithful, all things that were claimed by him through his faithfulness to the cross and to the word of God. Interestingly, in Numbers 24:14–20, Balaam's prophesy concerning Israel, the people of Israel are prophesied to be these bright lights in the world. Verse 17 says, "A star shall come out of Jacob, and a scepter shall rise out of Israel," tying together both the idea of the star and the scepter as in Revelation 2:27–28. Daniel 12:3 as well says, "And those who are wise shall shine like the brightness of the sky above; and those who turn many to righteousness, like the stars forever and ever." The glory of Jesus will become the glory of his people. He whose eyes are like blazing fire and whose feet are like burnished bronze, will establish the faithful as morning stars, shining in the universe.[8]

---

6. Ladd, *A Commentary on the Revelation of John*, 53.

7. Other passages that apply Psalm 2 to Jesus are Acts 13:33, Romans 1:4, and Hebrews 1:2, 5; 5:5; 7:28.

8. See also Philippians 2:15.

## Conclusion

Our world needs this kind of authority. The church needs that kind of authority. We need a ruler who grants true freedom to those who serve him, a ruler who gives his life when we give it to him, and a ruler who promises us a share in his rule rather than a despotic, cruel king who serves only himself. This is the King to whom we must submit, going to war against all the powers of this spiritual world that rail against his kingdom.

Like the church in Thyatira, the church today must boldly stand against compromise and any form of idolatry, the Jezebels of the world who try to seduce us by secret knowledge and offers of security. Rather, in a crooked and depraved world, we must shine like stars (like the Morning Star) in the universe.

# Revelation 3:1–6

Jesus' Message to the Church in Sardis

## Introduction

THE AMERICAN PEOPLE AND many in the western world were shocked on September 11, 2001, as they watched and listened with the nation when two planes flew into the World Trade towers and then watched these buildings collapse onto the people of New York City. I remember my first thought: What kind of horrible problem went wrong with the plane that would make it fall in New York and why on earth didn't the pilot do anything to miss the city? I could not believe it, and many others could not believe either, when we learned that the one piloting the plane was a terrorist. What was even more alarming was that those terrorists lived in the U.S., worked there, learned there, ate there, and were trained to fly there. They had infiltrated the nation and then struck a death blow upon the nation from the inside.

That is the worst kind of enemy, an enemy that you cannot see, that you are not expecting, an enemy that joins the ranks of your army and then turns the guns on your own, except in that case, the guns were petrol laden airplanes and the targets were not soldiers, but civilians. In the mind of the terrorists there were no civilians. To the radical terrorists of the world, all Americans are the enemy. And chances are there are still many walking and living among the American population, waiting for the opportunity to strike again, when the nation once again falls asleep.

I think this is a perfect parallel to what has happened to many churches around the world. We have had enemies enter into our churches, penetrate its leadership, lull the church to sleep, and then strike with a death blow— division, immorality, apathy, and bitterness. All of these are like petrol-laden airplanes crashing into the church of God. Some of these internal enemies, these penetrations to our church walls, have begun within. They were not enemies on the outside who went undercover in order to destroy. These are enemies who slowly grow on the inside, as the heart hardens, as unforgiveness builds, as apathy for the vision and purpose of the church grows. The church lulls itself to sleep only to be kicked by passers-by, because they think it is a dead corpse.

## Exposition

The church of Sardis was on its death-bed before it was personally visited by the Doctor. Sardis was fifty miles east of Ephesus. A large temple was dedicated to Artemis, destroyed in the sixth century B.C.[1] and then partially rebuilt and dedicated to a local Asian goddess, Cybele, by the time of Alexander the Great in the 4th century B.C. The city suffered a severe earthquake in 17 A.D. but was rebuilt with the financial assistance of the emperor, Tiberius. Gold and silver coins were first struck at Sardis.[2] Aune estimates that the population of the city was between 60,000 and 100,000.[3]

Jesus is identified, like in chapter 1, with the seven-fold Spirit and the seven stars. He is identified in this way because of his presence through the Spirit amidst the church in Sardis. Because Jesus alone is the One who sends the Holy Spirit and holds the fate of the church in his hand, we must submit to him and listen carefully to his diagnosis as the Great Doctor. The church in Sardis had a reputation of being a vibrant church. They maybe had a good community reputation. They had a good reputation among the churches of the area. They probably had visible leadership and good programs. They were outwardly prosperous, busy with externals of religious activity, but devoid of spiritual life and power. Deep down, under the surface, the church was really dead. And just like in the history of the city which fell because of unseen vulnerabilities, the church in Sardis must heed the warnings of its Lord.

Think about what this says to reputation. There are so many "doctors" giving churches a healthy report around the world, when actually they are sick to the core. But there is only one Doctor's diagnosis that matters. What does Jesus think? A church can have a great music program, ministries for all the age groups that are flashy and expensive and smartly run. A church can have a clean, sprucely kept building. A church can have a reputation in the community of being a great place to belong. "Wow! You belong to that

---

1. Osborne, *Revelation*, 171, notes that the surprise attack of one of Sardis's men against Sardis, when he found a weakness in the wall at an unobservable point, led to the downfall of the city after only a fourteen-day siege in 546 BC. This led to the phrase "capturing Sardis" in the Greek world for doing the impossible.

2. Mounce, *The Book of Revelation*, 109.

3. Aune, *Revelation 1–5*, 219.

church? How did you get to do that? It's a special honor to belong to that church!" A church can have a radio or television broadcast, or an audience of 5,000 people. It can have all these things and still be dead.

What was the Doctor's prescription for the church in Sardis? He commanded them to wake up and strengthen what remained and was about to die. There was still life in the church, but it was dying. What Jesus considered dead in verse 1 he then called asleep in verse 2. Thus, they are commanded to wake up. Their works had not been complete. In other words, there was no evidence of a full faith, or a fully-matured faith. Beale comments, "The so-called Christians of Sardis are living in such a way as to call into question whether or not they possess true, living faith in Christ."[4] Mounce writes that the "wake up" should be translated "show yourself watchful." This would be meaningful for Sardis because of the two times they had been attacked and conquered by their enemies because of their lack of vigilance.[5]

Jesus commanded them to remember what they had received. What is it that they had received? Probably the gospel message and instruction from the likes of Paul and/or his associates, or from John himself. They were commanded to obey and repent. Repent from their walking death. Repent from their lethargy. And repent from their neglect of their faith heritage. Thomas comments that there is a concrete action envisioned in this call. They are to be awakened, strengthen what remains, remember the things received, and heard, as well as keep those things.[6] If they continued in their lethargic spiritual state, Jesus promised to come to them like a thief, at an unexpected time. This can be understood both as reference to an imminent visitation as well to the Parousia of the day of the LORD. Jesus used the idea of thief for his second coming in Matthew 24:42–44.[7]

In application, the message is clear for the church today. Proverbs 6:9–11 says, "How long will you lie there, O sluggard? When will you arise from your sleep? A little sleep, a little slumber, a little folding of the hands to rest, and poverty will come upon you like a robber, and want like an armed

---

4. Beale, *The Book of Revelation*, 273. Ladd, *A Commentary on the Revelation of John*, 56, adds, "Here is a picture of nominal Christianity, outwardly prosperous, busy with the externals of religious activity, but devoid of spiritual life and power."

5. Mounce, *The Book of Revelation*, 110.

6. Thomas and Macchia, *Revelation*, 114.

7. Mounce, *The Book of Revelation*, 111. See also 1 Thessalonians 5:2 and 2 Peter 3:10. Johnson, *Hebrews through Revelation*, 449, believes Christ's threat of judgment is a coming of historical judgment, not the Parousia. Ladd, *A Commentary on the Revelation of John*, 57, understands this as a historical visitation as well. I think this can be fairly understood as a both/and situation. Jesus is threatening a coming and imminent judgment, but ultimately, they would face the judgment of the coming Judge and King when he comes back.

man." The enemy wants to penetrate the church from the outside and the inside. The church must be alert and prepared for battle. We cannot let him in and, when even the hint of disunity, immorality, or bitterness begin to creep in, the alarm must be sounded by those who see it.

There are a lot of depressed people in the world. With some of them, if you look at their sleeping habits, you begin to get a clue why they are depressed. Some stay up real late watching television, and then do not get up until 12:00pm or 1:00pm. The morning is gone, and the opportunity for productivity as well. This is going to contribute to depression. The church is the same. The longer we sleep, the more we flirt around with the night, the more depressed we will become and the more sleep we will want. It is a vicious cycle and only the Holy Spirit can break us from it. The prayer of the church must be, "Revive us, Lord. Wake us up. Keep us alert and on guard, against the desires of the flesh and the attacks of the enemy."

If the people of the church in Sardis did not wake up, they would miss the coming of the Lord. As in the parable of the wicked servant in Matthew 24, if the servant in charge of the Master's household begins to lose faith and begins to beat his fellow servants and to eat and drink with drunkards, "the master of that servant will come on a day when he does not expect him and at an hour he does not know and will cut him in pieces and put him with the hypocrites."

Not all in Sardis were asleep. There were a few who had not compromised or had not forgotten the heritage of faith. They had kept themselves clean, which implies that the problem in the church may have been a moral issue. It also means that their Sardis church friends had probably participated in the idolatrous feasts of the city, thus staining their clothes and their reputations as follower of Jesus. See the use of the word "defiled" in 14:4, 6–9. Those who remain faithful will be dressed in white (see Revelation 19), white clothes being the righteous deeds of the saints and *given* to them by the Lamb.

Literally the Greek in verse 4 means, "They will walk with me in white." The primary thrust of the white clothes and walking with Jesus is purity and holiness,[8] but a purity and holiness that came as the result of being justified by Jesus.[9] There is a parallel here with Revelation 7:9, 13–14 and possibly with Daniel 11:35 and 12:10 where the saints are made white through the fires of persecution.[10] 2 Corinthians 3:18 says, "And we all, with unveiled faces, beholding the glory of the Lord, are being transformed into the same

---

8. Osborne, *Revelation*, 179

9. Mounce, *The Book of Revelation*, 112.

10. Beale, *The Book of Revelation*, 277.

image from one degree of glory to another. For this comes from the Lord who is the Spirit." All purity, holiness, and glory come from Jesus. Romans 13:14 says, "But put on the Lord Jesus Christ, and make no provision for the flesh, to gratify its desires."

The one who proves faithful will show himself faithful. The one who overcomes will wear white clothes as well, and their names will not be blotted out of the book of life. For more on the book of life see Revelation 13:8; 17:8 and Revelation 20:12, 15; 21:27, as well as Daniel 12:1–2 and 7:10ff. In Revelation, there is a book of life and a book of judgment. The blotting out of the name means not that names that are there are erased, but that their nominal following of Jesus shows their lack of real commitment to him. For the faithful, Jesus will act as a witness to their status before God and the angels. The same word for "confess" in verse 5 is the word used in 1 John 1:9. Jesus will not be ashamed to confess our association with him as we stay faithful.[11]

## Conclusion

The Disney movie, *Sleeping Beauty*, is the story of a princess who was lured by the evil witch to the castle where she pricked her finger on the spinning wheel and fell asleep. She was awoken later by the prince who had to fight his way to the castle against a dragon and thorns and obstacles. The prince, Jesus, is coming for his church. But what is different in this story is that "Sleeping Beauty," the church, needs to be awake before he gets here. The church must be alert and vigilant for the coming of the Lord.

11. See also Matthew 10:32 and Luke 12:8.

# Revelation 3:7–13

Jesus' Message to the Church in Philadelphia

## Introduction

ONE SUMMER, IN JUNE, my son, Rick, and I got to go to our first Chicago Cubs game. We had a great time. Our tickets cost $18.50 a piece, and we were in the windy section. An icy wind kept blowing right in our faces, but we did not mind, because we had a hot dog to share, a Pepsi to share, a popcorn to share, a cotton candy to share, peanuts to share, and candy to share. And a stomach-ache to share. Before the game started, I took Rick down to the foul line seats, the seats closest to the field. We got to the park two hours earlier than the start of the game, so we got to see all the batting practice. It would have been great to sit there for the game. The wind wasn't blowing, and the sun was shining right on the seats. We still had a great time, and a very enjoyable day together, but I had an inward covetousness for those seats.

Would it not be great to have the place of honor every so often? The place of honor at the company banquet or the place of honor at the school program, or the place of honor at the family gathering, or at the Premier League Championship game? There is a place of honor reserved for the faithful follower of Jesus, a place in Heaven with Jesus. When my Step-Father was in the hospital the last few years of his life I got to see him on December 24th. There were a few things I wanted to say to him alone, before we left the hospital that day. After the family was gone, I kneeled down by his bedside, and told him that he had been a great father. I wouldn't have wanted any other than him. I then told him to save me a place at the Lamb's table, because I wanted to sit next to him when I got there.

Now, the more I think of that, the more I realized that my father doesn't have a say where I sit. I don't have a say where I sit. But God does. And he will give each of us a place of honor according to his own choosing. In fact, through our lives God is sustaining us for a place of honor. This is what the church in Philadelphia needed to know.

## Exposition

The city of Philadelphia was located about thirty miles north/northwest from Sardis. It was known as the gateway to the East, and this made it a commercially important city, with the imperial road passing through it. Because of the many fertile lands for grape growing, Dionysius became an important deity for the city. Philadelphia suffered much after a major earthquake in 17 A.D. that also impacted Sardis. Philadelphia was nearer the fault line. The name of the city comes from the love of the ruler of the 2nd century B.C. for his brother, who remained faithful to him.[1] Osborne writes that in 92 A.D. Emperor Domitian issued a decree that half of the grape vines be cut down. This was to encourage the growing of grain for the Roman Empire because of the famine. This caused a severe crisis in Philadelphia as well as some loosening of ties with the Roman Empire cult.[2]

Jesus is described here as the holy and faithful one who holds the key of David. This may be a parallel to the keys to death and Hades in chapter 1. Just as Jesus remained faithful and set apart for the task God gave him, bearing witness even unto death, so this church is called upon to stay faithful in the midst of persecution and trial.[3] Ultimate judgment is in the hands of Jesus. They need not fear or give up. In Isaiah 22:22 God says concerning Eliakim and Hilkiah, "And I will place on his shoulder the key of the house of David. He shall open, and none shall shut; and he shall shut, and none shall open." Eliakim was the palace administrator. As palace administrator, he would have had the keys to the King's palace. Here in Revelation, the application is made to Jesus, who has keys to the palace of his Heavenly Father's home. These "keys of David" refer the Messianic leadership over Israel, a leadership that is in Jesus' hands and that he has the right to give to the faithful. The doors of the true synagogue were open to the faithful ones, whereas the doors remained closed to those who rejected Christ, the keeper of the keys.[4]

Jesus keeps the door open when others want to shut it. While the people of the church may have been shut out of the synagogue, they are not shut out of the kingdom of heaven.[5] It seems that the Jews had kicked the small Christian congregation out of the privilege of synagogue worship.

---

1. Mounce, *The Book of Revelation*, 115.

2. Osborne, *Revelation*, 185.

3. For the title "Holy One", see Revelation 4:8 and 6:10. Also see in reference to Jesus: Mark 1:24, Luke 4:34, John 6:68, and 1 John 2:20.

4. Beale, *The Book of Revelation*, 283.

5. See Mounce, *The Book of Revelation*, 117 as well as Osborne, *Revelation*, 188. Aune (Aune, *Revelation 1–5*, 244) sees the open door as referring to the "reserved seats" in the heavenly kingdom.

They were not welcome to worship with the Jews because the Jews did not believe that God loved the followers of Jesus. They had been told that God had rejected them, and that they were not of the chosen ones. Jesus had previously already rebuked the Pharisees in Matthew 23:13, "But woe to you, scribes and Pharisees, hypocrites! For you shut the kingdom of heaven in people's faces. For you neither enter yourselves nor allow those who would enter to go in."

Jesus promised the Philadelphian congregation an open door into the palace of Heaven, and no one was going to be able to shut this door on them. In the history of religion, there occasionally have arisen groups that limited salvation to a select number of people. The Jehovah's Witnesses, a large cult today, used to claim that only 144,000 were going to heaven. When their group got bigger, they had to change their beliefs. Some groups of the 1830s and 1840s limited their number to only celibate people—obviously, their groups did not last for more than one generation. Still today, there are some that suppose they have the authority to decide who can get into Heaven.

But Jesus holds the keys in his hands and no one else. And as the key holder, he determines the entrance requirements. And as Savior, he has already paid the entrance fee with his blood and invites everyone to come to the Father through him. Jesus said of himself in John 10, "I am the gate for the sheep; whoever enters through Me will be saved. He will come in and go out and will find pasture." As members of the body of Christ, we do not have the key to the door, but we know the One who has the key. Our task is to lead people to the Key-holder, so that he can let them in.

But more than just holding the keys, Jesus also promises a restored honor to those who had it taken away by others. Jesus used harsh language to describe those who had prevented the church from participating in their religious activities, calling them a synagogue for Satan. The synagogue of Satan is probably similar to what was encountered in Smyrna. Those who are Jews were trying to oppress or persecute the followers of Jesus. The "real" Jews spiritually are those who hold the teachings of Jesus and stay faithful. These false Jews will one day acknowledge not only the rightness of the church members in Philadelphia, but by doing so they will also acknowledge the truth claims of Jesus and his love for the church. Whether this means they repent or not is not clear.[6]

6. Johnson, *Hebrews through Revelation*, 453, sees this as retribution on Christ's enemies, not that they will repent. It could also be that the bowing down at the feet is an allusion to Isaiah 45:14, 49:23, and 60:14. Isaiah 45:14 reads: "Thus says the Lord, 'The wealth of Egypt and the merchandise of Cush, and the Sabeans, men of sature, shall come over to you and be yours; they shall follow you; they shall come over in chains and bow down to you. They will plead with you, saying, "Surely God is in you, and there is

Because of the faithfulness to the command to endure patiently, Jesus promised that he would keep the Philadelphia church from the hour
of trial that would come upon the whole world. What is the hour of trial
to come upon the earth? Is this the final suffering and judgment upon the
earth? Or is this a reference to a more severe level of persecution that the
church will escape, while other congregations and followers of Jesus may
have to endure?

I think the context, as well as the general teaching of Revelation and the
rest of the New Testament, lead to the conclusion that the tribulation is the
punishment of the ungodly. The church of Philadelphia will be spared from
the wrath of God just as the Jews were spared from the plagues of Egypt.
The phrase, "hour of trial," is the technical phrase for judgment (see 6:10;
8:13; 11:10; 12:12; 13:8, 12, 14; 14:6; 17:2, 8). This is an intensification of the
end-times tribulation on the earth which has already been set in motion.[7]
The phrase "keep you from," κἀγώ σε τηρήσω (kago se tereso), is also used by
Jesus in John 17:15. There, Jesus prays that the disciples would be kept from
the evil one, but not taken out of the world. Thus, in Revelation 3:10 it is not
a rapture or protection from persecution, but a perseverance in the midst of
that persecution. Jesus will keep them spiritually safe.[8]

This final trial is also mentioned in Daniel 12:2; Mark 13:19; 2 Thessalonians 2:1-12; and Revelation 13:5-10. It is the three and a half years of
trial that the church must endure.[9] In other words, it is a limited time of
persecution under the sovereign rule of Christ. "Although the church will
be on earth in these final terrible days and will suffer fierce persecution and
martyrdom at the hands of the beast, she will be kept from the hour of trial
which is coming upon the pagan world. God's wrath, poured out on the
kingdom of Antichrist, will not afflict his people."[10]

Jesus promised the church that he was coming soon. The "soon" here
is the apocalyptic "soon," not necessarily a chronological reference. Because

no other, no god besides him.""" Beale, *The Book of Revelation*, 287.

7. Beale, *The Book of Revelation*, 290.

8. For other verses in the New Testament that speak about the reality of believers
going through physical suffering or persecution, see Romans 8:35-39; 2 Corinthians
4:16-5:10; 6:4-10; Philippians 3:10-11; Colossians 1:24, as well as the rest of Revelation, particularly 7:14. This sounds a death-knell on the dispensational view of the rapture of the church out of persecution. Mounce, *The Book of Revelation*, 119, writes, "It
is precisely because the church was faithful to Christ in time of trial that he in turn will
be faithful to them in the time of their great trial."

9. Mounce, *The Book of Revelation*, 119.

10. Ladd, *A Commentary on the Revelation of John*, 62. See also Osborne, *Revelation*, 194 who views this protection as protection from the wrath of God, not protection
from persecution.

the coming of Christ will take place "without delay,"[11] the church is encouraged to hold on to what they have: their teaching, their faith, their holiness as a congregation, and their ministry. If they do so, no one would be able to take their crown. The crown is the same word used in chapter 2, the reward for faithfulness and the wreath of the Olympic games.

Not only would the crown be permanent, the faithful would become pillars in the house of God. In an area that is accustomed to earthquakes, this is an image that would have much meaning. Often, when an earthquake shook a city, the buildings would fall down, except for the pillars of the temple. The image is real here. Jesus promised to make them pillars, so that even in the midst of the earthquakes of suffering and persecution, they would not fall, but would be fixed in God's presence. This is where Jesus exceeds the promises made to Eliakim, the palace administrator, in Isaiah 22. Eliakim would hold the keys, but after he was fastened like a peg in a sure place to bear the weight of his father's house, in time it would give way. Pillars planted by Jesus would not give way.

## Conclusion

Three names are written on this pillar, the one who is faithful to the end, even in the middle of persecution. First, the name of God, or the seal of God. He will belong to God forever. Exodus 28:36–38 says of the priests, "You shall make a plate of pure gold and engrave on it, like the engraving of a signet, 'Holy to the Lord.' And you shall fasten it on the turban by a cord of blue. It shall be on the front of the turban. It shall be on Aaron's forehead, and Aaron shall bear any guilt from the holy things that the people of Israel consecrate as their holy gifts. It shall regularly be on his forehead, that they may be accepted before the Lord."

Secondly, is the name of the New Jerusalem, God's city. The name of New Jerusalem brings to mind also the authority of the keys of David, and the assured promise of the presence of the faithful in the new kingdom, although they had been put out of the synagogue. Philippians 3:20 says, "But our citizenship is in heaven, and from it we await a Savior, the Lord Jesus Christ." A suitcase that is traveling overseas has a baggage tag on it. This shows where the suitcase is going. We have a tag or a stamp on us. The claim tag reads "New Jerusalem" because that is where we are going.

Thirdly, the pillar has on it the name of the Son, Jesus. Jesus said, "My sheep hear my voice, and I know them, and they follow me. I give them eternal life, and they will never perish, and no one will snatch them out of

11. Mounce, *The Book of Revelation*, 120.

my hand."[12] God is preparing us as pillars. his name is on us. He is sustaining us for a place of honor at his table. We need to hold on.

12. John 10:27.

# Revelation 3:14–22

Jesus' Message to the Church in Laodicea

## Introduction

L ORA AND I HAVE a good relationship of mutual trust. But sometimes she just does not seem to trust me as well as she trusts others. For example, if she is wondering about some decision—either a dress or a product to try out, or whether something will work well in the garden—she will often ask me my opinion. A lot of times I have good opinions. And so, I will give her my opinion. But then I can see the doubt in her face. She is not quite sure I know what I'm talking about. I do not blame her if that happens to refer to clothes because many times, I do not know what I'm talking about.

The funniest thing is when I hear that later she had a conversation with a friend, a doctor, or her mother. And she comes to me and gives me their opinion on her dilemma which convinces her of that course to take. And you know what? Many times, that opinion is the exact opinion I had given her days before. It could be an important issue to me. I could think, "Am I not sufficient enough?" "Doesn't she trust me? Are my opinions not good enough? Do they not rank with those people?" In matters where my opinion really is not that important, I realize that she is going to a better source anyway, so I'll give my opinion and see if my opinion matches the other person's opinion. And if so, I can quietly do a high five to myself.

Imagine how offensive we are to Jesus, however, when we live our lives with no concern with his opinion. This does not concern temporal matters of what to wear and how to plant our flowers. This concerns matters of the soul, matters of holiness and lifestyle. Imagine how offended Jesus is when we do not act like we need him in our lives? In living for Jesus, and in working for Jesus, there is no other one we need but Jesus. Unfortunately, we are so prone to forget him or get used to doing things without him, that we eventually almost completely leave him out of our decision processes. This was the problem in the congregation in Laodicea.

## Exposition

Laodicea was forty miles southeast from Philadelphia. It was named after the wife of Antiochus, Laodice. It was the wealthiest city in the Phrygian region, known for its black wool industry, banking industry, and medical school. One of the most famous ointments made was an eye salve made from Phrygian powder mixed with oil.[1] The city was so wealthy that after it experienced a significant earthquake that destroyed the city in 60 A.D., it rebuilt itself without outside help from the Roman government.[2] The main weakness of the city was its lack of water. Because of that, an aqueduct system was built to bring water into the city. Water was retrieved from the hot springs that came from the city of Hierapolis and from the cold springs of Colossae.

In verse 14 Jesus is identified as the Amen, the Faithful Witness, the Truth, and the Ruler of God's creation—there is authority and truth and judgment. His word is final. There is no other witness higher than Jesus. There is no opinion that is more worthy of query. Isaiah 65:16 says, "So that he who blesses himself in the land shall bless himself by the God of truth, and he who takes an oath in the land shall swear by the God of truth."[3] This verse could be understood as the God of the Amen. Jesus is the Amen. What he says *will* happen. In the Old Testament, "amen" is primarily an acknowledgement of that which is valid and binding. In referring to Jesus, it would mean the One in whom perfect conformity to reality is exemplified. Jesus made this claim in John 14:6, "I am the way, and the truth, and the life." All truth and true reality are found in Jesus. What the world needs today is someone to trust. We have tried programs and policies, but they have failed. But Christ never fails. He is as good as an "Amen." His "yes" means yes. The name, Amen," applied to Christ, guarantees the truthfulness and reliability of his words.[4]

Jesus is also the faithful and true witness, that which puts him in stark contrast to the character of the Laodicean church. But he is also the ruler of God's creation. Colossians 1:15 says, "He is the image of the invisible God, the firstborn of all creation." Surely this is enough to convince us that our sufficiency can only be found in Jesus, the "Amen," the end of all things, the perfect and faithful Witness, the very Creator. The word ἡ ἀρχὴ (*he arche*) can be translated "beginning" or "ruler." Implicit in the idea is inauguration,

---

1. Mounce, *The Book of Revelation*, 122.

2. Aune, *Revelation 1–5*, 249.

3. See also Isaiah 43:10–12. Isaiah 65:16 and Revelation 3:14 are the only two passages where "Amen" is a name. See Beale, *The Book of Revelation*, 299.

4. Ladd, *A Commentary on the Revelation of John*, 65.

supremacy over, and temporal priority.[5] All creation was begun by him, for him, and in him. Because of his resurrection, Jesus is the inauguration of and Sovereign over the new creation.[6]

Jesus considered the Laodicean church lukewarm, neither hot, nor cold. That is his primary criticism of the church body. Hierapolis was famous for its hot springs, used medically. These springs rose within the city, flowed across a wide plateau and spilled over the cliff directly opposite Laodicea. The cliff was about 300 feet high and encrusted with white calcium carbonate. As the hot, mineral-rich water traveled across the plateau, it gradually became lukewarm before spilling over the edge. You get a picture of sickly, insipid water seeping over slimy rock, which the unsuspecting visitor drank only to spit up on the ground. In contrast to the hot springs of Hierapolis were the cold, refreshing and pure waters of Colossae. By the time these flowed down toward Laodicea, these waters were also tepid or lukewarm and good for nothing.[7]

Again, Jesus called the Laodicean church lukewarm. The word for lukewarm is χλιαρὸς (chliaros). That meant that they were filled with disease and bacteria. They were neither hot nor cold. He wanted them to be useful for his kingdom, but instead they were good for nothing except to be spit out. Jesus' desire was that they would be either useful for healing or useful for refreshing, one or the other. But they were neither. Their purpose and ministry and usefulness in the kingdom were gone. This made the church distasteful to the Lord.

We don't need to investigate too many churches in the world to see that there are many churches very much like Laodicea. Many churches have ceased being useful vessels in the hand of the Lord, and he is about to spit them out of his mouth. He wants us to be cold waters of refreshment to the spiritually weary. Those who are burdened with life need the cup of cold water of encouragement from the church—the cold waters of the grace of God and mercies of Jesus. Instead, they often receive more burdens, more guilt, and more religion. Those who are thirsty for God must be able to find God among God's people. There is no other place to look. The reason Western Europe is spiritually dead now is because the Christian churches in Western Europe stopped relying on Jesus for their sufficiency, began to call into question the Word of God, began to doubt the supremacy of Jesus, and when the

---

5. Beale, *The Book of Revelation*, 301. Osborne (Osborne, *Revelation*, 205) also believes that *arche* should be understood here as "source" or "origin."

6. Beale, *The Book of Revelation*, 298.

7. Mounce, *The Book of Revelation*, 123.

starving and the thirsty unbeliever looked to the church for a cold drink of water, they found the well empty.

Jesus wants his church to be hot healing waters to the spiritually sick or dead. The Gospel is for the sick. Jesus said, "It is not the healthy who need a doctor, but the sick. I have not come to call the righteous but the sinner to repentance."[8] The church must be a clinic, a healing station for the spiritually sick around us. Unfortunately, many churches have turned into funeral homes themselves, and the sick do not go into funeral parlors seeking life. They need hospitals. Jesus wants us to be hot, healing waters, but again, the source of healing is found in Jesus, and in a proper understanding of who he is.

I gave an assignment one semester at the University of Toledo where the students had to go to churches in the area before and after Thanksgiving Day to evaluate how those churches celebrated or recognized Thanksgiving. The responses in their papers and as they shared their experiences in class was sad to hear. Many of these students had not been in church for many years, some of them never. And the stories they told revealed how sick some of the churches themselves were. One young man, who had a long ponytail, and wore an army jacket, said that no one talked to him. He really felt like an outsider. Another mentioned how catty and gossipy the choir ladies were before they went up to sing.

How can the sick find spiritual healing among the sick? Does this mean that the church today must be perfect, and everyone in the church spiritual giants? No. But the church is a hospital, and hopefully hospitals are places people go to find healing. There should be many sick people there, and we should all be in process of getting healthier, not sicker or more stagnant.

From the perspective of the Laodicean church, there was no problem. They were very wealthy. Material wealth had clouded their spirituality. The wealth source in Laodicea would have been clothes, healing balm for the eyes, and precious metals. They had these, but they did not have the spiritual wealth from Jesus. And from his perspective they were wretched, pitiful, poor, blind, and naked, like a homeless infant in the middle of a dirty sewer-filled city street. Mounce accurately paints the problem by writing, "Their pretentious claim was not only that they were rich but that they had achieved it on their own."[9]

Woe to the church if it ever thinks that it has attained completeness in its life and ministry so that they do not any longer need the sufficiency and help of Jesus. There is never a level of righteousness that we can attain where

---

8. Luke 5:31.
9. Mounce, *The Book of Revelation*, 126.

we can say that we have done it on our own. As soon as we begin to strive after internal righteousness without Christ, we will find ourselves on a path toward spiritual ruin and hypocrisy.

By his grace, Jesus exhorted the church to seek true riches, riches that have their source in him. Those true riches are gold refined in the fire so they can be truly wealthy—faith and perseverance. This is what makes us truly rich, not the worldly riches of a big house, fancy clothes, and gold rings; but the fiery furnace where we are melted into an eternal blaze of holiness in service to the Lord. In Job 23:10, Job said, "But he knows the way that I take; when he has tried me, I shall come out as gold."[10]

Jesus also exhorted the church to seek after white garments to cover their shamefulness. In a land rich from textiles, Jesus knew what they needed—the righteousness of Christ. The shameful nakedness of Israel was pointed out in Isaiah 43:3, Ezekiel 16:36 and 23:29, and Nahum 3:5 in the context of idolatry. This possibly means that the Laodicean church was caught up in idolatrous practices as well. In fact, any time we prioritize something or someone other as more important than Jesus we are committing idolatry. In God's sight, we are properly clothed only when we are clothed with the righteousness of Christ.

Lastly, Jesus exhorted them to buy salve for their spiritual blindness. Regardless of their medical schools, they were blind where it counted—spiritually. Second Corinthians 5:7 says, "For we walk by faith, not be sight." Unfortunately, for many churches around the world, it has become so easy to walk by sight, because we have the money, the doctors, and the clothes. We can claim sufficiency in our material resources more than others. But are we wealthy where it counts—in our hearts, in our love for Jesus, in our reliance on him?

Jesus called the church to repentance and to earnestness—to come to Jesus in repentance and then zealously continue in him as a daily practice. God disciplines those he loves. When we go through the refining fires of trial, it is because God loves us and knows that on the other end of the trial, we will be truly wealthy. Has the church been lukewarm, good for nothing in Christ's kingdom, rather than hot or cold? We know that real spiritual fulfillment cannot be found there. It must be found in Jesus. That is why he invites the church to fellowship with him on a deeper and more intimate level.

It is interesting that the One who has a key to the door, as in Philadelphia, willingly stands at the door and waits to be let in. This is not a call to salvation, but to a greater level of fellowship.[11] Jesus stands at the door and

---

10. See also Proverbs 27:21, Malachi 3:2–3, and Zechariah13:9.

11. Cf. Johnson, *Hebrews through Revelation*, 459, who believes that the invitation

knocks. He wants us to open the door of our stubborn hearts and allow him to give us his wealth and his riches—the wealth of sweet fellowship with him. He will dine with us and we with him. Osborne views this as a foretaste of the final messianic banquet (see Revelation 19:6–9; Luke 13:29; 22:29–30), saying, "The depth of sharing with Christ attained through spiritual growth of this kind anticipates the total unity to be achieved with God and Christ in eternity."[12]

## Conclusion

In most Asian cultures, the sharing of a common meal indicated a strong bond of affection and companionship. Jesus offers us that increased bond, that intimacy with him. What an act of unbelievable condescension by Christ! He actually requests permission to enter and re-establish fellowship, a fellowship that is broken off by our self-sufficiency and pride. He does not break the door down. He does not force his way in or go through the window. He waits for us to answer the door. He waits for us to open it. And not only is this just an invitation to fellowship with a dear Friend, it is an invitation to rule with the King.

What will Jesus find of us? Will he find us hot or cold, useful for his kingdom? Will he find us seeking after the wealth of righteousness rather than the wealth of the world, which corrupts and will fade away? Will he find us finding our fulfillment solely in him?

Bryan Chapell tells a story in his book, *Holiness by Grace*, about his wife and kids. He writes,

> Several years ago my wife, Kathy, and a friend gathered up the kids and made a trip to the St. Louis Zoo. A new attraction had just opened called "Big Cat Country," which took the lions and tigers out of their cages and allowed them to roam in large enclosures. Visitors observed the cats by walking on elevated skyways above the habitats. As my wife and her friend took the children up one of the skyway ramps, a blanket became entangled in the wheel of the friend's stroller. Kathy knelt to help untangle the wheel while our boys—ages three and five—went ahead. When next she looked up, Kathy discovered that the boys had innocently walked right through a child-sized gap in

of Jesus is more evangelistic than admonitory because the Laodiceans were not really Christians. After all, Jesus was going to spit them from his mouth. I think, however, that Jesus is speaking to the church in general, as a church body, rather than to individuals in the church. Certainly, there were some who truly believed in him.

12. Osborne, *Revelation*, 213.

the fencing and had climbed up on the rocks some twenty feet above the lion pen. They had been told that they would be able to look down on the lions, and they were doing just that from their hazardous vantage point. Pointing to the lions below, they called back to their mother, 'Hey, Mom, we can see them.' They had no concept of how much danger they were in. Kathy saw immediately. But now what could she do? If she screamed, she might startle the boys perched precariously above the lions. The gap in the fence was too small for her to get through. So she knelt down, spread out her arms, and said, 'Boys, come get a hug.' They came running for the love that saved them from danger greater than they perceived. [13]

When the church loses its focus of Christ being its sufficiency, of Christ being the only protection, the church is living life very dangerously. Jesus is knocking at the door. Like the mother who spread out her arms to her boys, Jesus is knocking and hoping we will answer, and get out of the danger into his safe arms. The church must answer the door!

---

13. Chapell, *Holiness by Grace: Delighting in the Joy that is our Strength*, 107.

# Revelation 4:1–11

## The Vision of the Throne of God

### Introduction

T HERE IS ONE CONCEPT that is increasingly missing in today's churches, and in the worship service of today's churches. This concept goes beyond our intellectual capacity to comprehend, a concept both glorious and terrifying, a reality that causes the knees to buckle and bend, our voice to tremble, and our hair to stand on end. This concept is the holiness of God. Do I dare even write of such a topic for this commentary, except that with Jeremiah the prophet I can agree, who said, "The word of God is like a fire inside that I cannot keep in." And the Apostle Paul said similarly, "Woe is me, if I do not preach the gospel."

Older generations today complain and cry and lament over the lost sense of respect among the present and future generations, the young people. It comes down to one primary cause: we have forsaken a Biblical picture of the holiness and awesomeness of God. We have come to the end of the portion of Revelation where Jesus is speaking directly to the church. Some of these passages are like shot guns from God's word. Now we come to the portion of the book where the plan of God, the Lord of history, is going to be revealed.

In this chapter, the focus is on God and his throne. In the next chapter the focus shifts to the Lamb of God. We learn about God and why we worship him on Sunday morning in our churches and why he is worthy of our worship and praise all throughout the week. There is no challenge to our character necessarily, no message against lukewarm faith, no warning against idolatry, no plea for sexual purity and holiness, except that we are forced to those decisions when we come face to face with the holiness of our Creator. When we view his holiness, and understand why he is worthy of our worship, we will want to alter our character to conform to his. We will want to be far from lukewarm. We will want to put off idolatry and sexual impurity before him. We will want to be zealous before God as we realize how far we are from him still.

## Exposition

Chapters 4 and 5 have to be thought of as one unit, a growing crescendo of praise to God and to the Lamb by the angels of heaven and then by every living creature with breath. This is all part of one vision, the overcoming Lamb who sits on his throne just as God sits on his throne. There is no contradiction between thrones (who sits on which throne). But, as members of the Trinity, God and the Lamb occupy the same throne and yet can be said to have different thrones. There is an innate and a given authority. Both are possessed by the Lamb of God.

Beale believes there is a similar structure between Revelation 4–5 and Daniel 7. He sets up the parallel as follows:[1]

| | | |
|---|---|---|
| Introductory vision phraseology | Dan. 7:9 | Rev. 4:1 |
| A throne set in heaven | Dan. 7:9a | Rev. 4:2a (also see 4:4a) |
| God sitting on the throne | Dan. 7:9b | Rev. 4:2b |
| God's appearance on the throne | Dan. 7:9c | Rev. 4:3a |
| Fire before the throne | Dan. 7:9d–10a | Rev. 4:5 |
| Heavenly servants before the throne | Dan. 7:10b | Rev. 4:4b; 6b–10; 5:8, 11, 14 |
| Books before the throne | Dan. 7:10c | Rev. 5:1–5 |
| The books opened | Dan. 7:10c | Rev. 5:2–5, 9 |
| A divine (messianic) figure approaching God's throne to receive authority to reign forever over a kingdom | Dan. 7:13–14a | Rev. 5:5b–7; 9a, 12–13 |
| The kingdom's scope "All peoples . . ." | Dan. 7:14a | Rev. 5:9b |
| The seer's emotional distress | Dan. 7:15 | Rev. 5:4 |
| The seer's receptivity to heavenly counsel | Dan. 7:16 | Rev. 5:5a |

1. Beale, 314–15.

| The saints given authority to reign | Dan. 7:18; 22, 27a | Rev. 5:10 |
| Concluding mention of God's reign | Dan. 7:27b | Rev. 5:13–14 |
| An image of a sea | Dan. 7:2–3 | Rev. 4:6 |

I would say that while there are definitely similarities between the two visions, there is not an exact one-to-one correspondence. And we cannot forget about Ezekiel's obvious influence. It is actually not important to know whether Daniel or Ezekiel was the more dominant influence. If John actually saw the vision of heaven, and I believe he did, of course there would be similarities with what Ezekiel and Daniel (and Isaiah) saw.

Mounce correctly describes the purpose of Revelation 4–5 as a vision that "serves to remind believers living in the shadow of impending persecution that an omnipotent and omniscient God is still in control."[2] All the difficulties of what these congregations faced in the first century and what congregations may face in the twenty-first century come into clear perspective before the throne of God. And it is to that throne that John was called up.

Jesus is the voice calling John up to the next stage of his vision (see 1:10–11). A door was standing open in heaven. Literally this could read "The door which had been opened," a divine passive which could indicate that God had opened the door, or that Jesus had opened the door, as the possessor of the key.[3] Aune notes that divine *epiphanies* connected with a heavenly door were particularly important in southwest Asia Minor in the Hellenistic and Roman periods, hinting that John could have been using this tradition to describe his vision.[4] But John did really see an open door. He was not just borrowing from local pagan tradition. And it must be remembered that this is an apocalyptic vision, filled with symbolism. John is told to come up to heaven to see. Maybe this vision or experience could be compared with Paul's experience (see 1 Cor.12), or to Isaiah's vision in Isaiah 6, or to Ezekiel's vision. There are a lot of similarities between this kind of prophetic experience and the experience of the Old Testament prophets.

---

2. Mounce, *The Book of Revelation*, 131.

3. Thomas and Macchia, *Revelation*, 135.

4. Aune, *Revelation 1–5*, 281. It is very difficult, if not impossible, to see an implicit reference to the rapture in 4:1, as the dispensational interpretation requires. This is a case of forcing an issue into a text. Rather, the language used seems to be clearly prophetic visional language that continues the vision or continues on to a subsequent vision from the same speaker, Jesus.

It will be evident in Revelation that John moves from the vision in heaven to earth (chapter 10) to heaven again (11) and to earth again. This is not overly important. In a prophet/ecstatic state it is not surprising that he would be able to see visions of heaven and earth and move between them with ease.[5] This vision of heaven takes place "after this." This simply refers to the order of visions, not necessarily to an historical order.[6] But with the door open in 4:1, the final stages of the consummation are announced. In Revelation, the door open continues to have a message of hope for the suffering believers.[7]

John is said to have been "in the Spirit" in verse 2. This is a reference to the prophetic influence of the Holy Spirit upon him. So, the vision he sees, he is allowed to see because of the overpowering Spirit, just as he described in 1:10. The same phrase is used there.[8] John sees a throne in heaven and one sitting on the throne. He does not give the name, but it is clear that this is God from the descriptions that follow. The word for throne occurs seventeen times in Revelation 4–5 (of thirty-eight occurrences in Revelation 4–22). This high frequency emphasizes that although God's realm is separated from the earthly, he is nevertheless in control over earth's affair.[9] All the judgments later to be issued upon the ungodly come from the throne.

Who else but a king sits on a throne? And as king, what rights does God have? He has the right to judge and the right to show mercy. God said to Moses in Exodus 33:19, "I will be gracious to whom I will be gracious, and will show mercy on whom I will show mercy." The Apostle Paul, in Romans 9:20, writes, "But who are you, O man, to answer back to God? Will what is molded say to its molder, 'Why have you made me like this?'" God also has the right to rule by his law. Praise God that his laws are always just and always

---

5. See Ladd, *A Commentary on the Revelation of John*, 71. According to Aune, *Revelation 1–5*, 275, the switching of scenes between earth and heaven is evidence of the hand of a redactor, but I don't think this is necessarily true. Rather, aligning with Ladd, I think John is seeing a vision of both scenes in heaven and on earth in his visionary state.

6. Beale, *The Book of Revelation*, 317. See also Osborne, *Revelation*, 223.

7. Osborne, *Revelation*, 224. Although Beale interprets "What must take place after this" as both realized and unrealized, it seems clear that John is about to receive words of God's sovereignty primarily over the rest of history, not necessarily going back to the resurrection of Christ alone, though that is certainly an important aspect of the overall message of victory, as will be clear in Revelation 12.

8. See Ezekiel 11:1, 5 for a parallel of the carrying away in the Spirit. Thomas (Thomas and Macchia, *Revelation*, 136), comments that there is no hint that John's "in the Spirit" state stopped. There is continuity between the vision before and this vision, a new movement in Revelation.

9. Beale, *The Book of Revelation*, 320.

put into effect for our best interests. Those who break the laws of God suffer the consequences of their actions. Those who obey them inherit the blessings of God. God, as king, also has the right to be honored. Kings command honor. And if earthly kings through the generations have been given honor and respect (even though many of them did nothing to merit that respect), how much more is God worthy of our honor and praise!

As servants of the King, what rights do we have? None, except the privilege of serving and worshipping him. For he deserves nothing less than our right obedience and loyalty. Anything less than this must be considered unacceptable. But we also have the privilege of audience with the King, relationship with the King, and the inheritance of the King because of the new identity we have in Christ as sons and daughters of the King. This holy King deserves our worship.

John came face to face with the holy King in all his beauty. The description of the One on the throne is similar to Ezekiel's vision in Ezekiel 1:26, 28; 9:2; 24:10; and 28:13, 17–20. John used known terms with the word of "like," ὅμοιος (homoios), to describe something heavenly. It may not have been exactly a throne made of jasper and carnelian. It looked like that. A rainbow or something that looked like a rainbow encircled the throne. These are images of glory and power and exalted royalty. The brilliance of the stones reflects the overwhelming brilliance of God's glory, creating a dazzling affect in heaven and on John. Mounce astutely comments that while various meanings have been ascribed to the stones (Jasper suggests such qualities as majesty, holiness, and purity; sardius is often interpreted as wrath or judgment; and the emerald as mercy), it is best to understand the gems to be part of an overall description which displays the majesty of God, clothed in unapproachable light.[10]

Our cultures think they have a clue as to what is beautiful, but God's beauty comes from his character of holiness, glory, and majesty, which is real beauty in his eyes. What we consider beautiful is skin, teeth, and hair, but God's beauty goes so much deeper. If we think about some comparisons, we can see this more clearly. We consider a great mountain range to be beautiful. We consider a bouquet of roses beautiful. We consider an ocean wave on a clear sandy shore beautiful. Why? Because God, the Creator, gave us a sense

---

10. Mounce, *The Book of Revelation*, 135. See 1 Timothy 6:16. Johnson (Johnson, *Hebrews through Revelation*, 462), notes that the earlier mysticism in Jewish thought is throne mysticism, or *merkabah* mysticism. Its essence is not absorbed contemplation of God's true nature, but perceptions of his appearance on the throne, as described by Ezekiel. Beale (Beale, *The Book of Revelation*, 321), notes that the rainbow reminds us of the Noahic covenant. The judgments that will be revealed and that will proceed from the throne will be tempered with mercy for God's people.

of beauty to appreciate these things. And if God can give a sense of beauty in us, and can create beauty, just imagine how beautiful he must be.

As the holy and beautiful God, he is the center of all praise. Similar to the visions of Ezekiel, Isaiah, and Daniel, in the throne room were other figures, angelic figures of power, reflecting the glory of God. John first sees twenty-four elders surrounding the throne of God. There are several suggestions as to the identity of these elders. Some believe them to be faithful witnesses, like the Lord himself. They are saints who have persevered to the end. That is why they have white robes and golden crowns, as promised to those who overcome in chapter 2–3.[11] Others, like, Beale, view the elders as symbolic, representing the twelve tribes of Israel and the twelve apostles, thus all the saints of the Old and New testaments.[12] More likely, the twenty-four elders are angelic beings dressed in white because they reflect the glory of God. Their crowns are symbols of authority, authority we learn later was given to them from the throne, and thus given back to the One on the throne (4:10).[13]

The throne-room of God is a place of God's thundering and power. God is a God of thunder as well as fire and a still small voice. The seven lamps of verse 5 are a symbolic way of describing the Spirit of God. The Spirit of God hovers before the throne, an image reminiscent of the Spirit of God hovering over the creation of the world. The fact that the Spirit of God is standing next to the throne indicates that when God acts, he acts, and is the means by which this revelation is experienced.[14]

In Psalm 29:3–4, thunder and loud rushing waters describe the voice of God. John could be referring here in verse 5 to the voice of the Lord that was coming from the throne of God, his word continually going forth in power. This is also what the children of Israel saw from Mount Sinai

11. This is the view of Thomas and Macchia, *Revelation*, 139.

12. Beale, *The Book of Revelation*, 322. Beale (Beale, *The Book of Revelation*, 324), also sees a possible reference to Isaiah 24:23, which reads, ". . . for the Lord of hosts reigns on Mount Zion and in Jerusalem, and his glory will be before his elders" and Exodus 24:10.

13. This is the viewpoint of Osborne (Osborne, *Revelation*, 229), who believes a close examination of the role of the elders shows a distinct differentiation between the elders and the saints (see 5:8; 7:13–14; 11:18; 14:3; 19:4). Therefore, elders must be viewed as angels, not saints. Ladd (Ladd, *A Commentary on the Revelation of John*,75) also views them as angels who serve as a sort of heavenly counterpart to the elders in Israel (Exodus 24:1). See also 7:9–11. And Mounce (Mounce, *The Book of Revelation*, 135, 136), rather convincingly, shows that these elders are the heavenly counterpart to the twenty-four priestly and twenty-four Levitical orders of 1 Chronicles 24:4 and 29:9–13. Their function is both royal and sacerdotal, and may also be judicial.

14. Thomas and Macchia, *Revelation*, 139.

in Exodus 19. Exodus 19:18–19 says, "Now Mount Sinai was wrapped in smoke because the Lord had descended on it in fire. The smoke of it went up like the smoke of a kiln, and the whole mountain trembled greatly. And as the sound of the trumpet grew louder and louder, Moses spoke, and God answered him in thunder."[15]

The crystal sea of glass before the throne is similar to Ezekiel's vision as well. It reveals a purity and glory that surrounds and exudes from the throne of God. Ezekiel 1:22 says, "Over the heads of the living creatures there was the likeness of an expanse, shining like awe-inspiring crystal, spread out above their heads." Whether the sea was below or above is not important. What is space in heaven? What is clear is the throne was enveloped in praise and glory. In Revelation 15:2 John sees another sea (the same sea?), pure as glass, and mixed with fire, and the song of Moses was sung, the song of redemption. Could this sea be the redemptive power of God?[16]

The four living creatures are similar to those in Isaiah and Ezekiel. They are exalted orders of angels who are in charge of the heavenly worship of God.[17] Osborne writes, "Since they are nearest the throne (v.6) and take the lead in worship (4:8; 5:14), it is likely that they are the leaders of the heavenly court. In essence, all we can know for certain is that they represent the highest order of celestial beings, perhaps angels, and lead in worship and judgment."[18] These four living creatures are described as animals, in pure form, not in the corrupted form of the visions of Daniel, especially in chapter 7. These represent, possibly, authority (lion), power (ox), wisdom (man), and vision/insight (eagle). But this is only a guess, at best. It could just be a description of the created normalcy or purity of these creatures.[19]

These creatures have six wings, similar to the seraphim in Isaiah 6. They are covered with eyes, and the chorus was similar to what Isaiah heard. Is this a case of John bringing in prophetic visions that Isaiah and Ezekiel saw to

15. See also Psalm 77:18: "The crash of your thunder was in the whirlwind; your lightnings lighted up the world; the earth trembled and shook." See Revelation 8:5, 11:19, and 16:18 for important events accompanied by thunder and lightning, usually in anticipation of God's final judgment.

16. Beale (Beale, *The Book of Revelation*, 328) believes that John sees the chaotic powers of the sea, a source of wickedness, as calmed by divine sovereignty. But I think it more likely reflects the purity and holiness of God associated with Ezekiel's vision and Isaiah's vision (with the four seraphim) in Isaiah 6.

17. Mounce, *The Book of Revelation*, 138.

18. Osborne, *Revelation*, 235.

19. See Ezekiel 1 for a depiction of a creature with four sides (the lion, man, ox, and eagle). The four creatures could also refer to the created order, as each represent the head of its species. (See Beale, *The Book of Revelation*, 330 and Thomas and Macchia, *Revelation*, 141.)

make his point or did John actually see the same thing? I think that John saw what he saw, and it was the same kind of vision that Isaiah and Ezekiel saw, though they used different words to describe it, and rightly so, given the different cultures and times they represented. And it is important to remember Mounce's caution that, "Here as elsewhere we are dealing with visions which were meant to stir the imagination, not yield to the drawing board."[20]

The song is important, as it celebrates the holiness of God. When something is named twice in the Bible, it is very important. The three-fold calling of God's holiness emphasizes his infinite character and his complete holiness. He is "Lord God Almighty" and "The One who is and was and is to come." This emphasizes that the God who transcends time is sovereign over history. The suffering readers can rest in the truth of God's control.[21] Thus it is important for the readers of Revelation to understand that God is outside of time and holds time in his hands (see Revelation 5). He is above and in and around all eternity and nothing escapes his sovereignty, the sovereignty of the Lord God Almighty. In verse 9, this sovereignty is repeated. God is described as "him who is seated on the throne and who lives for ever and ever." This is eternal authority, eternal power, and absolute sovereignty. God is the King, and he is always the King and always has been the King.

The response of the twenty-four elders is a response of worship. They fall before the throne of God whenever the four living creatures give glory, honor, and praise. That means they are doing this eternally, because the four living creatures are always giving praise to God. There is eternal praise and worship before the throne. Their laying of their crowns before the throne is a sign of the recognition of God's sole sovereignty and worth of honor. They are not worthy to wear a crown in the presence of God because only he is worthy of such authority and power. God is exalted in the song of the twenty-four elders because he has authority as Creator and Sustainer, two characteristics that were commonly used by Jews to describe God.

## Conclusion

Isaiah 40:18 asks, "To whom then will you liken God, or what likeness compares with him?" We rightfully ask this question in light of what John saw in Revelation 4. Even the most powerful, the special elite squad angels, bowed before him, and removed their thrones.

The playing of Handel's Messiah has traditionally ended with the audience standing for the Hallelujah Chorus, the final crescendo of praise

20. Mounce, *The Book of Revelation*, 138.

21. Beale, *The Book of Revelation*, 333.

offered to Jesus, the King of kings. Ought we not rather fall on our faces as the twenty-four elders do in heaven? It is time we re-evaluate the holiness of our worship in light of what kind of perspective we have of God. How will a proper image of the exalted King of kings impact our Sunday worship? How will it impact our daily sacrifices of praise? How will it impact our offering of ourselves on the daily altar of Romans 12:1?

# Revelation 5:1–14

The Lamb is Worthy to Open the Scroll

## Introduction

I TOOK A WALK IN my neighborhood the other day. I decided to walk outside our housing complex. It was hot, as the rainy season is letting up, and
the dry season is allowing the sun to bake the earth, and those who choose
to take a walk at 1:30pm, when the sun is at its hottest. As I made my turn
to come back to the house, there was a group of goats feeding in the grass,
near a large house. Two of the younger goats had strayed from their mother.
One goat bleated for its mother as I approached it. It was funny, because it
sounded like it was saying, "Mama." The goats were small, vulnerable, and
certainly not intimidating. I was not afraid at all.

Now suppose I had come across a little lamb. That would have been
even less intimidating. When we want to think of a ferocious animal, we
typically do not think of a little lamb or a goat. There are not too many
sports teams with the mascot of a lamb. There are lions, and bears, and
eagles, and foxes, and cobras, and wolves. These animals are intimidating.
But not lambs. And yet, that is what we see in Revelation 5 as the representative of the Son of God, the One who has the right to take the scroll from
the right hand of the One on the throne. Jesus is the center of attention in
chapter 5. And he deserves the center of attention. But the image we see of
Jesus is profound and deep with meaning.

## Exposition

Besides the centrality of the Lamb of God in chapter 5 is the opening of
the scroll that is in the hand of God. Aune sees the text of chapter 5 as
divided into three sub-units, each introduced by the formula, Καὶ εἶδον (Kai
eidon), meaning "and I saw" (5:1–5; 5:6–10; 5:11–14). The chapter also must
be viewed as depicting the investiture of the Lamb based not on ancient
enthronement customs but rather on the literary adaption of Dan.7 and

Ezek. 1–2, as opposed to the enthronement of the Lamb or the commission of the Lamb in the heavenly court. Jesus always sits on his throne. Investiture refers to the ratification of the office that somebody already holds informally.[1] Aune is correct is viewing this as an investiture. But John is not only adapting the visions of Daniel 7 and Ezekiel 1–2 to his context. He is actually seeing this scene through his own vision.

What was the first thing John saw in chapter 5? He saw a scroll in the right hand of the One on the throne (chapter 4). This means that God has all authority in his hands and holds judgments and future histories in his hands. This reminder of God's sovereignty helps the suffering church bear under their persecution. They know that God is in control and that his kingdom, and the kingdom of the Lamb, will win out over the kingdom of Rome or any other earthly kingdom that pretends to set itself up in opposition to God.

The reader may know the song, "He's got the whole world in his hands." Annie Murray made that song popular when I was young. I used to picture, as a child, the earth in the safe position of God's cupped hands. And, indeed, the world would be in utter chaos if it were not in God's protective care and sustaining power. But situations like the bombing of the World Trade towers, terrorist attacks in Paris, France, famines in Bangladesh, or when a mother drowns her five children in her own bathtub, when divorce strikes a home, or when the economy collapses, cause many around us to question whether God has the world in his hands. It may even bring doubt to our minds. "Is God really in control when so much around us goes wrong?"

In a sense, these are some of the questions that the rest of the book of Revelation is trying to answer: Does God have it all under control? Will justice triumph over injustice? Will good win over evil? Will the wicked be paid back for the wrongs they inflict upon humanity? The answer to these questions is "Yes!" God has it all under control. He will win. The righteous will be rewarded, and the wicked will perish. In the meantime, we hold on.

What gives us a huge booster shot of confidence and hope, even when we find ourselves in confusing situations, is to take a look at Jesus and realize the center of importance that he occupies. John had already been called up to the throne room of Heaven into the very presence of God through a vision. Now we experience with John the dilemma which takes place in the throne room. John sees a scroll in the right hand of the One on the throne. The scroll was sealed with seven seals with writing on both sides.

In those days, there were no "books" as we know them. The bound document with hard covers on the outside and leafy pages on the inside had not

---

1. Aune, *Revelation 1–5*, 329, 332, 336.

yet been invented. They used scrolls, rolled up pieces of heavy paper, usually papyrus. Most of the common scrolls were written on one side. They simply rolled the scroll down and as they rolled the bottom side down, they followed that with the top side until they were finished. Scrolls were then sealed thus, often with a waxy substance that they melted on the seam of the scroll. The unique thing about these scrolls is that they could only be opened by the owner himself. The seals were his own and only he could break them.

When I was in high school, we used textbooks that had been used by other students who had taken the course in the previous years. There was nothing special about those textbooks. Anyone could use and read them. But if I had a diary that was my very own, only I would have the key to that diary. Only I could open it and read what was inside. No one else could, because no one else had the key. This was the type of scroll that John saw in the hands of God. It could only be opened by its owner.

For background on the scroll we can read Daniel 7:10 and 12:8–9. There, Daniel is told to seal up the book until a later time. That later time was the time of John's vision. Beale discusses several interpretive suggestions for the identity of what is written in the scroll: 1) It is the book of redemption (like the Lamb's book of life); 2) It is the Old Testament; 3) It is a book containing events of the future "great tribulation;" 4) It is a book containing God's plan of judgment and redemption. Beale chooses this last choice based upon the parallelism of the hymns in 5:9–10 and 5:12.[2] Ladd also writes that "an adequate interpretation of the scroll must make room for the inclusion of God's judgmental acts as well as the positive aspect of the inheritance bestowed upon the saints."[3] Both Mounce and Johnson believe that the contents of the scroll are more than just a description of judgment and redemption, but the full account of what God has determined for the destiny of the world, the consummation of all history, and how things will ultimately end for all people, which includes the judgment of the world and the final reward of the saints (see 11:18).[4] There is truth in all of these opinions. The scroll contains the judgments that will be revealed; that is, the trumpets that are declared after the seventh seal is opened by the Lamb, and the bowls of wrath that are introduced with the sounding of

2. Beale, *The Book of Revelation*, 339–40.

3. Ladd, *A Commentary on the Revelation of John*, 80.

4. Mounce, *The Book of Revelation*, 142; Johnson, *Hebrews through Revelation*, 467. Aune (Aune, *Revelation 1–5*, 374) believes the contents of the scroll to be the eschatological scenario from 6:1—22:9: "The scroll represents the final and fully predetermined stage in God's redemptive purpose for the world, which will unfold between the heavenly exaltation of Christ following his death and resurrection and the final inauguration of the eternal reign of God."

the seventh trumpet. As part of that judgment is the redemption of God's faithful. This judgment and redemption will come to completion at the end of all things, thus all of history is included in the scroll and held in God's hands, and later, in Christ's hands.

The scroll is sealed with seven seals. The number seven, as in chapter 1, is here a symbol of completion or perfection. The seven seals are a complete pre-unveiling of the judgments of God. Beale sees some intriguing similarities between the double-written scroll of John and the legal background of Roman wills. The contents of a Roman will were sometimes summarized on the back. A will had to be witnessed and sealed by seven witnesses, and only on the death of a testator could a will be unsealed, and the legal promise of the inheritance be executed. Lastly, a trustworthy executor would then put the will into legal effect.[5] Jesus is worthy to open the scroll, as we will see, because his death, as the testator, and the executor, allows the seals to be undone.

An angel in the throne room called out in a loud voice concerning the worthiness of who could open the scroll. The scroll was in the right hand of God, the place of power and prestige. Why did he not just open the scroll? Because he gives the authority to the Son. The question from the angel may remind us of the call for servants in Isaiah 6, "Who will go up for us?"[6] Isaiah answered the call, and it was a call to give the judgment of God to the nation of Israel, who had ears but would not hear. The unfolding of the seals of the scroll would be similar. Though the world would hear the pronouncements of judgment, they would not repent.

No one could open the scroll or even look inside it. No one, that is, until the Lamb of God. A sense of anticipation and literary build-up is used to set the stage for the revelation of the worthiness and the centrality of the Lamb. John wept because no one was worthy. Why would he weep? He didn't really know yet what was in the scroll. But certainly, he knew it was an important part of his vision and he wept because of its importance and that it was not yet revealed. He wept because the judgments of God would not be realized (similar to Habakkuk's complaints). And he wept that there would be no divine and glorious relief for the people of God.

The answer to this dilemma in heaven is answered in dramatic fashion. One of the elders, probably one of the twenty-four elders, tells John not to weep because of the One who is worthy. And he points to the Lion of the tribe of Judah, the root of David. The Lion reference is from Genesis 49:8–12, the prophesy of Judah and his descendants. From the tribe of Judah would

5. Beale, *The Book of Revelation*, 344.
6. Aune, *Revelation 1–5*, 373.

come a lion. The root of David refers to the prophesy of Isaiah 11:1, "There shall come forth a shoot from the stump of Jesse, and a branch from his roots shall bear fruit." A Lion would make sense. A lion! The Jewish people for ages had expected a conquering hero to put an end to the wicked world and all its injustices. For the Jewish people, that meant the Roman empire. They had expected a warrior, someone like the king of beats.[7]

But then we witness one of the greatest literary paradoxes of the Bible. John hears about a Lion of Judah who is victorious. What he sees is a Lamb looking as if it had been slain. Jesus' victory comes from his death and sacrifice, and herein is an important theme of Revelation, one we have already seen in the first three chapters. "In one brilliant stroke John portrays the central theme of New Testament revelation—victory through sacrifice."[8] The Lamb does not cease being the Lion. This dialectical imagery means that the Lion cannot be considered any longer without the concurrent identity of the slaughtered Lamb.[9] This eternally is true. Christ was found worthy to take the scroll because he suffered final judgment as an innocent sacrificial victim on behalf of his people, whom he represented and redeemed.[10] And he remains forever the Lion/Lamb. Only Jesus was worthy to open the scroll, because only Jesus adequately represented humanity before God and God before humanity.

John saw Jesus as the sacrificial sufferer. Here, in a graphic picture, is the great paradox of salvation. In God's upside-down kingdom, the first are the last and the last first. The meek will inherit the earth. God will make the foolish to be wise, and the weak to be strong. Only by dying to ourselves can we then begin to truly live. And here, only by the given of his own life, as the sacrificial Lamb of God, could Jesus conquer the forces of Satan.

John saw Jesus in the middle of the throne of the four living creatures. The authority, and sovereignty possessed by God is possessed by the Lion/Lamb as well. There is no need to be concerned about the exact position of Jesus, that is, is he on the throne, next to it, or to the right of it? We ought not force our own spatially limited categories on the text. The placement of the Greek of the word, throne, first in the sentence, emphasizes its place in heaven. The focus is on the throne, and then on Jesus' worthiness to occupy that throne.

---

7. Ladd (Ladd, *A Commentary on the Revelation of John*, 84) notes that in contemporary Jewish literature, the lion was a symbol for the conquering Messiah (IV Ezra 11:37; 12:31).

8. Mounce, *The Book of Revelation*, 144.

9. Thomas and Macchia, *Revelation*, 148.

10. Beale, *The Book of Revelation*, 341.

The background of the slain Lamb could either be the Passover Lamb of Exodus, or the Isaiah 53:7 Lamb/servant of the Lord. The perfect participle for "slaughtered" or "having been slain" expresses an abiding condition as a result of the past act of being slain. Jesus continues to exist as the "slaughtered Lamb."[11] It bears repeating that Jesus conquered through his sacrifice. This is a reality whose impact and consequences (or fruit) are still realized today and will be realized until the final consummation of all things at Jesus' return. His seven horns and seven eyes reveal the perfection of his power and presence, transcendence and immanence. He is above all, on the throne, and he is with us as the Spirit is sent throughout the earth.[12]

Like the Son of Man in Daniel 7 who received power and authority from the Ancient of Days, so the Lamb who was slain receives the scroll from the right hand of the One on the throne. Though Mounce says that "this is not to be taken as a coronation, but as an event yet to take place at the end of time,"[13] I think it is more accurate to say that Jesus is not waiting for authority. He already has it. His authority will not wait. He won that authority because of his sacrifice.

After Jesus, the Lamb, took the scroll, the four living creatures and the twenty-four elders fell down before the throne and praised the Lamb. The Lamb is worthy of praise just as the One on the throne in Revelation 4. They had in their hands harps and golden bowls full of incense which are the prayers of the saints. This is a clear indication that these elders are not saints (as we discussed in chapter 4), but angels who come to God in a priestly fashion with the prayers of the saints. The prayers are identified in 6:9-11 and 8:4 and beyond. They were praying for divine vindication of their suffering. Ladd sees these saints as "All of God's people on earth who have prayed for the coming of God's kingdom; and the foremost among such saints must be believers who constitute the church."[14]

The four living creatures and the twenty-four elders (part of the crescendo from chapter 4) sing a new song. Beale writes that in the Old Testament a new song is always an expression of praise for God's victory over

11. Beale, *The Book of Revelation*,352; Mounce, *The Book of Revelation*, 146.

12. See also Daniel 7:7-8:24 and Zechariah 3 and 4. Beale (Beale, *The Book of Revelation*, 355) writes that as a result of the death and resurrection of Jesus, these spirits become the agents of Christ throughout the world, who figuratively represent the Holy Spirit himself. The Spirit carries out the sovereign plan of the Lord in the world.

13. Mounce, *The Book of Revelation*, 146.

14. Ladd, *A Commentary on the Revelation of John*, 90. See 11:18; 16:6; 18:24. These saints are not Jews as in the dispensationalist view. In these passages, we see a list of saints, apostles, and prophets. Apostles would not be an appropriate term for Jews, as they had no apostles. The natural way to understand this is to see it as a reference to the church.

the enemy, sometimes including thanksgiving for God's work of creation. Here the new song celebrates the defeat of the powers of evil and sin.[15] It is new because, through the death of Christ, a new covenant has been established, a better covenant, as Hebrews teaches. Men were purchased for God, for his glory and for his honor. They were purchased for God because God is the Creator. God was exalted as the Creator. Jesus is exalted as the Redeemer. Isaiah 42:10 says, "Sing to the Lord a new song, his praise from the end of the earth, you who go down to the sea, and all that fills it, the coastlands and their inhabitants."

This new covenant and redemption are not just for the Jewish nation alone. This makes the song new as well. Every tribe and language and people and nation have been purchased for God. This is a way of saying that people from all parts of the earth, every tribal group, every racial identity, benefit from the spilled blood of the Lamb of God. This is a universal redemption for people of all kinds. A similar list can be found in Daniel 7:14.[16]

In verse 10 we see a fuller fulfillment of the purpose of God. Just as the nation of Israel was made to be a kingdom and priests to serve God (see Exodus 19:6), so now the redeemed of the Lamb. What is different in this case is that now the kingdom and priests (like in Revelation 1) is from every tribe, tongue, people, and nation. This is the power of the redemption of the blood of Jesus. Is this reigning of the peoples as kingdom and priests taking place right now, or is this only something in the future? Both the present and the future are supported by good textual evidence. But the context determines that the present is preferred. The church now has authority and reigns because of Jesus' death and resurrection and will reign ultimately on the earth. This is a case of now and now yet eschatology.[17]

In the third "And I saw" in verse 11 (the second was in verse 6), John sees many angels join the four living creatures and the twenty-four elders in an ever louder crescendo of praise. The number of the angels here is not, most likely, literal. The "thousands upon thousands, and ten thousand times ten thousand," is meant to be figurative to show that this number is beyond count. It would be like saying angels number google times google.

15. Beale, *The Book of Revelation*, 358.

16. Beale, *The Book of Revelation*, 359, notes that this not a redemption of all peoples without exception, but of all without distinction.

17. See 1 Peter 2:9–10 . Cf. Mounce (Mounce, *The Book of Revelation*, 149) and Ladd (Ladd, *A Commentary on the Revelation of John*, 92), who believe that even though the text is in the present tense, it should be read as a futuristic present. The church is to share in the eschatological reign of Christ and all that it will involve. I don't think we need to split the two realities. We reign in the present as the church. We have been given Jesus' authority (Matthew 16:18–20 ; 28:19–20). But we will also reign with Christ on the earth when he returns (1 Thessalonians 4:17).

The identity of the Lamb again becomes the focus of the praise, as the One who was slain. His fulfillment of his purpose on the earth becomes a part of his nature and character. And then a litany of words is used to emphasize his worthiness. He receives power (*dunamis*) and wealth and wisdom and strength and honor and praise. Does not he have these already? Yes, but this is a reminder again of his glory and worthiness.

The final elevation of the crescendo of praise is when every creature gives praise to the One who sits on the throne and to the Lamb. On the apparent paradox of praise to both God and Jesus, as part of the divine Trinity, Bauckham writes, "John does not wish to represent Jesus as an alternative object of worship alongside God, but as one who shares in the glory due to God. He is worthy of divine worship because his worship can be included in the worship of the one, true God."[18] The simple response of the four living creatures and of the elders is to fall down and worship God and the Lamb.

## Conclusion

Is Jesus the center of attention in our lives? He deserves to be. There was once a little boy who was desperately ill. His parents recognized that he probably soon would die. They sent for the local pastor. He came at night to visit the child, who was semiconscious. He was unable to speak and apparently never spoke in any acknowledgment of the pastor's presence. That pastor was alone in the child's upstairs room and left late at night. He returned early the next morning after the boy had died. He did his best to console the parents. He prayed with them. He grieved with them.

Later the parents asked the pastor if he had any explanation for something that had happened. They told the pastor that in the hours before their son died and at the time of his death, he was holding the ring finger of one hand with his other hand. He died in that position. It was then the pastor explained what he had said that night in the child's room. He had wanted to explain to that child on the edge of eternity not only the importance of being a Christian but, in a child's language, how to become one. He said he had taken their son's hand and first held his thumb and had said, "*The . . .* , because, we're talking about one of a kind." Then he held his next finger and said, "*Lord.*" For the next finger, he said God himself *is* right here. The next finger: *my*, a personal commitment and relationship. For the last finger:

18. Bauckham, *New Testament Theology*, 60–61. John never uses a plural verb or a plural pronoun to refer to both God and Jesus. It's clear that he places Christ on the divine side of the distinction between God and creation, but he wants to avoid ways of speaking which sound to him polytheistic.

*shepherd*, the one who owns, who died, who cares and loves: Jesus. While he had not spoken, the child had heard. Before he died, he put his hand around his finger to say, "The Lord is *my* shepherd."

Is Jesus the center of our lives? May we let our lives be a chorus of praise to him every day. He is the Lamb who was slain and is worthy of our lives and praise.

# Revelation 6:1–17

## The Opening of Seals 1–6

### Introduction

H AVE YOU EVER BEEN afraid of punishment, I mean really afraid of punishment? Have you ever been terrified of something? When I was in class five of elementary school, my family lived in a cemetery, a national cemetery in Virginia. My father was a superintendent and so part of the benefit was the free house . . . in the cemetery. My brother, Kelly, is five years older than I am, so when he was in the last year of middle school, he had me convinced of the legend of the blue civil war ghost. There was a large unmarked tomb in the middle of the cemetery that marked the burial place of dozens of confederate soldiers. Kelly told me the blue civil war ghost would come out when it was raining and the moon was full. So, when the next full moon was out, and it was raining, he convinced me to go out with him to prove our bravery and walk through the cemetery in the dark. We did, and I was terrified.

Have you ever been afraid of a wild dog on the street? Have you ever been afraid of a shark while swimming in the water? Have you ever been afraid of a snake in the garden? Have you ever been afraid of a lamb on a hillside? What a minute! A lamb?! Yes. There will come a day when a Lamb, though no ordinary Lamb, will strike terror in the hearts of all the inhabitants of the earth who have opposed him. At that time, he will come as King.

### Exposition

Revelation 6 begins the revelation of the judgments to come. The interpretive question is whether these judgments begin after the resurrection and ascension of Jesus or are they events that are signs of the coming Day of the Lord, in other words, do they happen just before the return of Christ? We actually need to consider the seven seals as introductory judgments to the seven trumpets and the seven bowls of wrath. Osborne lists seven helpful major themes in the great judgments of the seals, trumpets, and bowls: 1) They are judgments of God poured out on the earth; 2) These judgments are God's response to the prayers of the saints for justice and vengeance; 3) The sovereignty of God is stressed throughout the judgments; 4) God does not command evil to do something. He allows it to operate; 5) The response of the earth dwellers proves their total depravity for they refuse to repent; 6) The outpourings of God's wrath have a redemptive purpose; and 7) There is a progressive dismantling of creation (1/4, 1/3, total).[1]

When are the judgments revealed? Are they revealed beginning with the opening of the seals, or only after the seals are opened, beginning with the sounding the trumpets? Bauckham believes that the opening of the seals prepares for the revelation of the contents of the scroll. In other words, the scroll is closed, and so the contents are not yet revealed, only until the seventh seal is opened.[2] Ladd, as well, views the breaking of the seals as not part of the great tribulation itself, but only preliminary and preparatory to the great tribulation. So also, the opening of the seals is preliminary to the opening of the scroll and the end of time.[3]

On the other hand, as Aune points out, the events accompanying the breaking of each seal (except the fifth) belong to traditional Jewish and Christian conceptions of the tribulations that will introduce the end.[4] It is not so important to know the exact timing of the judgments, whether the seven seals are events that have been experienced since the ascension of Christ or are events that are in the future, as precursors to the great tribulation. What is important to remember is that each of the seven seals is opened by the Lamb of God, and that he controls the timing and time of the judgments. It seems clear that the seven trumpets are contained within the opening of the seventh seal, and the seven bowls of wrath are poured out after the sounding of the seventh trumpet. And whether the judgments of a more severe nature are begun only with the blowing of the trumpets, the judgments of the seven seals do seem severe in and of themselves. Beale comments, "Revelation 6:1–8 is intended to show that Christ rules over such an apparent chaotic world and that suffering does not occur indiscriminately or by chance."[5]

Where is the church during this whole period? This is a question that has caused much debate for the last 150 years. Some believe the church will

---

1. Osborne, *Revelation*, 270–71. There is disagreement about whether the judgments actually have a redemptive purpose. We will discuss that soon.

2. Bauckham, *New Testament Theology*, 80. See also Mounce, *The Book of Revelation*, 151.

3. Ladd, *A Commentary on the Revelation of John*, 96.

4. Aune, *Revelation 6–16*, 424.

5. Beale, *The Book of Revelation*, 370.

be taken out of this period of persecution and tribulation through what is called the rapture of the church. So, the judgments we see relate to only the ungodly on the earth and any who come to Christ during that period. Some believe the church will have to go through the great tribulation and be cleansed of its impurities as if in a crucible. The church, because of this suffering (through persecution, not the wrath of God), will be cleansed of those who hold onto the church just as if it was a social club.

Unfortunately, we have lost much of the central message of the book of Revelation because we have labored so long on these debates, some to the point of starting separate denominations or churches because they held strongly to their views. Whether the church goes through the tribulation or doesn't seems to be particularly an issue for churches in the West, where persecution has not historically been strong. It is the view of this commentary that the church will be present through the great persecutions, but be spared from the wrath of God, just as the nation of Israel was separated from the plagues of Egypt. What we do know is that those who do not know Jesus will go through the sufferings described in the book of Revelation without the protection of God. And, if they do not repent, the sufferings or the wrath of the Lamb of God will be great and terrible.

This Lamb opens the seals of the scroll in verse 1 just as John had heard in chapter 5. He alone is worthy to open the seals. The background of the four horses has to be Zechariah 6:1–8, except that those were chariots. Zechariah was prophesying the completeness of God's judgment in that it would cover the whole earth. The idea here is the same.[6] The four living creatures have authority to command the horses to come. The first horse was commanded by the first living creature, the second was commanded by the second living creature, and so on. It is as if they have charge over the appointed horses of judgment and that may have something to do with their position before the throne.

The first horse was a white horse. This is different than the white horse of Revelation 19. This horse, and its rider, are signs of judgment. The judgment of the first horse is the authority to conquer. The bow is a tool of war and the crown a sign of authority and power. Beale lists several arguments for this rider being identified with Christ: 1) This may be an allusion to Psalms 45:3–5, a Messianic passage applied to Christ in Hebrews 1:8; 2) In Revelation 19:11–16 Christ rides with crowns on his head on a white horse; 3) In 14:14, a figure like Christ is carrying a weapon in his hand and rides

---

6. Mounce (Mounce, *The Book of Revelation*, 152) also sees Luke 21 and the end-times discourse of Jesus as background. The seven woes of Luke are included within the six seals of Revelation. It could very well be that John intended a double reference, first to Zechariah and the obvious connection with color, and then to Jesus' prophesy.

on a white horse—but it is not clear that this is Jesus; 4) Christ "conquers" elsewhere in the book (3:21; 5:5; 17:14); 5) Part of the synoptic tradition places the universal preaching of the gospel before the beginning of the woes before the Son of Man's coming; 6) White is used without exception in Revelation (14 times) in a good sense in descriptions associated with the holiness of God, Christ, or the saints; and 7) The first horseman is different than the others. Arguments against the rider being identified with Jesus: 1) The language of "conquering" is used elsewhere of the beast oppressing the saints; 2) In Zech.1:8–15 and 6:1–8 the horses are identified together as being the same in nature and this must be the case in Revelation 6:1–8; 3) Revelation 12–13 portray Satan and his minions as deceiving by imitating Christ's appearance; 4) Prophesy of "false Christs and false prophets" predicted that they will come (Mk.13:5–6; Matt.24:4–5; Luke 21:8); 5) The four horsemen seem to be a set; 6) It may be awkward to have Christ open a seal, in which he is the object; 7) If the fourth horseman, death, is a summary of the first three, then all must be considered evil; and 8) In 9:7, demonic agents of judgment are likened to "horses prepared for battle."[7]

The view of this commentary is that the rider is not Jesus, but part of the judgments of God sent by God and commanded by Jesus, who opened the seal. The rider is given authority (divine passive) only because of God. He comes to judge the earth, and maybe also to persecute the saints (see the fifth seal). The rider could either be considered an antichrist-type of figure whose forces seek to conquer the followers of Christ,[8] or a human force. God was allowing human depravity to run its course. The description of the rider closely resembles the Parthians, the only military force in the world at that time that was feared by the Romans. They were known for their effective cavalry and their ability to accurately shoot arrows from horseback. They had made several incursions into Rome in the 60s and 70s. The crown would then indicate a sovereignty outside of Rome.[9]

Rather than white standing as a symbol for the purity of Christ, white here, and the other colors in Revelation 6, corresponds to the character of the rider and symbolize conquest (white), bloodshed (red), scarcity (black), and death (pale, livid).[10]

The second horse was red or fiery. The passive voice of the verb, "was given" is again used to show that this is authority and power that is bestowed

---

7. Beale, *The Bok of Revelation*, 375–76; See Aune, *Revelation 6–16*, 393–94, for a list of reasons for and against as well. Thomas (Thomas and Macchia, *Revelation*, 156) views the rider to be Jesus.

8. See Johnson, *Hebrews through Revelation*, 473.

9. Osborne, *Revelation*, 277.

10. Mounce, *The Book of Revelation*, 152.

on them. This is not a power they have on their own. It is a power granted to them. This rider is given power to take peace away from the earth. The literal translation is, "He was given to take."

Beale believes this absence of peace is a reference to the persecution of Christians as well as general strike on the earth. In Matthew 10:34, Jesus says, "Do not think that I have come to bring peace to the earth. I have not come to bring peace, but a sword." As in this passage, the word μάχαιρα (*mach-aira*), sword, is used in contexts of persecution in Rom.8:35; Heb.11:34; and Revelation 13:10. And the word used for "kill" is used by John without exception to refer to the death of Christ or his followers (see 5:6, 9, 12; 6:9; 13:8; 18:24).[11] However, while it may refer to persecution, it seems more likely to refer to the general anarchy and bloodshed that will occur, and has several times occurred in localized places, around the world in history. Anarchy and bloodshed were common in John's era. In 68–69 A.D. alone, Rome had been ruled by four different emperors.[12] What is clear is that the Lord would punish with the sword, as was prophesied in Isaiah 27:1; Jeremiah 32:24; and Ezekiel 21:14. "The great sword" would be a tool of judgment on the nations as they would turn their swords against one another.

The third horse is black, and the rider holds a pair of scales in his hands. The scales have to do with famine, as the scale was the common device for measuring and buying and selling. As part of the curses of God upon unfaithful Israel, God warns in Leviticus 26:26, "When I break your supply of bread, ten women shall bake your bread in a single oven and shall dole out your bread again by weight, and you shall eat and not be satisfied." Also, Elisha warned in 2 Kings 7:1, "Hear the word of the Lord: thus says the Lord, Tomorrow about this time a seah of fine flour shall be sold for a shekel, and two seahs of barley for a shekel, at the gate of Samaria." This was in reference to a great famine that would come upon the people because of their unfaithfulness. See also Ezekiel 4:10, 16.

A voice speaks from the middle of the four living creatures. This was most likely another angel. This being declares the standard prices for wheat and barley but commands the protection of the oil (probably olive oil) and wine (the grapevines). The price listed is about 10–12 times higher than the normal prices at the time, indicating a severe famine.[13] According to Ladd, the warning against hurting the oil and the wine is not a reference to the

11. Beale, *The Book of Revelation*, 379.

12. See Mounce, *The Book of Revelation*,155. Aune (Aune, *Revelation 6–16*, 395) also points out that the function of the second rider of taking peace from the earth is portrayed as a universal phenomenon, perhaps as a conscious reversal of the *Pax Romana* proclaimed by Augustus.

13. Beale, *The Book of Revelation*, 381.

wealthy being immune from the famine, but the phrase "grain, oil, and wine" is a common phrase in the Bible representing the basic necessities of life (see Deuteronomy 7:13; 11:14; 28:51; 2 Chronicles 32:28; Nehemiah 5:11; Hosea 2:8, 22; Joel 2:19; and Haggai 1:11).[14] This was a famine, but not a complete famine, again indicating the limited nature of this judgment.

The fourth horse was a pale horse, or a speckled horse. This is the first time a number is used. A fourth of the earth would suffer from the judgment of this rider. The name of the rider is Death, and Hades was his companion. Death and Hades have the power to kill through four means, that is, sword, famine, death or plague, and by the wild beasts of the earth. In Hosea 13:8, God says, "I will fall upon them like a bear robbed of her cubs; I will tear open their breast, and there I will devour them like a lion, as a wild beast would rip them open." And even more clearly linked is God's warning in Ezekiel 14:21, "How much more when I send upon Jerusalem my four disastrous acts of judgment, sword, famine, wild beasts, and pestilence, to cut off from it man and beast!" Whether this fourth horse is a summary of the judgments brought by the first three, or a separate judgment, it is clear that these are satanic forces that are ultimately under the governance of the throne.[15] Later, Death and Hades deliver up the dead for judgment in Revelation 20:13–14, but before then, their task is to inflict judgment upon those who have rejected the Lamb.

We see unleashed the beginning of the bad fruit or consequences of the sin of mankind. When Adam and Eve sinned, that set into motion the destruction of the world, as sin and all its devastation crept in like a snake in a field of mice. When do these judgments takes place? During the fourteenth century many in the Christian church in Europe thought they were seeing the beginning of the distress of Matthew 24. The black plague killed 3/5 of much of Europe. It followed a series of brutal wars against the Muslims from the south. On the other hand, the world has never seen the kind and extent of war as we saw in the twentieth century. Russia lost twenty-five million men alone during WWII. Man has turned against man unlike any time before, but now has the capability of wiping out whole cities with a single weapon. It becomes all the more real when we think of how close we as a human race are to fulfilling the task of the four horsemen. Where there has been war, there has been much famine and plague. Death and Hades have been active grave diggers in the near past, and I believe it will get worse. We should not be fooled by the apparent economic power of this nation or that

14. Ladd, *A Commentary on the Revelation of John*, 101. Aune (Aune, *Revelation 6–16*, 397) makes an interesting point that one liter of wheat and three liters of barley are mentioned because that was the appropriate amount for a cavalryman and his mount.

15. Beale, *The Book of Revelation*, 382.

nation. The world will continue to turn its dagger on one another as long as nations try to rule their people without reference to God.

In verse 9 we see a vivid contrast. There are those (1/4 of the earth) who are killed by the means mentioned in verse 8, killed because of the judgment of the fourth rider. And in verse 9, when the fifth seal is opened, we see those who were killed because of their testimony and the word of God. These are the faithful who have continued in their faith despite the persecution they have faced, like those in the Philadelphia church and those in the church in Smyrna.

Persecution was already common is some areas of the Christian church during the time of John. The little word, διὰ (*dia*), used twice in this verse, shows that the souls of these people were slain "on account of" or "because of" the word of God and their testimony. That they are under the altar is evidence of their sacrifice to God and their eternal protection in his presence. They were slain just as the Lamb was slain. They, as followers of Christ, will have their sacrificial suffering and their apparent defeat turned into ultimate victory.[16] From God's perspective, their untimely deaths are a sacrifice on the altar of heaven.[17]

Those under the altar call out with a loud voice. There is an anguish in their emotions. How long until their blood is avenged? Their lives were taken from them by the wicked. They want to know how long before justice is done, and the Lord makes things right. This question, "how long," can be found as well in Psalm 6:4; 12:2; 73:10; 78:5; 88:47; 93:3; and Daniel 8:13.[18] It is a common call for help in the midst of a difficult trial or case of injustice. Even the angel is Zechariah 1:12 asks, "O Lord of hosts, how long will you have no mercy on Jerusalem and the cities of Judah, against which you have been angry these seventy years?" God is addressed in verse 9 as the Sovereign One, Holy and True or faithful. Because God is holy and faithful, he will judge those who have slain the righteous and he will make things right.

And so, God gives comfort to the saints under the altar. There is a limit to those who will suffer for the sake of the word of God. They are told to wait "a little time longer," χρόνον μικρόν (*chronon mikron*). The word used to describe time as event, *Kairos*, is not used here. There is a definite clock/calendar time-limit to their suffering. The saints are given white robes to wear, either as evidence of their righteousness and victory before the judge of the

16. Beale, *The Book of Revelation*, 392.

17. See also Mounce, *The Book of Revelation*, 157; Thomas and Macchia, *Revelation*, 159; and Aune (Aune, *Revelation 6–16*, 404), who shows that the location of the souls under the altar indicating a nearness to God is apparently the same motif at work in early Jewish traditions.

18. Beale, *The Book of Revelation*, 392.

earth, [19] or as a vindication of the purity of the saints (and thus not their guilt as determined by the world). They had proved faithful and had shown to be "in the right."[20] There would be more who would suffer as they did, "fellow servants and brothers." This informs us that these are members of the body of Christ. There are some that have already suffered for the word of God; there are others who will still yet join them in their suffering.

Have you ever asked God, "How long, O LORD?" How long are the wicked going to get away with their wickedness? How long are the ungodly going to rule politics and kingdoms? How long will the arrogant get away with his brashness and pride? How long will the child pornographer continue to prey on innocent children? How long will the child slave traffic continue in this cold world? How long will the unfeeling continue to abort babies? How long will we have to suffer from speaking the truth? God says, "Wait a little while longer." And the picture we see in the sixth seal is a glimpse of the terror that will fall upon those who oppose God.

What are revealed with the opening of the sixth seal are various apocalyptic signs of the coming of the Day of the Lord. In Joel 2:30–31 we read, "And I will show wonders in the heavens and on the earth, blood and fire and columns of smoke. The sun shall be turned to darkness, and the moon to blood, before the great and awesome day of the LORD comes." These signs will precede the coming of the Son of Man. Jesus, quoting from Joel 2 in Matthew 24:30 says, "Then will appear in heaven the sign of the Son of Man, and then all the tribes of the earth will mourn, and they will see the Son of Man coming on the clouds of heaven with power and great glory."

Other signs of the day of the LORD are in verse 13 and 14: the stars falling from the sky and the skies receding and the mountains and islands being remove from their place. Isaiah 34:4 prophesied in the context of judgment against the nations, "All the host of heaven shall rot away, and the skies roll up like a scroll. All their host shall fall, as leaves from the vine, like leaves falling from the fig tree." See also Isaiah 13:10–13; 24:1–6, 19–23; Ezekiel 32:6–8; and Habakkuk 3:6–11. This language is clearly symbolic of the coming day of the LORD, but it is not merely symbolic but describes a real cosmic catastrophe whose actual character we cannot conceive.[21] It is like a window to the final day is being opened for us through this sixth seal. We have not

19. Johnson, *Hebrews through Revelation*, 475.

20. Beale, *The Book of Revelation*, 394. See Ladd (Ladd, *A Commentary on the Revelation of John*, 106), who says that the white robe is a symbol of blessedness and rest, knowing that the state of final rest awaits the return of Christ and the resurrection of the body.

21. Ladd, *A Commentary on the Revelation of John*, 108.

seen these things take place, and it is quite clear that these signs directly precede the coming of the day of the LORD.

At that time, all the peoples of the earth will mourn. There will be no difference between slave and free in those days. All will be on the same level field before the Lamb. Thomas comments that there are seven distinct classes of human society listed in verse 15. These respond in unison, indicating that humanity in its entirety is represented as mourning the coming of the wrath of the Lamb.[22] This reaction of the peoples is prophesied in Isaiah 2:19, "And people shall enter the caves of the rocks and the holes of the ground, from before the terror of the Lord, and from the splendor of his majesty, when he rises to terrify the earth."

In the case of the sixth seal, it is the wrath and glory and majesty of the Lamb. It will be clear on the Day of the Lord that judgment will come from the One who sits on the throne and from the Lamb, who has authority to open the seals. Beale aptly writes, "The gentle Lamb who was slain on the cross is now in an exalted position over the whole cosmos (1:5; 3:21; 5:5–6) to pour out his wrath."[23] The wrath from the throne is both a present reality (1:18) and an eschatological event (Revelation 19:15). It is a response of God's holiness to persistent and impenitent wickedness (see also Zephaniah 1:14–18; Nahum 1:6; Malachi 3:2).[24] And on that great and terrible day of the LORD, no one will be able to stand, or withstand the judgment and wrath of the Divine Lamb of God.

## Conclusion

Our response before the Lamb on his throne is determined by our response before the Lamb on the cross. We will either be rejoicing because the final day of our redemption in Christ will have come, and we had already responded to the Lamb on the cross, recognizing that he is our Savior. Or we will be asking the rocks and mountains to fall on us, because we will be terrified to face the One we rejected. We will be terrified to face the One who sent messengers to us and witnesses to pray for us, plead with us, and explain to us, the urgency of our decision.

This is a terror we do not need to face, and a terror that our relatives and friends do not need to face. 1 John 4:16–18 says, "God is love, and whoever abides in love abides in God, and God abides in him. By this is love perfected with us, so that we may have confidence for the day of

22. Thomas and Macchia, *Revelation*, 163.

23. Beale, *The Book of Revelation*, 403.

24. Mounce, *The Book of Revelation*, 163.

judgment, because as he is so also are we in the world. There is no fear in love, but perfect love casts out fear. For fear has to do with punishment, and whoever fears has not been perfected in love." We do not need to be afraid if we have already knelt before the Lamb on the cross and received his salvation for us.

# Revelation 7:1–17

First Interlude (A Picture of the End)

## Introduction

I HAVE NEVER KNOWN THE agony of having to wait for my wedding day because I had to go off to war. It must be very hard and painful, a reason why many young couples quickly get married before military service. But I have known the wait of an engagement period of fourteen months. Lora and I were engaged shortly before she graduated from high school, and all through her freshman year at Moody Bible Institute. The ring (the engagement ring) was a symbol to all those other young men training to be pastors and missionaries that she was already spoken for.

When a young man gives his bride-to-be a ring in the western culture, he is declaring to everyone that this young woman is engaged to be his wife. She is taken. He is hers. No one else may interfere in this relationship. The ring is a symbol of the covenant to come. When a soldier goes to war as an engaged man, his girl has the ring on her finger to ward off pursuers of her affection, to remind all others that there is another coming for her. That he will be home from the battle lines soon and that she belongs to him.

What a great picture this is of the relationship between Jesus and his bride, the church. The metaphor is a little different from reality, however. Jesus has already won the battle on the cross and the resurrection. He has fought the fight and the victory is his. We, his bride, are still actively engaged in a spiritual war on the earth, battling with the prince of darkness, the warlord of this world, Satan and all his forces. We now await the return of our Groom, Jesus, who will take us to his home forever. This is the great hope of the church—the end of time, God's people will dwell with him forever. We get a glimpse of this in Revelation 7.

## Exposition

Revelation 7 is not a continuation chronologically from chapter 6. It is the first of several interludes. According to Osborne, the interludes serve several purposes: 1) The two interludes that occur between the sixth and seventh seal and the sixth and seventh trumpets are closely linked to the six judgments that are associated with each; 2) They provide information about the situation regarding the saints (7:1–17) and the conflict (10:1–11:13; 12:1–13:18); and 3) They stress even more the sovereignty of God in the process.[1] Beale likewise notes that chapter 7 serves parenthetically after the opening of the six seals and before the opening of the seventh seal in chapter 8. But it also has a future aspect, especially toward the end. The chapter, then, is also an answer to the question of 6:17, "who is able to stand?" before God and not suffer the wrath of the Lamb? Those who have been sealed. Chapter 7, then, is not a new series of events. 7:1–8 immediately precedes the time of 6:1–8 and 7:9–17 focuses on the scene after the final judgment.[2]

A big question of interpretation concerns the identity of the two groups mentioned in 7:1–8 and 7:9–17. Are they different groups? Are they descriptions of the same group? Who are the 144,000? There are many different options, one being that the 144,000 are the Jews who have been saved in the tribulation period (the dispensational view). I think more likely, as Bauckham explains, that the two images depict the same reality. These are the victorious followers of Christ. They are parallel to the two contrasting images of Christ in 5:5–6: the 144,000 "Israelites" are the followers of the Davidic Messiah, the Lion of Judah; and the innumerable multitude are the people of the slaughtered Lamb, ransomed from all nations (see 5:9). Also, the 144,000 are an army, listed in a census-like manner as a reckoning of the strength of the nation. And the multitude celebrates their robes as washed in the blood of the Lamb. This means they are martyrs, who have triumphed by participating, through their own deaths, in the sacrificial death of the Lamb.[3]

More specifically and more clearly, Mounce believes that in the case of both groups, the church is in view, but from two different vantage points. Prior to the trumpet judgments (not before the four horsemen, as in Beale), the last generation of believers is sealed so as to be saved from the destruction coming upon the earth. The second vision is a picture of all believers, when they realize their reward at the end in the presence of God.[4] I don't

---

1. Osborne, *Revelation*, 301.

2. Beale, *The Book of Revelation*, 405–06.

3. Bauckham, *New Testament Theology*, 76–77; see also Aune, *Revelation 6–16*, 436. Osborne (Osborne, *Revelation*, 313) sees this as a secondary image.

4. Mounce, *The Book of Revelation*, 164; see also Osborne, *Revelation*, 303.

think we need to limit the first group to only those who are saved from God's wrath just prior to the judgment of God. This group could also represent the body of Christ as a whole, the new Israel of God, who are sealed from God's wrath by the blood of Christ. The saints are protected from the wrath of God (see 7:1–8), but are not protected from the wrath of the beast (7:9–17; see also 13:1–8).[5] See also Romans 5:3–5; 8:12–39; 1 Corinthians 4:8–13; 1 Thessalonians 4:4–7; Hebrews 12:4–11; James 1:2–4; 1 Peter 1:6–7; and 3:13–4:19 as examples of exhortations in the midst of suffering.

In verse 1, John sees four angels standing at the four corners of the earth and holding back the four winds of the earth. There is similar language used in Zech.6:1–8, particularly in verse 5, when the angel describes to Zechariah the identity of the four chariots, "These are going out to the four winds of heaven, after presenting themselves before the Lord of all the earth." (see also Zech. 2:6). In Daniel 7:2, Daniel saw, "four winds of heaven were stirring up the great sea." The four angels are assigned the task to hold back the judgment of God, symbolized by the winds of the earth. These angels are given power to harm the land, the sea, and the trees, but only when the time is right.

Several times in the Scripture the idea of "four" symbolizes the whole world. So here, "standing on the four corners of the earth" is a reference to the whole world. In Isaiah 11:12 we read that God will "assemble the scattered people of Judah from the four quarters of the earth."[6] For reference to "four winds" as a symbol of the entire world see Jeremiah 49:36, "I will scatter them to the four winds, and there will not be a nation where Elam's exiles do not go," meaning they will go throughout the entire world. In Matthew 24:31 Jesus very clearly references the whole world, "And he will send his angels with a loud trumpet call, and they will gather his elect from the four winds, from one end of the heavens to the other."[7]

Are the winds evil or angelic forces? The word, "winds" could be translated "spirits" and refer to the demonic powers bent on destruction but dependent upon the sovereignty of God. Mounce does not see this. He sees them as angels only, and believes that the references above (Jeremiah 49 and Daniel 7) are important.[8] Whether these are angels who bring the

5. Osborne, *Revelation*, 302.

6. See also Ezekiel 7:2 and Revelation 20:8.

7. See also Daniel 8:8, 11:4, and Mark 13:27. Thomas (Thomas and Macchia, *Revelation*, 165) notes that the emphasis on the number four points to God's complete control of the earth, and that the four points of the earth point to the earth in its totality.

8. Mounce, *The Book of Revelation*, 166. Osborne (Osborne, *Revelation*, 305) points out that it was the wind at the Exodus that brought the locusts and took them away, and parted the Red Sea (Exodus 10:13, 19; 14:21). The "four winds" developed in

destruction or demons who are given power (divine passive) by God to unleash chaos and judgment is less important than seeing this ultimately as judgment from God upon the whole earth, while still limited in scope in terms of the extent of the judgments.

An angel comes from the east to place a seal on the foreheads of the servants of God. Only then would the destruction come. The angel would come from the east possibly because this is the place where traditional judgments came from, or the enemies of God's people (for example, Babylon and Assyria). The angel is carrying a seal of the living God. This seal is the identity marker (like an engagement ring) of those who belong to God. The seal was placed on the foreheads of the people of God. The forehead was the place of the seal for the priests in Exodus. The inscription upon that seal was "holy to the Lord." So also, this seal, written metaphorically upon the foreheads of the servants of the Lord, is a seal that sets them apart from the judgments that would come, and declares that they belong to God. They are not sealed from physical harm, as we see several examples of the saints' sufferings in Revelation. But they are spiritually sealed so that they may maintain their testimony until the end.[9]

Another possible background for this is the seal of the blood of the lamb that marked the doorposts of the children of Israel so that they would not be touched by the plague of death against the firstborn in Egypt. Ezekiel 9:4 may also have been influenced by this Passover blood seal. The people, in Ezekiel's case, were marked with a Hebrew *Tau* to show that they were deeply troubled over the sins of Jerusalem, and thus repentant. The Tau is not the shape of the English or Greek T, but in early Jewish tradition, the + sign or the x sign was used. Later, for Christians, the sign of the cross was used. In any case, what seems clear is that the believers are marked from the judgment to come, probably by the blood of the Lamb of God. But again, Ladd gives us an important reminder, "Apocalyptic language does not convey its message in precise photographic style, but more in the style of modern surrealistic art with great fluidity and imagination." The message is simply that the judgment of God will be withheld until God's people are sealed.[10]

For thousands of years, shepherds around the world marked the ears of their sheep by notching their ears with a sharp knife. Each shepherd had his

---

the prophetic period to depict a universal disaster from every direction.

9. See also Beale, *The Book of Revelation*, 411. He says that the seal could designate belonging to God (the word *doulos* is used, meaning "slave"), and membership in God's covenantal community. This seal is the name of God (i.e., "this one belongs to God") and parallels the mark or seal of the beast on the foreheads of the sinful in Revelation 13.

10. Ladd, *A Commentary on the Revelation of John*, 111.

own distinctive notch for the ear of his sheep. If the sheep gathered in a cluster, he could see even from a distance which ones are his. The people of God are marked or sealed by the mark of the blood of Jesus. The blood of Jesus, God's Son, cleanses us from all unrighteousness. Like the doorposts of the Israelites were marked with the blood of the lamb against the wrath during the tenth plague, God's people are marked from his wrath with the blood of Christ, and the seal of the Holy Spirit, like the engagement ring. 2 Corinthians 1:22 tells us, God "has also put his seal on us and given us his Spirit in our hearts as a guarantee." We need not fear the wrath of God.

Beginning in verse 4, John hears the number of those who were sealed. Notice the emphasis on the number. There is perfect symmetry. 12 tribes of 12,000 each. So, there must be a clear symbolism here for a number that means completion. That is why it is very possible that these groupings indicate the same group as in verse 8, the number that was beyond count.[11]

The list of tribes, who is in and who is out, is intriguing as well. The tribe of Judah is listed first, an unusual position because Judah was the fourth born, not the first. Could it be that Judah was listed first because of David, and the Descendant of David, the Lion of the tribe of Judah? In Ezek.34:23 God promised, "And I will set over them one shepherd, my servant David, and he shall feed them: he shall feed them and be their shepherd." Also, Joseph is listed as part of the tribes of Israel. Joseph received a double inheritance from Jacob/Israel, as his two sons Ephraim and Manasseh each inherited land in Canaan. Ephraim is not listed, however, but Manasseh is. Maybe Ephraim is not listed because Ephraim becomes the representative name for the nation of Israel, the northern kingdom that turned away from the Lord. Ephraim is also associated with idolatry in Hosea 4:17–14:8. Dan is also not listed. Dan was a rebellious tribal group as well and was closely associated with idol worship. In 1 Kings 12:28–30 we read that King Jeroboam set up two golden calves to be worshipped; one in Bethel and the other in Dan (see also Judges 18:16–19). The twelve tribes are listed in about eighteen different orders in the Old Testament, none of which agrees with the order in Revelation.[12]

So, who are these 144,000? There are at least five different possibilities, according to Beale: 1) The number 144,000 is literal and these are a remnant of ethnic Israelites who come to believe in Christ during the tribulation period (Since Christians have already been taken away from the earth because of the rapture); 2) The 144,000 in 7:3–8 is linked to the prophesy of Romans

11. See Mounce, *The Book of Revelation*, 168; Thomas and Macchia, *Revelation*, 167. Twelve squared and multiplied by a thousand, a two-fold way of emphasizing the completeness.

12. Mounce, *The Book of Revelation*, 170.

11:24–26 in which all Israel will be saved at Christ's second coming; 3) A Christian remnant of ethnic Jews living in the first century, contrasted with unbelieving Jews at the time. This remnant rose up after the destruction of the temple in 70 A.D.; 4) The number is figurative, since nearly all numbers in Revelation have a figurative sense. So, the number sealed is the complete number of God's people. The 12 tribes multiplied by the 12 apostles, times 1000 (a number of completeness). The identity of the group is qualified by the fact that they are Israelites; and 5) The 144,000 is a figurative number for the totality of the redeemed.[13] Option 5 is the position of this commentary.

I agree with Osborne, who writes, "The list of the tribes stresses the completeness of the people of God seen as the messianic army of the lion of Judah." They have been "sealed" by God from the outpouring of his wrath and given a two-fold task: being witnesses for the eternal gospel as they call the nations to repentance (12:11a) and participating in the defeat of the dragon both by martyrdom (12:11b) and by forming the army of the victorious Christ at his return (17:14).[14] Thus, the 144,000 are the number beyond count in 17:9–17. They are the redeemed army of the Lord, washed in the blood of the Lamb, the Lion of the tribe of Judah.

So, as an extension of the vision of 17:1–8, John sees a great multiple in heaven that no one could count from every nation, tribe, people and language. The people of God, first the nation of Israel called out from the nations to be a blessing to the nations, and then the nations of the world as those who have been redeemed and standing before the throne of the Lamb of God. The number that no one could count reminds us of the promises to Abraham in Genesis 13:16 and 17:4–6 (see also 35:11 and 48:19). The multitudes of Revelation 7:9 are the ultimate fulfillment of the Abrahamic promise and appear to be another of the many ways in which John refers to the Christians as Israel, or the new Israel.[15]

13. Beale, *The Book of Revelation*, 416–422. Beale also notes that ten of the tribes had lost their national identity in the Assyrian exile, and the same fate fell upon Benjamin and Judah in 70 AD when the temple and Jerusalem were destroyed. There was a strain of Jewish tradition that held that the ten tribes would never be restored (b. Sanhedrin 110b). It is improbable that John expected either a literal restoration or salvation of a remnant from each of the tribes of Israel. However, there was a broader Old Testament tradition that held that there would be a restoration of all the tribes of Israel in the latter days (Isaiah 11:10–13; 27:12–13; Jeremiah 31:7–9; Ezekiel 37:15–23). But John, if he were aware of this tradition, would have adopted it and applied it to the church. Thomas (Thomas and Macchia, *Revelation*, 169) also notes that Judah is listed first and Benjamin last as an inclusion of the two tribes of the south that survived the exile. The other ten were lost.

14. Osborne, *Revelation*, 315. See also Mounce, *The Book of Revelation*, 168; Thomas and Macchia, *Revelation*, 167.

15. Beale, *The Book of Revelation*, 427.

These saints were wearing white robes and they held palm branches in their hands. Was this the same group as in 6:11? It appears a strong possibility. Those who had shed their blood in faithfulness to Christ, along with the others who were to be added. Palm branches were tools for praise to the Lamb on the throne, like the palm branches used by the adoring crowd at the time of Jesus' triumphal procession (see Matthew 21). Beale notes that palm branches and white robes were also associated with military victory (see 2 Macc.11:8; 13:51).[16] But the victory is ironic here, because it is a victory won through sacrifice, just as the victory of Jesus on the cross.

Imagine the noise, and the crowd, and who will be there. We will be singing with King David, Martin Luther, and Charles Wesley. Denominationalism won't matter. Jesus will be the focus. We will be worshipping with Augustine, Aquinas, St. Francis, Fanny Crosby, D.L. Moody, and A.B. Simpson. We will be worshiping with believers from Russia, China, Mali, Saudi Arabia, Indonesia, Afghanistan, Ecuador, Cuba, India, and New Guinea. Family members who belong to Christ and have since died will be there with us, friends from the past who have helped us come to know Jesus. No sorrow. There will be only joy as this great multitude is caught up in Jesus.

Similar to the burst of praise from everything that has breath in Revelation 5, this group beyond count praises both God and the Lamb. Salvation is the possession and right to give of both God and the Lamb. Here is a high Christological statement about Jesus. Just as God has the authority to grant salvation, so does the Lamb. The response of the angels is proper. They fall down and worship before the throne, and the chorus sung is similar to the chorus of 5:12, a song sung to the Lamb as well. There is a two-fold "Amen" introducing and concluding the praise formula in order to confirm emphatically the certainty and factual truth of the redemption won by God through the Lamb.[17]

The angel explains to John that these in white robes are those who have come out of the great tribulation. For background of the great tribulation, τῆς θλίψεως τῆς μεγάλης (tes thlipseos tes megales), we can refer to Daniel 12:1, "And there shall be a time of trouble, such as never has been since there was a nation till that time. But at that time your people shall be delivered, everyone whose name shall be found written in the book." Jesus quotes this in Matthew 24:21 as well. The great tribulation is something that is to take place still in the future. But, like a telescope, we view the tribulations that have been a part of history, as a smaller scale version looking toward the

16. Beale, *The Book of Revelation*, 425.

17. See Beale, *The Book of Revelation*, 432 and Mounce, *The Book of Revelation*, 172.

great tribulation to come. The great tribulation will be one final calamity faced by the church, which it has experienced throughout its entire existence, when Satan, with one final rage of persecution, will try to turn the hearts of God's people away from God.[18]

The white robes are explained as that which is given to those who have been faithful. The paradoxical image of the white robes washed in the blood of the Lamb is powerful. In Isaiah 1:18 God says, "Come now, let us reason together, says the Lord: though your sins are like scarlet, they shall be as white as snow; though they are red like crimson, they shall become like wool."[19] The tribulation (s) has refined and will refine the faith of the saints, and their perseverance through trials has proven their faith as genuine.[20] See also Revelation 22:14, where those who wash their robes are contrasted with those who are unbelievers, and are not able to enter the New Kingdom.

Because of the faithfulness of the saints they are given the privilege of serving God day and night in his temple and dwelling in his presence. The word for serve, λατρεύουσιν (latreuousin), is a priestly word. Those who worship the Lamb are his kingdom and priests, the people of God who forever will joyfully and willingly give him glory. That is where the greatest joy and human satisfaction lies. Whereas the judged of Revelation 6:16–17 flee from the wrath of the Lamb, those whose clothes have been washed are allowed entrance into the salvation and eternal rest of God's presence, as Hebrews 4 promises also. The promise of God spreading his tent over the faithful reminds us of God "tabernacling" with the people of Israel through the tabernacle in the wilderness (Leviticus 26), the pillar of cloud and of fire (Exodus 13:21–22), and the shekinah glory, the radiance of God's presence in the midst of his people (Exodus 40:34–38).[21] No longer do we enter a tent. God spreads the tent over us. He is that tent.

Isaiah 55:1–4 is fulfilled in verse 16. The people of God will no longer need to struggle for life and bread and drink. They will never be deprived again. The sun will not oppress them because the sun will no longer be there. The sun will no longer be necessary (see Revelation 22). Isaiah 49:10 is fulfilled here as well. That verse reads, "They shall not hunger or thirst, neither scorching wind nor sun shall strike them, for he who has pity on them will

18. See Ladd, *A Commentary on the Revelation of John*, 118. Also see Mounce (Mounce, *The Book of Revelation*, 173), who notes that the definite article in the phrase, "the great tribulation," indicates that the angels are referring primarily to that final series of woes that will immediately precede the end.

19. See also Ezekiel 37 and Isaiah 4:4–6 for more background to the idea of white robes.

20. Beale, *The Book of Revelation*, 436.

21. See Mounce, *The Book of Revelation*, 175.

lead them, and by springs of water will guide them." In the context of a prophesy of the restoration of Israel, the church becomes the fulfillment of this prophesy. The Lamb is at the center. The Lamb is the shepherd (see Ezekiel 34), and he will lead the saints to eternal life and eternal joy.[22]

## Conclusion

What a wonderful scene heaven will be. The image of it in all its beauty compels us to continue living for God now, even when this world is slowly slipping away. There is a story of a little boy whose mother died when he was just a baby. His father, in trying to be both mother and father, had planned a picnic. The little boy had never been on a picnic, so they made their plans, fixed the lunch, and packed the car. Then it was time to go to bed, for the picnic was the next day. The little boy couldn't sleep. He tossed and turned, but the excitement got to him. Finally, he got out of bed, ran into the room where his father had already fallen asleep, and shook him. His father woke up and saw his son. He said to him, "What are you doing up? What is the matter?" The boy said, "I can't sleep." The father asked, "Why can't you sleep?" The boy answered, and said, "Daddy, I'm excited about tomorrow." His father replied, "Well, son, I'm sure you are, and it is going to be a great day, but it won't be great if we don't get to sleep. So why don't you just run down the hall, get back into bed, and get a good night's rest."

So, the boy trudged off, down the hall, to his room and got into bed. Before long the father fell asleep. It wasn't long thereafter that back came the little boy. He was pushing and shoving his father, and his father opened his eyes. Harsh words almost blurted out until he saw the expression on the boy's face. The father asked, "What's the matter now?" The boy said, "Daddy, I just want to thank you for tomorrow."

Have we paused to think about the great scene that is coming, the great fulfillment of the engagement ring on our finger, the seal of the living God? Have we paused to thank Jesus for the tomorrow that we don't have yet?

---

22. For shepherd images, see also Psalm 23. Isaiah 25:8 prophesies the removal of tears and the removal of disgrace.

# Revelation 8:1–13

## Introduction

S ILENCE CAN BE VERY loud sometimes. When I was a freshman at Wheaton College in Illinois, I attended a football game one Saturday afternoon. It was a good game for Wheaton. We were good that year and we were soundly beating the team we were playing that day. A lot of students were in the stands, and it was loud for a Wheaton College game. Then, during the game, one of the opposing players got hurt. This is not so unusual for a football game, but it soon became obvious that this player was seriously hurt. The doctors and trainers were out on the field for a long time. What had once been a noisy, joyful atmosphere in the stands, became a hushed silence. Our Wheaton football team circled together, knelt on the field, and began to pray for this player. Quiet, whispered prayers were heard all through the stands. It was a silence that was very loud.

Children know this loud silence. When children do something particularly disobedient, one of the hardest things they might have to endure is the silence of their parents right before the punishment. The quiet, disappointed shaking of the head, the long silent stare from the father, maybe even the quiet tear down the cheek of the mother as she ponders how naughty her child has been. This is a silence that is very loud. In Revelation 8, we meet the most deafening silence ever—what I call the Silence of Heaven. Silence signals importance, soberness, solemnity, and seriousness. And God takes the prayers of his people seriously and the coming judgment of the world.

## Exposition

In chapter 8, the seventh seal is opened, and the way is prepared for the seven trumpets to be sounded, an intensification of the judgment of God upon the earth. Indeed, the first four trumpets seem to be judgments against the universe: the earth, the sea, the rivers, and the skies (the sun, moon, and stars). Mounce notes, and this commentary agrees, that the visions of John neither follow a strict chronological sequence nor do they systematically recapitulate one another. They are not intended to represent a corresponding historical development. There is obvious progression, but not without considerable restatement and development of detail.[1]

There is a strong relationship between chapter 8 and chapter 6, with the 7th chapter serving as an interlude, a look back and a look forward. There is obvious parallelism between the seals and the trumpets. So, while recapitulation is not systematic, there does seem to be some measure of it. The narrative backs up and recovers some of the same ground. For example, in 6:17 and 11:15, both the seals and the trumpets bring us to the end, like looking through the window to the end of time. The seven trumpets are the contents of the seventh seal, or of the scroll after the seventh seal is opened. The six seals relate the forces leading up to the end, and the seven trumpets relate the beginning of the end itself, particularly the time of the great tribulation that will introduce the end.[2]

In verse 1 of chapter 8, we "hear" the deafening silence of heaven. It is a silence of a half an hour. Habakkuk 2:20 says, "But the Lord is in his holy temple; let all the earth keep silence before him." Could the silence be related to Psalm 46:10? "Be still and know that I am God. I will be exalted in the earth!" God's desire to reveal his glory and greatness to the nations is again repeated in the seals/judgments and in preparation of the opening of the scroll. The earth must be silent before the final plunge.

Or was heaven silent to hear the prayers of the saints? Could God not hear the prayers of the saints even if there was a cacophony of noise? Yes, he could. The silence was a preparation for the nations of the world to know that God is God, the Lamb is true, and his judgments are just (see chapter 15). Ladd writes, "The silence suggests an attitude of trembling suspense on the part of the heavenly hosts in view of the judgments of God which are about to fall upon the world. It is the silence of dreadful anticipation."[3]

In Exodus 14:14, Moses says, "The LORD will fight for you, and you have only to be silent." Also in Isaiah 47:5 God says to Babylon, "Sit in

1. Mounce, *The Book of Revelation*, 178.

2. See Ladd, *A Commentary on the Revelation of John*, 121–2. For another viewpoint, see Beale, *The Book of Revelation*, 463. Beale's view is that by connecting the trumpets with the prayer for judgment in 6:9–11, this indicates that the first four seal woes were primarily trials to test the faith of God's people, but the trumpet woes depict trials that punish the unbelieving persecutors during the same period of the entire church age when the faith of believers is tested. The dual purpose of the trumpet plagues is modeled after the Exodus, where the elements that struck the Egyptians were transformed to protect the Israelites.

3. Ladd, *A Commentary on the Revelation of John*, 122

silence, and go into darkness, O daughter of the Chaldeans; for you shall no more be called the mistress of kingdoms." Tyre also is silenced by the judgment of God in Ezekiel 27:32. Beale sees a multi-faceted dimension to the silence metaphor. Silence is an indication that God has heard the saint's prayers; an indication of a revelatory announcement by God; and in relation to the temple liturgy.[4] First Samuel 12:16 says, "Now therefore stand still and see this great thing that the Lord will do before your eyes." The earth will be awestruck at the end of history in response to God's revelation of his sovereignty, as seen in this dramatic pause.[5]

In verse 2, there are seven angels who stand before God. These are the angels who hold the seven golden trumpets. The "Before God" is placed in an emphatic position in the Greek. They represent his judgments from the throne. Could these angles be the seven angels of the seven churches? Most likely not, as these angels have a very different task, that of sounding the trumpet of judgment. Aune notes that the appearance of the definite article with the angels, THE angels, seems to indicate that these seven angels were known to the readers.[6] It may also be an emphatic way of indicating their important place in the judgment of God.

Before the seven trumpets are sounded, there is a brief interlude for the angel with the golden censer at the altar. The censer in the Old Testament was offered by Aaron on the altar of incense every morning (See Exodus 30:1 and others). This angel, playing the part of the priest, offers the offering before God along with the prayers of the saints. He was given a lot of incense to offer (Gr: *polla*) so that (*hina*) the prayers of the saints could be offered up before the throne of God. These prayers are the prayers of the saints of chapter 6. They are heard by God and the time of judgment is now at hand, the time of recompense for the wickedness of the nations against God's people.[7]

---

4. Beale, *The Book of Revelation*, 451–2. Johnson (Johnson, *Hebrews through Revelation*, 488), also sees this silence as a time to hear the cries for deliverance and justice for God's persecuted servants. The choirs are subdued because of God's concern for his persecuted saints. And also, I think, for the judgment to come. Interestingly, Beale (Beale, *The Book of Revelation*, 453) also sees a connection between the half hour and the apocalyptic use of "half" in numerical designations elsewhere in Revelation and Daniel that confirms that the number here involves a time of crisis and judgment (Revelation 11:3, 9; 12:6–9; 13:5; Daniel 7:25; 9:27; 12:7).

5. Mounce, *The Book of Revelation*, 179.

6. Aune, *Revelation 6–16*, 509. Mounce (Mounce, *The Book of Revelation*, 180) notes that Jewish apocalyptic literature (1 Enoch 20:2–8) names these angels: Uriel, Raphael, Raguel, Michael, Saraqael, Gabriel, and Remiel.

7. Beale, *The Book of Revelation*, 455, agrees. That the altar of 8:3 is the same as the altar of 6:9 is confirmed by the repetition of the words "altar," "much incense," and

The prayers of the saints, mixed with the incense, went up like smoke from the angel's hand to God. "From the angel's hand" is first in the sentence, emphasizing it. In Psalm 141:2, David prays, "Let my prayer be counted as incense before you, and the lifting up of my hands as the evening sacrifice!" Associated also with the saints' prayer in 8:3–4 is the idea that believers have suffered and even given their lives sacrificially because they have remained faithful to Christ. The saints' prayers of 6:10 have been accepted by God because they have offered their bodies as sacrifices to him.[8]

These are the prayers of "all" the saints. It doesn't say that only the prayers of the pastors or elders are heard, or only the prayers of seminary professors who say the right words, or only the prayers of deacons and Sunday School teachers. These are the prayers of all the saints. As we saw in chapter 6, these are anyone who has received the sacrifice of Jesus on the cross as payment for their sins and has persevered, in the light of possible or real persecution. A saint is not a statue in an old church. It is not someone you pray to for a good harvest or a good vacation. A saint is anyone who knows Jesus, the Lamb of God. And God hears all the prayers of his saints. He takes them seriously.

Why is the censer, which was just offered with the prayers of the saints, filled with fire from the altar and then hurled to the earth? This, again, shows the connection between these prayers and the those prayed in 6:10. That is, the prayers for God's justice to be done and the blood of the martyrs answered by God, are now being set in motion through the judgments that will come in the blowing of the seven trumpets. In Ezekiel 10:1–8, when the glory of the Lord departed from the temple, one of the cherubim took burning coals from among the cherubim and scattered them on the city, as an act of judgment. Judgment in Revelation is also accompanied by thunder and earthquake as we see in verse 5 (see also 11:19; 16:18). That 8:5 is a window to the last judgment is confirmed by the appearance of a similar angel in 14:18–19, also a clear context of the last judgment. There is a progressive expansion of the judgment.[9]

---

"to the prayers of the saints."

8. Beale, *The Book of Revelation*, 456–7; Aune (Aune, *Revelation 6–16*, 514) notes that during the incense offering, coals from the altar were heaped in the fire pan and the incense was sprinkled on top of the coals. Thus, the smoke went up like a fragrant offering. The smoke is not spiritualized or interpreted figuratively as the prayers of the saints, but rather the analogy between smoke and prayer is emphasized.

9. Beale, *The Book of Revelation*, 459. Beale views this as evidence of a recapitulation. I see it as a progressive intensity of judgment, though when an earthquake is involved, it is like a sneak peek at the final end. See Exodus 19:16–18 and Psalm 68:8 and 77:18 for examples of an earthquake and an eschatological event.

The first angel blew his trumpet and a third of the earth was burned up. This is a judgment on the land, the trees, and the grass (see 7:1). For a parallel judgment, we could refer to Exodus 9:22–26, the plague of hail that burned the areas of Egypt but not the land of the Israelites. Consider also Ezekiel 38:17–23, and the prophesy against Gog, particularly verse 22–23, "With pestilence and bloodshed I will enter into judgment with him, and I will rain upon him and his hordes and the many peoples who are with him torrential rains and hailstones, fire and sulfur. So I will show my greatness and my holiness and make myself known in the eyes of many nations. Then they will know that I am the Lord." Interesting that this is the same declaration as in Psalm 46:10.

What is the purpose of the trumpets? Is it retribution or a way to invite the wicked to repentance? Mounce sees this as similar to Ezekiel 3, and the warning of the watchman of the impending and final judgment. The fraction (1/3) indicates that although God is bringing punishment upon the earth, it is not yet complete and final.[10] Osborne writes, "The purpose of the first four trumpets is primarily to disprove the earthly gods and to show that Yahweh alone is on the throne."[11] The answer to the purpose of the trumpets may lie somewhere in between. It is legitimate to ask: would God provide an opportunity to repentance when there is no one who repents? We see no one repenting in chapter 9 or chapter 16. Or is this simply an expression of God's judgment and the further hardening of the hearts as in the plagues of Egypt and Pharaoh? The judgments of the trumpets and the seals, as in the case of the plagues in Egypt, have a declarative purpose—declaring the justice and glory of God among the nations that have rejected him and have attacked his people.

The second trumpet judgment is on the sea, the water itself, the living creatures, and the ships. This again is limited to one-third. This is like the plague against the Nile when the waters of Egypt turned into blood in Exodus 7:20. A mountain is thrown into the sea. In Jewish apocalyptic literature, and in the Old Testament, the likeness of a mountain could be interpreted to be a kingdom.[12] See, for example, Revelation 18:21, where Babylon is cast into the sea. This is likely a reference to Jeremiah 51:25 that says of Babylon, "Behold, I am against you, O destroying mountain, declares the Lord, which destroys the whole earth; I will stretch out my hand against you, and roll you down from the crags, and make you a burnt mountain." And verse 27 says, "Set up a

---

10. Mounce, *The Book of Revelation*, 184–5.

11. Osborne, *Revelation*, 357.

12. Beale, *The Book of Revelation*, 475.

standard on the earth; blow the trumpet among the nations;" The fires of the blazing nations will be quenched by the judgment of God.

The third trumpet turns the waters bitter. A question that arises is: what is the nature of the star and why is it named? One possible background is Jeremiah 9:13–16. The Lord speaks judgment against the people of Jerusalem because they have followed the Baals, just like their fathers had taught them. They would be given bitter food and poisoned water to drink. Another allusion may be Isaiah 14:12–15. The morning star (in the context of Isaiah 14, this is the king of Babylon), has fallen from heaven. "How you are fallen from heaven, O Day Star, son of Dawn! How you are cut down to the ground, you who laid the nations low!" Because of the pride of Babylon, who said, "I will ascend to the heaven; above the stars of God I will set my throne on high; I will sit on the mount of assembly in the far reaches of the north," verse 15 promises, "But you are brought down to Sheol, to the far reaches of the pit."[13] Why the star is named "wormwood" most likely has to do with the bitterness of the substance and the bitter judgment upon the nations of the world.

For the fourth trumpet, the judgment that is sent affects the celestial world, the sun, the moon, and the stars. This is a common image of the day of the LORD, when the celestial beings are impacted by the judgments of God. Isaiah 13:9–10 says, "Behold, the day of the LORD comes, cruel, with wrath and fierce anger, to make the land a desolation and to destroy its sinners from it. For the stars of the heavens and their constellations will not give their light; the sun will be dark at its rising, and the moon will not shed its light."[14] This parallels also the plague of darkness upon Egypt in Exodus 10:21. Beale believes the darkness is not probably literal, but refers to all those divinely ordained events intended to remind the idolatrous persecutors that their idolatry is folly and they are separated from the living God.[15] Actually, whether it is literal or not is hard to conclude. Are we looking through that window to the last judgment or is this a figurative symbol to the end? I tend to lean toward the idea of the window to the final judgment. Revelation is not strictly chronological, though there seems to be a progressive nature to the judgments.

In verse 13, we see an eagle calling out a warning because of the woes of the other three angels, trumpets 5–7. The intensity of God's judgment upon the earth continues to increase. Beale also notes that the spiritual intensity

13. That the morning star in Isaiah 14 refers to the king of Babylon and not to Satan is the most straightforward interpretation of the text, given the context of the chapter.

14. See also Ezekiel 32:7–8 and Joel 2 and 3.

15. Beale, *The Book of Revelation*, 482.

of the next woes is highlighted by the direct involvement of demons. These are not even called trumpets, but woes, because of their severity.[16] Old Testament announcements accompanied by the image of an eagle are common. Deuteronomy 28:49, a warning to Israel, if they do not live faithfully, says, "The Lord will bring a nation against you from far away, from the end of the earth, swooping down like the eagle, a nation whose language you do not understand." (see also Jeremiah 4:13; 48:40; 49:22; Lamentations 4:19; Ezekiel 17:3; Hosea 8:1; Habakkuk 1:8).

## Conclusion

The weekend following the September 11, 2001 attack on the World Trade Towers in New York City, syndicated columnist and former presidential speechwriter, Peggy Noonan, drove to Lower Manhattan to witness the relief effort taking place at Ground Zero, the place where the towers had stood. She found herself focusing on the convoy of trucks filled with rescue workers coming off their 12-hour shifts. The men in the trucks were construction and electrical workers, police, emergency medical workers, and firemen. It was a procession of the not-so rich and famous.

Nonetheless, these New Yorkers were celebrities in a human drama more significant than any Broadway act. Noonan joined the growing crowd of onlookers cheering the workers with shouts of "God bless you!" and "We love you!" They clapped and blew kisses. Noonan writes:

I looked around me at all of us who were cheering. And saw who we were. Investment bankers! Orthodontists! Magazine editors! In my group, a lawyer, a columnist, and a writer. We had been the kings and queens of the city, respected professionals in a city that respects the professional class.

And this night we were nobody. We were so useless, all we could do was applaud the somebodies, the workers who, unlike us, had not been applauded much in their lives . . . I was so moved and, oddly I guess, grateful. Because they'd always been the people who ran the place, who kept it going, they'd just never been given their due.[17]

This reversal that Peggy Noonan witnessed is a foreshadowing of what things will be like on the day of the LORD, a great reversal, the last will be first, and the first will be last. Those persecuted will see justice be done. And the proud will fall like stars from the sky. The loud silence in heaven is a signal that God would hear the prayers of his people and that he would begin the judgment upon the earth.

16. Beale, *The Book of Revelation*, 490.

17. Noonan, *A Heart, a Cross, and a Flag: America Today*, 28–29.

# Revelation 9:1-21

Trumpets 5-6 (The First Two Woes)

## Introduction

T HERE IS A DISEASE that is impacting many people around the world. This is the disease of the heart. It is not heart disease, as in clogged up arteries, or a blood flow issue. It is the disease of the spiritual hardening of the heart. This disease is so consuming and dangerous that many are unaware they have it. Even when God sends judgments and clear messages about his character, his justice, and his holiness, they cannot see it. They only experience a greater hardening.

Pharaoh was like that. Moses warned him of the plagues that God would send. God sent the plagues, even to the point of the advisors and other leaders of Egypt despairing and begging Pharaoh to send the Hebrews away. But Pharaoh's heart was increasingly hard. It is not the scope of this commentary to determine whether Pharaoh's heart was hardened because of his own sinfulness or because God hardened it for his greater purposes. We can study Exodus and Romans 9-11 for some of those answers. What is clear is that in spite of the greatness and glory of God displayed through the plagues sent upon Egypt, Pharaoh did not repent. We see a similar situation explained in Revelation 9.

## Exposition

As parents, we often give warnings to our children that they will get into trouble if they do something not nice. The conversation may go something like this: "Timmy, if you do that one more time, you are going to your room." The problem that the parent creates, at times, is that when Timmy does do that disobedient thing one more time, his parent does not send him to his room, but gives him the warning again. "Timmy, if you do that one more time, you are going to your room." The message that is communicated to the child is that discipline, or the judgment from the parent, is not really a sure thing, therefore, there is no reason to change the course of disobedient or naughty behavior. Because the mother or the father is not keeping his word.

But with God, this is different. He has told us in his word, "If you deny the Son of God, you will be judged and condemned." (See John 3:17–18). He will keep his promise. The judgments that are in Revelation 9 are horrible. They are the fifth and sixth trumpet blast, things that are yet to appear on the earth. These are events to come that precede the final return of Christ. They are also the first and second woe in the listing of three woes. The third woe is the opening up of the seventh trumpet which announces the judgment of the bowls of wrath.

Where the first four trumpets were plagues against the natural world, the next two, discussed in Revelation 9, are plagues against mankind—those who are not sealed with the seal of God on their foreheads. Again, we may ask the question: are these judgments meant to cause repentance or just judgment? This is difficult to answer. But as we briefly discussed in the last chapter concerning chapter 8, these are either to show that God was still offering out the possibility of repentance, or only proving the hardness of heart of the people of the earth who oppose God.

The fifth trumpet introduces a star that had fallen from the skies and was given the key to the shaft of the Abyss. The fifth trumpet is also the first of the three "woes" that the eagle announced in 8:13. This star *was given* the key, another use of the divine passive showing that the authority of the angel was only possessed by God's authority. And Jesus has the keys of death and Hades (1:18). The abyss is the place of holding those to be judged, as well as those demons who have been cast there (see Luke 8:31). Beale, referring to several Old Testament background references, notes that the abyss is the abode of the cosmic sea dragon (Job 40:17; 40:25; 41:10; Isaiah 27:1; Psalm 73:12–13; and Amos 9:3). It is also synonymous with the concept of Hades (Job 38:16; Ezekiel 31:15; Jonah 2:6) and is the realm of suffering (Psalm 70:20) and death (Exodus 15:5; Isaiah 51:10; 63:3).[1]

2 Peter 2:4 says, "For if God did not spare angels when they sinned, but cast them into hell and committed them to chains of gloomy darkness to be kept until the judgment." And Jude 6 reiterates this picture, "And the angels who did not stay within their own position of authority, but left their proper dwelling, he has kept in eternal chains under gloomy darkness until the judgment of the great day."[2]

1. Beale, *The Book of Revelation*, 493.

2. The word for "hell" in 2 Peter 2:4 is *Tartarus*. This is similar to 1 Enoch 20:2, where the archangel Uriel is placed in charge of "eternity and Tartarus," the Hellenistic place of final judgment. See also Osborne, *Revelation*, 362.

Was this star that had fallen[3] an angel or a demon or something else? Beale holds that the angel is an evil angel that had fallen from heaven. He refers to Isaiah 14; and also, Luke 10:17–20, Jesus' description of Satan falling like a star from heaven.[4] Mounce, on the other hand, sees this star as a divine agent, one of the many, sent to carry out the will of the Lord, in this case the judgment of the fifth trumpet.[5] Consistent with the rest of Revelation, it seems clear that the angels carry out God's judgment, and that part of those judgments are the unleashing of the demonic. The angels do the unleashing. The evil horde brings the harm.

Similar to the judgment of the fourth trumpet (8:12), the apocalyptic darkening of the sun and the sky appear again here, darkened this time by the smoke from the abyss. In speaking of the army of locusts, Joel 2:10 says, "The earth quakes before them; the heavens tremble. The sun and the moon are darkened, and the stars withdraw their shining." (See also 2:31; 3:15). The judgment formerly limited to the realm of the abyss is now to be extended to the earthly realm. As the result of Christ's death and resurrection, the devil and his horde have already begun to be judged. The effect of their judgment will be released upon humanity.[6]

Similar to the locusts of the prophet Joel and the plague of locusts in Exodus 10:12–15, locusts are sent to judge the nations. But these locusts seem also to have a demonic quality. They come from the abyss, bent on destruction, not against the vegetation but against those without the seal of God. The divine passive is again used to emphasize that they were given authority to torment only because they were allowed to do so by God. God is the sovereign Judge in this play. Aune sees these as "demons in the guise of locusts, for

3. Perfect tense is used here to show that the star had already fallen, and not that John was seeing it fall. See Beale, *The Book of Revelation*, 491.

4. Beale, *The Book of Revelation*, 492. However, as we noted in our exposition of Revelation 8, and the star, wormwood, I don't think that Isaiah 14 can be properly used as an example of an evil angel (Satan?) falling from heaven. I interpret Isaiah 14 as a description of the king of Babylon falling from his self-exaltation. Also, it is certainly not clear that Jesus is referring to Isaiah 14 in Luke 10.

5. Mounce, *The Book of Revelation*, 192. See also Ladd (Ladd, *A Commentary on the Revelation of John*, 129), who believes that in Revelation there is no reason to identify the star with Satan or an evil power. The star represents some angelic figure divinely commissioned by God. Satan is not specifically confined to the underworld (see Ephesians 2:2; 6:12). Aune (Aune, *Revelation 6–16*, 525) also agrees that the star should be identified as an angelic messenger and not with the angels of the abyss named Abaddon (verse 11) or Satan as in 12:9.

6. Beale, *The Book of Revelation*, 494.

their king is Abaddon, the angel of the abyss.[7] It should be noted as well that in 11:7 and 17:8 the beast ascends from the abyss.

The demonic locust-horde was not to harm the plants or the trees, or the grass, like the judgment of the first trumpet (already a third of that had been destroyed). But they were to harm those who did not have the seal of God on their foreheads. This is not a plague against nature (like the first four trumpets), but now begins the plagues against mankind. Just as in 7:1–4, Ezekiel 9:4 is important here. A mark is put on the foreheads of any who still feared God. This is a woe that makes a distinction. Only those not marked as belonging to God are subject to this judgment.

The power given to the locusts (divine passive) was not for death, but for great suffering. There seems to be here a physical suffering, not simply a metaphorical suffering, as the pain inflicted upon humanity from the sting of these locusts from the abyss is a pain that is like a scorpion sting. But this does not mean there was not spiritual and psychological suffering as well, besides the physical. Beale notes that the Greek word used for suffering (*basanismos*) connotes a spiritual and psychological suffering, since this is the connotation of the word in other places in Revelation with reverence to trials both before and during times of judgment (11:10; 14:10–11; 18:7, 10, 15; 20:10).[8] For other examples of spiritual and psychological judgment see Deuteronomy 28:28–29, 34, 65, 66–67.

Why five months? While Mounce notes that this is the life cycle of the locusts in the dry season,[9] it is more likely the case, with Aune, that the number five is symbolic. It is frequently used in contexts in which it obviously functions as a round number meaning a few. One example is 1 Corinthians 14:19. Paul says, "Nevertheless, in church I would rather speak five words with my mind in order to instruct others, than ten thousand words in a tongue."[10]

The suffering from the sting of the scorpions would be so intense that men will want to die rather than suffer the pain. But they will not be able to die. See Jeremiah 8:3, where, in the context of a prophesy against the people of Judah who had done evil in God's eyes (7:30), they would prefer death to life in the midst of the judgment, though Mounce does not see Jeremiah 8:3 as relevant because that passage refers to corpses that have been unearthed,

---

7. Aune, *Revelation 6–16*, 527. Mounce (Mounce, *The Book of Revelation*, 194), notes that in the desert, locusts are known to travel in a column a hundred feet deep and as long as four miles in length, easily acting as clouds to darken the sun.

8. Beale, *The Book of Revelation*, 497.

9. Mounce, *The Book of Revelation*, 195.

10. Aune, *Revelation 6–16*, 530.

not the desire to die.[11] I think, however, that although speaking of the bones of the ancestors, those who would prefer death in Jeremiah 8:3 are not the corpses, but rather those who were to be banished by the Lord because of their unfaithfulness. Regardless, it is clear that the judgment of the locusts will be very intense. And this desired (but not attained) death of the ungodly is a dramatic contrast to Paul's desire to die and be with Christ, if that be God's will (Philippians 1:23).

Verse 7 begins a vivid description of this locust horde. This is somewhat similar to the description in Joel 2:5, where the locusts were compared to horses and chariots. These seems to be some organization to their destruction, as if they are under command. As a reminder of the apocalyptic nature of these visions, John uses words like *homoiwmata* (likeness) and *homoias* (like) to show that he is trying to describe something that is almost impossible to describe. The crowns on their heads are symbols of authority, divinely given authority. The human like features of these locusts are not something new from John. An Arabian proverb spoke of the locusts with the head of a horse, a breast like a lion, feet like a camel, the body of a serpent, and antennae like the hair of a maiden.[12]

The description continues with what appears to be abominations and distortions of the natural order so that the creatures that were locusts take on horrifying and frightening images. Could we expect anything less than demonic figures? They have long hair like a woman, and teeth like a lion. Joel 1:6 says of the locusts, "For a nation has come up against my land, powerful and beyond number; its teeth are lions' teeth, and it has the fangs of a lioness." The mention of the hair is not a mark of femininity, but simply to point out the flowing mane of these creatures, like the hair of a woman which was typically long in that cultural context. Aune notes that long and possibly disheveled hair had several connotations in the Old Testament: 1) As a sign of uncleanness for people with leprosy (Leviticus 13:45; 2) As a sign of mourning (Leviticus 10:6; 21:10); and 3) As a part of the sacrificial protocol for a woman accused of adultery. Also, in the Jewish literature, the loose hair of ugly angels who carry off the souls of the wicked and cast them into eternal punishment is similar to that of a woman's hair (see Apoc. Zeph.4:4). The hair of the accuser (Satan) is described as "hair was spread out like a woman's" in Apoc. Zeph.6:8.[13] It seems apparent that the long hair, and the teeth of a lion are signs of demonic ferocity.

---

11. Mounce, *The Book of Revelation*, 195, no.17.

12. Mounce, *The Book of Revelation*, 196.

13. Aune, *Revelation 6–16*, 532.

These are creatures bent on war. They have breastplates (thoraxes?) of iron and they are rushing into battle (again see Joel 2:4–9). Beale also sees Jeremiah 51:14 and 27 as background. Verse 27 says, "Set up a standard on the earth; blow the trumpet among the nations; prepare the nations for war against her; summon against her the kingdoms, Ararat, Minni, and Ashkenaz; appoint a marshal against her; bring up horses like bristling locusts." This is an announcement of a coming vindication for Israel against idolatrous Babylon.[14] The locusts of Revelation 9 are a coming vindication for the church against the idolatrous nations of the world.

Jeremiah 8:16–18 provides background for verse 10. Verse 16–17a reads, "The snorting of their horses is heard from Dan; at the sound of the neighing of their stallions the whole land quakes. They come and devour the land all that fills it, the city and those who dwell in it. For behold, I am sending among you serpents." Beale notes that early Jewish writings held that the antichrist was to come from Dan, just as these horses in Jeremiah 8. But wherever they are from, it is clear that their ultimate source is evil. Abaddon and Apollyon are names given for the leader of the hoard of locusts. He is called a king and an angel. There are similarities between this angel and the destroying angel of Exodus 12:23 and the plague on the firstborn in Egypt.

Who is this Abaddon? This destroyer is most likely a representative of the devil. Revelation 12:3–4 and 13:1ff make this conclusion more certain. Mounce concludes that this is the prince of the underworld.[15] The title for the angel (*anggelos*) is articular. This either means that the angel from the abyss was a familiar figure, none other than Satan or Belial,[16] or that the readers were familiar with the name "Abaddon" rather than assuming that this meant that he was Satan.[17] Given the appearance of Satan in chapter 12, this is probably simply a representation of Satan, a demon of extensive responsibility over the demonic hoard of the fifth trumpet.

The first woe is past, and the second one, or the sixth trumpet is announced. A voice from the horns of the golden altar before God. This reminds us again that there is a relationship here between the prayers of the saints who are under the altar in chapter 6 (the fifth seal) and the answer of

14. Beale, *The Book of Revelation*, 502.

15. Mounce, *The Book of Revelation*, 198. There are also some, including Mounce, who see a reference or play on words to Apollo. Emperors claimed to be the incarnation of the god Apollo, particularly Domitian, the probable emperor at the time of the writing of Revelation (see Introduction). In the fifth century BC, the Greeks pictured Apollo as a locust, one of his many symbols. Ladd (Ladd, *A Commentary on the Revelation of John*, 134), however, sees no such connection.

16. See Aune, *Revelation 6–16*, 534.

17. See Osborne, *Revelation*, 373.

God through the judgments of the trumpets. With the mention of the four angels bound at the river Euphrates, we are reminded of Zechariah. If these horses are the same as angels in chapter 7, restrained before the sealing of the saints, then it is safe to say that now that the saints are sealed, the horses no longer need to be restrained.[18]

Unlike the locust beings of the fifth trumpet, who were not to kill mankind, the demonic beings released from the sixth trumpet are given authority to kill a third of mankind, a limited amount. The four horses kept ready for this hour are leading the larger horde of 200 million demonic forces. They were kept ready for "This very hour and day and month and year." Could it be that this is another answer to the question from 6:9, "how long?" Maybe. But what is certain is that the angels are released according to God's own time-table.[19]

Is the number 200 million significant? Interestingly, some estimates show that the world population at that time was about 200 million. Does that mean the number of the demonic horde was equivalent to the number of humans on the earth? Or should we not make this an important point of exposition? How was John to know the world population at that time, except by the inspiration of the Holy Spirit? All we can safely say is that this is another number of symbolic significance. *Murias* indicates an incalculable number without exception wherever it is used without any numerical adjective.[20] The literal translation is double myriad of myriads. Thus, this is a symbolic number for a vast number beyond count and imagination.

These demonic horses and riders are again distortions of God's creation. They had breastplates the colors of fire, sulfur and smoke. They had heads like lions but out of their mouths they breathed fire like dragons. John reiterates that he is describing a vision, a reminder of the apocalyptic, and therefore symbolic, nature of the trumpet judgment. Beale writes, "The piling up of monstrous metaphors underscores that the demons are ferocious and dreadful beings that afflict people in a fierce, appalling, and devastating

---

18. Though Beale sees a parallel (Beale, *The Book of Revelation*, 507), Ladd (Ladd, *A Commentary on the Revelation of John*, 136) does not. Osborne (Osborne, *Revelation*, 379) sees a connection with 1 Enoch 56:5–57:3. The angels of punishment turn to the east to the Parthians and Medes and get them to attack Israel. This is very similar because these angels were also "bound at the great river Euphrates." The Parthians figure in as an important background, for they were a force east of the Roman Empire, feared by the Romans and known for their long hair. See Jeremiah 46 for more background for this passage. It's also possible that the four angels represent four nations, based on Daniel 10:13, 20–21. See Aune, *Revelation 6–16*, 538.

19. See also Beale, *The Book of Revelation*, 508; Mounce, *The Book of Revelation*, 201; Aune, *Revelation 6–16*, 537.

20. See Beale, *The Book of Revelation*, 509, referring to Walter Bauer's Lexicon, 199.

manner."[21] We are reminded of Genesis 19:24 when "Then the LORD rained on Sodom and Gomorrah sulfur and fire from the LORD out of heaven." It looked like smoke rising from a furnace (see Genesis 19:28). The judgment that would fall upon mankind from these evil creatures would be similar to the judgment on the wicked cities who rejected God.

Though these beings had the ability to kill all of mankind, especially given the incalculable number, a limited number of mankind was killed. Is the possibility of repentance legitimate? Or, like the Egyptians, did their hearts just get harder? There are some who believe that repentance is a possibility.[22] There are others who see this as a judgment and a curse upon mankind who had rejected God's forgiveness in Christ.[23] I think it is fair to make the parallel between these plagues upon mankind in the end, and the purpose of the plagues of Egypt, to show the extent of the wickedness of mankind and the justice of God's judgments.

The primary sin is the sin of idolatry as noted in verse 20, worshipping man-made images rather than the one true God. Paul explains in 1 Corinthians 8–10 that the demonic is behind idol worship. Belshazzar's judgment was the loss of his kingdom because he "did not honor the God who holds in his hand your life and all your ways." His idol worship led to his downfall and judgment. The other sins listed are the sins of murder, sorcery (use of dark powers), sexual immorality, and stealing. These sins are either part of the activities associated with idolatry or they actually become acts of idolatry themselves. Either way, idolatry is the root cause of the sins of verse 21,[24] as idolatry has been the root cause of every sin since sin entered the world. Whether Adam and Eve were elevating knowledge above God, or mankind elevating their own names over the name of God, whenever something is placed ahead of God in the estimation and worth of our minds and hearts, it is idolatry. This is one of the chief of all sins.

## Conclusion

One day I borrowed my friend's digital video camera, and I thought that I had ruined it beyond repair. It began eating the tape that was on the inside

---

21. Beale, *The Book of Revelation*, 510.

22. Thomas and Macchia, *Revelation*, 189; Osborne, *Revelation*, 374.

23. See Beale, *The Book of Revelation*, 517 and Ladd, *A Commentary on the Revelation of John*, 139. Ladd writes that God pours out his judgments, not because he takes pleasure in wrath, "but in order to warn men that the way of sin and defiance of God can only lead to disaster."

24. See Beale, *The Book of Revelation*, 520.

and I couldn't get it out. I was preparing myself to pay my friend for the cost of a new camera. But he told me that he had bought a service contract, so that if anything went wrong with it, they would fix it for free. The repair guy told him, if he did not have that service contract, the cost of the repair would have been $400.

God paid the cost of the guarantee with the life of his Son. In a way, he paid the service contract on our lives. We mess up, we sin, we break. There is no way we can afford to fix ourselves. Nor is there any way we can fix ourselves. But God paid the service contract for us, when he sent Jesus to pay for our sins. But there is no limit to the life of the service contract. This payment is forever.

We send our warranty in when we seek him in repentance, confessing our sin, and asking him for forgiveness. The guarantee is that he will forgive us if we confess our sin to him. He has promised us, and in Christ, all the promises made by God are "Yes!" But the time to receive his forgiveness is now. Just as sure as his forgiveness is guaranteed, so also the surety of his coming judgment. We still have time to respond. But as 2 Corinthians 6:2 says, "Now is the favorable time; behold, now is the day of salvation." Let us make sure we are sealed for the day of judgment and will be spared the judgment of the first and second woe.

# Revelation 10:1–11

Second Interlude (The Little Scroll)

## Introduction

NO ONE LIKES TO share bad news with someone else. Good news is easier to share—the birth of a baby, a good report card, a great buy during a closeout sale, or the announcement of an engagement. But bad news is very hard to give, like the death of a loved one. Some are old enough to remember the days when a knock was heard at the door, or at a neighbor's door, and a soldier was waiting to bear the sad news of the passing of a loved one in combat. I still remember the day I was told of my parents' divorce. It was tough to hear. I'm sure it was even harder for my mother and older brother to relay that news.

The truth of God's word is also sometimes difficult to proclaim. We see that in Revelation 10. This chapter is an interlude between the judgments John saw—between the judgment of the trumpets, and the judgment of the bowls of wrath, which are about to be announced with the sounding of the seventh trumpet. After the seventh trumpet is sounded, the beast from the earth and the beast from the sea and the antichrist will be released upon the earth and deceive mankind. After they are allowed to reign for a specified and limited period of time, the bowls of wrath are poured out on the earth, upon the worshippers of the beast, and those that bear his mark. It is too late to turn. After the distress of those days, then Jesus will come back with power and might and set up his kingdom on the earth. John literally gets to taste the bitterness of the message and then is compelled to proclaim it. That is the central point of chapter 10.

## Exposition

Chapters 10 and 11 form a unit, a unit to explain the activity of the believers during the judgments of the seals and trumpets. Believers are symbolized by John in chapter 10 and by the two witnesses in chapter 11. They are called to witness and suffer, leading to vindication and victory.[1] The main Old Testament text that provides background for this chapter is Ezekiel's little scroll and the judgment that would come. This is the announcement of the end. "There will be no more delay" (v.6). The prophesy of John is not over (v.11), but the beginning of the end will be announced by the blowing of the 7th trumpet.

John uses the familiar phrase, "Then I saw" (*kai eidon*) to indicate that this is another vision, connected with the previous visions, concerning the end. The figure that came down from heaven is called "another angel." Though the description matches the description of Jesus in chapter 1, it is clear that this is not Jesus. This is "another" angel and he swears by God who created the heavens. The glory and brilliance of the rainbow, his face, and his legs are reflections of the glory of the Lamb and of the One on the throne.

There are some, however, that believe this is too close to the description of Christ to simply dismiss the possibility. Beale, for example, believes that this angel may be identified with Christ, or at least with the "one like a son of Man" because of the divine aura around him. In the Old Testament, only God comes in heaven or to earth in a cloud, with the exception of Daniel 7:13, the son of man. Because of the parallel also with Revelation 14:14–15, this being is probably the angel of Yahweh, like in the Old Testament, who is referred to as Yahweh himself (see Genesis 16:10; 22:11–18; 24:7; 31:11–13; Exodus 3:2–12; 14:19; Judges 2:1; 6:22; 13:20–22; Zechariah 3:1–3; Jude 9). Also, the rainbow reminds us of Ezekiel 1:26–28 and the throne of God.[2] Beale concedes as well that the angel of Revelation 10:1 may merely be an angelic representative of Christ, who therefore possesses Christ's traits. If so, Michael would be a good candidate, since he represents Christ in 12:7–9.[3]

On the other hand, Mounce believes that the identification of the angel with Christ should be rejected, because in Revelation Christ never appears as an angel, and his use of an oath in verse 6 would be inappropriate for Christ.[4] Thomas makes the point that John and his hearers would view this angel as being intimately associated with God and Jesus, authorized to act

1. See Osborne, *Revelation*, 391. See also Beale (Beale, *The Book of Revelation*, 521), who holds that the believers are sealed to bear an enduring and loyal witness to the gospel.

2. Beale, *The Book of Revelation*, 523. The article in the Greek with the rainbow, according to Beale (Beale, *The Book of Revelation*, 524), is probably an article of previous reference, referring back to the rainbow of 4:3.

3. Beale, *The Book of Revelation*, 526.

4. Mounce, *The Book of Revelation*, 207. Concerning the oath, however, God does swear by himself. It would not be inappropriate, then, for Christ to swear by himself as well.

according to divine will and representing divine presence and glory, but a different being than Christ.[5] We also see that there is no worship addressed to the angel, something that frequently accompanies the appearance of Christ in John's vision. Angels are always angels in Revelation. They are not called angels, but stand as Christ, the Lamb. As Osborne notes, the angel is simply another mighty angel, like the one in 5:2, who now holds the opened scroll of chapter 5 in his hand. The angel is not Christ, but a special herald of Christ and "shares in his glory and his mission."[6] I would hesitate, however, to say than an angel, or any created being, shares in Christ's glory since God will share his glory with no one. Rather, it is more accurate to say that he reflects the glory of Christ.

This mighty angel, then, is holding a little scroll in his right hand. Eze-kiel 2:9–3:3 provide the background for this scroll. The words of Ezekiel's scroll were filled with mourning, lament, and woe. There is a good chance that the little scroll given to John was like that which was given to Ezekiel, a word of judgment. Was this the same scroll as in chapter 5? I think not. This scroll is called a little scroll and is held by an angel, if the interpretation above is correct. This little scroll is not sealed, unlike the scroll of chapter 5, which could only be opened by the Lamb. There are some parallels, as Beale points out. Both scrolls are opened, though one was only able to be opened by Jesus, and we don't know who opened this scroll. Both scrolls are associ-ated with a strong angel who "cries out." Both are associated with God who lives forever and ever. Both seem directly related to the end-time prophesy of Daniel. In both visions, someone approaches a heavenly being and takes a scroll out of the being's hand. There is similar commissioning language communicated to John in both. And both scrolls concern the destiny of "peoples, nations, tongues, and tribes/kings."[7]

5. Thomas and Macchia, *Revelation*, 192.

6. See Osborne, *Revelation*, 393–4; see also Johnson (Johnson, *Hebrews through Revelation*, 496). Aune (Aune, *Revelation 6–16*, 556) notes that John's conception of the angel may be based on Colossus of Rhodes, the famous bronze statue erected around 280 BC by Chares of Lindos. His legs represented pillars of fire and his face was sup-posed to represent the sun. It was destroyed in an earthquake in 224 BC. But if it was destroyed, how was John supposed to know about it? I think there's no external refer-ence, just what he saw in his vision. I would also hesitate to conclude that the scroll is the same scroll held by Jesus in chapter 5. Jesus was the only one worthy to open the scroll. Did he then give it to the angel in chapter 10? This doesn't seem likely.

7. See Beale, *The Book of Revelation*, 527. Beale also includes as parallels the fact that both scrolls are held by Christ and in both cases, the divine being is likened to a lion. But I do not see these parallels as significant—they fail if the angel in chapter 10 is indeed an angel. See Aune (Aune, *Revelation 6–16* 558), who believes this to be a different scroll and Thomas (Thomas and Macchia, *Revelation*, 192), who believes it's the same scroll as chapter 5, declares: "John and his hearers are finally encountering the

The angel is standing on the land and on the sea as a sign of the judgment of God against all the nations of the earth and against all the evil forces behind those nations. The sea is a traditional source of evil in the Jewish worldview. This is a universal sovereignty, as the placing of feet on something is a symbol of sovereignty over that which is underneath. Both the sea and the land are underneath the angel's feet, meaning that God has sovereignty over all and is right is sending the judgment that is to come.[8]

The shout of the angel was like the roar of a lion, maybe indicating the ferocity of the judgments that were contained in the little scroll. When the angel shouted, the voices of the seven thunders spoke. This is the announcement of judgment from heaven. Daniel was told to seal up the scroll in Daniel 12. John is also told to seal up what the seven thunders speak and not write it down. This is the perfect, complete, and final judgment of the Lord against the world. Mounce writes that the thunders are associated with the seven trumpet plagues in 11:19 and in 16:18 with the final bowl of God's wrath. Here, they are foreboding the coming peril of divine retribution.[9]

John was about to write what the seven thunders spoke, but a voice from heaven commanded him not to write it down. The seven thunders may represent another set of judgments, after the bowls, based on the model of four sevenfold plagues, as in Leviticus 26.[10] It is too, late, however, for any extra set of warnings. The judgment was set, and there was no more need of another set of judgments or warnings. This is the "time of trouble, such as never has been," as foretold in Daniel 12.

Why is this so? We see the answer in verse 6. "There will be no more delay." Literally, this can be translated, "because the time (*kronos*) will be no more." There is no more delay in terms of God's judgments. The prayers of the saints in Revelation 6 are being answered. Their appeal, "how long?" Is now clear—there will be no more delay after the sounding of the seventh trumpet. This also answers the question asked in Daniel 12:5–10, "how long until the end." Had the seven thunders not been cancelled, there would have

opened book!"

8. Beale, *The Book of Revelation*, 529. See Job 11:9, Psalm 146:6, Proverbs 8:29, Isaiah 42:10, and Jonah 1:9 as examples.

9. Mounce, *The Book of Revelation*, 209. Mounce also notes that with the definite article, "The thunders," the readers may have heard of them, possibly a reference to Psalm 29:3: "The voice of the Lord is over the waters; the God of glory thunders, the Lord, over many waters." See also Amos 3:7: "'For the Lord God does nothing without revealing his secret to his servants the prophets. The lion has roared; who will not fear? The Lord God has spoken; who can but prophesy?'" In parallel, in poetic form, the lion would be equivalent to the Lord.

10. Beale, *The Book of Revelation*, 536.

been another delay.[11] The angel, while saying this, swears an oath to God. God is described as the eternal Creator and, therefore, rightful Judge of all that is on the earth. He is just in the judgments he is going to bring because he has been opposed by those who dwell in the sea (the evil forces of the world) and those who dwell on the land (the nations of the world). We see this expression of God's justice again in 15:5–6.

With the sounding of the seventh trumpet, the mystery of God would be accomplished. What is the μυστήριον τοῦ θεοῦ *(musterion tou Theou)*? It is that the nations are redeemed by the blood of the Lamb and that those who reject him will be judged permanently and completely (either through the seven thunders, but more likely through the seven bowls of wrath). This has been prophesied many times in Isaiah, Jeremiah, Ezekiel, Daniel and the other minor prophets. It has been clearly proclaimed. It is the evangel, the *eueggelisen*, the good news that there is salvation by the blood of the Lamb, but that those who do not respond to that salvation will be judged.

See Amos 3:4–8 combined with Daniel 12. The mystery is also that the saints of God must suffer, but that in that suffering (as in the suffering of the Lamb) there would be victory and God's vindication upon the wicked. Paul speaks of this mystery in Romans 16:25–26, "Now to him who is able to strengthen you according to my gospel and the preaching of Jesus Christ, according to the revelation of the mystery that was kept secret for long ages but how now been disclosed and through the prophetic writings has been made known to all nations, according to the command of the eternal God, to bring about the obedience of faith." The mystery of the gospel is made known in Christ, the Lamb. And those nations that oppose him will know the other side of that mystery, the scroll of judgment.[12]

When exactly this mystery of God will be accomplished is not so clear. Ladd believes the translation should read, "in the days of the trumpet call." This suggests that the sounding of the trumpet is not a simple one-time action, but it indicates a period of time. The period of the seventh trumpet includes the seven bowls of wrath and the final judgment of the ungodly.[13] Persecution and martyrdom preceded the seventh trumpet, but the overthrow and destruction of those persecuting will follow it. From this point on in Revelation, the action of the apocalypse will be a "multi-dimensional presentation of the final triumph of God over evil."[14]

11. See Mounce, *The Book of Revelation*, 211.

12. See also Ephesians 3 and Colossians 2.

13. Ladd, *A Commentary on the Revelation of John*, 145.

14. Mounce, *The Book of Revelation*, 213.

From John's vantage point on the brink of eternity, he unveils the evil forces which operate behind the scenes of history and in the last days will mount a final and furious assault on the faithful. It is like reading a book about WWII, with each chapter of the book describing a different scene of the war: one about Italy, one about Japan, one about Russia, and one about Germany. None of the chapters are in any particular chronological order, but all about the same war. Revelation 11–18 is like that—a description of the different enemies of God, and how each of them controls the world and then is subsequently defeated.

In verse 8, John hears another voice speaking. Whose voice is this? Is it the angel who swore by God with arm lifted high, or is it the voice from heaven in verse 4 who told John to seal up what the seven thunders had said? It is probably the voice associated with the seven thunders since he tells John to take the scroll from the angel who stands on the earth and the sea. John is then instructed to take the scroll and eat it, just as in Ezekiel's case. And like in Ezekiel's case, the scroll is sweet to the taste but sour in the stomach. It is sweet because it is the word of God. It is bitter or sour because it is the judgment of God. Jeremiah as well declared the word of God as his heart's delight even though the message was difficult. He said in Jeremiah 15:16, "Your words were found, and I ate them, and your words became to me a joy and the delight of my heart, for I am called by your name, O LORD, God of hosts."[15]

What are the contents of the scroll? What did John just eat? Mounce believes the contents to be the message of 11:1–13, a message for the church that they will triumph as they go through this ordeal on the earth.[16] Beale thinks that the contents of the scroll are at least Revelation 11–16, and may also include 17–22, depending upon whether John is recommissioned in 17:1–3 or not.[17] Because of the close association with Ezekiel's scroll, and Daniel's prophesy of distress in the end, associated with the thunders, it is likely that the contents of the scroll are the rest of Revelation, the judgment of God, the final judgment of all time.

And so, John is commissioned again in verse 11. He needed to prophesy again to the nations. The judgments of God were coming. Though the voice of the seven thunders was sealed, the seventh trumpet was yet to be declared. John is recommissioned to the prophetic task. Osborne observes

15. See also Psalm 19:7–11; 119:97–104; Proverbs 16:21–24; 24:13–14. Beale (Beale, *The Book of Revelation*, 550) writes, that the sweetness of the words also represents the "positive and joyous effect God's words have in instructing and guiding those who submit to them."

16. Mounce, *The Book of Revelation*, 216.

17. Beale, *The Book of Revelation*, 527.

that the command to prophesy "again" probably refers back to 1:19, though John had not specifically been called a prophet.[18]

A small, but important, translation issue has to do with the small Greek pronoun, *epi*. Was John told to prophesy "about" many peoples, nations, languages, and kings," or was he to prophesy "against" them or "to" them. The word could mean any of these. But given the context of judgment contained in the little scroll, and the context of the rest of Revelation, it is fair to say that John must prophesy against these nations as a means of warning and judgment, just as Jonah prophesied against the people of Nineveh. But in prophesying against them, he is also prophesying to them and about them. So, it is best to keep a broader perspective of translation and interpretation here.

## Conclusion

Why do we call the word of God bitter? In Jesus' parable of the sower, he told about a sower who went out to sow his seed. He threw the seed on all kinds of soil, and depending upon the kind of soil, the seed either took root and flourished, or did not. When his disciples asked him to explain the parable, Jesus said the seed represented the word of God. The nature of the seed never changed. It is always good seed in the hands of the sower. What changed was the character of the soil. The word of God is good, the soil can either be hard and reject the seed, or soft and receptive so that the seed can take root.

So also, the word of God is bitter, not because of the bitter nature of the word of God, but because of the bitter nature of the reception of the judged. Those who have rejected the word, to them the word is bitter. It is a word of judgment because they have rejected the word of God.

It should be bitter for us to tell someone that God is going to judge them. Painful not because we are embarrassed for God's sake, but painful because we are concerned over the choices of our loved ones. It should be painful for us to think about people separated from God and having to go through the judgment of the Lord because of their own stubbornness and rejection of him. It should not make the preacher joyful to speak of the judgments of God, happy that the wicked will end up in hell. The message of judgment is necessary in the church, but it should never bring us joy. Paul was so burdened

---

18. Osborne, *Revelation*, 390. This is not, according to Johnson (Johnson, *Hebrews through Revelation*, 498), a mere recapitulation in great detail of previous visions, but a further progression of the events connected with the end.

about the future of Israel and their rejection of the Messiah, that he said in Romans 9, "I have great sorrow and unceasing anguish in my heart."

This is a bitter message for us also because this is a message that affects all of humanity. This is not just a message of judgment against the obviously wicked, but against all who have not turned to Christ. Sometimes, if we are honest with others, we would admit that we get an internal satisfaction at seeing the really wicked get their due—the child molesters, the serial killers, and the corrupt politicians. But the judgments of God will come against all who have forsaken his Son, Jesus. Any who turn their back on his salvation and seek to justify themselves on their own will be judged by God. That may mean our relatives, our teachers, our policemen, our neighbors, co-workers, friends, philanthropists, queens, athletes, and even pastors who do not know Jesus. It is a bitter message because we are compelled, like John, to proclaim it. We cannot hold it in.

# Revelation 11:1–19

Third Interlude (The Two Witnesses) and
Trumpet 7 (A Picture of the End)

## Introduction

WE ARE LIVING IN a day when it is not popular to talk about knowing the truth or holding to the truth. Is it intolerant to tell a friend that he or she is wrong in what they believe? Or is it an act of love? Media types in the West are telling Christians that evangelism and witnessing and trying to win others over to the faith is arrogant, narrow minded, and intolerant hate mongering. The "intelligent" are trying to reconcile the search for truth with their belief system that does not give room for truth. As our societies abandon the truth and the importance of the truth more and more, the more lost and chaotic those societies will become and the more illogical its arguments will become.

The mission for the church has never changed, regardless of the position of society regarding truth and intolerance. God's call to us, and Jesus' great commission for his church, is still the same. We are called to continue to be witnesses for Jesus in this world, even in a context of suffering and persecution, even in a context of increased ungodliness, and even in a context of increased nonsensical reasoning.

## Exposition

Chapter 11 in Revelation announces the final judgment of God. John heard the angel declare in chapter 10, "there shall be no more delay." Chapter 11 ends with flashes of lightning, thunder, an earthquake, and a hailstorm, evidences of judgment.

There seems to be a finality to this judgment. Verse 15, the sounding of the seventh trumpet, announces that the kingdoms of the world now belong to Christ. It seems clear that chapter 11 describes the larger picture of what is happening between the people of God and the nations of the earth who have rejected Christ. The people of God are submitted to persecution after a specified and limited period of time (1260 days). After this limited time, they rise up and are taken to heaven, like Elijah. Exodus and 1 Kings provide a strong background for what is happening here—the ministries of Moses and Elijah, two faithful servants of God who brought the word of God first to Israel as a young nation, and then to Israel in rebellion. There is also much symbolism taken from Daniel and Ezekiel in Revelation 11. Mounce views the entire chapter 11 as symbolic of the fate of the witnessing church during the final period of opposition and persecution. These are the contents of the little book of chapter 10.[1] Bauckham writes, "The people of God have been redeemed *from all the nations* (5:9) in order to bear prophetic witness *to all the nations* (11:3–13).[2]

In verse 1, John was given a reed, like a measuring rod, and was told to measure the temple of God and the altar. The background for this must be Ezekiel 40:1–4, when Ezekiel saw a measuring rod in the hand of the angel who was to measure the temple. Also, see Zechariah 2:1–5. There, another man had a measuring line in his hand. He was measuring Jerusalem and it was found to be a city without walls because of the great number of people living there. Beale believes the measuring represents the security of the city's inhabitants against the pollutants of the unclean people outside. This temple community will be composed of both Jewish and Gentile Christians. The measuring can also connote God's presence, which is guaranteed to be with the temple community living on earth before the consummation.[3] This does not necessarily mean a literal temple, but rather a community of faith, as congregations are the temples of the Holy Spirit now.

It is also possible that the worshippers were to be counted to see (or insure) that the total number of saints who were to be martyred had come in, and that now it was time (see 10:6) for the prayers of the saints in 6:9–10 to be answered. The full number of God's people had come in. There will be no delay for the judgment of God against the ungodly.

Beale lists as least five common interpretations of 11:1–2 and variations of those interpretations: 1) Dispensationalist future—these verses describe the time of the tribulation immediately preceding Christ's *parousia*. The temple and altar are literally restored in the literal city of Jerusalem. The outer court is usually identified with Gentiles who will persecute the

---

1. Mounce, *The Book of Revelation*, 218.

2. Bauckham, *New Testament Theology*, 84.

3. Beale, *The Book of Revelation*, 559. See also Revelation 21:15–17. The measuring has the same meaning as the sealing in 7:3–8. See Beale, *The Book of Revelation*, 560.

remnant and overrun a literal Jerusalem; 2) Preterist—this is a similar approach, but not of the future. What is portrayed here is what happened in 70 AD; 3) Modified futurist—the descriptions in chapter 11 must be understood figuratively. The images of the cultic things represent those within ethnic Israel whose salvation is secured by the measuring. Those outside represent Jewish unbelievers. Both groups will undergo persecution; 4) The outer court are those of the professing but apostate church which will be deceived and join together with the persecutors; 5) The text must be understood figuratively, but the outer court is the physical expression of the true, spiritual Israel, which is susceptible to harm and persecution.[4]

Remembering that John is describing visions with apocalyptic language and given the nature of the overall themes of John (the church overcoming in the face of suffering), it is less likely that a physical or literal temple is being described. Thomas rightly notes that *naos*, temple, appears three times in John's gospel, each time with reference to Jesus' body (2:19–21). This suggests that the temple in view here is not the literal temple complex but is filled with theological significance. In other words, it is linked to God's temple in heaven. Johnson as well notes that in Paul's letters the word for temple is used metaphorically as a way of referring to the either the physical bodies of Christians, or to the church of God. Only in Thessalonians could it possibly refer to the actual temple.[5]

So, believers are preserved, or sealed as in chapter 7. This preservation is a spiritual preservation from the wrath of God that is coming through the blowing of the seventh trumpet. But it is not a physical preservation from persecution and suffering at the hands of the wicked, as will be clear in the rest of chapter 11.[6]

We continue this thought from the distinction that is made in verse 2. A distinction is made between those within the temple (those who are counted as holy, the people of God), and those outside of the city (the nations of the world). Those outside the city, or those outside of the people of God, will come against them for a limited time—forty-two months (see Daniel 8:9–14). While those outside of the city, or the "Gentiles," are the nations of the world, there is a segment of the people of God (the outer court) that are not measured. They are excluded. For John, the outer court is not necessarily something negative. Gentiles are accepted on an equal footing

---

4. Beale, *The Book of Revelation*, 557–8.

5. Thomas and Macchia, *Revelation*, 199; Johnson, *Hebrews through Revelation*, 500.

6. See Osborne, *Revelation*, 410; Mounce, *The Book of Revelation*, 219.

with Jews into the new covenant community.[7] Mounce also believes that the outer court refers to the church viewed from a different perspective. It is to be cast out and not measured; that is, it is to be given to persecution in the last days. This distinction is used to point out the limitations placed upon the pagan hostility.[8] As we have seen already in Revelation, while God will spiritually protect the believers, there would be some of them (those outside) that would suffer under persecution. But this is a limited time only.[9] They are handed over to the power of the Gentiles in the outer court, the traditional place of the Gentiles in the temple.

This is a limited time. The number forty-two should be interpreted figuratively for the eschatological period of tribulation prophesied by Daniel (7:25; 9:27; 12:7, 11–12). This could also be connected to the forty-two encampments (forty-two years?) of Israel's desert wondering, or to Elijah's ministry of judgment which lasted for forty-two months or three and a half years.[10] The church must undergo a period of persecution, figuratively three and a half years, but they are protected from spiritual harm. Until the victorious return of Christ, they must continue in their faithful witness in the world, even in the face of severe threat and persecution. Mounce notes that the primary reference for the forty-two months is the time of Antiochus Epiphanes in 167–164 BC. This became the conventional symbol for a limited period of time during which evil would be allowed to reign. See also Luke 21:24 where the phrase "The time of the Gentiles" is used.[11] It is best not to try to determine when this will be as if the forty-two months was a literal number. Three and a half years is half of seven years, meaning not a full, all-out persecution. It is limited by God, and his people will stand firm to the end.

In verse 3, we are introduced to two witnesses who will be empowered to prophesy for 1,260 days, clothed in sackcloth. Consistent with the view of the temple, as described above, it is clear that these two witnesses represent the church. We will see this kind of drama played out again symbolically in chapter 12. The church, or God's faithful witnesses, will give testimony for the same time period as the opposition. Forty-two months is the same as 1,260 days. Why did John not simply use forty-two months again? Because John wants to tie this closely with Daniel's prophesy, which talked about

7. Beale, *The Book of Revelation*, 560,

8. See Mounce, *The Book of Revelation*, 220; see also Thomas and Macchia, *Revelation*, 200. Ladd (Ladd, *A Commentary on the Revelation of John*, 152), however, sees Jerusalem as standing for the Jewish people, rather than symbolically representing the church.

9. Osborne, *Revelation*, 415.

10. Beale, *The Book of Revelation*, 565.

11. Mounce, *The Book of Revelation*, 201.

time, times, and half a time, or three and a half years. Again, this is limited compared to the more complete seven years.

The two witnesses are clothed in sackcloth because of the message of repentance and the appeal for the people of the earth to repent and be in sorrow for their sinfulness and rebellion against God. This was the apparel of both Elijah and John the Baptist. Moses and Elijah, as these figures seem to represent as well, do not stand for the law and the prophets. Both are prophets. As prophets who both confronted the world of pagan idolatry, they set the precedent for the church's prophetic witness to the world.[12]

Although both Ladd and Osborne feel that the two figures could be two eschatological historic figures, just as the beast and the antichrist will be actual figures in the future, they also concede that they could be symbolic of the witness of the church, in its suffering and triumph.[13] I think it is more consistent to understand these two figures corporately. They represent the whole community of faith, whose primary function is to be a prophetic witness. Like John the Baptist was not a literal reappearance of Elijah, but came in the spirit and power of Elijah, so the church must testify in the same spirit and power of Moses and Elijah. According to Beale, the corporate identification is supported by six considerations: 1) They are identified as "two lampstands." See chapters 1 and 2; Verse 7 says that the beast will make war against them. See Daniel 7:21; 3) Verses 9–13 shows that the entire world will see the defeat and resurrection. The witnesses are visible throughout the earth (not on television like Hal Lindsey argued); 4) The two witnesses prophesy for three and a half years, the same time that the "holy city," "the woman," and "those tabernacling in heaven" are to be oppressed (11:2; 12:6, 14; 13:6; 5) The time of tribulation comes from Daniel 7:25; 12:7 and this is against the community, not particular individuals; and 6) "Testimony" to Jesus is attributed to the community of believers elsewhere in the book (6:9; 12:11, 17; 19:10; 20:4).[14] The case seems fairly strong for a corporate understanding of the two figures.

In verse 4, this is even more emphatic, as the two symbols from Zechariah 4:3, 11–14 are used. In Zechariah, the two lampstands are identified as the word of the Lord (verse 6: "Not by might, nor by power, but by my

---

12. See Bauckham, *New Testament Theology*, 85 and Johnson, *Hebrews through Revelation*, 54.

13. Ladd (Ladd, *A Commentary on the Revelation of John*, 154) views this as possibly symbolic of the witness of the church to Israel; Osborne, *Revelation*, 418.

14. Beale, *The Book of Revelation*, 573-4. Aune (Aune, *Revelation 6–16*, 631) agrees. Placing emphasis on the idea of the two olive trees and the lampstands representing Zerubbabel and Joshua as kings and priests, it is likely that these two witnesses represent the church in its prophetic witness.

Spirit"). The two olive trees are those anointed to serve the Lord of all the earth (4:14). The olive tree (and so anointing oil) and the lampstands are references to the lampstands of the churches and the presence of the anointing Spirit of God. By the power of the Spirit, and as the light of the world, reflecting the light of Christ, the church triumphant boldly continues to testify for God and preach to the nations.

The image of the church, if we continue this line of thinking, is a bit surprising as they are clothed in sackcloth, except that this could be symbolic again, as is the calling down fire from heaven as Elijah did, as well as shutting up the skies (verse 6), and turning the waters to blood and calling down the plagues, as Moses did. In other words, God's witnesses will continue in the powerful ministry of the Spirit, proclaiming the word of God, and doing miraculous signs of wonder among the ungodly, just as the early church apostles did in the book of Acts. In this way, the church will minister from the fulfilled power of Christ, who, according to Isaiah 11:4, "shall strike the earth with the rod of his mouth, and with the breath of his lips he shall kill the wicked." God had told Jeremiah in Jeremiah 5:14, "I am making my words in your mouth a fire, and this people wood, and the fire shall consume them."[15]

Jesus promised that if the church would be faithful in its witness, he would not remove the lampstand, but keep the light of his word burning through them. So, no matter what oppression, no matter what attempt the world uses to snuff out the light of our witness, by the power and anointing of the Holy Spirit, our light will continue to burn, even when the world tries to snuff it out by death. But even in death, the message remains a message of power and punch.

The witness of the church has power because the church has the Holy Spirit. The Holy Spirit is a dangerous power. And if the church truly understood its authority to witness on the earth, the world would once again witness the power of the awesome and living God. Hebrews 12:29 says, "for our God is a consuming fire." The message of the church should be like fire from its mouth, cleaning the dross of sin and igniting and burning up the wickedness of men. The church is an army that is called to be an army of grace and compassion to the lost and the seeking. But to those opposed to God, we also rise up to be an army representing the God of the universe, and Satan and all his demons cannot stand against the church of Jesus, empowered by the Holy Spirit.

---

15. Beale, *The Book of Revelation*, 585, notes that the three and a half year torment inflicted by the witnesses corresponds not only to the length of Christ's ministry, but also to Elijah's ministry of judgment (Luke 4:25; James 5:17).

In verse 7, we see a divinely permitted power of the wicked beast against the people of God. This is clear in Revelation 13 as well. The power of the message and messengers of God does not preclude or protect the church from suffering, even death. 2 Timothy 3:12 says, "Indeed, all who desire to live a godly life in Christ Jesus will be persecuted." In Daniel 7:21, the horn, the wicked nations, "made war with the saints." The source of the power against God's people is the wicked abyss, the source of the evil spirits and powers of judgment against the nations. The people of God would be protected from the wrath of God, but not from the wrath of the beast. But even in that there is victory. The phrase, "And when they have finished their testimony," indicates that this is the end of history. The church will have completed its witness to the world and will appear defeated.[16] Jesus prophesied this as well in Matthew 24:9–22. This also parallels Revelation 6:9 and 11. The wicked will defeat God's people, but that will signal the end of the wicked as they will have to face the final judgment. Paul refers to this in 2 Thessalonians 2:4, "who opposes and exalts himself against every so-called god or object of worship, so that he takes his seat in the temple of God, proclaiming himself to be God."

The people of God will be subject to ridicule and shame in the world, their bodies figuratively being left out for the world to see after they have fallen. According to Beale, this is a hyperbolic statement that the true church will seem to be defeated in its role of witness and will appear small and insignificant in the eyes of the world.[17]

Where is this "great city" of verse 9. There is a clear reference to Jerusalem, although the city is not named. Jerusalem was the place where Jesus was crucified. If John means the literal Jerusalem, then it is also identified as Sodom and Egypt, a reference made by Jesus as well. The judgment against the villages of Galilee would be greater than the judgment against Sodom and Gomorrah, because the Jewish cities rejected the Son of God. Also, in Isaiah 1:10, Jerusalem is called Sodom and Gomorrah.

But John refers to Jerusalem as "Sodom and Egypt." In John's days, with the city of Jerusalem no longer significant, the great city could be none other than Rome, or metaphorically, Babylon. The main characteristic of the city is persecution. And like Jerusalem, which had become like other ungodly nations that persecuted God's people (e.g., Sodom and Egypt), and even worse, killing the Son of God, this city is the site where the witnesses meet their death, a universal dominion epitomized by the power of Rome,

16. Beale, *The Book of Revelation*, 587. Beale (Beale, *The Book of Revelation*, 589) also notes that the description of the beast rising out of the abyss refers to the final onslaught against the saints directly preceding his ultimate demise.

17. Beale, *The Book of Revelation*, 590.

or Babylon. The reference to the crucifixion is a symbolic clue, not a historical one. This is the response of the ungodly to the righteous.[18] Johnson rightly concludes that John sees five places as one: Babylon, Sodom, Egypt, Jerusalem, and Rome. Wherever God is opposed, and his people harassed and persecuted, there is the "great city."[19]

For three and a half days the peoples of the world will gloat over the broken church and heap shame upon it. Again, the time is limited, three and a half days, and should not be interpreted literally, but figuratively as a time that is limited by the sovereign God. This reminds us of the time period of the period Christ was in the tomb. Also, the contrast of a short three and a half days compared to the three and a half years of witness shows that this "victory" of the antichrist is brief and insignificant.[20] But wasn't Jesus in the tomb three days only? Bauckham answers this by reminding us again of John's apocalyptic purpose. He has converted the three days of the resurrection in the gospels into the conventional apocalyptic number, three and a half. It is the witness of Jesus himself that the witnesses continue, and their death is a participation in the blood of the Lamb.[21]

A worldwide celebration will take place because of the demise of God's people. How had the witnesses tormented those who live on the earth? The people of the world were tormented by the truth of God's word, proclaimed in power. From the perspective of those who heard the piercing truth, it was torment. But certainly, not from God's perspective. The people of the earth have underestimated the power of God and the power of God's church. You can't kill what is always alive. Jesus said, "Do not be afraid of those who can only kill the body."

After a limited time, the church, or God's people, would rise up again in triumph and this renewed people of God will bring terror to the people of the earth. This is very similar to the strange parabolic story of Ezekiel 37, when the dry bones, having been given the breath of God, God's life, and empowering Spirit, they rise up to testify and declare the word of God. This will strike terror on all those who had gloated over them. Though some may see this as a reference to some kind of rapture, it is really the resurrection of the saints at the coming of Christ. Thus chapters 12–18 are recapitulations,

18. See Beale, *The Book of Revelation*, 592; Mounce, *The Book of Revelation*, 226; Thomas and Macchia, *Revelation*, 206. Ladd, *A Commentary on the Revelation of John*, 157, sees this as the actual city of Jerusalem, but that fits with his interpretation of the two witnesses being historical figures.

19. Johnson, *Hebrews through Revelation*, 506.

20. Beale, *The Book of Revelation*, 594–5.

21. Bauckham, *New Testament Theology*, 85. See Psalm 79:1–13 for a good comparison of this wording.

or the same story from different perspectives, of what is described symbolically in chapter 11. This is very clear from verse 13 as the traditional signs
of final judgment take place. This is just before the third and final woe, and
thus the opening of the seven bowls of wrath and the final victory of God
over the nations of the world.[22]

"At that hour" in verse 13 could be a reference to the day of the LORD
and the final end. When the dead in Christ are raised up from the dead, and
the church has its final victory with the end of wickedness. Whether the seven
thousand who were killed in the earthquake is a literal number or a symbolic
number is not clear. Though there are some[23] who see this a partial conversion
of the wicked, it is more likely that a conversion must be ruled out because
it is placed after the commencement of the last judgment, signaled in verse
13. The terror and giving glory to God, then, would be similar to the "forced"
worship of the Messiah in Zechariah 14. If they do not worship, they will
be punished.[24] In the context of a judgment on the nations, Micah 7:16–17
prophesies that "The nations shall see and be ashamed of all their might; they
shall lay their hands on their mouths; their ears shall be deaf; they shall lick
the dust like a serpent, like the crawling things of the earth; they shall come
trembling out of their strongholds; they shall turn in dread to the Lord our
God, and they shall be in fear of you."

The second woe has ended, and third woe is said to be coming soon.
But the third woe is never announced. This must mean that the sounding
of the seventh trumpet is the third woe and announces the end. The imper-
fect tense is used in the phrase, "The kingdom of the world has become the
kingdom of our Lord and of his church." This means that the kingdoms of

22. Beale (Beale, *The Book of Revelation*, 599) understands this as a spiritual rapture in which the witnesses are restored and called further into prophetic ministry.
Osborne, *Revelation*, 432, understands this to be a "proleptic" anticipation of the "rapture" of the church, rather than the rapture itself. See also Ezekiel 38 for background,
especially verses 19–20, where a great earthquake is prophesied before the time of the
end.; also Zechariah 14:15.

23. See Osborne, *Revelation*, 435–6. Osborne calls this "the one evangelistic victory in the book." God does not send judgment only to punish, but to call to repentance.
But not if this is the final judgment and the temple has been closed (see chapter 15),
with no opportunity for sacrifice. Johnson, *Hebrews through Revelation*, 507, views this
as a genuine conversion as opposed to 16:9, but I think the same reason 16:9 is not a
genuine conversion holds true here. Bauckham says that because of the witness of the
two witnesses (or the church), the judgment of God is always salvific. But as with the
case of Nebuchadnezzar, one can give glory to the God of heaven (the same phrase as
in Daniel 2:18–19, 37, 44) as the sovereign God over events of the earth, but not yet
commit one's life to that God. This is an intellectual acknowledgment, not necessarily a
statement of the will or repentance.

24. See Beale, *The Book of Revelation*, 607.

the world have already begun to belong to Christ because of the cross and the resurrection but will finally belong to Christ at the announcing of the seventh trumpet, the announcement of the seven plagues and the return of the Lamb (see chapter 19). The contents, indeed, of the seventh trumpet, are found in chapters 15-19, after the interludes and recapitulations of chapter 12 and 13, and on overview of the great harvest in chapter 14.

We see the twenty-four elders again in verse 16, and again they fall on their faces before the throne and worship God. They declare him to be the One who is and who was, similar to 1:4, 8; 4:8; and 19:6. God's reign is coming to full completion on the earth. "Have begun to reign" looks forward to the millennial reign described in chapter 20.[25] With the blowing of the seventh trumpet, all of history is quickly cascading toward the final end with Jesus' reign on the earth, and the enemies of God finally and completely judged, and the people of God vindicated.

The finality of this is repeated in verse 18, as part of the praise song of the elders. The wrath of the nations came, but the wrath of God overcame them. The time (*kairos*) for judgment and reward is come. Those who are faithful will be rewarded, those who are wicked will be judged and destroyed. This is similar to Daniel 12:2, a prophesy of the final resurrection, the righteous to eternal life, and the wicked to judgment. Mounce writes, "The reign of God is established by a great demonstration of divine wrath against the defiant anger of the world."[26] We have a summary here of the remaining chapters of Revelation—the nations will rise up against God's people, but they would be victorious in their suffering, and God will reward his servants the prophets and the saints and those who reverence the name of God, that is, all those who remain faithful to him unto the end.

In verse 19, we again read of lightning, rumblings, thunder, and an earthquake and hailstorm, all signs of divine judgment (see 8:5; 16:18, 21). The ark of the covenant becomes visible. Why? There are two possible answers and maybe a combination of the two is best. First, the ark of the covenant becomes a symbol of Israel's rebellion before God. Within the ark are the rod of Aaron that had budded, the broken tablets of the Law, and a jar of manna. All of these are memorials to the rebellion of Israel, and so also the rebellion of the world. Because of their rebellion, the people will be judged, as the presence (and so wrath) of God will come upon the ungodly.

Secondly, the ark can also be understood as a symbol of God's faithfulness in fulfilling his covenantal promises. For the days of wrath to come,

25. Johnson, *Hebrews through Revelation*, 509.

26. Mounce, *The Book of Revelation*, 232. See also Psalm 2:5, 110:5, and 115:13 for songs praising God for his promised victory over the wicked and his punishment of the ungodly.

believers will need to be assured that God will bring his own people safely into their eternal reward.[27] Just as the blood of the lamb or goat was sprinkled on the ark once a year for the atonement of the sins of the nation, and thus covering their sins with the blood before the face of God, so also the faithful are covered with the blood of the Lamb of God, sealing them from the day of wrath, and reminding the faithful of the mercy, loving kindness, and faithfulness of God.

## Conclusion

Persecution and suffering have been common themes in the history of the church. Whether we speak of local persecutions in the first two centuries, or more general persecutions like those under Nero, Domitian, Marcus Aurelius, and others, it is something that the church has endured. In the twentieth century, when the number of the followers of Christ has increased dramatically, persecution has escalated in areas where Christians are the minority again, just as they were in the Roman Empire. And with that increased strength has come increased persecution. There have been more followers of Jesus put to death in the twentieth century than in the previous nineteen centuries combined. Suffering has become part of the culture of the church in many parts of the world.

But that is not the final word in chapter 11. The final word is victory, even in the midst of suffering. Jesus wins. His church wins. And just as in their Savior's case, sometimes the church will win when it suffers. The end is near in Revelation. The rest of the book goes quickly toward the second coming of God. The call to faithful perseverance is still relevant.

---

27. See Mounce, *The Book of Revelation*, 233.

# Revelation 12:1–18

The Vision of the Woman and the Dragon

## Introduction

B ARRY MERRIT TELLS THE following story:

> When we lived in St. Petersburg, Florida, we would go to the
> beach. It was always hard to relax and have a good time with our
> children, though, because there were too many threats: jellyfish,
> stingrays, sharks, and the undertow. One time we had some
> relatives that came to St. Petersburg and brought their boat with
> them. We decided to go out to an island a couple of miles off
> shore called Egmont Key. We had a great time because we didn't
> think we had to worry about the normal threats. The water was
> blue, the sand was white. We swam with our children carefree
> in the Gulf of Mexico. A few days later we were telling some
> friends about our wonderful day. Being more familiar with the
> area, they informed us we had been swimming in one of the
> most shark-infested areas around! We were in danger, but com-
> pletely oblivious to it.[1]

The church knows it is in a struggle. It has been a struggle that is all
too familiar and has been going on a long time, not just in one culture, but
with all those who follow Jesus down through the ages, and in every part
of the globe. That struggle will continue between good and evil until Jesus
comes. That is the message of Revelation 12. There is a war. But the church
must continue to follow the example of Jesus, even unto the final sacrifice.

## Exposition

Ever since Adam and Eve first gave in to the temptation of the serpent, there
has been a long struggle between good and evil. If you were to summarize

1. "Alert to Satan's Work", Christianity Today.

143

the Old Testament, you would see that it is a story of God's work among his people against the designs of the enemy against them. From the very beginning, after the fall of Adam and Eve, God pronounced the future battle and the ultimate end of Satan. In Genesis 3:15, God tells the serpent, "I will put enmity between you and the woman, and between your offspring and her offspring. He will bruise your head, and you will bruise his heel."

The offspring of the woman were those who followed and worshipped God, those who were faithful to the covenant and looked toward the coming of the Messiah. Hebrews 11 mentions quite of few of them, but we could here list Abel, who offered an acceptable sacrifice, Abraham and his seed, Joseph, the righteous son of Jacob, as an example of what the Messiah would be like, Moses, King David, who was a man after God's own heart, the prophets Elijah, Elisha, Isaiah, Jeremiah, Daniel, and others, and Joshua the high priest of Zechariah.

The offspring of the serpent, or Satan, have been all those who yielded themselves to his wicked designs. Some of them were Cain, who killed his brother and allowed sin to fester in his heart and corrupt his family line, Lamech, the seventh generation from Cain, who boasted of his murderous acts, and all those political leaders who became tools of oppression against God's people: Pharaoh of Egypt, Balaam, the prophet of Baal who caused the Israelites to be seduced into sexual sin, the Ammonites and the Philistines, the Syrians, Assyrians, Babylonians, Medes, and Persians. What John sees in this vision in chapter 12 is the pinnacle of the battle, the high point of the age-old struggle.

Chapter 12 is not a chronological continuation from chapter 11. Rather, this is another apocalyptic picture of the victory won by the Lamb of God and the defeat of the dragon, the great enemy of the people of God. This, alongside chapters 13 and 14, give further definition and clarity to the victory of the Lamb and the temporary victory of the beast against the saints. His "defeat" of the saints is nothing more than a path to their victory. The interpretive key is the symbolic identity of the woman and of the child. The woman seems to be the nation of Israel, or at least the people of God, combined with the new people of God, the church. The child seems to be the Messiah, and then by extension, those who follow him. The dragon pursued Jesus during his ministry, through Herod the Great, through temptation, through Pilate, and others, and now he pursues the church through the various evil rulers of the world.

Bauckham notes that the story takes us back to the confrontation between the serpent and the woman in the garden of Eden. The woman is not only Eve but also Zion (see Isaiah 66:7–9). The dragon is Leviathan (see Isaiah 27:1), and the ancestry of the dragon goes back to it (see Daniel 7:2–8), since he rises out of the sea. The combination of the sea monster and the monster of the earth (13:1, 11) reflects the typical pair of monsters, Leviathan and Behemoth.[2] Bauckham is right is seeing a link to the initial battle between Eve and the serpent, but the ramifications of that, and the applications, goes deeper and must be applied to the church and its current struggle with the enemy of our souls. Beale points out that there are four beasts introduced in chapter 12–20, the second half of the book of Revelation. They are introduced and then meet their demise in reverse order, highlighting that the devil is the initiator of all resistance to God's people.[3]

Ladd, as well, writes that this vision transcends the traditional categories of time and space. This is not a vision which is to take place at the end. It is a highly symbolic vision which describes a warfare between God and Satan, which has its counterpart in history in the conflict between the church and demonic evil. "The experience of the church in suffering tribulation on earth is the manifestation in history of a spiritual battle."[4]

The first part of this vision is a wondrous sign, σημεῖον μέγα (*semeiov mega*), showing that this vision is apocalyptic and should be interpreted as such. The source of the sign is heaven. This is a God-initiated sign for John to see and to use to encourage the believers. Who is this woman? A clue may be the twelve crowns. Could this be a reference to the twelve tribes of Israel and/or the twelve apostles? If so, then this is a symbol of God's people. She is clothed with the sun and the moon is under her feet, a sense of authority and glory, given to her by the God of heaven.

Aune lists several options for the identity of the woman: 1) The ancient and Catholic understanding is that the woman is Mary; 2) Another ancient understanding is that the woman represents the church; 3) The woman is sometimes identified with the bride, the Heavenly Jerusalem of Revelation 19:7–8; 21:9–10; 4) From a Jewish perspective, the woman could represent the persecuted people of God from whom the Messiah comes; 5) The woman is an astrological figure—the constellation Virgo, whose Greek name was "virgin"; 6) The woman is Isis, queen of heaven, since Egyptian sources understood Isis as connected with the sun and the stars.[5]

---

2. Bauckham, *New Testament Theology*, 89.

3. Beale, *The Book of Revelation*, 623.

4. Ladd, *A Commentary on the Revelation of John*, 166. Aune (Aune, *Revelation 6–16*, 668) sees a parallel between Revelation 12 and combat myths of the ancient near east. The Jewish community also had their own versions, the primary function of which was to show the experience of suffering and evil in the world to an independent cosmic adversary, Satan.

5. Aune, *Revelation 6–16*, 680.

Osborne addresses the possibility of option six above because it is so similar to Revelation 12. In Egyptian mythology, the mother goddess, Isis, is pursued by the red dragon, Set or Typhon, and flees to an island where she gives birth to the sun god, Horus. Osborne wonders why John set this story in themes so similar to the myths of the pagan nations? He writes, "What the Greeks have known as myths has now been actualized in history." The New Testament demythologizes Greco-Roman myths by historicizing them. What the pagans longed for in their myths has now become true in Jesus. This could be called a form of redemptive analogy to present the gospel in a way that captures the minds and interests of non-Christian readers.[6] This is possible. In other words, John used a story-line well known to his readers, and retold the story with historical characters, the church, Christ, the dragon (or Satan). Symbolically, the point is the same. A woman would bear a child. The dragon would pursue that child, and then the other offspring of the woman.

This background, combined with what we know in the Old Testament, all point to the identity of the woman as both Israel and the church. Zion as a mother for the people of God, according to Mounce, is a common theme in Jewish writings. Paul himself wrote in Galatians 4:26, "But the Jerusalem above is free, and she is our mother," in reference to the identity of the true people of God, children of Abraham by nature of their faith. So, as the woman symbolized Israel, the same woman comes to symbolize the church. Mounce writes, "The people of God are one throughout all redemptive history. The early church did not view itself as discontinuous with faithful Israel."[7]

In verse 2, we read that the woman was pregnant with a child. The child here can be both the Messiah, and by extension, those who follow him. The word used for "birth" a child is not used elsewhere in the New Testament for childbirth, but as an expression of physical distress. A double meaning is present in this verse of the birth of the Messiah and the Messianic community, and the messianic woes of the people of God throughout history as they desire to "give birth" to the Messianic age.[8] A close parallel

6. Osborne, *Revelation*, 454. Beale (Beale, *The Book of Revelation*, 624), also refers to the story of the birth of Apollo, the son of Zeus. His mother was Leto. She was attacked by the dragon, Python, because he knew that Apollo had been set apart to kill him. But she was carried to safety by Zeus by four winds to an island that was hidden by Poseidon. Four days after Apollo was born, he slew the dragon. Beale asserts that although John may have used this story or similar, or those from Ugarit, Babylon, Persia, Egypt, or Greece, it's more likely that he used the Old Testament as his primary filter. I would agree.

7. Mounce, *The Book of Revelation*, 236.

8. See Mounce, *The Book of Revelation*, 237, no.6; Osborne, *Revelation*, 458. Beale (Beale, *The Book of Revelation*, 629) notes that the birth pains represent the persecution

of this travail is found in Isaiah 26:17–19a, "Like a pregnant woman who writhes and cries out in her pangs when she is near to giving birth, so were we because of you, O Lord; we were pregnant, we writhed, but we have given birth to wind. We have accomplished no deliverance in the earth, and the inhabitants of the world have not fallen. Your dead shall live; their bodies shall rise." What Israel failed to do, in bringing the kingdom of God to the nations, the Messiah did; and through the Messiah, so also his followers. Jesus promised this victory in similar language in John 16:21–22, "When a woman is giving birth, she has sorrow because her hour has come, but when she has delivered the baby, she no longer remembers the anguish, for joy that a human being has been born into the world. So also you have sorrow now, but I will see you again, and your hearts will rejoice, and no one will take away your joy from you."

If there is indeed victory, then that victory is against whom? That question is answered in verse 3. This is the second apocalyptic sign to appear in heaven in this chapter—the seven-headed dragon with the ten horns and the seven crowns. The identity of the dragon is Satan or the Devil, as we know from 12:9. The dragon has some authority, authority associated with the reign of the empires of the earth. But his authority is nothing compared to the authority of Christ with many crowns. His seven heads and ten horns emphasize completeness, but this is a completeness of oppressive power and its world-wide effect.[9] This is a complete dominion of evil opposed to the people of God. The Greek word, *drakon*, was a serpent or sea monster usually connected with demonic powers in the ancient world. For example, there is a Sumerian myth from the 24th century B.C. where a seven-headed dragon was destroyed. In Canaan, the enemy of Baal is a serpent.[10]

John only needs to look to the Old Testament, however, for ample evidences of the dragon's representation of the evil enemies of God. Isaiah 27:1 says, "In that day, the Lord with his hard and great and strong sword will punish Leviathan the twisting serpent, and he will slay the dragon that is in the sea." Psalm 74:12–14 as well says, "Yet God my King is from of old, working salvation in the midst of the earth. You divided the sea by your might; you broke the heads of the sea monsters on the waters. You crushed the heads of Leviathan; you gave him as food for the creatures of the wilderness." In Ezekiel 29:3 Pharaoh is called, "the great dragon" (see also 32:2–3).

---

of the covenant community and the messianic line during Old Testament times and during the intertestamental period (see Matthew 8:6, 29; 14:24; Mark 6:48; Luke 8:28; 2 Peter 2:8).

9. Beale, *The Book of Revelation*, 634. See Daniel 7:7, 24 for a reference to a beast with ten horns and who came out of the sea.

10. Osborne, *Revelation*, 458.

And Babylon as well was often referred to as dragon. Jeremiah 51:34 says, "Nebuchadnezzar the king of Babylon has devoured me; he has crushed me; he has made me an empty vessel; he has swallowed me like a monster; he has filled his stomach with my delicacies; he has rinsed me out." Readers would have known that the dragon was the biggest enemy of God, representing traditional enemies like Egypt and Babylon, and now Rome and other empires opposed to God and his people.

The tail of the dragon swept a third of the stars from the sky and flung them to the earth. There are several possibilities as to the identity of the stars. Are they angelic forces that joined the dragon in his fight against God's people and God's plans? Or are the stars a reference to a judgment that he inflicts upon the earth? Does he have the authority for such a judgment, unless it is a judgment given (divine passive) by God? Or, as with Beale, referring to Daniel 8:10, are the stars thrown to the earth a reference to persecution against God's people? Israel's saints were often portrayed as stars or angels in Daniel (see 10:20–21; 12:1, 3).[11] But we could also say that stars symbolize angels as in Revelation 1:16, 20, and the angels represented the early churches. Osborne notes that *surei* is a strong word that pictures a dragging away of an individual or a fish (see John 21:8; Acts 8:3), always with a negative result. This seems to lead to the conclusion that the dragging here is a suffering inflicted on the angels in heaven who were dragged away and enticed by the Devil.[12] I think this is a better way to read this passage. The third of the angels would mean a limited portion of the servants of heaven became tools of the Devil, the Great Dragon, and would wage war together against the saints. These angels are with the dragon in verse 8 warring against Michael and his angels.

The intention of the dragon is clear. He stood in front of the woman so that he might devour the child as soon as he was born. Again, we could refer to Jeremiah 51:34 where Nebuchadnezzar devoured Zion "like a dragon" or "serpent." Here is a close reference to Mary, and her giving birth to the Messiah in the face of danger (Herod). But we should not limit our understanding to only Mary. This is Mary, Eve, Israel, and the church, all wrapped up in this woman in Revelation opposed by the dragon. This is the chosen people of God who would be pursued by the dragon but would ultimately have the final victory, even in the face of suffering and death.

The male child that was born was the Messiah. We know this from the reference to Psalm 2:9, which reads, "You shall break them with a rod of iron and dash them in pieces like a potter's vessel." But what does it mean

11. Beale, *The Book Revelation*, 636.
12. Osborne, *Revelation*, 460–61.

that the child was snatched up to God and to his throne? Is this a reference to the holy family's flight to Egypt in Matthew 2 to escape the clutches of the wicked Herod the Great? Most likely, this is a reference to the resurrection. So that the child grew, ministered, died on the cross, and then was raised from the dead. Both Beale and Mounce correctly interpret this with this understanding. This is a snapshot of Christ's entire life—his birth, his kingship (the iron scepter), his resurrection, and his assent to the heavenly throne. We see similar views in John 3:13; 8:14; 13:3; 16:5, 28; Romans 1:3–4 and 1 Timothy 3:16. The evil designs of the Devil are foiled by the completion of Christ's messianic ministry, from his birth to his ascension.[13]

John then sees the woman fleeing into the desert for a period of 1,260 days, where she can be cared for. This harkens again back to Daniel. God will continue to strengthen his church, his people, after the resurrection and ascension of Jesus. They will be able to spiritually stand against the persecutions of the dragon, just as was emphasized in 11:2–3. In Hosea 2:14, God says of Israel, "Therefore, behold, I will allure her, and bring her into the wilderness, and speak tenderly to her." For a limited period of time (3 ½ years is the same as 1,260 days), God will spare his people from his wrath. They are sealed from the wrath of God (see chapter 7), but not from the wrath of the dragon as we see in 13:8.

The desert here may also be a reference to the wanderings of Israel in the desert for forty years, when God continued to sustain them and strengthen them. Beale points out several examples of Old Testament desert experiences when God cared for his people: Israel's flight from Egypt and safety in the wilderness can be seen in Exodus 16:32; Deuteronomy 2:7; 8:3, 15–16; 29:5—32:10; Joshua 24:7; Nehemiah 9:19, 21; Psalm 78:5, 15, 19; 136:15; and Hosea 13:5; Elijah's flight into the wilderness (1 Kings 17; 193–8); Moses' time in the wilderness in Exodus 2:15.[14] For John, the desert was not a place inhabited by evil spirits and unclean beasts, but a place of spiritual refuge.[15]

The vision shifts places. John had seen God's care of his people in verse 6, and in verse 7, the scene shifts to a war in heaven. When did this war take place? Was this at the time of the cross? Mounce believes this verse explains the cosmic prelude to the consummation, the intense hostility to be poured

---

13. Beale, *The Book of Revelation*, 639 and Mounce, *The Book of Revelation*, 239.

14. Beale, *The Book of Revelation*, 643.

15. So Mounce, *The Book of Revelation*, 239. Beale (Beale, *The Book of Revelation*, 647) also notes that some Judeans fled Jerusalem during the three and a half year persecution under Antiochus Epiphanes. Jews also fled to the wilderness during the three and a half year siege of Jerusalem by the Romans.

out on the church in the days of the final tribulation.[16] But that needs much more explaining. I think it is more reasonable to see this as an expulsion of Satan associated with Christ's victorious and vicarious sacrifice on the cross.[17] Satan had been in heaven before God in Job 1–2, and as the accuser in Zechariah 3. But in Christ Jesus, because of his death and resurrection, the whole Messianic ministry, there is now no longer any condemnation. Our Advocate is in Heaven, and the accuser is no longer. This event took place at the cross and the resurrection of Jesus, one packet, one set—his victory over the enemy of God's people. This will be completed at his second coming, but Satan's ability to accuse has been severely curtailed. Christ's work on the cross unleashes the impact of Michael's victory of the dragon. Notice, Jesus doesn't even fight against Satan. The angels are strong enough for that.

The dragon lost his place in heaven in his war against Michael and the angels, because of the cross. Jesus disarmed the powers and principalities by the cross, triumphing over them (see Colossians 2). In Daniel 2:35, we see that the Rock that struck the statue of gold, silver, bronze and metal, destroying it, became a great mountain. The rock is Christ. He has the victory. The church must be reminded that those who meet conflict or opposition on the earth can be assured of the victory already won by Jesus in heaven.[18] Satan was hurled to the earth, along with his fallen angels. It is clear who this dragon is from verse 9. He is the ancient serpent. He is the devil. He is Satan, the accuser. He is the deceiver who leads the whole world astray. He had a place of authority in heaven, it appears, but no longer. He now roams the earth, seeking whom he may devour.[19]

We get a further clue about what actually defeated the dragon from the chorus of praise in verses 10–12. He was hurled down because of the blood of the Lamb and the testimony of God's people. The authority is fully given to Christ because of his cross and the continued testimony (even unto death) of his followers. The accuser can no longer be in heaven as accuser, because of the blood of Christ. There is now no condemnation for those

16. Mounce, *The Book of Revelation*, 240.

17. Cf. Osborne (Osborne, *Revelation*, 469), who views this as the primordial fall of Satan, but there is a telescoping of time in chapters 11–12, and that all three "bindings" of Satan (in the primordial past, the death of Jesus, and at the second coming) are intertwined in chapter 12.

18. Ladd, *A Commentary on the Revelation of John*, 171.

19. 1 Peter 3:8. This is in opposition to the amillennial view that believes chapter 12 describes the binding of chapter 20 as the same event. But I think the casting out of heaven is a different event from the binding. The binding will take place at the end. It is clear from other passages of Scripture like 1 Peter 3:8 and the explained activity of the enemy of God's people, that the dragon has been cast out, not bound. He is still active on the earth, very active.

who are in Christ Jesus (see Romans 8:1, 33–7). A parallel to this is found in Jesus' words in John 12:31–33. He said, "Now is the judgment of this world; now will the ruler of this world be cast out. And I, when I am lifted up from the earth, will draw all people to myself. He said this to show by what kind of death he was going to die." Jesus interpreted his crucifixion as the final death-blow upon the head of the serpent, and the glorification of the Son of Man. This interprets the use of Psalm 2 from verse 4. Beale points out that the combination of God or "Lord" and "his Christ" is found only in Psalm 2:2. There is a high probability this Psalm provides the background for this chorus of praise,[20] and we understand his kingdom and victory won through his cross, a common theme in John's theology.

The faithful testimony of the followers of the Lamb was more important than even their own lives. The serpent may win a battle against our bodies, but he cannot win the battle for our souls. The Greek preposition *arxi*, can mean "until the time of death" as in 2:10. Suffering may include death, but does not necessarily mean that all the faithful of Christ will die. So, we should understand this as referring to all the saints who remain faithful to Jesus, not a limited group of martyrs. This suffering of the believers in 12:11 partially fulfills God's promise in 6:9. The saints can be confident that their suffering is part of God's greater plan and it brings us closer to the final consummation of Jesus' end-time coming and final victory over Satan and the beasts.[21]

Within this song of praise a warning is given to those who are still on the earth, because the dragon knows his time is short. The word *kairon*, important event or era, is used rather than *kronos*, chronological time, because his period of rule and authority is limited; limited by the sovereignty of God and limited by the majesty of the victory of Jesus. This "little time" is the same three and a half year period as in 11:2–3; 12:6, 14; and 13:5. The time of the dragon's activities against God's people is limited and he knows it.[22] Jesus already warned his followers in John 10:10, "The thief comes to steal, and kill, and destroy." It is the nature of the enemy of God's people to pour out his wrath on those who follow God, and others who dwell on the earth, because they are objects of God's love.[23]

When the dragon saw that he had been hurled down, he pursued/persecuted the woman. But the woman was given two wings of an eagle so that

20. Beale, *The Book of Revelation*, 658.

21. Beale, *The Book of Revelation*, 665–66; contra Johnson (Johnson, *Hebrews through Revelation*, 517), who views the group of martyrs as limited.

22. See Beale, *The Book of Revelation*, 667.

23. Osborne, *Revelation*, 479.

she might be protected for time, times, and half a time, or three and a half years. The people of God are sealed and protected from the pursuits of the dragon, but only for a limited time. The use of "time, times, and half a time" is a direct and purposeful reference to Daniel to remind the reader that John is seeing a vision that is a fulfillment of this prophesy. God had done this before. In Exodus 19:4, he says to Moses, "You yourselves have seen what I did to Egypt, and how I carried you on eagles' wings and brought you to myself."[24] And God promised his people in Isaiah 40:31, "But they who wait for the Lord shall renew their strength; they shall mount up with wings like eagles; they shall run and not be weary; they shall walk and not faint."

But the enemy would not stop the pursuit. He spews out water like a river from his mouth to overtake the woman, or God's people. What else comes from the mouth of the dragon, or the Devil, except for deception and lies? 1 Timothy 4:1 says, "Now the Spirit expressly says that in later times some will depart from the faith by devoting themselves to deceitful spirits and teachings of demons." 2 Timothy 2:26 also warns against needless quarrels and to warn those who are entrapped by them, "And that they may come to their senses and escape from the snare of the devil, after being captured by him to do his will." Beale notes that flood waters are symbols of persecution and deception in the Qumran. The Damascus Document (CD 1:14–15) pictures a time "when the man of mockery arose who by his preaching let flow over Israel the waters of falsehood and led them astray in the roadless desert."[25] Though John may have been familiar with the document, it is more likely he was calling up images of his contemporary apostles or remembering the words of the Lord who called the Devil the father of lies in John 8:44.

The earth opened up and swallowed the waters to protect the woman. Likewise, God protects the church from potential demise and deception by swallowing up the deceptive waters of the devil. There are two times in the Old Testament where the earth opened up and swallowed God's enemies. One is when the Red Sea collapsed upon the armies of Egypt and delivered the Israelites in Exodus 15, and the other when the earth opened up and swallowed up the sons of Korah and others who opposed the leadership of Moses and Aaron in Numbers 16:12–14. While not a one-to-one correspondence, there are some similarities, primarily that God spared his own from the attacks of the enemy, or those who opposed God; and that the natural world was called on to compete God's work.

---

24. See also Deuteronomy 1:31–33 and 32:10–12.
25. See Beale, *The Book of Revelation*, 673.

Finally, in verse 17, we see the offspring of the woman identified, beyond that of the clear reference to the Messiah earlier in the chapter. They are those who obey God's commandments and hold to the testimony of Jesus. These are the faithful in the church of Christ, those who face the persecutions and sufferings from the dragon and all his minions. Ladd makes the helpful point that this suffering (in verse 17) depicts the suffering of the saints from the perspective of the people on earth. The suffering of verses 13–16 is from the perspective of heaven.[26] While the dragon continues to make war against God's people, God will continue to limit his impact, and to spiritually protect his people.

The dragon standing on the shore of the sea in verse 18 reminded the reader that he is the ruler of the evil powers (the sea is traditionally thought of as the source of evil for Jewish 1st century thinkers), and he will continue to work against the purposes of the church. But even in their death, he will be thwarted and defeated.

## Conclusion

The enemy of God's people will continue to pursue God's people and try to disrupt their work and their faithful pilgrimage toward God. He will try to destroy families, create disunity in churches, cause division among those who love one another, and breed discontent into the lives of Jesus' followers. We are not ignorant of his schemes. He puts temptations before us and tries to lull us to complacency and apathy. The devil need not worry about an inactive church. In those instances, he has already won. But for those of us who care, we know that the Devil is a roaring lion, seeking whom he may devour. But God has given us the tools to counter him. We are not unaware of his strategies against us.

The Battle of Antietam in 1862 lasted for twelve hours and ranks as the bloodiest day of the American Civil War, with 10,000 Confederate (southern) casualties, and even more on the Union side. One historian writes, "At last the sun went down and the battle ended, smoke heavy in the air, the twilight quivering with the anguished cries of thousands of wounded men." Though militarily a draw, the mediocre Union General, George McClellan, was able to end the brilliant Robert E Lee's thrust into Maryland, forcing him to retire across the Potomac River. How as this possible? Two Union soldiers had found a copy of Lee's battle plans and had delivered them to McClellan before the conflict.[27]

26. Ladd, *A Commentary on the Revelation of John*, 167, 174.
27. Catton, *Hallowed Ground: A History of the Civil War*, 168.

In some respects, we are no match for our enemy, Satan, whose wiles we are to be wary of. But as with General McClellan, our enemy's plans have fallen into our hands. We know his usual strategies—to entice us with lies, lust, greed, and the like. With such knowledge, given us by God's word, and God's Spirit within, we too can resist the enemy's advances. And what is more, we know that he is a defeated foe because of the cross of Christ.

We, the church of Jesus today, must join the battle. We cannot expect to be protected in the war if we are content to watch from the sidelines. In this war, there are no innocent bystanders. Jesus said, "You are either with me, or against me." Bystanders are not protected by the armor of the Lord. We need to actively put his armor on and take the battle seriously. 1 Peter 1:13 says, "Preparing your minds for action." Be aware of the tactics of the enemy, but more importantly, get to know your Commander the most. We can only know what the Commander wants from us if we know him. The battle is indeed real, and it gets more intense as Revelation 13 reveals, but the King of Kings is coming.

# Revelation 13:1–18

### The Two Beasts Oppose the Servants of the Lamb

## Introduction

C.S. Lewis, in an allegorical story of his conversion, talks of a man who is looking for meaning. He pictures himself bound by the Spirit of the Age. He is offered food and calls it by its right name. The rationalists laugh at him and describe the food in crude and horrible terms. Lewis is too stunned to respond. Time goes by, and Reason Alone comes riding on horseback to rescue him. As they ride away, Reason turns and says to the Spirit of the Age, "You lie! You don't know the difference between what nature has meant for good and what nature has meant for garbage."[1]

Evil in this world has always taken the beautiful of God and made it into something that is worthy of the garbage heap. And it has always called what is beautiful and created by God, a piece of trash. The dragon and those who follow him will continue to attempt to deceive, and indeed, they will deceive many. They will come as the unholy trinity, the imposter of justice and power. Bu their end has already been broadcast in chapter 12. Chapter 13 is a further description of the conflict between the forces of the dragon and the people of God.

## Exposition

The forces of the dragon, the beast from the sea and the beast from the earth, are given power to make war against God's people and to conquer them. The irony is that in conquering the people of God physically, the people of God win the battle spiritually, just as was declared concerning the defeat of the dragon by the blood of the Lamb and the testimony of God's people. There are several instances of the divine passive (he was given) used in chapter

---

1. Zacharias, quoting C.S. Lewis, "Bound by the Spirit of the Age", Christianity Today.

13 to show that this action is only by the authority and will of God. In fact, Osborne says this is a key theme of the chapter, because everything that happens, only happens because God allows it to happen.[2]

As we saw at the end of chapter 12, with the dragon standing on the shore of the sea, so in the beginning of chapter 13, a beast is coming out of the sea. As in the case of the dragon, so in the case of the beast, the sea is the traditional source of evil. In the Greek, the word for sea is placed forward to emphasize this. It is also clear that the authority or identity of the beast from the sea has its source in the dragon. Similar to the dragon, this beast from the sea has ten horns, and seven heads, and crowns on his horns. This is a sign of authority, though limited, that is possessed by this beast. It could also mean that this beast acts on behalf, and in concert with, the dragon. Beale notes that the seven heads and ten horns express the completeness of power possessed by the beast from the sea. In John's day, the beast from the sea would have been identified with Rome, the contemporary possessor of earthly power and authority.[3]

The blasphemous names on the heads of the beast remind the reader that this beast is opposed to everything that is good and holy and that he is in opposition to the people of God and in opposition to the Lamb of God. While the dragon tries to usurp the authority of God, the first beast from the sea tries to usurp the authority of Christ, the Lamb. This is the Antichrist who stands against Christ.[4]

The description of the beast in verse 2 is an obvious reference to Daniel 7:4–6, which describes the four beasts that come out of the sea, one of which was a lion, one a bear, and one a leopard. The beast in John's vision is a corrupted conglomeration of those animals, a deformity of God's intended beauty in creation. The power of the beast comes from the dragon. The source of all evil authority is found in Satan. There is no mistaking the place/pit of evil, but this is a power that is allowed (divine passive). Though we can think of the beast of the sea as representative of Rome (as John's readers would have thought, and Rome was believed to have been Daniel's fourth beast), it is really representative of all earthly kingdoms from the past, the present Rome, from John's perspective, and even the kingdoms of the future.

---

2. Osborne, *Revelation*, 487. Aune (Aune, *Revelation 6–16*, 726) views chapter 13 as a perverse reflection of the investiture of the Lamb in chapter 5. Just as the Lamb received the sealed scroll from the One on the throne, and power and authority, so the beast receives power and authority from the dragon.

3. Beale, *The Book of Revelation*, 684. See also Mounce (Mounce, *The Book of Revelation*, 251), who identifies the beast with the Roman Empire, but sees its complete fulfillment still lying in the future, at the end of history.

4. See Osborne, *Revelation*, 490–91.

Osborne agrees. He notes that the beast does not represent an empire but will be a person who is an embodiment of every evil empire. The rest of the New Testament assumes the Antichrist to be a person (2 Thessalonians 2; 1–2 John), and since the dragon was an individual, it makes sense to assume that the Antichrist will be one as well.[5] Thus, the beast out of the sea is an individual, a creature of the future, but he represents all the kingdoms opposed to God.

The beast from the sea appears to recover from a serious setback. Whether this is a physical wound, or a metaphorical wound is up for question. What is clear is that this recovery causes the people of the earth to be amazed and follow the beast. "People of the earth" here is a technical term for those on the earth who do not follow the Lamb of God. There are two ways to interpret why the beast has the wound, not necessarily in contradiction. First, it can be understood that God is the unmentioned "source" of the beast's wound, because the Greek word for wound, *plege*, has been elsewhere used for God's plagues against humanity. Secondly, we also can understand the death and resurrection of Christ as providing the death stroke upon the beast, as a fulfillment of Isaiah 27 and Psalm 74:13 (see discussion on 12:17). Underlying these thoughts are Genesis 3:15. The wound looks fatal; and it was. But from John's perspective the beast continues his assault on God's people.[6]

The continued revival of the beast after an apparent defeat throughout history reminds the reader that he is a defeated foe, trying to convince a gullible world that he is indeed restored and ready to conquer God and God's people. But he has already been conquered, and any attempt to have power again is ultimately in God's hands. But as the Antichrist, this "resurrection" becomes a parody of Christ's death and resurrection.[7] See 2 Thessalonians 2:1–12 for Paul's treatment of this Antichrist.

Worship of the beast from the sea leads as well to the worship of the dragon. The phrase, "Who is like the beast?" is an evil plagiarism of the question/praise that was sung when the people of Israel left Egypt in Exodus 15. Miriam, Moses' sister, sung in 15:11, "Who is like you, O Lord, among the gods? Who is like you, majestic in holiness, awesome in glorious deeds,

---

5. Osborne, *Revelation*, 495.

6. See Beale's discussion, *The Book of Revelation*, 688.

7. Osborne, *Revelation*, 495. Mounce (Mounce, *The Book of Revelation*, 253) notes that some commentators point to the suicide of Nero and his rumored future return (*Nero Redividus*) from the Parthians as the background for this beast. But this seems too fantastical, and by the eighties and nineties this rumor had died down. Thomas (Thomas and Macchia, *Revelation*, 231) also makes the interesting observation that the same word for "slaughtered" used here was used for the Lamb in chapter 5. This indicates that the beast offers a salvation of sorts to those who follow him.

doing wonders?" The people of the earth have the audacity to imitate this verse of praise for the wicked beast of the sea. The same question is asked concerning God in Deuteronomy 3:24; Isaiah 40:18, 25; 44:7; 46:5; Psalm 35:10; 71:19; 86:8; 113:5; and Micah 7:18.[8]

Unlike God, who is praised for his majesty and holiness and glory, this beast is known for his proud and blasphemous words. His authority is limited by God; again, we see the typical forty-two months, or three and a half years. See also Daniel 7:6, 8, 11, 20, 25. Mounce writes, "The reign of the beast is by divine permission. He operates only within the limitations determined by God."[9]

Through the activities of this beast, we see that he opposes and blasphemes all that is holy. He sets his words against God himself, against God's temple (here the temple could be interpreted as the people of God, since the place of his dwelling is now among his people),[10] and against the saints who dwell in heaven as well as the heavenly host there. In Daniel 7:25, the fourth beast "shall speak words against the Most High, and shall wear out the saints of the Most High, and shall think to change the times and the law; and they shall be given into his hand for a time, times, and half a time." The parallels to Revelation 13:5–6 are too obvious here to ignore. Also, in Daniel 11:36 we read of the king who magnifies himself above every god and does what he pleases, "and he shall speak astonishing things against the God of gods." See also 2 Thessalonians 2:4 where the Antichrist "opposes and exalts himself against every so-called god or object of worship, so that he takes his seat in the temple of God, proclaiming himself to be God."

The beast "was given" power to make war against the saints and to conquer them. The divine passive should be noted. In Daniel 7:21, the horn wages war against the saints, just as the beast of the sea wages war against the saints in Revelation 13:7. He also was given authority to rule over the peoples of the earth—every tribe, people language, and nation. This is the opposite reaction of the representatives from those who praise the Lamb on his throne in Revelation 7. It should be noticed that the beast was given authority to conquer the saints. But this means conquer physically. The saints are sealed from the wrath of God, but not from the wrath of the beast. But with this defeat is ultimate victory as the saints stand firm until the end, as John will explain in the rest of the chapters of Revelation.

---

8. Beale, *The Book of Revelation*, 694.

9. Mounce, *The Book of Revelation*, 254.

10. See 21:3 where *skenen* and *skenountas* occur together, seeming to indicate that the dwelling place is the people of God, since God becomes their dwelling place, and a temple is no longer necessary.

All of these inhabitants of the earth—those from every tribe, people, language, and nation—will worship the beast. The only exceptions are those whose names are written in the book of life belonging to the Lamb. Osborne notes that the universality of this worship is emphasized. And while aorist verbs are most common in 13:5–7, John uses the future tense here to stress the futurity of this event.[11] In other words, this is not something that has happened on this kind of scale before in the history of the world. There will be those who are defeated physically by the beast. It is for that reason that John once again reminds the reader to stand firm and listen well.

It is a very profound and powerful concept that the Lamb was slain from the creation of the world. Before sin entered into the world, the Lamb was already considered slain. God's plan was already set in motion before Adam and Eve fell into sin. This understanding fits the Greek word order, as "from the foundations of the world" could refer to "slain" or to "written." Either way, the plan of God and the people of his elect were determined from before the foundations of the world.[12]

This book of life contains the names of those who belong to the Lamb. This book is mentioned again in 17:8; 20:12, 15; and 21:27. The book, a strong possibility the same book, is also referenced in Daniel 7:10 and 12:1–2. The book is the possession of the Lamb. It is his book. He is worthy to own and possess this book by virtue of his sacrifice and his authority.

After encouraging the readers to pay careful attention, John calls for patient endurance from the saints during the time of persecution and testing. For some, the opposition and war from the beast will mean captivity. For others, it will mean death. Has this taken place already? Has not this patient endurance been needed since the time of the first church who endured hardship at the hand of the puppets of the dragon? But there will be an intensity or activity even greater in the days to come against the people of God. At that time, the people of God must stay faithful.[13]

The second beast that John sees comes out of the earth. This seems to be again a blasphemous attempt to copy Christ. The beast has horns like a lamb, but he speaks like a dragon. His mouth betrays his true character.

11. Osborne, *Revelation*, 502.

12. Thomas (Thomas and Macchia, *Revelation*, 236) notes that the use of the word "slaughtered" again, or slain, shows the drastic contrast between the Lamb and the beast. The Lamb was slaughtered from before the foundations of the world. There is a similar reference found in John 17:24.

13. Mounce (Mounce, *The Book of Revelation*, 257), in contrast, believes the first phrase is calling the believer to accept what God has ordained, while the second warns against any attempt on the part of the church to defend itself by the use of force, Osborne (Osborne, *Revelation*, 509) more rightly sees both couplets as mandating passivity and dependence upon God in light of persecution, even unto death.

Daniel provides the background, most likely, for this beast as well. Just as the beast who came out of the sea, this beast from the earth is given power and authority, the authority of the dragon, again the source of all that is wicked and evil. This beast is most likely the false prophet of the Olivet discourse in Matthew 24:24. "For false christs and false prophets will arise and perform great signs and wonders, so as to lead astray, if possible, even the elect." Jesus earlier warned in Matthew 24:5, "For many will come in my name, saying 'I am the Christ,' and they will lead many astray." Even the two horns serve as a parody of the Lamb in 5:6. Possibly, two horns are used to mimic the two witnesses, the two lampstands, or the two olive trees. These two horns may also reflect the evil ruler of Daniel 8.[14]

The purpose of the beast from the earth is to force the inhabitants of the earth (the catch phrase again for those who do not worship the Lamb), to worship the beast from the sea. The marker of the beast from the sea is the recovery from the fatal head wound. This beast from the earth performs miracles like the miracles of Elisha, fire from heaven, and like Moses (Exodus 4:17, 30: 10:2; 11:10), and because of these miracles he is able to deceive the people of the earth. It is clear from verse 13 that power or miracles is not an automatic sign that God is involved, or that things are done by the power of Jesus. The Antichrist will be able to imitate miracles through the power given him from the dragon.[15]

The sole purpose of the power is to deceive the inhabitants of the earth. The people of God will not be deceived. The blasphemies that come from his mouth will be clear. It is only those who have not bent the knee to the Lamb of God who will be fooled by the beast. The deception is so thorough that the people of the earth will be led astray into false worship of an idol. This image (*eikona*) was set up to honor the beast. Daniel 8:25 provides background for this, "By his cunning he shall make deceit prosper under his hand, and in his own mind he shall become great. Without warning he shall destroy many. And he shall even rise up against the Prince of princes, and he shall be broken —but by no human hand."[16]

The penalty for non-conformity to the beast, in this case, is death. Any who do not worship the image of the beast would be killed. How different this is from the rule of the Lamb! The followers of the Lamb willingly give

14. Beale, *The Book of Revelation*, 707 and Thomas and Macchia, *Revelation*, 238, though Mounce (Mounce, *The Book of Revelation*, 259) doesn't think so. Aune (Aune, Revelation 6–16, 755) notes that the beast is referred to as *therion* only here in Revelation. Elsewhere, the personal pronoun is used (it or he) or the title "false prophet."

15. See Matthew 24:24, 2 Thessalonians 2:9, and 2 Peter 2:1–3.

16. Mounce (Mounce, *The Book of Revelation*, 260) notes that according to *Ascension of Isaiah* 4:11, the antichrist is to set up his image in every city.

their lives up in service to him, being faithful even unto death. The followers of the beast are killed if they don't worship him. A parallel again may be found in Daniel 3. Nebuchadnezzar ordered the execution of any who did not bow before the image of his glory. This kind of prophesy of persecution and forced worship makes sense in light of the situation in Ephesus at the time. Domitian was requiring worship of his image and his person, and those who did not were persecuted, some even put to death.

The power of the statue would not have sounded that uncommon or unusual for John's readers. Ventriloquism and other magic tricks involving statues that spoke were common in the first century in the Roman world and in oriental cults (see Acts 13:6–8).[17] Aune also notes that special effects equipment was used to produce speaking and moving statues as well as simulated thunder and lightning in the imperial cult.[18] I do not think, however, that tricks will be needed in the last days. Satan has power to deceive with power beyond the natural, and not just through the use of material devices. This is the world between the worlds that western people forget exists because everything is sought to be explained through natural causes.

Whereas the followers of God are marked, or set apart, from the wrath of God, this does not set them apart from the wrath of the beast (a point reiterated several times). In verse 16, the followers of the beast receive a mark on their forehead or hand, another blasphemous replica of that which is done by God for us. There is no distinction in the obtaining of the mark. It is forced upon the rich and the poor, the small and great, and the free and slave. This mark will be visible just as the emperor's seal on business contracts and the impression of the Roman ruler's head on coins was visible, the emperor's stamp of approval of those who choose to worship him, or the beast's stamp of approval on those who worship him.[19]

17. Mounce, *The Book of Revelation*, 261.

18. Aune, *Revelation 6–16*, 764.

19. Beale, *The Book of Revelation*, 715. It is interesting, however, that Beale, after providing this important background, then goes on to state that just as the seal of God on the saints is invisible and thus metaphorical, so is this mark or seal. But Mounce (Mounce, *The Book of Revelation*, 262), believes the mark will be visible and will symbolize, "unqualified allegiance to the demands of the imperial cult." Beale (Beale, *The Book of Revelation*, 717) also notes an interesting parallel with 3 Macc. 2:28–32, another example of a visible sign. The evil Greek king decreed that entrance to their (the Jews) own temple was to be refused to all who would not sacrifice, and all Jews were to be registered among the common people, that those who were not registered were to be forcibly seized and put to death, and that those who were thus registered were to be marked on their persons by the ivy-leaf symbol of Dionysius and set apart with these limited rights.

The purpose of the mark is economic oppression. No one could buy or sell or take part in any market system of the earth without the mark. The mark is the name of the beast, meaning that those who receive the mark are identified as belonging to him. This was more than the Roman government ever did. They persecuted Christians, but did not use economic sanctions against them.[20] This tells us that this kind of oppression and wickedness, in its ultimate form, is something that has yet to be seen on the earth.

Chapter 13 ends with the interesting call for wisdom from the reader to understand that this beast, the antichrist, and the beast from the sea as well as the dragon, does not measure up to the perfection of the lamb. While Mounce believes that John is referring to a historical person,[21] I am not convinced. I think the sense of incompleteness is more telling. Beale writes, "The triple repetition of sixes connotes the intensification of the incompleteness and failure that is summed up in the beast more than anywhere else among fallen humanity."[22] It is as if John is saying that there is no way in the world, in the universe, and in heaven, that the beast can measure up to the perfections of Christ. This is important for the reader to remember and continue to stand firm.

## Conclusion

It is clear that this conflict is real. The enemies of God, empowered by the dragon, will come against God's people. What are believers supposed to do in the light of such evil? Firstly, from 2 Thessalonians 2:12–17, we must choose to believe. We must choose to believe in God and everything that God has said to us in his word. Only then will we not be deceived by the evil that is everywhere around us, and that will intensify until the beast and the false prophet are unleashed on the earth. We must not be deceived by any form of evil until then or in the midst of that time.

John calls for patient endurance on the part of the saints. Those whose names are not written in the book of life do not bend their knees to Christ. And they sometimes actively seek to fight against the church in the world. But the church's responsibility is not to fight back with the sword. This is not what God has asked us to do. We should seek justice in light of the law, but not pick up the sword to defend ourselves. We need patience and steadfast endurance in the midst of persecution and a steadfast faith that never waivers.

20. See Johnson, *Hebrews through Revelation*, 532–33.
21. Mounce, *The Book of Revelation*, 264.
22. Beale, *The Book of Revelation*, 722.

Lastly, we must be people of praise and thanksgiving, as 2 Thessalonians 2:14–15 admonishes us. We have been saved through the sanctifying work of the Spirit, and by our belief in the truth. So we must stand fast, hold on to the truth, and look to Jesus who strengthens us and encourages us. Just as the Lamb was slain to take away the sins of the world, his saints will be asked to testify, even to the point of death, to defy the sin of the world.

# Revelation 14:1–20

## The Lamb, The Angels, and the Harvest

### Introduction

**M**Y WIFE ENJOYS GARDENING. It is one of the things she does for relaxation. That is hard for me to understand. I look at a garden, and I see work—weeds to pull, soil to cultivate, plants to water, especially in the dry season in Indonesia where it could go several months without raining. But Lora loves it. She loves pulling the weeds. She loves the colors of the flowers and watching the little seedlings grow to become large, thriving plants. My problem is that sometimes I don't know the difference between weeds and plants. This becomes a real problem if I try to help Lora, by weeding in the garden. To her dismay, in the past, there have been several times when she has found a plant inadvertently mistaken for a weed by her husband.

When we talk about the end of the earth, or the great harvest of humanity, we can be confident that God will know the difference between the weeds and the wheat, between those ungodly and the godly. Those who belong to him are marked with a seal. Those who belong to the beast are marked with the mark of the beast. While it may be difficult sometimes for us to distinguish between the two, it is not difficult for God.

### Exposition

Chapter 14 is a continuation of the symbols and apocalyptic images describing the victory of the saints and the defeat of the wicked kingdoms of the earth and of all that follow the dragon, the beast from the sea, and the beast from the earth. The harvesting is a fulfillment of the promise of the wine of God's wrath on the earth (see Isaiah). The wrath of God will be poured out in power and in final judgment on "Babylon," the symbol of all the wicked nations that have opposed God. Ladd asserts that just before the outpouring of the wrath of God, John is again assured that the consummation of all things is in God's hands. The wicked, those who worship the beast, will be judged, and the saints will be victorious, standing with the Lamb.[1]

In verse 1, we see the Lamb, standing with the 144,000 who had his name and his Father's name written on their foreheads. Mounce writes, "John moves quickly beyond the storm about to break to the bright morning of eternity with the Lamb and his followers standing on the heavenly Zion with the anthem of redemption everywhere resounding like the roar of a mighty waterfall and the echo of thunder."[2] The number, 144,000, is the same number as in chapter 7, and as in that chapter, this 144,000 symbolizes the faithful who have followed the Lamb. In Revelation 22:4 we see that those with the mark of the Lamb are the entire community of the redeemed throughout history. As opposed to the wicked, who have the mark of the beast written on their foreheads (or hands), these faithful have the name of the Lamb and the name of the Father written on their foreheads.[3]

Where is Mount Zion? Does this refer to a literal Jerusalem as in the dispensationalist view, or the New Jerusalem as we see in Revelation 22? There is probably a now and not yet sense depicted here. This is the heavenly city, the dwelling place of God that will be established on the new earth with the Lamb in the center. If true, this enforces the interpretation of the 144,000 as the complete community of the redeemed, not only those who were in alive at the time of Christ's return. It is probably best, in terms of the placement of Mount Zion, to take Thomas' view that whether this is on earth or in heaven is not as important, as it seems that heaven and earth are coming together. What is important is that the Lamb's location on Mount Zion indicates the beginning of the eschatological promises being fulfilled.[4]

1. Ladd, *A Commentary on the Revelation of John*,188. Beale (Beale, *The Book of Revelation*, 731) believes it is best to view 14:1–2 and 15:2–4 as another prophetic narrative of the actual, future final judgment and reward, rather than a transition or parenthesis in the midst of a chronological presentation. I agree. It's important to remember that we cannot interpret Revelation through a strict chronological framework.

2. Mounce, *The Book of Revelation*, 266.

3. There are a few differing opinions concerning the identity of the 144,000. There are those, as in the explanation above, who view them as the redeemed of Christ. See Mounce (Mounce, *The Book of Revelation* 268), who believes that the same number is used as in chapter 7 to show that not one of them has been lost. Aune (Aune, Revelation 6–16, 804) thinks the 144,000 are probably the group of believers that survive until the end, the remnant of the faithful still alive when the Lamb stands on Mount Zion. Thomas (Thomas and Macchia, *Revelation*, 251) also views them as those who have overcome and stand with the Lamb, ready to fight. Osborne (Osborne, *Revelation*, 525) puts the two ideas together. Primarily, posits Osborne, the 144,000 are the victorious saints who have not worshiped the beast but have been faithful to Christ, and, secondarily, the people of God throughout the ages.

4. Thomas and Macchia, *Revelation*, 250.

Ladd as well, contends that Mount Zion stands for the eschatological victory which is the new Jerusalem that will come down from heaven (21:2). Men will not leave the earth to go to heaven at that time (as in the view of the pre-judgment rapture), but heaven will come down to earth.[5]

For Old Testament background, John may have had in mind Psalm 2:6, "I have set my King on Zion, my holy hill." This, combined with the reference to Psalm 2:9 in Revelation 12:5, seems to point to a time of fulfillment of the messianic promises. Hebrews 12:22 picks this them up, "But you have come to Mount Zion, and to the city of the living God, the heavenly Jerusalem, and to innumerable angels in festal gathering,"[6] Jesus victoriously stands as a warrior with the redeemed. Here is another window view to the end, as we see the final victory before the final judgment, described via the image of the harvest.

John hears a sound from heaven like the voice of many waters. This is similar to the voice that came from Jesus in 1:15, except that these are the voices of angels, reflecting the powerful voice of their Creator and Lord. John hears the same voice again in 19:6, before the coming of the Lamb. The same sound was heard by Ezekiel in Ezekiel 1:24, "And when they went, I heard the sound of many waters, like the sound of the Almighty, a sound of tumult like the sound of an army. When they stood still, they let down their wings." The voice is also compared to many harpists playing their harps. They are singing a new song.

What is the new song? It is the song of the redeemed. It is the song of those who have been redeemed from the earth, of the 144,000 who have the name of the Lamb and of their God on their foreheads. The "they" indicates that these many voices are of the angels in heaven, most likely besides the four living creatures and the twenty-four elders. This new song is an expression of praise for God's victory over the enemy, which sometimes included thanksgiving for God's work in creation (see Psalm 33:3; 40:3; 96:1; 144:9; 149:1; and Isaiah 42:10).[7]

We see a further description of the 144,000 in verses 4–5. The phrase, "Have not defiled themselves with women," stresses the commitment of these faithful ones. Unlike the nation of Israel, who fled to the gods and women of the nations around them, these people of God who have the name of the

---

5. Ladd, *A Commentary on the Revelation of John*, 189–90.

6. Beale (Beale, *The Book of Revelation*, 731–32) notes that the phrase "Mount Zion" is used nineteen times in the Old Testament, nine of which allude to a remnant being saved or to God's sovereign rule, and sometimes both (see 2 Kings 19:31; Isaiah 4:2–3; 10:12, 20; 37:30–32; Joel 2:32; Obadiah 17, 21; Micah 4:5–8; Psalm 48:2, 10–11; 74:2, 7).

7. Beale, *The Book of Revelation*, 736 and Thomas and Macchia, *Revelation*, 253.

Lamb on their foreheads, have not defiled themselves. They are virgins because they belong to Christ, not literal virgins, in that they are celibate. They
belong to Jesus and have not given themselves over to other gods before the
great wedding of the Lamb, the marriage supper in chapter 19.[8]

These saints follow the Lamb wherever he goes, not only reflecting
the same character and godliness, but also being willing to suffer even to
the point of death, so as not to worship the dragon, but to be faithful to
the Lamb. Aune correctly notes that this is a discipleship that may result in
death.[9] As part of this faithfulness, they are also called the first-fruits. They
belong to the Lamb and to God. The dative used here could be either a dative of location or a dative of identity. They are the first-fruits "that belong"
to God and to the Lamb. Jeremiah 2:3 says, "Israel was holy to the Lord, the
firstfruits of his harvest;" These first-fruits in Revelation 14:4 are the totality
of believers throughout the ages.[10]

The 144,000 are also described as saints honest before God. They will
not fall to the great deceiver. They are blameless in that they have been
redeemed. They are not blameless in order to be redeemed, but blameless
because they are redeemed. Zeph.3:13 prophesies, "Those who are left in Israel; they shall do no injustice and speak no lies, nor shall there be found in
their mouth a deceitful tongue. For they shall graze and lie down, and none
shall make them afraid." Also Isaiah 63:8, in the context of God's judgment
(Isaiah 63:1–6), says, "For he said, 'Surely they are my people, children who
will not deal falsely. And he became their Savior. Like the Lamb in Isaiah
53:9, in whose mouth was found no deceit, these followers of the Lamb will
be people of integrity, ethically pure.[11]

Following the song of the redeemed, John sees another angel flying
in midair and proclaiming the eternal gospel. Is this message a message of

---

8. See Beale (Beale, *The Book of Revelation*, 739) and Mounce (Mounce, *The Book
of Revelation*, 270) who believe the Greek word for Virgins (*parthenoi*) refers to all true
saints who have not compromised with the world, because they have remained loyal
as the faithful betrothed bride of Christ. See also 2 Kings 19:21; Isaiah 37:22; Jeremiah
14:17; 18:13; 31:4, 13, 21; Lamentations 1:15; 2:13; and Amos 5:2, where the term "virgin" is applied to the nation of Israel in the Old Testament. By extension, then, as the
new people of God, the term now applies to the church, the faithful followers of Jesus.
Also, note that the term "virgin" in verse 4 is in the masculine form, perhaps indicating
that they have not given themselves to the great prostitute of Revelation 17.

9. Aune, *Revelation 6–16*, 813.

10. See Ladd, *A Commentary on the Revelation of John*, 192. Aune (Aune, *Revelation 6–16*, 818) believes "first-fruits" should be understood as people devoted to the
Lord as servants. See also James 1:18, where the same word is used to describe saints as
the beginning of the new creation. See Beale, *The Book of Revelation*, 742.

11. See Osborne, *Revelation*, 531; contra Aune (Aune, *Revelation 6–16*, 822), who
sees this as ritual purity.

warning or a message of repentance? This is before the seven bowls of wrath are poured out, but we may not want to be so time specific or chronological concerning the timing of the declaration of this message. This gospel is called "the eternal gospel," the gospel message from the beginning of time. God is the Lord of all the earth. He must be feared, glorified, and worshiped. The eternal gospel was proclaimed to all those who live on the earth—every nation, tribe, and language. According to Mounce, and I agree, this is not the gospel of God's redeeming grace in Christ, but a summons to fear, honor, and worship the Creator, a final appeal to all men to recognize the one true God.[12] This is good news to those who have suffered under persecution and are finally seeing justice fulfilled, but it is not good news to those who have worshipped the beast. It is a word of doom and judgment.[13] What supports this position is the position of the angel flying overhead, the same position as the eagle in 8:13, a message delivered as a word of judgment.

The command of the gospel in verse 7 is to fear God, give him glory, and worship him. Why? Because the judgment is coming, his judgment. God is right to judge because he is the Creator. He is the One who made the earth, the sea, and the springs of water. He is just to bring judgment upon them. The angel is not telling the people of the earth to repent in order to avoid judgment, but is giving a decree that, at last, they acknowledge, or see, the mighty hand of the Creator.[14]

John sees a second angel in verse 8. This angel announces the fall of Babylon, which we see again in Revelation 18. Babylon is the representative name for the nations of the world who oppose God. This is not literal Babylon, but a conglomeration of all the wicked systems against God. Babylon is portrayed as a female, a prostitute who led the nations astray in sexual immorality. Those led astray are not those who are called virgins and stayed committed to the Lamb. Mounce writes that Babylon "is a symbol for the spirit of godlessness which in every age lures men away from the worship of the Creator."[15] For John, Babylon was Rome. For the faithful in other parts of the world today, Babylon may be the political power that oppresses them. What

---

12. Mounce, *The Book of Revelation*, 273.

13. Ladd, *A Commentary on the Revelation of* John, 193. Beale (Beale, *The Book of Revelation*, 748) also sees this as the judicial side of the gospel, rather than an offer of grace. See Isaiah 40:9, 52:7, and 61:1. Cf. Aune, *Revelation 6–16*, 825; Osborne, *Revelation*, 535; and Johnson, *Hebrews through Revelation*, 541, for different opinions. They see the call as a call for repentance. Johnson writes, "The announcement of divine judgment is never separated from the proclamation of God's mercy." It may be best to leave the decision in God's hands as to whether he is offering the call as a call of repentance or a call of judgment. We may not know until that time comes.

14. Beale, *The Book of Revelation*, 753.

15. Mounce, *The Book of Revelation*, 274.

is sure is that the source of the wickedness of Babylon and all her daughters is the dragon who makes war against the saints.

A third angel follows the first two in verse 9. He gives out a warning against those who join the beast and worship him. If anyone unites with the beast, he will be made to drink the wine of God's fury. The word for fury, *thumou*, is a very passionate word for anger that can mean the "white hot" anger of God. Because the wicked drink from the cup of Babylon and her sexual immorality, they will be required to drink from the cup of God's wrath. Revelation 16:19 says, "God remembered Babylon the great, to make her drain the cup of the wine of the fury of his wrath." This wine is poured full strength, undiluted. In the Jewish world, people would only drink undiluted wine if they wanted to get drunk. That is the idea here.[16]

This fall of Babylon was prophesied in Isaiah 21:9, "And behold, here comes riders, horsemen in pairs! And he answered, 'Fallen, fallen is Babylon; and all the carved images of her gods he has shattered to the ground.'" Babylon and those who love her will be tormented in the presence of the holy angels and of the Lamb. They will be tormented with the realization that they defied the Lamb, and continually will defy the Lamb. They will be forced to confess his rightness and justice as they are suffering before him because of their rejection. For other verses related to the wine of God's wrath see Psalm 60:3; 75:8; Isaiah 51:17, 21–23; 63:6; Jeremiah 25:15–18; 51, and Obadiah 16.

What is clear from verse 11 is that the torment and suffering of the ungodly is an eternal suffering. There is no annihilation. Those who reject the Lamb and follow the beast will be forever tormented. Beale notes that the word for torment, *basanismou*, is used nowhere else in Revelation or in Biblical literature for the idea of annihilation. Without exception, Revelation uses it of conscious suffering on the part of the people (9:5; 11:10; 12:2; 18:7, 10, 15; 20:10). See also Matthew 4:24; 8:6, 29; 18:34; Mark 5:7; 6:48; Luke 8:28; 16:23; 2 Peter 2:8.[17] We could also parallel this suffering with the never-ending praise to God offered by the four living creatures in 4:8, an unforgettable contrast of unceasing worship and unceasing torment.[18] What

16. Osborne, *Revelation*, 540. Mounce (Mounce, *The Book of Revelation*, 275), notes that the wine is poured out mixed and unmixed. It is mixed (prepared) so as to increase its strength, and it is unmixed (not diluted with water) so as to be un-tempered by God's mercy and grace. This is the "response of a righteous God to man's adamant refusal to accept his love."

17. Beale, *The Book of Revelation*, 762.

18. Aune, *Revelation 6–16*, 836. Mounce (Mounce, *The Book of Revelation*, 277) comments that a vivid description of torment will not be put aside by "euphemistic redefinition." Ravi Zacharias refers to Ajith Fernando, in his book, *A Universal Homecoming*, where he "reminds us that sixty-four times the same word, eternal, is used to

is clear is that we either belong to the Lamb or to the beast. There is no third option. We cannot belong to ourselves.

Smoke is an image used in the Bible for terrible suffering because of the wrath of God. Isaiah 34:10 says of the day of the LORD's vengeance and the blazing pitch and sulfur, "Night and day it shall not be quenched; its smoke shall go up forever. From generation to generation it shall lie waste; none shall pass through it forever and ever." (speaking of Edom). We see the smoke also in Revelation 18:18 and 19:3. For those who remain faithful to Jesus, the reality of the coming judgment calls for patient endurance (see 13:10; 13:18).

In vivid contrast to those who drink the fury of God's wrath are those who die in the Lord because of the hope they have. They are promised the rest, the Sabbath rest for the people of God (Hebrews 4:9–11). The "from now on" refers to those who after the resurrection of the Lord, die in the Lord, and refuse to lose faith. This does not refer to a chronologically specific time in the future. Their deeds will follow them does not mean that they have the victory because of some legalistic work that merits eternal joy, but that their deeds are a manifestation of their devotion to Christ.[19]

D.L. Moody, the famous evangelist of the nineteenth century, said, "Someday, you will read in the papers that D.L. Moody, of East Northfield, is dead. Don't you believe a word of it! At that moment, I shall be more alive than I am now. I shall have gone up higher, that is all-out of this old clay tenement into a house that is immortal; a body that death cannot touch, that sin cannot taint, a body fashioned like unto his glorious body. I was born of the flesh in 1837. I was born of the Spirit in 1856. That which is born of the flesh may die. That which is born of the Spirit will live forever."[20]

John sees another figure in verse 14. This figure has the same traits as Jesus in chapter 1. He is seated on a cloud like the Son of Man in Daniel 7. And he has a golden crown on his head. Because of this, there are several interpreters who believe this is Jesus. Beale bases this on the parallels in Matthew 24:30; Mark 13:26; and Luke 21:27. In the Old Testament, God alone comes

---

remind us of heaven's eternality. He goes on, "Would it not be logical to conclude that in the seven occurrences of 'eternal' to describe the antithesis of these blessings (eternal punishment), the idea is that of duration without end?" (see "The Eternality of Hell", Christianity Today.)

19. Mounce, *The Book of Revelation*, 278. See Beale, *The Book of Revelation*, 768. This is a faith that endures in trouble and hardship, which is its normal meaning in the New Testament.

20. Quoted in Rick Curtis, *Early Discovery: Growing in the Community of Believers*, 124–125.

in heaven or to earth in a cloud, like we see in Daniel 7:13.[21] If this is Jesus, it could be that Jesus is coming as the harvester of his people.

As the Harvester, he is instructed by the angel (really by God through the angel. No way is an angel going to tell Jesus what to do, if indeed the figure in verse 14 is Jesus, and not an angel[22]) to swing his sickle and harvest the grain. Joel 3:13 likewise says, "Put in the sickle, for the harvest is ripe. Go in, tread, for the winepress is full. The vats overflow, for their evil is great." In Mark 4:29, Jesus compares the kingdom of God to a man who is harvesting his grain. "But when the grain is ripe, at once he puts in the sickle, because the harvest has come." Jeremiah 51:33, with a more negative twist to the harvest, reads, "The daughter of Babylon is like a threshing floor at the time when it is trodden; yet a little while and the time of her harvest will come."

Do we have here a harvest of the unrighteous and wicked, or a harvest of the righteous? If we understand the harvest of the grapes as negative (the fury of God's wrath), it could be that the harvest of the grain is a positive harvest, the harvest of the redeemed.[23] When Jesus spoke to the disciples of the harvest in Matthew 9:36; Luke 10:2; John 4:35–38, he meant those who had not yet heard the gospel but were ready to respond. Jesus' parables of the wheat and the weeds and the good fish and the bad fish (see Matthew 13:24–30, 47–50) seem to indicate that there will be a harvest of the good (the good wheat and the good fish); and a harvest of the wicked (the weeds and the rotten fish). Though, in those parables, and in Jesus' explanation (see 13:36–43), it is clear that the harvesters are the angels. The Son of Man is the sower. Could it be then, that this harvest in chapter 14 is speaking of the final harvest of the righteous when Jesus comes back in Revelation 19? It may be a case of both, not either/or. We cannot pin John down in a tight understanding of who is harvesting when, given the nature of apocalyptic language.[24]

Two more angels appear in verses 17 and 18. The angel that come from the temple in heaven is to harvest the clusters of grapes from the earth's vine. Just as the grain was ripe for harvest (the harvest of the righteous), so the grapes are ripe for harvest (the harvest of the wicked). Two different words

21. Beale, *The Book of Revelation*, 771; see also Mounce, *The Book of Revelation*, 279; Thomas and Macchia, *Revelation*, 263; Ladd, *A Commentary on the Revelation of John*, 199; Osborne, *Revelation*, 550.

22. Beale, *The Book of Revelation*, 772, defends his view that this is Christ in that he is acting in submission to the word of command of the Father, not the angel. The angel only delivers the message of God.

23. See Ladd, *A Commentary on the Revelation of John*, 200; Osborne, *Revelation*, 556.

24. Bauckham, *New Testament Theology*, 96, views this as two reapings, the first reaping of the first-fruits of the harvest of all those who believe among the nations., the second, a harvest of judgment.

are used for "ripe" for the grain and the grape, possibly indicating two types of harvest. The word for ripe could be translated "overripe," or "withered." In other words, the harvest is over. Workers are no longer needed in the harvest because the harvest time is over, and the final reaping must be accomplished by these harvesting angels. We had a mulberry bush in our back yard in the U.S. For many years, it seemed that we went on vacation just as the mulberries were ready to be picked. When we would get back, either the birds had eaten them all, or they were overripe and no longer good for eating. That is how it will be with the earth when the final time for judgment has come.

In verse 19, the angel swings his sickle on the earth, as instructed by the other angel, and gathers the grapes into the winepress, a reference to the judgment of God, as the grapes are thrown into the winepress of the fury of God's wrath. As discussed previously, the wine of the wrath of God is a common theme in the Old Testament, as a symbol of the blood of the condemned. The judgment of God's wrath was so complete, that the blood flowed as high as the horse's bridle (note the blood on the robe of the Rider on the white horse in chapter 19). Zechariah 14:3 says, "Then the Lord will go out and fight against those nations, as when he fights on a day of battle."

Why was the winepress outside of the city? The city was the city of God, and those outside are the unrighteous whose blood flowed in judgment. Revelation 22:14–15 says, "Blessed are those who wash their robes, so that they may have the right to the tree of life and that they may enter the city by the gates. Outside are the dogs and sorcerers and the sexually immoral and murderers and idolaters, everyone who loves and practices falsehood," in other words, all those who bowed to the beast. The LORD is asked in Isaiah 63:2, "Why is your apparel red, and your garments like his who treads in the winepress? He answers in 63:3, "I have trodden the winepress alone, and from the peoples no one was with me; I trod them in my anger and trampled them in my watch; their lifeblood spattered on my garments, and stained all my apparel."

The blood flowed for a distance of 1,600 stadia. The length of Palestine (from Tyre to the border of Egypt) was 1,665 stadia. 40 is also the number of judgment at the time and this is 40 times 40, or 4 times 1000.[25] The length of Palestine indicates that the judgment be symbolically complete, on a world-wide scale.

---

25. Beale, *The Book of Revelation*, 782.

## Conclusion

A harvest is coming. It will not be like the case where the farmer who was too lazy to get out into his field and the harvest, or when we got home from our vacation and missed out on the fruit of the mulberry bush. This is a harvest called for from the throne of heaven, from God himself as he directs his holy angels to gather in the elect, and the wicked. What should be our response until then?

Jesus has commissioned his church to be harvesting now because the fields are white for harvest. The church must actively be engaged in Jesus' mission so that many will be spared the fury of God's wrath on the final harvest, when there is no more time to wait.

# Revelation 15:1—16:21

## The Seven Bowls of Wrath

## Introduction

WHEN DOES "TOO LATE" really mean too late? If I show up to a wedding reception in Makassar at 7:30pm when the invitation may say 7:00pm, I am not too late. In fact, the activities may not begin until 8:00pm. If I show up to class at 2:15pm, when I am supposed to start teaching at 2:00pm, I may be late, but I am not too late. But if the Queen of England issues an invitation to come to her birthday party, and I show up a day later, then I am too late. I will not be allowed into Buckingham Palace, because there is no longer a party.

As we know, there are various levels of lateness with various degrees of consequences. Some of the consequences may be minor, like a detention after school for a student who continuously shows up late for class, or a late payment penalty fee of a small amount of money because the house owner is late on his water bill. But other consequences are much more serious. Some people get fired from their job because they are consistently late. Some get thrown into debtor's prison, as in nineteenth century England, if they are late with the repayment of their loans.

As far as God is concerned, there is a "too late." And in Revelation 15–16 we encounter this "too late" when the temple doors are closed and the angel of the seventh bowl announces, "It is done." There is no longer any sacrifice for sin. There is no longer any opportunity for forgiveness. There are no longer any more chances offered to the ungodly. When the seven bowls of wrath are unleashed, it is certainly too late.

## Exposition

The last breath before the final storm continues in chapter 15. Beale views 15:1–4 as linked to 14:14–20.[1] We ought not be too precise with chronological issues here. The visions are intended "more to confront man with vivid portrayals of eschatological truth than to supply him with data for a precise chronology of the consummation."[2] We will consider, in this commentary, chapter 15 and chapter 16 as part of the same unit. The seven bowls of wrath are poured out and the final judgment will be complete. There is no interlude between the sixth and seventh bowl, like there was between the sixth and seventh seal, and the sixth and seventh trumpet. The time of repentance is over, and the bowls of wrath will come quickly and decisively. The response of the peoples of the earth will be discussed in Revelation 17–18. Johnson sees chapter 15 as preparatory and interpretive and chapter 16 as descriptive.[3] The reader is set up to understand the completeness of the final judgment of God.

In verse 1, we see that John views another sign in heaven, the seven angels with the seven plagues. With these plagues the wrath of God is completed; in other words, this is the final and complete judgment of God upon the wicked. The aorist passive of "completed" (*etlesthe*) is used, another divine passive to remind us that all is in God's hands. Though Beale does not believe that "last" must mean at the end of the age, thinking it could mean also any time between the first coming of Christ and the second, Osborne does not agree. He sees the word "wrath of God is complete" as important and as indicating this is the end of God's judgments.[4] Aune also notes that in the New Testament, wrath or the anger of God is primarily used in the eschatological sense of the final judgment of God (see Luke 3:7; Romans 1:18; 2:5, 8; 3:5; 5:9; Colossians 3:6; Ephesians 5:6). This wrath can only be escaped through Christ.[5]

John sees the saints who were victorious over the evil trinity (mentioned in verse 2 as "the beast, the image, and the number"). The saints

---

1. Beale, *The Book of Revelation*, 785.

2. Mounce, *The Book of Revelation*, 284.

3. Johnson, *Hebrews through Revelation*, 546.

4. Beale, *The Book of Revelation*, 787; Osborne, *Revelation*, 561. Also, Ladd, *A Commentary on the Revelation of John*, 203; Mounce, *The Book of Revelation*, 2844; and Johnson, *Hebrews through Revelation*, 545–46. All believe the seven last plagues are part of the last trumpet, and thus signal the end of all things.

5. Aune, Revelation 6–16, 870. Ladd, *A Commentary on the Revelation of John*, 204, notes that the plagues do not precisely complete the totality of God's wrath since the dragon and the false prophet have not yet been thrown into the lake of fire.

had harps in their hands, like the angels before singing praise before God. They join the throng of loud praises before the victorious God. The sea of glass mixed with fire is symbol of purity and judgment, and the glory and presence of God. Daniel saw a similar scene before the Ancient of Days in 7:10–11, "A stream of fire issued and came out from before him; a thousand thousands served him, and ten thousand times ten thousand stood before him; the court sat in judgment, and the books were opened. I looked then because of the sound of the great words that the horn was speaking. And as I looked, the beast was killed, and its body destroyed and given over to be burned with fire." Parallels like this cause Beale to say that in 15:2 the sea of glass is a reminder of the Red Sea during the time of the Exodus. The chaotic powers of the sea are calmed by the victory of Christ. And the saints are standing by the sea of glass to show that they themselves were involved in the great victory over the forces of evil.[6] It is fair to say that there is a combination of judgment, victory, glory, and purity in the sea of glass before the throne.

The saints before the throne sing the song of Moses and the song of the Lamb. The song of Moses is the song of redemption of Exodus 15:1–18 and Deuteronomy 31:30 (see also Deuteronomy 32). But this is also the song of the Lamb. There is a unifying theme of redemption, the atonement of the blood of the Lamb, deliverance, and God's victory over the enemies of God. The song of Moses was fulfilled in the song of the Lamb.[7] We see a sharp contrast between this song of deliverance sung by all the saints and the song of "worship" of the peoples of the nations who worship the beast.

The saints praise God for his great and marvelous deeds, as well as his justice and truth. God's justice and truth are parallel with his great and marvelous deeds, showing that God's sovereign acts are not demonstrations of raw power but moral expressions of his just character. He demonstrates his justice through the redemption given through Christ.[8] He is just in his judgments because he is the sole Creator of the universe, and all that he does is great. See also Hebrews 3:5; Job 37:5; Psalm 111:2; 139:14; 145:17 and Hosea 14:9 for other references to the great works of God.

The theme that God is worthy of praise continues in verse 4. The promise of the nations worshipping the Lord is the fulfillment of the prophesies of Scripture and the picture of Revelation 7. All nations, languages, tribes, and peoples will worship God. The "all" in this phrase of "all nations," is not

6. Beale, *The Book of Revelation*, 789, 91.

7. See Osborne, *Revelation*, 564, who interprets the Greek *kai* as epexegetical (describing a word that is added in order to clarify meaning)—the song of Moses and the song of the Lamb.

8. Beale, *The Book of Revelation*, 795.

the idea of without exception, in that everyone will repent; but all without distinction—from every nation, tribe, and people. Ladd comments that the kingdom of God will be a fellowship of people from all nations who gladly give themselves in worship and devotion to God.[9]

In another movement of action in the story, John sees that the tabernacle of the testimony in heaven was opened (see Hebrews 9). It was opened to prepare for the final judgment. In Rome, according to Aune, the *templum Iani*, "the temple of Janus," was opened as a prelude to war or as a declaration of war. It was closed by Augustus three times to restate the *Pax Romana*, the peace of Rome, the first time in January 29 BC at the end of the civil war, the second time in 25 BC, and the third time at a date unknown.[10] We also may note that in Revelation 11:19, the temple was opened as well, in the context of judgment. The temple is open here to prepare for the unleashing of the seven bowls of wrath.

Out of this tabernacle come the seven angels with the bowls of wrath. These angels reflect the glory of the Lamb. They are clothed in bright clothes with golden sashes around their chests, the symbol of priesthood and the kingdom in Leviticus 16:4, 23; and 1 Samuel 2:8. Osborne sees a connection with Ezekiel 9:2–3, which says, "And behold, six men came from the direction of the upper gate, which faces north, each with his weapon for slaughter in his hand, and with them was a man clothed in linen, with a writing case at his waist. And they went in and stood beside the bronze altar." (See also Daniel 10:5; 12:6–7).[11] These are angels specifically tasked with the judgment of God upon humanity.

These seven angels are given the seven bowls of wrath from one of the four living creatures. The seven bowls of wrath remind us of the pouring out of the fury of God's wrath on the wicked of the world. We soon see come to fruition what was metaphorically described as a harvest in chapter 14. Isaiah 51:17 says, "Wake yourself, wake yourself, stand up, O Jerusalem, you who have drunk from the hand of the Lord the cup of his wrath, who have drunk to the dregs the bowl, the cup of staggering." (Also verse 22). The bowls of the seven angels are the final answer to the request for vengeance from the saints under the altar in chapter 6 ("How long, O Lord?")

When the summons is given to the seven angels, the temple is filled with smoke from the glory of God and no one could enter the temple. No

9. Ladd, *A Commentary on the Revelation of John*, 206; also Beale, *The Book of Revelation*, 798. Aune (Aune, *Revelation 6–16*, 876), lists several examples in the Old Testament where you can find themes of the nations coming to worship God in Jerusalem (Isaiah 2:2–4; 14:1–2; 45:14; 60:1–3; 66:18; Jeremiah 16:19; Zechariah 8:20–23).

10. Aune, *Revelation 6–16*, 878.

11. Osborne, *Revelation*, 569.

one could enter the temple because the opportunity for forgiveness and repentance is over. Too late. The final wrath of God would fall upon the earth, and the final judgment would be complete and ultimate. In Ezekiel 10:2–4, the glory of God departs the temple in Jerusalem. There, the glory of God, the radiance of his glory that is represented by a thick cloud of smoke, filled the temple, and then left. Beale says that John combined the passage of Ezekiel 10 in the context of judgment and that of Isaiah 6 to convey the image of the glory of God and judgment.[12] Mounce writes, "The time for intercession is past. God in his unapproachable majesty and power has declared that the end has come. No longer does he stand knocking: he enters to act in sovereign judgment."[13]

Chapter 16 continues the theme from chapter 15. The angels who had the seven bowls of wrath are commanded to pour them out. There is no hesitation between the sixth and seventh bowl, as there was an interlude between the sixth and seventh seal, and between the sixth and seventh trumpet. The obvious differences between the trumpet and the bowls are plain to see. The trumpets are a partial judgment upon the earth (1/3 of the earth), and the bowls are universal. The bowls of wrath also are directly poured out upon man. Mankind, in other words, becomes the primary recipient of the judgment. In chapter 16, just as somewhat with the seals and the trumpets, the plagues of Egypt form the background canopy.

The command is given from the temple to pour out the bowls of wrath. The temple had been filled with smoke (15:8) and no one could enter the temple until the seven plagues were completed. This is the voice of God (see 15:5–8). Only here in Revelation does the adjective "great" precede "voice," which makes it even more certain that this is God speaking.[14] The idea of God pouring out his wrath is a common idea in the Old Testament, as we have already seen. He said in Ezekiel 14:19, "Or if I send a pestilence into that land and pour out my wrath upon it with blood, to cut off from it man and beast." (see also Jeremiah 10:25; Zephaniah 3:8).[15]

Like in Egypt, these plagues (the bowls of wrath) are directed against those who are set apart, those who have the mark of the beast. This

---

12. Beale, *The Book of Revelation*, 807.

13. Mounce, *The Book of Revelation*, 290. For other passages describing the glory of God and the cloud, see Exodus 40:34–35 (Moses is not able to enter the tabernacle because of the cloud filling it. The glory of God and his power are all-consuming); Isaiah 6:4; Haggai 2:7; 1 Kings 8:10, 11; and 2 Chronicles 5:13–14.

14. Beale, *The Book of Revelation*, 812; Mounce, *The Book of Revelation*, 293; Ladd, *A Commentary on the Revelation of John*, 210; Osborne, *Revelation*, 578; Thomas and Macchia, *Revelation*, 277; Aune, *Revelation 6–16*, 882.

15. Beale, *The Book of Revelation*, 812–13.

assumes that there are those who do not have the mark of the beast, and so there is a differentiation between those who belong to God and those who do not, just as there was in the Exodus during the time of the plagues of Egypt. The painful sores of the first plague are similar to the plague of boils in Exodus 9:10.

Similar to the plague on the Nile river (see Exodus 7:14–27; Psalm 78:44), when the river became blood, the second plague affects the sea. This sea is turned into blood. Whereas the Nile was fresh water, here the salt waters become blood. The source of life, the sea, becomes a source of death. But this could also be a judgment against the sea, a traditional place of wickedness. Beale sees this as a judgment upon the economic systems of the world (see chapter 18). The sea and all that came from the sea dies. This would cripple the shipping industry around the world.[16] Thomas writes, "The events accompanying the pouring out of the second bowl reveal a comprehensiveness and intensity that make clear the unparalleled nature of this bowl."[17] This is a judgment that has not yet been unleashed upon the earth, in this kind of magnitude.

In the third plague, continuing the blood theme of the second plague, the fresh waters become blood. An angel calls out in verse 5 and declares the acts of God just. There is a reference to 1:8, the One who is, who was, and who is to come. God is just because he is holy. His justice is based upon his holiness. God could not be anything other than just because of his holiness. The angel who declares this is in charge of the waters. It is as if he saw his commission impacted by the sinfulness of mankind and recognized the justice of God in it. Mounce says it well, "The judgment of God is neither vengeful nor capricious. It is an expression of his just and righteous nature." God is righteous in his judgments, and his exposing of evil is appropriate for a moral universe.[18]

Because the blood of the saints and prophets had been shed by mankind, their seas would become blood and they would be given blood to drink. The punishment will fit the crime/sin. The Greek word is *axioi*, "worthy." In other words, this people who have rejected God and have killed his people are worthy of judgment. Isaiah 49:26 says, "I will make your oppressors eat their own flesh, and they shall be drunk with their own blood as

---

16. Beale, *The Book of Revelation*, 815. Mounce, *The Book of Revelation*, 294, notes that this is an arid region of ancient civilization, and water was considered critical as one of mankind's basic requirements.

17. Thomas and Macchia, *Revelation*, 278.

18. Mounce, *The Book of Revelation*, 295. See also Psalm 119:137. It is interesting to note the Greek word translated here, *dikaios*, contains both the idea of justice and righteousness (or rightness).

with wine. Then all flesh will know that I am the Lord your Savior, and your Redeemer, the Mighty One of Jacob."[19]

The altar answers in response and agrees with the angel in charge of the waters. There is agreement in heaven, and it is announced that God is right and just in bringing these punishments upon the people of the earth. In Deut.32:4 Moses praises God, saying, "The Rock, his way is perfect, for all his ways are justice. A God of faithfulness and without iniquity, just and upright is he." Interestingly, as Beale points out, the phrase, "The Lord, the Almighty God," is used here and elsewhere for the absolute sovereignty of God over the historical affairs of his people.[20] Because the altar is the source of this voice, maybe there is a connection between the concept of judgment and the concept of sacrifice. The sacrifice of the Lamb has already been made. But, because mankind does not respond in worship to the Lamb, the altar speaks out as a witness of judgment against them.[21]

The plagues continue to come. The sun is impacted by the fourth bowl of wrath, so that the sun is scorching hot. This may refer to a famine of extra-ordinary proportions, or simply to a level of heat intensity that cannot be borne. It was so hot that humanity is scorched with fire. But rather than repent and give God glory, the people of the earth are set in their stubborn rejection of God. They do not bless God or praise him as the angels of verses 5–7. They curse his name instead.[22]

The fifth bowl of wrath, like the plague of darkness (see Exodus 10:21), brings the world into a deep darkness so that men suffer greatly. The throne of the beast is crippled, and this impacts the rest of mankind. The darkness is an appropriate context in which to suffer the wrath of God. Darkness is a symbol of judgment in 1 Samuel 2:9; Amos 6:20; Joel 2:2; Zephaniah 1:15; ignorance and wickedness in Psalm 82:5; Proverbs 2:13; Ecclesiastes 2:14; and death in Psalm 143:3.[23] Jeremiah 13:16 says, "Give glory to the Lord your God before he brings the darkness, before your feet stumble on the twilight mountains, and while you look for light he turns it into gloom and makes it deep darkness."

19. See further descriptions of blood in 17:6; 18:24; 19:2 (Beale, *The Book of Revelation,* 819).

20. Beale, *The Book of Revelation,* 821.

21. Aune (Aune, *The Book of Revelation,* 888) wonders whether this voice is one of the voices of 6:10, requesting a response from God against the wicked.

22. Aune (Aune, *Revelation 6–16,* 889) describes an ancient myth where the son of Helios, the sun god, whose name is Phaethon, drove the chariot of the sun too close to the earth, blacking the skin of the Ethiopians and scorching the mountains, forests, meadows, and cities of the earth with fire.

23. Aune, *Revelation 6–16,* 890.

The refusal to repent continues. Does this mean that there still is an opportunity to repent? Or is this merely a way of expressing the stubbornness and wickedness of men who reject God and are thus worthy of these judgments? Beale would call this lack of repentance, "irremediable," according to the theological pattern of the hardening of Pharaoh and the Egyptians.[24] I would agree. Maybe we should not say that it was impossible for Pharaoh to repent. But God knew his heart. He knew that it was hardened and that it would be further hardened. The plagues only entrenched his wickedness and set further alight the glory of God over the earth. So shall it be in the end. The heart of mankind will be blackened before God. The judgment of God will not turn him toward God, only away in bitterness and anger.

The sixth bowl of wrath was poured out upon the river Euphrates, a traditional source of evil. And sure enough, when dried up, we see the demonic coming out of the river in 13ff. In the Old Testament, great redemptive works are associated with the drying up of water such as the Exodus (Exodus 14:21) and the entrance to Canaan (John 3:14–17), as Mounce notes.[25] But, just as there may be a note of redemptive analogy or language here, so there is also a strong note of judgment. The Egyptian army was judged in the midst of the dried-up Red Sea, after the waters swallowed them up; and the dried-up Jordan River prepared the way for the destruction of the wicked populace in Canaan. And just as those dried-up rivers symbolized the spiritually dried and worthless conditions of the hearts of those local peoples, the dried-up Euphrates stands as a symbol of the judgment of God to come upon a mankind that has rejected him. This is not the actual river, but symbolic of a universal judgment, just as Babylon becomes a symbol of the universal empires that oppose God.[26]

What comes out of the dried-up Euphrates are not particular kings or groups of nations, but a demonic host bent on the destruction of mankind. This demonic host is further represented by the appearance of three evil frogs that come out of the mouth of each member of the evil trinity, reminding us of the plague of frogs in Egypt (see Exodus 8:2–11). They came out of their mouths because each evil member of the evil trinity is a liar and replicates the character of lying from the beginning. Thomas sees the contradiction with the 144,000. Whereas the 144,000 had no deceit in their mouths, in the mouths of the evil trinity were demonic frogs and deception.[27]

---

24. Beale, *The Book of Revelation*, 825.

25. Mounce, *The Book of Revelation*, 298.

26. See Beale, *The Book of Revelation*, 828.

27. Thomas and Macchia, *Revelation*, 285.

The demonic frogs continue the deception of the dragon, as they go out into all the earth to perform miraculous signs and convince the kings of the whole world to make war against God. These are kings from the *whole* world. This is a united front against God's purposes and his people. Actually, frogs represent the demons of the nations, as the frogs were represented by the goddess Heqt in Egypt, overpowered by the God of the universe. See Psalm 104.30. That the definite article is used to define the war probably means this is a war that the audience knew was coming. *The* war between the forces of evil against the forces of God. The forces of evil will gather only to face their final judgment (see Revelation 19). Christ will defeat them with the breath of his mouth (2 Thessalonians 2:8).

Jesus interjects a word of encouragement in verse 15. While the intensity of persecution may very well increase, we are reminded that Jesus is coming and will set all things straight—a foreshadowing of chapter 19, when Jesus comes back. The one who stays awake and keeps his clothes with him will not be shamefully exposed. What clothes are these? They are the clothes of the overcomer. The believer must stay faithful and committed so that he will not be ashamed (see Revelation 3:3; Luke 12:39–40). Jesus' coming as a thief reminds us that it could be at any time. If the believer stays awake, he will not be caught off guard (1 Thessalonians 5:2).

The kings of the earth are led by the demonic frogs to a placed called Armageddon. A lot of ideas have been espoused as to the location of this final battle. Rather than waste time trying to figure out where it is, as if that is important, it is better to admit that it is most likely symbolic, like much in Revelation, for the place of mankind's resistance and evil rejection of God. Beale, Mounce, and Johnson believe it to be symbolic. It is symbolic for the whole world, a typological symbol for the last battle. There is a place called Megiddo that lies on the north side of Carmel Ridge and occupies the strategic pass between the coastal plain and the valley of Esdraelon. But it is difficult to know that the text should be read *Harmegiddo* or *Armegiddo* (mountain or valley). It is best to view it as an eschatological confrontation, rather than a strict geographical place.[28]

When the seventh angel pours out his bowl of wrath, the judgment is over as is announced by the angel, "It is done." The end of all things is at hand. Chapters 17 and 18 describe this final judgment before Jesus' return and final victory. And just like in other passages of Revelation, when the final judgment is described, there is thunder, lightning, earthquakes, hail, and general chaos in the universe. See 8:5; 11:13, 19. The earthquake seems

---

28. Beale, *The Book of Revelation*, 838; Mounce, *The Book of Revelation*, 301–2; Johnson, *Hebrews through Revelation*, 552.

to be an unusually big one, unseen or not-yet-experienced by men before this time. This fulfills the prophesy of Daniel 12:1.

The great city, Babylon, probably a symbolic name for Rome, is split into three parts. But not Rome specifically, but the city Babylon stands for the kingdoms of the world that position themselves against God. The division of the city into three parts connotes the severity of the destruction.[29] Haggai 2:7 says, "And I will shake all nations, so that the treasures of all nations shall come in, and I will fill this house with glory, says the Lord of hosts." The world will be shaken with the final earthquake, and the desired One will come to claim his own and establish his glory. The natural world will be turned upside down by the plagues of the angels. The beauty of the earth is taken away as the mountains and the islands flee. And once again, the people of the earth do not repent, but curse God on account of the hail and the plague.[30]

## Conclusion

In 2 Peter 3:8–9, we are told, "But do not overlook this one fact, beloved, that with the Lord one day is as a thousand years, and a thousand years as one day. The Lord is not slow to fulfill his promise as some count slowness, but is patient toward you, not wishing that any should perish, but that all should reach repentance." But after the seven bowls are poured out, and based on the exposition above, while the bowls are being poured out, there will no longer be a time for repentance. It will be too late.

Verse 10 continues, "But the day of the Lord will come like a thief, and then the heavens will pass away with a roar and the heavenly bodies will be burned up and dissolved, and the earth and the works that are done on it will be exposed." Where does the church stand today in regard to this surety? We must not be like the five foolish virgins who were left out of the wedding banquet because they were unprepared (see Matthew 25:1–10). For those women, it was too late. Let us continue, then, to live holy and godly lives as we look to the day of the LORD and speed its coming (2 Peter 3:11–12). The reality and certainty of the events of chapter 15–16 should not frighten the church. We are marked with the seal of Christ. But it should motivate the church, to continue to work while it is still day, before it is too late for the world.

29. See Mounce, *The Book of Revelation*, 304.

30. See Exodus 9:23 for the plague of hail, except these are about 100 pounds each. Mounce (Mounce, *The Book of Revelation*, 305) notes, citing Ezekiel 38:18–22, that hail was part of the accepted arsenal of divine judgment.

# Revelation 17:1–18

The Vision of the Prostitute and the Scarlet Beast

## Introduction

O NE DAY I DID an internet search of the words "eternal life", and I thought it interesting that eBay was one of the hits. So, I clicked the link and found the following items for sale: Jesus Christ Eternal life cross stitch kit, 3 "eternal life religious art print lighthouse" for bids of $3.25, $0.01, and $1.00, a silver and amber eternal life cognac pendant, Cronos Eternal Life Vampires VHS, Eternal life skeleton of Pharaoh, and a CD by Jeff Buckley, called Eternal Life Aussie. How sad a picture our world has of the concept of "forever." It has now become a successful marketing strategy. That, along with all the silly items for sale we find in the typical Christian book store: "testamint" gum, cross trinkets, angel earrings, and many other things I think would make God want to vomit.

The reality is that all that is in this world will pass away one day. When all is said and done, only Jesus and his word will remain. All the meaningless and superficial trappings of religion will no longer be of any use to anyone. We see in chapter 17, and then later, in chapter 18, that the world and all its systems of opposition to God will pass away. The seventh bowl has already announced the beginning of the end. Chapters 17 and 18 tell us that story.[1]

## Exposition

Chapter 17 describes in more symbolic imagery the vileness of the kingdom of the earth, in alliance with the wicked beast of chapter 13 who makes war against the saints and is drunk with their blood. All of this is still under the sovereignty of God (we remember the Lamb has the scroll of history and

---

1. Osborne (Osborne, *Revelation*, 603) goes a bit further, 17:1—19:5 recapitulate the events of the seals, trumpets, and bowls, telling why Babylon was judged (17:1–18) and then detailing the effects of that judgment (18:1—19:5).

authority in his hand). God allows the woman and the beast to exercise authority so that his word is fulfilled (v.18). As we seek to understand this passage, it is pointless to try to figure out historically (more on this later) who the seven hills represent and who are the ten kings. What is important is that their rule is brief (only one hour) compared to the eternal and unending power of the Lamb of God. The seventh bowl has already announced the beginning of the end.

Chronological accuracy or preciseness is not important here. What is important is that the image that John sees beginning with verse 1, is of the destruction of the kings of the earth who ally with the beast and war against God's people. The angel is showing John the punishment of the great prostitute, called Babylon in verse 6, the mother of prostitutes. The Old Testament background for this prostitute/Babylon is Jeremiah 51 where Babylon is described as making the earth drunk (51:7) and living by many waters (51:13). The Lord's vengeance was promised to come upon Babylon (51:5). In chapter 17, we have that destruction and vengeance renewed.

Interestingly, the definite article is used with prostitute, "*the* great prostitute." It is as if she is known to the readers. Perhaps we should understand her to be Rome, Babylon, and all the cities that have opposed God's peoples in the past. There are points of identification for both Rome and Babylon. Beale notes that there is a coin that depicts the goddess Roma sitting on the seven hills of Rome. This may be behind John's imagery but may only be used as a backdrop as well.[2] Ladd reminds us, however, that Rome did not sit on many waters. Babylon did. This is a personification of ancient Babylon as a representative of the wicked nations of the world.[3] Babylon and Rome could also be considered hand-in-hand in John's mind as symbols of nations opposed to God and who oppressed his people.

One of the angels with the seven bowls of wrath shows John these things. This ties chapter 17 in with the final judgment of the seven bowls upon the earth. Perhaps hearers at the time would have seen in the judgment of the great prostitute in 17:1 an ultimate fulfillment of the prophesy of Jesus to the church in Thyatira in 2:20–23.[4] Mounce writes, "When the great harlot

---

2. Beale, *The Book of Revelation*, 848.

3. Ladd, *A Commentary on the Revelation of John*, 222. See also Isaiah 23:17 and Nahum 3:4 where Tyre and Nineveh, respectively, are compared to harlots because of their dependence upon the idolatry of economic gain. Aune (Aune, *Revelation 17–22*, 929), notes that the many waters must remind us of Babylon, crossed through by the River Euphrates and crisscrossed with ancient canals.

4. See Thomas and Macchia, *Revelation*, 292.

with all her seductive allurements is exposed and destroyed, then the Bride of Christ will be seen in all her beauty and true worth."[5]

Through the deceptions of the great prostitute, the kings of the earth were led astray by the lure of wealth and political promises offered by the great kings. From Nebuchadnezzar to Nero to Domitian to every other super power since then, the leaders of the world fall to the power of money and comfort. As in Jeremiah 51:7, the putrid relationship is explained as fornication and adultery or idolatry. Isaiah 23:17, speaking of the judgment against Tyre, says, "and will prostitute herself with all the kingdoms of the world on the face of the earth."

John is then carried away in the Spirit, where he saw a more detailed description of the woman. Carried in the Spirit to the desert probably refers to an ecstatic vision that was given to John, similar to what he had experienced in chapter 1, when he was in the Spirit on the Lord's day. Aune views the desert negatively, because the prostitute was there.[6] In this vision, he saw the prostitute united with the beast with seven heads and ten horns, similar to the beast described in chapter 13, that is, the beast out of the sea. There is an interesting contrast of images in verse 3. John is taken to the *desert* or wilderness to see the woman sitting on many *waters*. Both the desert and the sea are sources of trials and sometimes wickedness in Jewish literature. See 12:15–16 where the dragon unleashes water to overtake the church (cf. Isaiah 21:1).

The beast is scarlet, probably reflecting the red color of the dragon, a color of bloodshed and war. And like Ezekiel was carried into the desert to pronounce judgment (see Ezekiel 3:12, 14, 24; 11:1), John is carried to the desert to witness the finalization of that judgment.[7] Isaiah 21:9 says, "And behold, here come riders, horsemen in pairs! And he answered, 'Fallen, fallen is Babylon; and all the carved images of her gods he has shattered to the ground.'" Ladd notes that the woman was seated on many waters representing her relationship to the kings of the earth. That she was seated on the scarlet beast represents her relationship to the antichrist.[8] She has sold her soul and her eternity to the wicked trinity and would reap the horrible fruit of her decisions.

5. Mounce, *The Book of Revelation*, 307.

6. Aune, *Revelation 17–22*, 933; Osborne, *Revelation*, 610; Thomas and Macchia, *Revelation*, 293—all, however, view the wilderness positively, as a place to meet with God (John 1:23; 3:15; 6:31, 49; 11:54; Revelation 12:6,14) or as a place of safety.

7. Beale, *The Book of Revelation*, 850.

8. Ladd, *A Commentary on the Revelation of John*, 223.

The woman is adorned with the signs of wealth and prosperity—a purple and scarlet robe, gold, precious stones, and pearls.[9] The golden cup in her hand was filled with the blood of the saints which she had persecuted. Far from anything remotely pure and good, the cup was filled with abominable things and the filth of her adulteries. Her sins are clearly on display. A common word used in the Septuagint for idolatry or idolatrous practices is used here for "adulteries," which strengthens the idea of the association between the fornications and idolatrous practices.[10]

On the forehead are the titles of the woman, just as the seal of God is upon the forehead of the faithful and the mark of the beast is on the forehead of the followers of the beast. The name on the forehead indicates the ownership of the wearer of that name. Her titles betray not only her character but her master. She is a mystery, but a mystery revealed by the angel to John.[11] See 1:20; 10:7. She is Babylon the Great, or Rome, the ancient city that opposed God's people and symbolic of all the cities of the earth that persecute or will persecute the church. See Daniel 4:27, 30. She is also the mother of prostitutes—the source of abomination and wickedness. Close Old Testament parallels would be Old Testament passages in which apostate Israel is pictured as a mother who prostitutes herself (Hosea 2:2–7; Isaiah 50:1).[12] Mounce quotes Tacitus, who said that Rome was a place "where all the horrible and shameful things in the world congregates and find a home." Seneca called Rome "a filthy sewer."[13]

In verse 6, John sees that the woman is drunk with persecution, a vivid image of the violence inflicted upon the faithful (see Revelation 13:8). Those who bore testimony to Jesus unto death are the victims. But in reality, they are the victors. Through their death, the great prostitute and the beast upon

---

9. Beale (Beale, *The Book of Revelation*, 854) notes that the expensive and attractive clothing reflects the outward attractiveness by which prostitutes try to seduce others. Jeremiah 4:30 reads, "And you, O desolate one, what do you mean that you dress in scarlet, that you adorn yourself with ornaments of gold, that you enlarge your eyes with paint? In vain you beautify yourself. Your lovers despise you; they seek your life." Mounce (Mounce, *The Book of Revelation*, 309) also notes that scarlet was used to display magnificence. See Nahum 2:3.

10. See Beale, *The Book of Revelation*, 856; Osborne, *Revelation*, 611. See also Jeremiah 13:27; Ezekiel 6:9, 11; 20:28–30.

11. Aune (Aune, *Revelation 17–22*, 926–37) wonders if this mystery could be a reference to a popular thought that the secret name of Rome was *Amor* ("love" in Latin), or Roma spelled backwards, and that this may have motivated John to portray Rome as a prostitute, a perversion of love? On the face of the coin that has the goddess Roma sitting upon seven hills is the image of Caesar Vespasian Augustus.

12. See Aune, *Revelation 17–22*, 937; Osborne, *Revelation*, 613.

13. Mounce, *The Book of Revelation*, 310.

whom she sits, are defeated. This persecution seems to be world-wide and universal. Nothing in the first century provides an accurate counterpart of this level of persecution. John is looking to a day in the future when the chief city of the beast will unleash a great persecution upon the faithful.[14]

John was astonished when he saw the image of the woman, the great prostitute. Aune thinks that John's marveling may be an indication of his confusion in interpreting the details of the vision.[15] He is confused because he anticipated seeing the judgment of the prostitute, not the apparent victory she was experiencing. The angel rebuked John for being surprised, or at least strongly questioned why he is astonished. The angel assured John that he would show him the meaning of the woman, and that of the beast upon whom she sits. "Marveled" here could be understood as "appalled." John was appalled by the vision, in the sense that there was shock and fear, which brings the rebuke of the angel. John should not have been afraid.[16] See Daniel 4:19 when Daniel was also greatly perplexed by the vision and terrified by his thoughts.

Some believe John's marvel had the nuance of adoration or admiration. She was adorned beautifully. "Could she really be all that bad?" This would certainly earn the rebuke of the angel. But Beale gives the following valid reasons why John's marvel should be understood as shock or fear: 1) This is the meaning from Daniel 4:2) The vision is not presented as a glorious image but as a horrific one. She was full of abominations. It is hard to conceive John admiring this; 3) John's response should not be compared to his wrong response in 19:10 and 22:8, since there he is confronted with the muted glory of the angelic being, not a horrible abomination; 4) The angel had already told him the nature of the woman in the beginning of the vision. He would not be lured as well.[17]

The angel begins to describe the beast in verse 8. This is the antichrist who once was, is not, and will come again—similar to the beast with the mortal wound that was healed (see chapter 13 as well as Daniel 7:7).[18] The source of the beast is the abyss, the place of evil, and this is also his future. He comes out of the abyss and he goes to it, to his destruction. Those who have rejected the Lamb of God and have chosen to follow the image of the beast, and receive his mark, will be deceived by his apparent return/resurrection and will be astonished. They will follow the beast because their

14. Ladd, *A Commentary on the Revelation of John*, 225.

15. Aune, *Revelation 17–22*, 938

16. Beale, *The Book of Revelation*, 861.

17. Beale, *The Book of Revelation*, 862–63.

18. See also Osborne, *Revelation*, 616.

names are not written in the book of life from the creation of the world (see 13:8—a clear connection to that verse, tying the identity of the beast in 17 with the beast in 13).

Just as wisdom was required for understanding in chapter 13, so the angel tells John that he needs to have a mind of wisdom to understand these things, not necessarily to understand who the woman and the beast are, but to understand what is required of God's people when they face these opponents to the truth. But where are these seven hills, or who are they? And why seven? As in 12:3 and 13:1–2, the fullness of oppressive power is in mind here. This is not a reference to specific kings in history but represent the oppressive power of world governments throughout the ages. For example, in Daniel 7:3–7 the kingdoms span many centuries.[19] Also, actually eight or nine hills can be counted in Rome, so the concept of specific seven hills is lost a bit.[20]

It is much wiser, therefore, to conclude that the seven hills, or kings, do not have to be identified in order for us to see John's meaning. They are rulers who are allied with the beast and will be opposed to God's people. There are too many problems associated with trying to determine which historical emperors are included if we understand John literally. This discount many times that God uses the number seven for completeness. Ladd believes that it makes more sense to think of the seven heads as kingdoms, rather than emperors, in line with Daniel 7 (so Egypt, Assyria, Babylon, Persia, and Greece are the ones that were; Rome is the one that is: and an unknown wicked empire is still to come).[21] Still, this forgets about the figurative use of numbers in John. It may be a kingdom, but it is more likely a conglomerate of the wicked kingdoms of the world that oppose God.

To illustrate the various possibilities and the futility of trying to determine who are the seven kings, Aune provides a chart of the various possibilities. There is the historical approach with its many possibilities, the symbolic approach, and the combined symbolic and historical approach.[22]

---

19. Beale, *The Book of Revelation*, 868. See Isaiah 2:2; Jeremiah 51:25; Ezekiel 35:3; Daniel 2:35, 35; and Zechariah 4:7 for passages where mountains symbolize kingdoms in the Old Testament. See also Mounce, *The Book of Revelation*, 315. The number seven is symbolic for the power of the Roman Empire as a historic whole.

20. Johnson, *Hebrews through Revelation*, 563.

21. Ladd, *A Commentary on the Revelation of John*, 227–29.

22. Aune, *World Biblical Commentary*, 945–50.

| Ruler | Possibilities of who is the first-seventh king and who is the eighth to come | | | | | | | | |
|---|---|---|---|---|---|---|---|---|---|
| | a | b | c | d | e | f | g | h | i |
| Julius Caesar (101–44 BC) | 1 | 1 | | | | | | 1 | |
| Augustus (27 BC—14 AD) | 2 | 2 | 1 | 1 | | | | 2 | |
| Tiberius (14–37) | 3 | 3 | 2 | 2 | | | | − | |
| Gaius (37–41) | 4 | 4 | 3 | 3 | 1 | | | − | 1 |
| Claudius (41–54) | 5 | 5 | 4 | 4 | 2 | | | 3 | 2 |
| Nero (54–68) | 6 | 6 | 5 | 5 | 3 | 1 | | − | 3 |
| Galba (June 68–Jan 69) | 7 | − | 6 | − | 4 | 2 | 1 | − | − |
| Otho (69) | 8 | − | 7 | − | 5 | 3 | 2 | − | − |
| Vitellius (69) | − | − | 8 | − | 6 | 4 | 3 | − | − |
| Vespasian (69–79) | − | 7 | − | 6 | 7 | 5 | 4 | 4 | 4 |
| Titus (79–81) | − | − | − | 7 | 8 | 6 | 5 | 5 | 5 |
| Domitian (81–96) | − | − | − | 8 | − | 7 | 6 | 6 | 6 |
| The "other" (17:10b) | − | − | − | − | − | − | − | − | 7 |
| [Neronic antichrist] | − | − | − | − | − | − | − | 7 | 8 |
| Nerva | − | − | − | − | − | − | 7 | − | − |

The phrase "must remain" for the one king who is to come is again a clear pointer to the sovereignty of God. He must remain. But he must remain for only a little while. His power and rule and dominion are limited by the ultimate sovereignty of God. John's primary intent is to let his readers understand how far they stand from the conclusion of the full sequence of the seven oppressive rulers. He tells them that only one more short reign will elapse before the end of the oppressive dominance of Rome, which represents all ungodly powers opposed to the Lamb. The end is not far off but will come in God's time. Within God's control we see the idea of immanence.[23] When the end comes, it will come suddenly. And the whole world will know it.

In verse 11, we see that the beast is beyond the seven. He belongs to them in that he is also from a wicked foundation and his destruction is sure just as their destruction. Calling the beast the "eighth" is also another way of mimicking the resurrection of Jesus. Just as Christ died on the sixth day, was in the tomb on the seventh day, and rose on the eighth day, so this beast is

23. Beale, *The Book of Revelation*, 871.

an eighth king.[24] And though the terrible reigns of those opposed to Christ will continue through the eighth beast, believers should know that the same wicked origins are there, and the Lamb has defeated them on the cross.

The ten horns of the beast are also ten kings (see Daniel 7:24, "As for the ten horns, out of this kingdom ten kings shall arise") These are ten kings who are to come. These as well do not need to be named or determined from history. They probably come from the seventh horn and are thus figurative of future evil kingdoms that will be controlled by the beast.[25] Their reign will be limited just as the seven hills/kings reign for only a little while. These kings will only reign for one hour, a very short time compared to the limited time of suffering for the church. See also Revelation 18:10, 17, and 19 for a reference to the one hour. The sole purpose of the ten kings is to submit to the authority of the beast. There will be a united frontal assault on God's people and against the Lamb.

Even though a combined and united attack will come from the kings of the earth against the Lamb, there will be no threat to the Lamb, as we see in verse 14. Why? Because he is Lord of lords and King of kings. With Jesus will be those who have remained faithful, the overcomers. There is a three-fold identification used here. They are the called, the chosen, and the faithful. Daniel 7:21–22 depicts a similar scene. "As I looked, this horn made war with the saints and prevailed over them, until the Ancient of Days came, and judgment was given for the saints of the Most High, and the time came when the saints possessed the kingdom." Aune views two types of apocalyptic holy war texts as background for John's concepts: 1) Those in which God wins victory alone and his people are passive (Exodus 14:13–14; 2 Kings 19:32–35; Isaiah 37:33–36; and 2 Chronicles 20); and 2) Those in which God wins the victory along with his people. His people are active (Joel 3:11b; Zechariah 14:5b). Osborne sees both of these options or concepts occurring in Revelation. The active model in 2:26–27 and 17:14, and the passive model in 19:14.[26]

In verse 15, similar to other parts of Revelation that allied the peoples, multitudes, nations and languages with beast, the waters are symbolic of them as well. This is what makes the salvation of languages, peoples,

---

24. So observe both Beale, *The Book of Revelation*, 875; and Johnson, *Hebrews through Revelation*, 560–61. It is also quite possible, taking the historical-symbolic position, that this eighth king is the antichrist who belongs to another sphere of reality and will rise during the time of the great distress or tribulation of the final days; so Mounce thinks (Mounce, *The Book of Revelation*, 316).

25. See Beale, *The Book of Revelation*, 879; Mounce, *The Book of Revelation*, 317; Ladd, *A Commentary on the Revelation of John*, 231.

26. Aune, *Revelation 17–22*, 956; Osborne, *Revelation*, 624.

nations, etc. in chapter 7 so amazing. For representatives of every people, nation, tribe, and language will be gathered before the throne of the Lamb in praise and worship.

While these peoples of the earth are under the authority of the great prostitute and the beast, the wicked union will turn against the prostitute, as the kings of the earth, and even the great empires, will fall into destruction as the beast turns on them. Ezekiel 23:25–29 provides some background here. Verses 28–29 says, "For thus says the Lord God: Behold, I will deliver you into the hands of those whom you hate, into the hands of those from whom you turned in disgust, and they shall deal with you in hatred and take away all the fruit of your labor and leave you naked and bare, and the nakedness of your whoring shall be uncovered." See also Ezekiel 38:21, where in the judgment of Gog, everyone turns his sword against the other.[27] There is a complete ruin and destruction of the once proud city. They will be left naked, and the city will be devoured by the beast, and be burned in the fire.[28]

The nations of the earth were only pawns in the hand of the beast. But the beast was only acting in line with the deeper plans of God. The Greek word for "has put" is a past tense verb, and is equivalent to the Hebrew prophetic perfect, which emphasizes the certainty of fulfillment.[29] What is being fulfilled? Probably Daniel, Ezekiel, Jeremiah, and Isaiah; those passages that have been the basis for John's visions of judgment.

27. Osborne, *Revelation*, 625.

28. Ladd, *A Commentary on the Revelation of John*, 233. See Psalm 27:2, Jeremiah 10:25, Micah 3:3, and Zephaniah 33 for references to nakedness and total destruction.

29. Beale, *The Book of Revelation*, 887.

# Revelation 18:1–24

## The Fall of Babylon

### Introduction

W E MOVE QUICKLY TO chapter 18 which discusses what was only mentioned once in chapter 17, the demise of the woman, or Babylon. Chapter 17 set up the concluding descriptions of chapter 18. According to Beale, the lament sections of 18:9–19 are similar to Old Testament models of funeral dirges and serve to enforce the curse involved in Babylon's coming judgment.[1] Mounce writes that John is portraying the "ultimate collapse of a monstrous anti-Christian world order determined to defeat the purposes of God in history."[2] For the primary Old Testament influence on chapter 18, Aune makes a good case for Jeremiah. He sees the connection as follows:[3]

| | |
|---|---|
| 18:2a | Jeremiah 51:8; Isaiah 21:9 |
| 18:2b | Jeremiah 51:37 |
| 18:3 | Jeremiah 51:7 |
| 18:4 | Jeremiah 51:6 |
| 18:5 | Jeremiah 51:9 |
| 18:6 | Jeremiah 50:28; 16:18 |
| 18:8 | cf. Jeremiah 50:32, 34; 51:30, 32, 58 |
| 18:20 | Jeremiah 51:48 |
| 18:21 | Jeremiah 51:64 |
| 18:22c–23b | Jeremiah 25:10 |
| 18:23c | Jeremiah 7:34; 16:9; 25:10; 33:11 |
| 18:24 | Jeremiah 51:49 |

---

1. Beale, *The Book of Revelation*, 891.
2. Mounce, *The Book of Revelation*, 321.
3. Aune, *Revelation 17–22*, 983.

It is clear that Jeremiah has a strong influence of John's vision in chapter 18, but we also see the influences of Isaiah and Ezekiel throughout.

## Exposition

John sees "another angel," meaning that all those who brought the messages in chapter 17 were also angels. This angel was so glorious that the earth was illuminated by his splendor. His source was heaven as the other angels. In Ezekiel 43:2 we also see the earth radiant with the splendor of God's glory. Ezekiel wrote, "And behold, the glory of the God of Israel was coming from the east. And the sound of his coming was like the sound of many waters, and the earth shone with his glory." So, in Revelation 18:1, the angel is reflecting the glory of God who dwells in unapproachable light (1 Timothy 6:16) and covers himself with light as with a garment (Psalm 104:2). The angel reflects the glory of God like Moses coming from the presence of God and reflecting the radiance (see Exodus 34:29–35).[4]

This angel announces the fall of Babylon. It fell just as the angel had told John in chapter 17. For background from the Old Testament see Isaiah 13:21; 21:9; 34:11, 14; Jeremiah 50:39; 51:8. The great prostitute would become food for the birds and a home for demons, meaning a place filled with evil spirits.[5] There will no longer be life in Babylon—only death and darkness and evil. In fact, Babylon's association with the dragon and darkness and evil is emphasized with the position of those descriptors more toward the front of the sentence in Greek. Besides that, the fall of Babylon is narrated in the past tense though it is speaking of something in the future. This underscores its certainty. The fall of the old Babylon is a prophetic precursor to the fall of the future Babylon, and just as certain as the first fall was, so as certain is the future fall.[6]

---

4. See Mounce, *The Book of Revelation*, 323; Osborne, *Revelation*, 634. Beale, *The Book of Revelation*, 893, is open to the idea that the appearance of the angel here may be a Christophany, as he also thought of the angel in 10:1, because the word "glory" is associated in Revelation either with God (4:9, 11; 5:13; 7:12; 11:13; 14:7; 15:8; 16:9; 19:1; 21:11, 23) or Christ (1:6; 5:12–13). But angels also reflect the glory of God. How could they not when they dwell in his presence? So this angel in verse 1 is most likely just an angel, not a Christophany.

5. The Greek for "haunt," *phulakh*, which is technically a watchtower, may also be translated "prison," but may mean something more, a place of judgment, like a desert place. Babylon the Great, who imprisoned many by her dominion, will be imprisoned where every unclean spirit is captive. See Beale, *The Book of Revelation*, 895; Mounce, *The Book of Revelation*, 323; Thomas and Macchia, *Revelation*, 308; Osborne, *Revelation*, 636; Johnson, *Hebrews through Revelation*, 566.

6. See Beale, *The Book of Revelation*, 893; Mounce, *The Book of Revelation*, 323;

The Greek for "because" in verse 3 gives the reason for the darkness and death and despair. It becomes this way because it deceived the nations of the world, and the kings of the earth joined with her in her adulteries and idolatries. The wealth of the city blinded them to its evil and the consequences of that evil. The word "drank" refers to the willingness of kingdoms and peoples in the Roman Empire to commit themselves to idolatry in order to share in her wealth, and maintain economic security.[7] Economic prosperity, rather than truth or justice, controlled the decisions and wills of mankind, and the nations of the earth. With the fall of Babylon came crashing down the fall of every nation dependent upon her.

The call is then given in verse 4 to the people of God to disassociate with the wickedness of the world systems, and the kingdoms of the world. Wealth should not be the goal of God's people. Isaiah 48:20 and Jeremiah 50:8; 51:6, 45 exhort Israel to come out of Babylon and return to Israel during its restoration. These prophesies are thus applied metaphorically to the people of God now, who live among the world systems dictated by wealth and power.

Where do these people come from? In other words, who are these believers that are called to come out of Babylon? This is when we need to remember the apocalyptic nature of the book of Revelation. These could be believers all through the centuries who have needed to resist the economic temptations of the world systems and all its idolatry. Still today, Christians are to remain in the world to witness (chapter 11) and to suffer for their testimony (6:9; 11:7–10; 12:10, 17; 16:6; 17:6; 18:24), but they must not be part of the world (14:12–13; 16:15).[8] Christians must also separate from the world spiritually so that they will not be inflicted with the plagues that will come against the wicked, just as the people were unaffected by the plagues of Egypt. Isaiah 52:11 calls Israel to come out of Assyria, "Depart, depart, go out from there! Touch no unclean thing! Come out from it and be pure, you who carry the vessels of the Lord." Paul picks up that thought and applies it spiritually to the people of Corinth in 2 Corinthians 6:17.

God is just. He does not let the guilty go unpunished. The sins of the city of Babylon (Rome, or any city that opposes God and his purpose) will be judged for the multitude of sins within her and committed by her.

---

Aune, *Revelation 17–22*, 985.

7. Beale, *The Book of Revelation*, 896.

8. Beale, *The Book of Revelation*, 899. Aune (Aune, *Revelation 17–22*, 1012) also holds that the flight is not to be understood as a physical flight, but the avoidance of the temptations of corrupt features of the Greco-Roman culture. Mounce (Mounce, *The Book of Revelation*, 325) quotes Augustine from the *City of God*, xviii.18, "We must renounce our rights as citizens of this world, and flee unto God on the wings of faith."

"Remembered" is in the emphatic position in the Greek (placed first in the sentence), which reminds the people of God, that though the nations of the world grow wealthy, the Lord would indeed remember their sins and bring judgment upon them. See also Genesis 18:20–21 and Jeremiah 51:8–9.

As a God who is just, in verse 6 we see the Lord as avenger. He will pay back the wicked a double portion of judgment. The cup of wrath that is drunk by the prostitute (chapter 17) will become the cup of wrath poured out by God onto the wicked. Psalm 137:8 says, "O Daughter of Babylon, doomed to be destroyed, blessed shall he be who repays you with what you have done to us!" Jeremiah 50:29b says, "Repay her according to her deeds; do to her according to all that she has done. For she has proudly defied the Lord, the Holy One of Israel." Habakkuk 2:16 as well says, "You will have your fill of shame instead of glory. Drink, yourself, and show your uncircumcision! The cup in the Lord's right hand will come around to you, and utter shame will come upon your glory!"

The translation of *diploun*, as "double," is not absolute, according to Beale. It could be translated "duplicate, twin, or matching" in that the punishment upon Babylon matches their sin, so that their crime is paid back in full.[9] The idea of double the penalty, however, was a common theme in the Old Testament (see Exodus 22:4, 7, 9, where certain transgressions required a double payment). The prophets also emphasized double retaliation (Isaiah 40:2; Jeremiah 16:18; 17:18). Psalm 79:12, moreover, calls for a sevenfold retaliation.[10] We ought not be too over-concerned to correct God's perspective of retaliation and retribution. What is emphasized here, rather, is the justice of God. Whatever he brings upon the wicked nations of the earth will be a fair repayment for their sins.

The boasting of her glory and luxury will come back upon the prostitute/city with torture and grief. As she treated the others under her, and the people of God, so will she be treated. She feels herself invulnerable and outside the hand of judgment or the hand of retribution. She feels herself above the law.[11] Isaiah 47:7–9 displays this attitude in the mouth of the daughter of Babylon. "You said, 'I shall be mistress forever,' so that you did not lay these things to heart or remember their end. Now therefore hear

9. Beale, *The Book of Revelation*, 901.

10. Osborne, *Revelation*, 641.

11. Osborne (Osborne, *Revelation*, 642) notes that one is reminded of Messalina, the wife of Claudius, whose sexual appetite was so fierce that she would at times become a sacred prostitute in some of the temples. What a great contrast for a queen to act the part of the prostitute! Is this not what Babylon the great would become, a glorious queen mired in a bed of filth with her lovers, not knowing of the judgment and burning that would come to her?

this, you lover of pleasures, who sit securely, who say in your heart, 'I am, and there is no one besides me; I shall not sit as a widow or know the loss of children.'" The judgment of God was prophesied upon her. It will ultimately come in the last day. In that day, she would be overwhelmed by plagues and consumed by fire. Her glories and her exaltations will come crashing down in a moment. This is idolatry of the self, which must be judged.[12] It is only God who is mighty and exalted and eternal.

The kings of the earth will mourn over the loss of Babylon, not necessarily because of a love for her, but because of their loss of economic prosperity. There are three groups who mourn because of the fall of Babylon: kings, merchants, and mariners.[13] The kings here mourn over the smoke of the burning of Babylon, which may remind us of the Lord's judgment upon Sodom in Gen.19:28, as Abraham saw the smoke rise in the sky. These kings were in alliance with her for economic gain. We could say that they slept with the harlot to enjoy the benefits of her kingdom. The close connection between idolatry/adultery and economic prosperity was normal in John's time in Asia Minor, where allegiance to both Caesar and the patron gods of the trade guilds was essential for people to maintain good standing in their trades.[14]

The lament lifted up by the kings for Babylon indicate that her doom came in one hour. This emphasizes the quickness of the judgment. Her glory was great, but in only a matter of time, a limited time, it will crumble. The phrase "one hour" is placed in an emphatic position in the verse (see 17:12). There is most likely fear in the dirge. They had slept with Babylon. Now, because of its demise, their demise would surely come.[15] The dirge also reveals the continued fascination of the kings of the earth with the prostitute. They still refer to her as "Babylon, city of power."[16]

Like in Ezekiel 27, in the case of Tyre, the second group to mourn the loss of Babylon is the merchants because their economic source of selling power was gone with Babylon. No one would buy their cargoes anymore. In

12. Beale, *The Book of Revelation*, 903. Mounce (Mounce, *The Book of Revelation*, 326) notes that pride is condemned in many places of the Scriptures, such as Isaiah 3:16–17 and Proverbs 29:23.

13. See Ezekiel 26:16–17, 29–30, and 35–36, where these three groups express sorrow over the demise of Tyre. Mounce (Mounce, *The Book Revelation*, 328) and Ladd (Ladd, *A Commentary on the Revelation of John*, 239) believe these kings are different from the kings of 17:16 who turn upon Rome. But I don't think we need to make a distinction. An alliance and dependence on the one hand can become mutual destruction on the other. There is not a strict chronological pattern here.

14. See Beale, *The Book Revelation*, 905. See also Acts 19, and the association of the trade guild in Ephesus with idolatry.

15. Beale, *The Book of Revelation*, 906.

16. Thomas and Macchia, *Revelation*, 314.

John's day, Rome was known for its extravagance and ostentatious displays of wealth and luxury. From the Talmud we read, "Ten measures of wealth came down into the world: Rome received nine, and all the world one." Little wonder, then, that the merchants of the earth would mourn over her demise.[17] In verse 12, we see a list of the merchandise that will go unsold.

Fifteen of the twenty-nine items listed in Revelation 18:12–13 are also listed in Ezekiel 27:7–25 (Tyre). Silver, for example, was highly valued in Rome, with some Roman women only bathing in silver tubs, and generals eating from silver dishes in the field. Pearls were highly prized, and purple dye was extremely expensive, extracted a drop at a time from the shellfish, murex. Silk came all the way from China, and citrus wood from Africa.[18] The whole world was impacted by the Roman lust for stuff (sounds a lot like the Western lust for stuff now). The most telling cargo, however, was the last one in the list, "bodies and souls of men." They were actively engaged in human trafficking at the time, some estimations putting the total as high as 60,000,000 slaves in the Roman Empire.

The mourning continues in verse 14, but because there is no longer any source of the fruit of the city, their products, the once wealthy and splendid city will vanish in a flash. The alliteration in the phrase, *ta lipara ta lampra*, "riches and splendor," suggests that the false glitter and glory of the city's wealth will be taken away and replaced by the genuine divine glory reflected in God's people, city, and Son (see 21:11, 23–24 where "glory" is linked to "brightness."[19] And just as the kings stood off and mourned the loss of Babylon, so the merchants will stand far off and sing a similar dirge of demise. The wealth of the city is reflective of the glory of the vision of the prostitute in 17:4. But like she fell, the wealth will fall. Both are temporal. See Ezekiel 27:31, 36; 28:13.

In verse 17, we are introduced to the third group, the mariners. Like the merchants, the sailors and mariners will stand far off and mourn the fall of Babylon because they no longer will be able to participate in its economic system. John continues to follow the thought of Ezekiel 27 concerning the judgment of Tyre. As in verse 18–19, so in Ezekiel 27:30: "(the mariners) shout aloud over you and cry out bitterly. They cast dust on their heads and wallow in ashes." But contrasted with the intense grief of the mariners, as well as the kings and merchants, the people of God (saints, apostles, and prophets—all who suffered by the hand of the wicked cities of the earth) are called

17. Mounce, *The Book of Revelation*, 329. See further examples of opulence in Aune, *Revelation 17–22*, 998–1003.

18. Mounce, *The Book of Revelation*, 330.

19. Beale, *The Book of Revelation*, 910–11.

upon to rejoice over her demise. This is again an answer to the question from Revelation 6:10. God pays back the nations for the injustice inflicted upon the people of God. Mounce writes, "The church victorious is to rejoice that God the righteous judge has turned back the evidence laid against believers and in turn has served to bring judgment upon the accuser himself."[20]

A final word of judgment is spoken over the city along with a large boulder the size of a millstone being hurled upon it. The millstone would have been four to five feet in diameter, one foot thick, and weighing thousands of pounds.[21] It is clear, then, that the large boulder should not be understood literally, but metaphorically as the final judgment of God upon the city. With the loss of the city comes the loss of music and entertainment, the normal activities of work and trade, and the joys of living and marriage. As the city had taken these joys away from the believers, so these joys would be removed from them. See Isaiah 24:8; Jeremiah 7:34; 25:10; and Ezekiel 26:13 for parallel passages from the Old Testament. The merchants of Babylon were renowned, but their fame would fall. They had deceived the nations, but their power would be shattered.

We get a final vindication of the fall of Babylon in verse 24. In her was found the blood of the prophets and saints. The blood of God's people was found "on the hands" of the city of Babylon. Nahum 3:1, 5 reminds us, "Woe to the bloody city, all full of lies and plunder—no end to the prey! Behold, I am against you, declares the Lord of hosts, and will lift up your skirts over your face; and I will make nations look at your nakedness and kingdoms at your shame." The once mighty and arrogant foe of God's people, puppet of the dragon, will fall, and fall quickly. The glory that she depended upon, her wealth, her luxuries, her status, would crash and be burned in the fire. The stage is set for John to describe the coming of the only true Warrior, the One King of kings. This we see in chapter 19.

## Conclusion

Jesus said, "heaven and earth will pass away, but my words will never pass away." There is truth that will be forever, because Jesus is the truth, and Jesus will remain forever. The wicked, and all that is with them, will perish from the earth. Their money, their pleasures, and their sin will perish. All will be ashes and dust. But Jesus and all who belong to him will remain.

---

20. Mounce, *The Book of Revelation*, 332. See also Deuteronomy 32:43 and Jeremiah 51:48.

21. Johnson, *Hebrews through Revelation*, 568.

In the great city of Athens, Greece, there is a lasting testimony to the power of Jesus' word and his presence. Throughout all the city there are ruins of great buildings and temples. You can walk down the main corridor of the city and you see the Parthenon, the ancient temples, the baths where the ungodly would indulge in revelry and immorality. But the name of the street where Paul had his famous religious debate on Mars Hill (see Acts 17) is called Dionysius Areopagus, the name of the first convert of Athens, and later on the first bishop of the city. The power of the gospel still remains, for Jesus and all that is his will never fade away.

Annie Johnson Flint, many years ago, wrote this poem:

I See Jesus

I don't look back; God knows the fruitless efforts,
    The wasted hours, the sinning, the regrets;
I leave them all with Him who blots the record,
    And mercifully forgives, and then forgets.
I don't look forward, God sees all the future,
    The road that, short or long, will lead me Home,
And He will face with me its every trial,
    And bear for me the burdens that may come.
I don't look round me: then would fears assail me,
    So wild the tumult of earth's restless seas;
So dark the world, so filled with woe and evil,
    So vain the hope of comfort or of ease.
I don't look in, for then am I most wretched;
    My self hath naught on which to stay my trust.
Nothing I see save failures and shortcomings,
    And weak endeavors crumbling into dust.
But I look up—into the face of Jesus,
    For there my heart can rest, my fears are stilled;
And there is joy, and love, and light for darkness,
    And perfect peace, and every hope fulfilled.[22]

22. Johnson Flint, "I See Jesus", Homemaker's Corner.

# Revelation 19:1–21

The Consummation of the Lamb's Victory

## Introduction

L ORA AND I CELEBRATED our thirtieth anniversary a few years ago. I
was only twenty years old when we got married, and I still remember
that day like it was yesterday. We had scheduled Lora's grandparents to be
ushered down the aisle to the song, "Sunrise, Sunset," from the musical, "A
Fiddler on the Roof." Lora's grandparents had arrived at the church earlier
to make sure they knew where it was, but when they tried to get back to the
church, from the cafe, they got lost. The pianist played, "Sunrise, Sunset," I
think, one hundred times waiting for them to come.

Meanwhile, I was pacing in the hallway, with my brother trying to
calm me down, and my youth pastor doing the same. Finally, they came,
and the moment of my entrance into the sanctuary with the groomsmen,
had come. That is when the nerves really could be felt. I didn't really pay
attention to the bridesmaids as they entered before Lora. I was waiting for
Lora to come. And when I saw her appear in the door, I couldn't speak, or
hear, or control my emotions. I leaned over to my brother and whispered,
"I think I am going to really cry." He said something like, "just don't start
sobbing." We waited in the receiving line after the wedding, greeting guests
for what seemed like two hours. When we finally got to the reception, there
was no punch left, and a lot of the food had been eaten. We had arranged for
the guests to go ahead and eat and not have to wait for us.

When Jesus comes back for his bride, the church, things are going to
be quite a bit different than my experience. Rather than the groom standing at the front, waiting for his bride, in a Jewish wedding, the bride is
in her home, waiting for the groom to come. He would have been away
preparing his house for his bride and when he started his journey to get
her, his friends (or the friends of the banquet) would announce his coming
so that the bride could be ready, as well as all the bridesmaids (see Jesus'
wedding language in John 14:1; Matthew 25). So, the bridegroom is the

one who approaches. And similar to western weddings, after the wedding ceremony, there is a feast, sometimes in the case of Jewish weddings, celebrations that may for several days.

Jesus is the Bridegroom who is coming for his bride, the church. He told his disciples the night before he died, "I am going to prepare a place for you, and when I return, I will take you to be with me." This is no middle-class wedding. This is not even as lowly as an earthly, high society, high class wedding. This will be a wedding between the King of kings and his bride, the church, the faithful who have been waiting for his to come for thousands of years. This is what is celebrated in Revelation 19.

## Exposition

There are some[1] who consider 19:1–5 together with chapters 17 and 18. There is good reason to do this, as 19:1–5 is a praise response to the judgment of the prostitute, the city of Babylon. But, on the other hand, as noted by Aune, Revelation 19:1–8 and 19:9–10 could be considered textual units which function as transitions between 17:1–18:24 and 21:1–22:5. 19:1–5 could just as easily serve as the introduction to the last stage, the coming of Christ. Chapters 17 and 18 are completed by the coming of the conquering King on the white horse.

The "after this" of verse 1 signals another vision, after the vision of the fall of the prostitute. This chorus of praise reminds us of the praises of the angels in chapter 5. The great multitude is like the multitudes of those who praised God and the Lamb. The Lord possesses salvation and power and glory. The multitudes are the saints who have been redeemed. This is evident from the specific mention of salvation, and the concern for avenging the blood of the martyrs (see Revelation 6:10).[2] The content of their praise is a direct contrast to the laments of chapter 18, spoken by the kings, the merchants, and the mariners. The first of four hallelujahs are spoken by these saints. The word "hallelujah" is found only here in the New Testament.[3]

1. For example, Beale, *The Book of Revelation*, 926 and Aune, *Revelation 17–22*, 1019.

2. Mounce, *The Book of Revelation*, 337; Osborne, *Revelation*, 663. Salvation here means more than personal deliverance. It is the completion of God's working on behalf of the elect, the consummation of all things. Even creation is waiting for this day (see Romans 8).

3. Ladd, *A Commentary on the Revelation of John*, 244. Johnson, (Johnson, *Hebrews through Revelation*, 569) also notes the connection between this passage and the Hallel Psalms of 113–118.

God is again declared just (*dikaiai*) in his condemnation and judgment of the great prostitute. The prostitute is called great only in terms of her influence in corrupting the earth by her adulteries, and great because of the level of persecution she poured out upon the saints of God. Again, 19:2 is the answer for 6:10. Just as the seals, trumpets, and bowls are answers to the prayers of the persecuted saints, so here is further answer, the destruction of the great prostitute.[4] 2 Kings 9:7 possibly provides some background for this. The blood of God's servants, the prophets, were avenged by God upon the throne of Ahab and Jezebel, who becomes a symbol for idolatrous relationships with the world (see Revelation 2:20ff). God avenges his servants once again by destroying the final great prostitute.[5]

As the merchants and mariners in chapter 18 see the smoke of the city rising, indicating its destruction, so the smoke is seen again. But this is not an occasion of mourning, but of rejoicing. Isaiah 34:10, speaking of the judgment against the nations, says, "Night and day it shall not be quenched; its smoke shall go up forever. From generation to generation it shall lie waste; none shall pass through it forever and ever." As in Isaiah, so in Revelation, the judgment is eternal. Beale wonders whether the eternal nature of the judgment may be a play on words of the mythical name of *Roma eaterna* (eternal Rome), one of the names of the Roman empire.[6] Rome, Babylon, Sodom, Gomorrah, and any other city that opposes God, meets the same fate, eternal judgment and retribution because they poured out the blood of God's servants.

Verse 4 connects the vision back to the opening vision in chapter 4–5, when we met the twenty-four elders and the four living creatures. They are still before the throne and they respond to the song of the loud voice with "Amen, Hallelujah!" In Ps.106:48 we read a similar response, "Amen, Hallelujah," after the deliverance of the people of God from the nations. Just as in Ps.106, we see a deliverance of the people of God from the nations. A voice then comes from the throne, maybe from one of the angels surrounding the throne, exhorting all those who serve God and fear him to give him praise. He calls on everyone, from every strata of society, "both small and great," to respond in praise.[7]

---

4. Osborne, *Revelation*, 655.

5. See also Aune, *Revelation 17–22*, 1025.

6. Beale, *The Book of Revelation*, 929.

7. Mounce (Mounce, *The Book of Revelation*, 338), Thomas (Thomas and Macchia, *Revelation*, 329), and Johnson (Johnson, *Hebrews through Revelation*, 570) all agree that this voice is not the voice of God or the Lamb, because the Lamb would have said, "My God" rather than "our God." Aune (Aune Revelation 17–22, 1027) emphasizes that, while it is difficult to identify the speaker with certainty, the phrase, "from the

Continuing the sounds of praise in heaven, John hears a great multitude, like the roar of rushing water or loud thunder. These are sounds that
are not surprising for the readers of Revelation. The roar of rushing waters,
and the loud peals of thunder are not the sound of judgment here, but the
sound of praise and shouting, a loud chorus of welcome to the Lamb who is
to come. This great multitude repeats the Hallelujah and declares the reign
of "our Lord God Almighty." This phrase is similar to Psalm 93:1, "The Lord
reigns, he is robed in majesty; the Lord is robed; he has put on strength as his
belt."[8] Domitian had given himself the title, "Our Lord and God," so John's
title for God as "The Almighty," is a reminder of who really reigns.[9] With the
coming of the Lamb, Jesus, who has been on the throne of God in heaven,
will come to the earth to claim his reign there as well.

With the coming of Lamb is the consummation of the bride and
Groom. The loud voices of verse 6 command the citizens of heaven in verse
7 to "rejoice and be glad," and "give him glory." These are imperatival verbs.[10]
Why must the saints rejoice? Because the wedding of the Lamb has come.
The word for Lamb, *arniou*, is the same word used in chapter 5. The bride is
the church. She has readied herself (reflexive pronoun). How has she readied herself? She has persevered and overcome until the end. The concept of
the bride preparing herself also reminds us of the Jewish wedding context,
where the betrothed woman, already a legally binding relationship, prepares
herself in her father's house while she waits for the groom. She has already
been chosen as his wife, and based upon that new identity, she prepares
herself to receive him and enjoy the consummation of the marriage.[11]

---

throne" at least indicates the divine authorization of the speaker.

8. See also Psalm 97:1, 99:1, and Ezekiel 1:24, where Ezekiel heard a sound like
rushing waters when the creatures of heaven moved their wings.

9. Mounce, *The Book of Revelation*, 339. There is a grammatical difficulty in verse
6, but Beale (Beale, *The Book of Revelation*, 933) believes that the difficulty is there only
because John wanted to attract attention to its unusual syntactical function as an Old
Testament allusion. In other words, this is a purposeful reference to a Hebrew construction to highlight the reference to Psalms. Ladd (Ladd, *A Commentary on the Revelation
of John*, 246), calls the aorist in this verse an inceptive aorist that can be translated,
"The Lord our God . . . has entered on his reign!" The announcement is a proleptic announcement of an event that actually will take place with the return of Christ. Thomas
(Thomas and Macchia, *Revelation*, 330) calls it an ingressive aorist.

10. Though Thomas (Thomas and Macchia, *Revelation*, 330) calls the verbs
hortatory subjunctives, a form that would seem to intensify the eschatological joy.

11. Beale (Beale, *The Book of Revelation* 935) points out that justification is the
causal necessary condition for entrance into the eternal kingdom, but good works are
a non-causal necessary condition. This is similar to the one who tried to enter the banquet in Jesus' parable without the proper wedding clothes. The bride already belongs
to the Groom, by nature of her election. She lives and prepares herself in association

As a part of the bride's preparation, she is given fine linen to wear. John interprets the linen as the righteous acts of the saints. There is no theological tension here between the grace of Christ in justification, as briefly discussed above, and the righteous acts of the saints, her making herself ready. The bride's garments are interpreted as "righteous deeds" in order to describe an aspect of the intimate relationship between God and his people. The church's righteous faith and deeds were judged worthy of death by the wicked in the world but are vindicated by God through judgment and deliverance at the consummation of their union with him.[12] This idea is similar to what Paul describes in Ephesians 5:25–27. Jesus loved his bride, the church, so fully, that he gave himself up for her, "that he might sanctify her, having cleansed her by the washing of water with the word, so that he might present the church to himself in splendor, without spot or wrinkle or any such thing, that she might be holy and without blemish." In Revelation 19 also, the church's righteous deeds are righteous because Christ has made them so.

Because the bride belongs to the Lamb, her righteous deeds are consistent with his righteousness. The righteous deeds of God carried out on behalf of the saints (15:4), encourage the righteous deeds of the saints carried on behalf of God. Their righteous deeds are consistent with his righteous deeds.[13] Johnson also points out that the white linen, bright and clean, describing the church's garments, are in stark contrast to the purple linen of the great prostitute. Linen was an expensive cloth used to make the garments worn by priests and royalty. It has two qualities: bright as the color of radiant whiteness and glory; and clean as the purity, loyalty, and faithfulness she has proven in her steadfastness, the character of the New Jerusalem. See 21:18, 21.[14] Isaiah 61:10 also prophesied this union. "I will greatly rejoice in the Lord; my soul shall exult in my God, for he has clothed me with the garments of salvation; he has covered me with the robe of righteousness, as a bridegroom decks himself like a priest with a beautiful headdress, and as a bride adorns herself with her jewels."[15] Isaiah 62:1–5 continue the picture

---

with that calling.

12. Beale, *The Book of Revelation*, 940. See also 1 John 3:2–3 and 2 Corinthians 7:1. The reality of the coming of Christ is a belief that encourages a righteous commitment before God. The Greek, *edothe*, as has been used in other parts of Revelation to describe the divine passive (13:5, 7, 14, 15), is used here to show God's sovereign actions in the lives of the people of God. They "were given" clothes to wear.

13. Thomas and Macchia, *Revelation*, 333.

14. Johnson, *Hebrews through Revelation*, 571.

15. Beale, *The Book of Revelation*, 938. See also Hosea 2:14–20. Osborne (Osborne, *Revelation*, 673) notes that Ezekiel 16:7–14 may also provide some background.

of a bridegroom rejoicing over his bride, an incredible picture of the Lamb's rejoicing over his purified bride, the church.

In verse 9, the angel commands John to write another blessing.[16] The blessing was for those who are invited to the wedding supper of the Lamb. A parallel passage to this idea may be Jesus' parable of the wedding banquet in Matthew 22:1–14. This was a wedding banquet for the son of the king. Many are invited, but few are chosen. Thomas reminds us that those invited to the wedding feast are none other than the bride herself, the saints who have persevered. In apocalyptic imagery, one image morphs into another.[17] The wedding party will be the bride and the Groom, with maybe the angels as guests. Those invited to the wedding supper of the Lamb are blessed, because they have been chosen, elected. Jesus said in John 6:37, "All that the Father gives me will come to me, and whoever comes to me I will never cast out."

When John saw the angel, he fell at his feet to worship him. But the angel rebuked him and quickly identified himself with John and John's brothers as a "fellow servant." The emphasis of worship is God. This is, indeed, emphasized in the Greek. Literally, it can be translated, "To God you must worship!" Hebrews 1:7, quoting Ps.104:4 says, "He makes his angels winds, and his ministers a flame of fire." And in verse 14, "Are not all ministering spirits sent out to serve for the sake of those who are to inherit salvation?" Angels cannot even be on the same platform with Jesus. And like John must worship God and be faithful to the message attested by Jesus (subjective genitive),[18] the angels must worship God and serve him also.

The follow-up phrase spoken by the angel is a little hard to grasp. What is the purpose of the statement, "The testimony of Jesus is the spirit of prophesy?" Bearing up and persevering under trial and persecution will speak as loudly for the glory of God as the ministry of the angels. The essence of a prophetic proclamation is a faithful witness for the sake of Jesus, keeping in line with the faithful witness of Jesus. Thomas is worth quoting here, "The witness of Jesus and the Spirit of prophesy are thus intricately connected to one another and in Revelation cannot be understood apart from each other. The witness of Jesus is quintessentially pneumatic, prophetic, dynamic, and active. The Spirit who goes out into all the world is the same Spirit who empowers the church's prophetic witness."[19]

16. Johnson (Johnson, *Hebrews through Revelation*, 572) notes that this is the fourth of seven beatitudes in Revelation (1:3; 14:13; 16:15; 19:9; 20:6; 22:7, 14).

17. Thomas and Macchia, *Revelation*, 334.

18. So Mounce, *The Book of Revelation*, 342 and Ladd, *A Commentary on the Revelation of John* 251.

19. Thomas and Macchia, *Revelation*, 337.

Verse 11 is the culmination of the visions from chapters 14–18. John sees heaven standing open and a white horse, whose rider is called Faithful and True. The rider judges and makes war with justice. This is the Lamb who alone was worthy to open the seals of the scroll. This is the Groom coming for his bride. Heaven is open because the end of all things was being fulfilled in the return of Christ. Heaven and earth would be united. In Ezekiel 1:1 the heavens were opened for Ezekiel and his visions. Another scene of judgment begins.

This is a powerful description of Jesus, the Lamb. He is faithful. He never fails. He never goes back on his promises. He never lies. He comes to bring justice and to fulfill all the promises of God that are "yes" in Christ (2 Corinthians 1:20). He is True. He is the polar opposite of the dragon, the great serpent and the father of lies. He judges and makes war with justice. He is totally fair and all that he does is right, particularly in judging the beast, the false prophet, and all who follow them. Psalm 96:12b-13 says, "Then shall all the trees of the forest sing for joy before the Lord, for he comes, for he comes to judge the earth. He will judge the world in righteousness, and the peoples in his faithfulness." Revelation 19:11 connects the coming of the Lamb and his identity with God, in the context of God's worthiness to be praised among the nations (see also Psalm 9:8; 72:2; 98:9). This is fulfilling the prophesy of the Branch of Jesse in Isaiah 11:4, "but with righteousness he shall judge the poor, and decide with equity for the meek of the earth; and he shall strike the earth with the rod of his mouth, and with the breath of his lips he shall kill the wicked." (See also 2 Thessalonians 2:8; 1:7–10).[20] Mounce writes, "There is no doubt in the Seer's mind that the righteous retribution about to be enacted upon the beast and his followers is perfectly compatible with truth and justice."[21]

The description of the Rider on the white house that continues in verse 12 is similar to description of Jesus' eyes from Revelation 1. His eyes are like blazing fire, the fire of judgment, knowledge, and discernment. On his head are many crowns, diadems. The many crowns show the unlimited power and authority of the Lamb. This vision, like Revelation 1, is similar to Daniel 10:6 and the vision of the Man dressed in linen. First Corinthians 15:25 says, "For he must reign until he has put all enemies under his feet." Jesus'

20. Aune (Aune, *Revelation 17-22*, 1049) notes that parallels to Revelation 19:11–16 are commonly found in Jewish literature. One example is Wisdom 18:15, dependent upon Exodus 15:3–4: "The all-powerful word leaped from heaven, from the royal throne into the midst of the land that was doomed, as stern warrior carrying the sharp sword of thy authentic command, and stood and filled all things with death, and touched heaven while standing on the earth."

21. Mounce, *The Book of Revelation*, 344.

reign as King will be complete and unlimited, unlike the limited power and
authority of the beast from the sea or the beast from the earth.

The Rider has a name written on him that no one but him knows.
Could Isaiah 62:2–3 give us a clue? "The nations shall see your righteousness, and all kings your glory, and you shall be called by a new name that
the mouth of the Lord will give. You shall be a crown of beauty in the hand
of the Lord, and a royal diadem in the hand of your God." Though speaking
of Zion, and the new name associated with her salvation, maybe this has
something to do with the name of the Lamb. Philippians 2:9 tells us that
to him was given "the name that is above every name." But if we already
know his name as "Faithful" and "True" in verse 11, why does he have a
name written on him that no one knows? There is no contradiction here,
but a reminder that this unknown name must be understood symbolically.
In the Old Testament, to know someone's name is to have control over them.
Therefore, the fact that no one knows the name of Christ shows that he is
uncontrollable, and above all other authorities and powers, over humanity's
attempt to usurp his authority.[22]

Christ's robe is dipped in blood. The blood could be from one of two
sources. The first option is that this is the blood of the enemies which would
rise as high as a horse's bridle, enabling the robe of the Rider to be splattered
with it. Isaiah 63:3 seems to corroborate this idea: "I have trodden the winepress alone, and from the peoples no one was with me; I trod them in my
anger and trampled them in my wrath; their lifeblood spattered on my garments and stained all my apparel."[23] The other option is that the blood reminds us of the redemptive victory of the Lamb. He conquered by his cross,
a past act to which this perfect passive participle points.[24] Given the nature
of chapter 19, particularly the feast for the birds at the end of the chapter, it
seems best to understand this blood to be the blood of the enemies of God.
Understanding the time of when and how the blood got onto Christ's robe is
not important when we remember that this is apocalyptic imagery.

The Rider is more specifically identified as the Word of God, a very
Johannine way to refer to Jesus. In John 1:1 John wrote, "In the beginning
was the word, and the word was with God, and the word was God." In John
1:14 we know that the Word became flesh and lived among us. The Word

22. See Beale, *The Book of Revelation*, 955.

23. This is the view of Mounce, *The Book of Revelation*, 345, Aune, *Revelation*
17–22, 1057, and Osborne, *Revelation*, 683.

24. For this view, see Thomas and Macchia, *Revelation*, 340 and Johnson, *Hebrews
through Revelation*, 574, who sees a difficulty in the blood identified as the blood of
enemies, as he is just descending from heaven.

of God is actively fulfilling God's purposes. This is God speaking and God acting, and God fulfilling.

The Lamb is not alone as he rides. With him, in verse 14, are the armies of heaven, also riding white horses, and dressed in fine linen, white and clean. Who are these armies of heaven? Are these simply angels or are these the saints of God who have persevered and have held out until the end? If saints, then the people of God who have suffered under the rule of the beast, the Babylons of the world, will victoriously reign with Christ when he comes. This fits with the cultural understanding of 1 Thess.4:17. When Christ comes in the clouds, those alive who belong to him, will meet him in the air. This is not the rapture to be taken to heaven. This is a meeting of the saints of Christ who come back with him immediately to reign on the earth. Just as in the first century, if a king was returning to his city, the citizens of that city, upon hearing of the approach of the king, would leave the city, join the king on the road, and return with him in triumphant procession.

The clue that these are the saints, the bride, is that they are dressed the same way the bride is dressed in verse 8. The same word, *bussinon*, linen, is used here as in verse 8. Also, Beale notes, that in Revelation, only with one exception (15:6), only saints wear white garments (3:4–5, 18; 4:4: 6:11; 7:9, 13–14). The saints here and in 17:14 take part in the final judgment in that their testimony is the legal evidence condemning the oppressors.[25]

As in Revelation 1 again, we see similar descriptions of the Lamb. The sword from the mouth of the Rider is the sword of victory and judgment and punishment. The nations will be struck down by this sword, who really symbolically stand for his powerful word, or the breath of his mouth (2 Thessalonians 2:8). In Joel 3:13, the sickle is swung. Here it is the sword, or the word of judgment, but the results are the same, judgment against the unrighteous (see Isaiah 63:3 as well). In Isaiah 49:2, the Servant of the LORD says, "He made my mouth like a sharp sword; in the shadow of his hand he hid me; he made me a polished arrow; in his quiver he hid me away." Isaiah 11:4 is another Messianic passage fulfilled here, "He will strike the earth with the rod of his mouth, and with the breath of his lips he shall kill the wicked." The scepter, the sword, and the breath of Christ all point to the

---

25. Beale, *The Book of Revelation*, 960. I disagree with Beale about 4:4. There, those surrounding the throne and dressed in white are angels. The stronger evidence here is the close proximity between the two verses using the word for linen, white and clean (verses 8 and 14). Ladd (Ladd, *A Commentary on the Book of Revelation*, 255) thinks these are angels based on Zechariah 14:5, Mark 8:38, Luke 9:36, 1 Thessalonians 3:13, and 2 Thessalonians 1:7; as does Osborne (Osborne, *Revelation*, 684). But the context of Revelation 14 must win the day. These are the saints of God following their Lord.

powerful justice of his word.[26] That powerful word would tread (reap) the winepress of the fury of the wrath of God Almighty.

John reads the identification of the Rider, written on his robe and on his thigh. He is the King of Kings and Lord of Lords. There is no one who may be compared to him (see Philippians 2:10–11). Deuteronomy 10:17 says of God, "For the Lord your God is God of gods and Lord of lords, the great, the mighty and the awesome God, who is not partial and takes no bribe." Jesus comes as God of gods. Beale makes the helpful observation that the thigh was the typical place of the warriors' sword (see Exodus 32:27; Judges 3:16, 21; Psalm 45:3), and the symbolic place under which the hand was placed to swear an oath to God (Genesis 24:2, 9; 47:29). So, Christ's victory over the wicked will be a fulfillment of God's promises.[27]

The next vision that John sees is of an angel standing in the sun, calling on the birds to gather for the great supper of God. Ezekiel 39:17–20 provides the referential background to verse 17–18. The call is given for the carrion birds to feast on the flesh of all humanity who defied the glory and reign of the Lamb. This is a great and clear contrast to the invitation to the followers of the Lamb to join the wedding supper of the Lamb. The faithful are blessed and invited to a feast of eternal joy. The wicked are cursed and are the main course of a feast of eternal sorrow. Before the battle has even started, it is over. There is no contest, no strategy drawn up. The Lamb comes and the war is over, with the breath/sword from his mouth.[28]

The carrion birds feast on the flesh of kings, generals, the rich, the mighty, the slave and the free—everyone who turns his back on God. A person doesn't have to be an atheist-scientist, or a communist, or a member of ISIS, or a university rationalist to be part of this feast. One can be an average person who never killed another, or never stole from another. One can be a church-goer who even gives when the collection is passed and prays at meals. But if that person has rejected Jesus as the Lord, then he will be a part of this fleshly feast as well. No one would want an invitation to this wedding banquet, but many freely choose to go anyway, based on their rejection of the Lordship of Jesus.

As in Revelation 14 and 16, the wicked of the earth, the kings who have allied with the prostitute, make war against the Lamb and his followers. But they are defeated. The kings do not gather under their own power but are

26. Psalm 2:9 speaks of the iron scepter in the hand of the King, another Messianic reference fulfilled here.

27. Beale, *The Book of Revelation*, 963.

28. Thomas and Macchia, *Revelation*, 344, notes that "flesh" (*sarkas*), occurs five times in verse 18, which may connect this to 17:16, the only previous occurrence of "flesh" in Revelation.

under the demonic influence of the dragon.[29] There are several passages in the Old Testament that speak of the kings of the earth taking their stand against God. See Ezekiel 38:2–9 and 39:2; Zechariah 12–14; Zephaniah 3, as well as Psalm 2:2.

But there isn't even a war. The beast was captured, as well as the false prophet who had deceived the people. They were thrown into the lake of fire, the eternal habitation of those who defy the Lamb. Daniel 7:11 says, "And as I looked, the beast was killed, and its body destroyed and given over to be burned with fire." The background for "lake of fire" is most likely the concept of *gehenna*, common for the first century Jewish audience. It is used here only in Revelation 19–21.[30] After the beast and the false prophet were thrown into the lake of fire, the rest of those who opposed the Lamb were slain with the breath of the Lord.[31]

## Conclusion

A young lady walked into a fabric shop, went to the counter, and asked the owner for some noisy, rustling, white material. The owner found two such bolts of fabric but was rather puzzled at the young lady's motives. Why would anyone want several yards of noisy material? Finally, the owner's curiosity got the best of him, and he asked the young lady why she particularly wanted noisy cloth. The young lady answered, "I am making a wedding gown, and my husband-to-be is blind. When I walk down the aisle, I want him to know when I've arrived at the altar, so he won't be embarrassed."

When Jesus comes riding on a white horse, all will see him coming, even the blind and the spiritually blind. And there will be no more secrets. All will be revealed. A question for us to ask ourselves is this: How do we want to see Jesus? Do we want to see him as he is seated at the table of his wedding banquet? Or do we want to see him as he is seated upon a war horse coming to judge the nations?

29. See Beale, *The Book of Revelation*, 967, who interprets the passive voice this way.

30. See Osborne, *Revelation*, 690. Mounce, *The Book of Revelation*, 350, writes that a lake of burning brimstone would not only be hot, but putrid and rank, an appropriate location for the sinful and wicked of the world. See Ezekiel 38:22 for the words, "fire," and "brimstone" used of Gog and Magog.

31. See Revelation 19:15, based again on Isaiah 49:2 and 11:4.

# Revelation 20:1–15

The Millennial Kingdom of the Final Doom of Satan

## Introduction

HELL IS NEVER AN easy topic of discussion, not because it is not true or because it is non-biblical, but because of the reality of it, and many people just don't take it seriously enough anymore. For many people in the West, hell seems to be a state of depression, or suffering on the earth, rather than a pit of fire. A recent *U.S. New and World Report* polls revealed that 64% of Americans believe there is a hell, 25% say there is not a hell, and 9% don't know. Most respondents think of hell as "an anguish state of existence" or "an unpleasant solitary confinement," rather than a real place. If a preacher preaches on hell, then people say he is being too negative or too judgmental, fear mongering. If a preacher does not preach on hell, some say he is being too soft. It is interesting to note that Jesus preached on the topic of hell and its reality more times than he did about heaven.

Here are just a few of the problems that arise when the modern thinker thinks about hell. Some believe that we will be able to walk around, hold conversations and still see old friends. Some hold to the cartoonish edition—everyone walking around hell with a pitchfork in their hand and a pointy tail. The problem with these too-common portraits is that it emotionally and mentally reduces the torment of hell for us, both for the non-believer and the believer. We don't want to take it seriously and we don't. But because we don't take it seriously, we begin to defuse the urgency in our heart to keep being used of God to keep others out or the thanksgiving we should express in God's grace in keeping us out.

Becoming increasingly common in the Evangelical church is the idea that there really is no hell, that when the unbeliever dies, then he or she just ceases to exist. This is called annihilationism. This, however, assumes that Jesus was only speaking culturally when he spoke of a literal hell and really didn't presume a literal place to exist. A brief survey of the gospels and how many times Jesus referred to an "everlasting torment" should dispel that for us, if we take seriously what Jesus said. Jesus would not have spoken culturally about something that exists beyond the boundaries of earthly culture.

Part of the root problem on this misunderstanding or misinterpretation is that scholars may start with a human understanding of God, even a limited understanding of God, and then try to explain the existence of hell and the future of the wicked, seemingly making excuses on God's behalf. Instead, we should accept what Jesus teaches on the subject, without playing the fancy word games that people play, and then struggle with the existence of evil, rather than change our views about God and what the Bible says. We need, rather, to change our own views. Some have got that all backward. They change what the Bible clearly teaches about God to fit their view.

Revelation 20 gives us some concrete truths about hell and about final judgment. The final judgment is a process in chapter 20, ending with the reality of the eternal lake of fire. This chapter, along with the many truths in other portions of Revelation, teaches us that final judgment is a reality we must come to terms with.

## Exposition

The method of interpretation of chapter 20 (and there are many) is dictated by the interpreter's position on the millennium. Is it a literal 1000 years? Is it a literal reign of Christ on the earth? Is it only symbolic? The premillennial position would understand Jesus' reign on the earth as literal. Whether it is a literal 1000-year reign is not clear and not vitally important to the discussion. The postmillennial position sees the millennial reign as something ushered in by the church. Jesus' second coming is after this "utopia," when all the nations of the world are evangelized. The a-millennial position does not hold to any kind of literal reign. Jesus is reigning now and has been reigning since the resurrection. What will happen at the end will be the consummation of all things and the creation of the new heavens and the new earth immediately following Jesus' return.

Beale, a reformed Biblicist, argues for a "recapitulation" understanding of Revelation 20. Chapter 20 is recapitulating or saying in another way, what John already described in chapter 16 and 19.[1] The problem with this view is that it does not take the sequence of events that are in chapter 20 seriously enough. Ladd notes that chapters 18–20 move in a series of destructions. Chapter 18 describes the destruction of Babylon; chapter 19

---

1. Beale, *The Book of Revelation*, 976–982. He argues for a relationship between the battle, the "nations" in 19:13–20 and 20:3, and the relationship of the structure of Daniel 7 to 19:11–20:6.

describes the destruction of the beast and the false prophet; and chapter 20 describes the destruction of Satan himself.[2] This commentary takes the premillennial view, but we will try to show the strengths primarily of the a-millennial view, while also providing counter arguments that seem to weigh in favor of the premillennial view. The postmillennial view has too many weaknesses to be a viable option.[3]

In verse 1, remembering that Jesus has just come as a conquering King to the earth with the holy ones with him, John sees an angel coming down out of heaven, with the key to the Abyss and a great chain. The Abyss is probably the same as that mentioned in chapter 13. It is the source of evil, and the holding place of the demonic. It was thought to be a vast "subterranean cavern which served as a place of confinement for disobedient spirits awaiting judgment."[4] John is again on earth when he sees the vision, because he sees the angel "coming down from heaven." Just as Christ has authority over death and Hades and holds the key (1:18), so the angel here executes that authority on behalf of Christ.

Beale argues that the binding of Satan was probably inaugurated during the ministry of Christ (see Matthew 12:29; Mark 3:27; and Luke 10:17–19) and was climactically put into motion immediately after Christ's resurrection. It lasts most of the age between Christ's first and second comings. According to 20:7–9, the end point occurs immediately before Christ's final coming.[5] I understand the argument, but Satan has been active in the world since he was cast out of heaven. He is not bound now, like the image in Revelation 20:1–2, where he is bound and thrown into the Abyss. He is still the prince of the power of the air and is still quite active. The Devil's influence is clear in 2 Corinthians 4:3–4; 11:15; Ephesus 2:2; 2 Timothy 2:26; and 1 Peter 5:8. A roaring lion does not seem to be the proper image of one bound in the Abyss. Mounce believes that the recapitulation argument

2. Ladd, *A Commentary on the Revelation of John*, 261.

3. To its credit, this view takes seriously the task of the church in evangelism, but its viewpoint that the world will continue to get better is too optimistic. Interestingly, even where I live, Indonesia, that has a high level of poverty but has seen significant technological growth over the last several decades, not one of my students (of about sixty) feels Indonesia is better economically now compared to one hundred years ago. And slavery is a bigger problem now, it may be argued, than in several centuries. But all this is up for a healthy and cordial debate.

4. Mounce, *The Book of Revelation*, 352. Aune (Aune, *Revelation 17–22*, 1078) observes that in Hesiod's Theogony, the conquest of the Titans by Zeus and his allies is followed by the imprisonment of the defeated foes below the earth.

5. Beale, *The Book of Revelation*, 985.

(Beale's argument) at least bears the burden of proof, apart from the sequential understanding of the "I saw" statements.[6]

It is abundantly clear in verse 2 who the dragon is. He is Satan, the Devil, the ancient serpent who deceived Eve in the Garden of Eden. This places the reversal of the curse at its final end. The one who deceived is being locked up. There is no war. There is no conflict. The dragon is seized. He bends to the mighty will of God as expressed and carried out by the angel. 2 Peter 2:4 says, "For if God did not spare angels when they sinned but cast them into hell (*tartanus*) and committed them to chains of gloomy darkness to be kept until the judgment." Thomas observes that while Satan imprisoned the saints in Smyrna for 10 days, he will be bound for 1000 years; one hundred years for each day of binding.[7] This emphasizes again the symbolic nature of these numbers. The suffering of the saints at the hand of God's enemy is limited. The reign of Christ is complete.

The angel who bound the dragon threw him into the Abyss and locked and sealed it. He was sealed in the pit (the Abyss) for 1000 years so that (Gr. *hiva*) he might not deceive the nations for a time. Beale, supporting the a-millennial view, believes that "sealed so as not to deceive" would mean that the devil's activities are curtailed to a degree, but not totally stopped. He sees a parallel to this passage in 9:1–10. This parallel is "synchronous" with 20:1–3 and portrays those whom Satan is permitted to deceive and those whom he is not permitted to deceive.[8] Ladd does not agree with Beale. "Satan will never be loosed from bondage to Christ won by his death and resurrection."[9] Ladd makes a good point here, though Beale says he is missing the point. Beale says Satan is not released from his bondage to Christ. His very deception of people at the end of the age is part of Christ's plan.[10] But, with Mounce, it must be remembered that the elaborate measures taken to ensure that the deceiving activities of the Devil are curtailed seems to imply the complete cessation of his influence on earth, rather than a mere curbing of his influence.[11]

---

6. See Mounce, *The Book of Revelation*, 3552 and Thomas and Macchia, *Revelation*, 348, but not Osborne (Osborne, *Revelation*, 699), who believes there is a chronology, but that it cannot be proven from the "I saw" sequence.

7. Thomas and Macchia, *Revelation*, 350.

8. Beale, *The Book of Revelation*, 986.

9. Ladd, *A Commentary on the Revelation of John*, 263.

10. Beale, *The Book of Revelation*, 987.

11. Mounce, *The Book of Revelation*, 353. Thomas (Thomas and Macchia, *Revelation*, 350) who notes there is a progression of Satan's limitations in Revelation. In chapter 12, he is thrown out of heaven. In chapter 20, he is thrown into the Abyss.

Who were those who will be deceived on the earth after Satan is released? And why "is it necessary" (Gr. *dei*) for him to be released for a
short time? The second question may be answered first. It will be necessary
to release Satan for a short time in order to differentiate those who really
love the Lamb from those who only are going through the motions, who
are submitting to his leadership on their knees, but have yet to bow the
heart. And secondly, were not the nations of the earth destroyed in chapter
19 (A common question of criticism from those who support a-millen-
nialism). If so, who are those who are deceived? This must be describing
the response of the remaining survivors on the earth, the non-military
personnel, who stayed alive after the last battle, and come to worship Jesus
forcibly (see Zechariah 14).[12]

After the vision of Satan's binding, John next sees thrones, and upon
the thrones those who had been given authority from Jesus. He also sees the
souls of those who had been beheaded for the sake of the cause of Christ.
They came to life and reigned with Christ during the time of the millennium. There are several questions here. Who are these who reigned? What
is the nature of this resurrection?

Part of the answer to these questions is determined by what position
the interpreter takes on the millennium. Premillennialists believe that the
thrones are on the earth, and those seated on the thrones are those who have
followed the Lamb and have not submitted to the dragon. They have died
and will be raised to life to reign with Christ on earth. Amillennialists hold
that these thrones are in heaven and those seated on the thrones are those
who have been raised (their souls—spiritually) to be with Christ from the
time of Pentecost and on through the church age.

The problem with viewing this resurrection as a spiritual resurrection
is that the word, *anastasis*, in verse 5, which occurs over forty times in the
New Testament, is used almost exclusively for physical resurrection (Luke
2:34 is the only exception).[13] One who holds to the a-millennial position
needs to be grammatically creative to make verse 4 mean spiritual resurrection, and not physical resurrection. A natural reading of the text leads
to the natural conclusion that this verse is speaking about a physical resurrection. Also, "came to life and reigned" are in the aorist indicative tense.

---

12. See Ladd, *A Commentary on the Revelation of John*, 262; Osborne, *Revelation*,
702.

13. See Johnson, *Hebrews through Revelation*, 584. Also, Ladd (Ladd, *A Commentary on the Revelation of John*, 265), speaking more specifically about the word *ezesan*
in verse 4, says it should not be used of spiritual resurrection, but only of physical
resurrection. See John 11:35, Romans 14:9, Revelation 1:18; 2:8; 13:14, and most likely
verse 5.

This meaning is undefined grammatically. Does this mean they came to life and reigned at a moment in the past from the perspective of John's time, or from the perspective of the final vision of the end, that is, they came to life and reigned after Jesus came back? A natural reading of the text, given the building chronology of judgment, leans toward the latter view—they came back to life and reigned with Christ.[14]

The martyrs are the focus of 20:4, those beheaded for the cause of Christ, but all the saints are intended in the larger context. It is grammatically difficult to conclude that only the martyrs will sit on the throne. The martyrs are the past embodying the whole, namely all who have remained faithful to Jesus.[15] In other words, all who have remained faithful to Jesus means those who have lost their lives for his sake and those who have lived as if they were dead and he is alive in them. Those who have died in Christ before the return of Christ will come with him in triumphal process at his return. Those who are still alive in Christ at the time of his return, will meet the Lord in the air, and then return with him in victory as well. It is to these, those faithful to the end, that he will give the right to reign at his side for the length of the millennium, a time set by him and reflected in the symbolic 1000 years.[16]

The parenthetical comment in verse 5 refers to the rest of the dead who have not followed the Lamb. They are still in their graves, and they will face the judgment, the great white throne of God, the resurrection of the dead. See 1 Thessalonians 4 and 5. Almost all commentators agree that verse 5 refers to a physical resurrection. If that is the case, then it seems even more likely that verse 4 also refers to a physical resurrection (see discussion above). Besides this, a spiritual resurrection rather than a physical resurrection is quite foreign to Johannine hearers. For examples of this we could refer to John 20 and 21 and the descriptions of the resurrection as well as 1

14. See also Matthew 19:28; 20:21; 2 Timothy 2:11–12; cf. Daniel 7:18, referring to the promise of reigning with Christ. In Matthew 19:28, Jesus promises Peter: ". . . . Truly, I say to you, in the new world, when the Son of Man will sit on his glorious throne, you who have followed me will also sit on twelve thrones, judging the twelve tribes of Israel."

15. Osborne, *Revelation*, 705. Contra Mounce (Mounce, *The Book of Revelation*, 359), who understands those reigning as a special reward for those who have paid with their lives the price of faithful opposition to the antichrist and the reign of the beast.

16. Mounce (Mounce, *The Book of Revelation*, 357) notes that the background for the concept of the millennium comes from Isaiah 11:10–16; 65:20–25; and Daniel 7:14, 27. In II Esdras 7:28, the millennium lasts 400 years. In Slavanic Enoch, the world is to last seven days of 1000 years each, followed by an eighth day with time divisions (II Enoch 32:2–33:2). It is not surprising, then, that the millennium in Revelation is marked out as 1000 years.

John 3:2.[17] John actually never specifically mentions a "second resurrection" probably because for him it is not a true resurrection. In the New Testament, that is only reserved for believers.[18]

In verse 6, John mentions the fifth beatitude, or statement of blessing. Here those who share in the first resurrection, those who will be raised with Christ because of their faith in him, are blessed. They are blessed because they do not take part in the second death, the second "resurrection" unto judgment and death. These are also called "holy," reinforcing the idea of those faithful witnesses who have stayed awake and have not defiled their garments, nor worshipped the beast, but have made themselves ready for the wedding supper of the Lamb. Because of the commitment to life in Christ, they are free from the second death. The second death is a phrase referring to the final judgment. There is life only in Jesus, never apart from him. This second death will not touch those who belong to the Giver of life. Those who share in the first resurrection will reign with Christ (see verse 4) for 1000 years. They will be priests, just as was promised in 1:6.

The story shifts in verse 7. There was a set time of peace, a complete time, as the 1000 years indicates. But Satan will be released from his prison after that period of time is over. Why the release? Bauckham observes "The devil is given a last chance to deceive the nations. But is no re-run of the rule of the beast. The citadel of the saints proves impregnable."[19] Mounce offers another possible and reasonable explanation. Satan was released to show that "neither the designs of Satan nor the waywardness of the human heart will be altered by the mere passing of time."[20] Even after a blissful time of peace on the earth, with the King of kings on his throne, mankind, unwilling to bend the heart while bending the knee, will be quickly and tragically deceived by Satan one last time.

The nations who are remaining and who are deceived gather for battle one last time. Satan gathers the nations of the earth, the whole earth (four corners)[21] of those who did not want to stay faithful to the Lamb. They gather to do battle against the Lamb. The number of those in battle cannot be counted. They are like the sand of the sea. Ezekiel 38 provides background for this passage and the symbolic identity of Gog and Magog. It

17. Thomas and Macchia, *Revelation*, 354.

18. See Osborne, *Revelation*, 708.

19. Bauckham, *New Testament Theology*, 107.

20. Mounce, *The Book of Revelation*, 361. Ladd (Ladd, *A Commentary on the Revelation of John*, 269) adds that the rebellion of mankind after the millennium proves that man cannot blame their sin on their circumstances or their environment, but only on their wicked hearts.

21. See Isaiah 11:12; Ezekiel 7:2; 37:9; Daniel 7:2.

serves no purpose to try to determine what nations these names represent. The names Gog and Magog probably became proverbial in Jerusalem for any enemy that was violently opposed to God's people.[22] This is not the same war as was described in 16:13–16 and 19:17–21. This war follows the thousand-year reign.[23]

This gathering of the deceived marches against the people of God. The universalization of Ezekiel's prophesy suggests that the oppression of Israel in Ezekiel 38–39 is also universal, and so, the "camp of God's people," in verse 9, is to be understood as the church throughout the earth, those who have followed the Lamb and remained faithful.[24] The wicked march against the saints at the central city of the millennial reign. Jerusalem? It is unclear.[25] But again there is no battle. Fire devours them from heaven, just as fire devoured the pagan armies trying to attack Elijah. See 2 Kings 1:10–14.[26]

At the conclusion of this quick and decisive battle, Satan is thrown into the lake of fire, where the beast and the false prophet had been thrown. The fact that the devil is now thrown into the lake of fire to join the beast and the false prophet seems to indicate some chronological sequence. This means that the battle in chapter 20, after the millennium, cannot be the same battle as that of chapter 16 and 19. So also, Osborne concludes, "There is a distinct progression throughout chapters 19–22, from the return of Christ to the millennium to the final judgment and finally to the descent of the new heavens and new earth. The recapitulation theory does not do justice to this progression and to the difference of details at each level."[27] This is the final judgment of the dragon, the Devil. He, along with the false prophet and the beast, will be tormented forever and ever. The torment of the lake of fire is eternal.

Next, in verse 11, John sees the great white throne. The white throne is the throne of judgment. John sees the throne and the One on the throne. This is truly the end, the final judgment. The removal of the old heavens and earth (the earth and sky fled away), was foretold in Haggai 2:6 and Hebrews 12:26–28. The new heaven and earth (chapters 21–22) will be

---

22. See Beale, *The Book of Revelation*, 1025; Mounce, *The Book of Revelation*, 362.

23. See Mounce, *The Book of Revelatior*, 362; contra Beale (Beale, *The Book of Revelation*, 980, 1023), who links the deception of the nations to 16:12–16 as the same event because of the similarity of language of deception, and both are followed by a description of the destruction of the cosmos.

24. See Beale, *The Book of Revelation*, 1022.

25. "City he loves" may echo Psalm 87:2–3; Psalm 122:6; Isaiah 66:10; Zephaniah 3:14–17. This is the argument for the identity to be linked with the church as the Gentiles are part of the Zion of God. See Beale, *The Book of Revelation*, 1028.

26. Also see Ezekiel 38:22, 39:6, and Habakkuk 1:6.

27. Osborne, *Revelation*, 715.

coming, so the old must go. Isaiah 51:6 says, "Lift up your eyes to the heavens, and look at the earth beneath; for the heavens vanish like smoke, the earth will wear out like a garment, and they who dwell in it will die in like manner." 2 Peter 3:10–12 also speaks of the elements burning up in the fire. The old heaven and earth flee from the presence of the One on the throne. They flee because they have no more use. All that is important in eternity is the throne of God, the saints, and the eternal joy that will be present through the coming of the new Jerusalem and the new earth. The creation will finally and fully be renewed.

Who is he who is sitting on the throne? It could either be God at the last judgment,[28] or Jesus. The important point is the God/Jesus is on the throne, is the Judge of all the nations, and will execute his justice upon all those who have fallen under the control of the forces of evil. The whiteness of the throne indicates not only purity and justice, but also vindication. The wicked will be judged, and the righteous will be vindicated (see 6:10).[29]

John sees the dead. Who are these dead? These are probably all those who have died, not just the wicked, but the righteous. The book of life was opened. If names are found in the book of life, they receive life; if not, then they receive death—the second death. There is no distinction at the throne. Both the small and the great appear. 2 Corinthians 5:10 says, "For we must all appear before the judgment seat of Christ (good argument for the identity of the One on the throne being Jesus), that each one may receive what is due for what he has done in the body, whether good or evil."[30] There are multiple books. One is the book of life. One is the book of deeds, a record of what mankind has done. Mankind will be judged based upon those books. But if one's name is found in the book of life, then eternal life is the reward.

The sea, a traditional source of wickedness, and Hades, the holding ground for those who had died, all have to give up their dead to stand before the throne. Jesus has said in John 5:28–29, "Do not marvel at this, for an hour is coming when all who are in the tombs will hear his voice and come out, those who have done good to the resurrection of life, and those who have done evil to the resurrection of judgment."[31] Those whose names are in the book of life will enter the new heaven and the new earth (21:1).

Finally, the big enemy of mankind, Death, will be thrown down. Death was defeated on the cross and out of the grave. Its final hold on humanity

28. See Mounce, *The Book of Revelation*, 364 and Thomas and Macchia, *Revelation*, 360.

29. Beale, *The Book of Revelation*, 1032. See Ezekiel 1:26–28 and Daniel 7:10 for images of the throne.

30. See also Romans 2:6–11.

31. See also Matthew 16:27 and Acts 17:3.

in the old system of the old earth will be broken, and there will be no more death in heaven, nor sorrow or pain. Paul says in 1 Corinthians 15:26, "The last enemy to be destroyed is death." Jesus also refers to the cessation of death in Luke 20:36, speaking of the resurrection. The faithful will no longer die, for death will no longer have a hold on them. Those who are thrown into the lake of fire experience the second death. Those who participate in the second death will forever be separated from God, the source of life. They will be outside the holy city (21:8; 22:15; see also Luke 15:24, 32; Ephesians 2:1; Colossians 2:13.[32]

Chapter 20 ends fairly clear. If your name is not in the book, you are thrown into the lake of life. If your name is in the book, you enter the new heaven and the new earth. If your name is in the book of life, you belong to the Lamb who already suffered the punishment of separation from God so that those who belong to him do not have to suffer it.

## Conclusion

Malachi 3:16–18 speaks about this book. "Then those who feared the Lord spoke with one another. The Lord paid attention and heard them, and a book of remembrance was written before him of those who feared the Lord and esteemed his name. They shall be mine, says the Lord of hosts, in the day when I make up my treasured possession, and I will spare them as a man spares his son who serves him. Then once more you shall see the distinction between the righteous and the wicked, between one who serves God and one who does not serve him."

The important distinction for us is whether or not our names will be in the Book. Jesus told his disciples, "Do not rejoice because the spirits submit to you but rejoice that your names are written in heaven." Our names are entered into the Book of Life when we receive the forgiveness that Jesus offers and believe. Actually, the names of the elect have been there since the beginning

---

32. Beale, *The Book of Revelation*, 1036. Beale (Beale, *The Book of Revelation*, 1034–35) also gives several possible explanations of how Death and Hades can be thrown into the lake of fire: 1) It could mean that death is annihilated forever; 2) It could be a figurative way of saying that in the eternal, consummated state, physical death will no longer be a reality; 3) "Death and Hades" may be a metonymy in which the container is substituted for the contained. That which once contained the souls of men will be forever contained in the lake of fire; 4) "Death and Hades" is the location of those who have suffered the physical death (the first death) in the pre-consummation age, but it has come to an end and has been incorporated into the lake of fire; 5) Death and Hades may be Satanic forces governing the regions of the dead. These forces are thrown into the lake of fire. Of these options, 3, 4, and 5 are the best choices.

of time according to Revelation 13:8. And the reality of it is that those whose names are not there will face the final judgment, the lake of fire.

The lake of fire is real. We can dismiss it because it doesn't make sense to us. We can deny its existence because it doesn't line up with our feeble conceptions of God. We can soften it by creating silly images of those who are there, but we cannot change the reality of the lake of fire. It does not help us to try to imagine what this will be like. Jesus never asked us to figure that out. But we must acknowledge both the horror of this reality and the joy of the final consummation.

# Revelation 21:1–27

## A New Heaven and a New Earth

### Introduction

Over time, the longer a couple is married, the more alike they become. They copy one another's facial expressions and mannerisms. They begin to laugh and cry about the same things. They like many of the same restaurants and foods, assuming, of course, that they are growing closer to one another. For the church and Jesus, the head of the church, this should also be true. The church must increasingly look like Jesus, the Groom, the longer she knows him, so also, we individually must increasingly act and think and speak like Jesus as we grow in our faith and in his grace. But for the church (for the believer), the wedding with Jesus has not yet begun. We are waiting in that period of betrothal, or engagement, when we look forward to the coming of the Bridegroom. That is when we shall be like him and see him face to face. The character of the church must ultimately pattern the character of God.

There are picture puzzle books that are made of a grid, 10 squares by 10 squares. Each square had an associate number like A–1, B–1, C–2, and so on. On the other side of the page is an empty grid of 100 squares (10 x 10) with the letters on the side and the numbers on the top. The point was to draw the appropriate square to the left into the grid pattern on the right, until the drawing was complete, filling in all 100 squares. For me, it was always easier to draw in the small, individual squares if I looked in the back of the book for the answer key. There I was able to see the completed picture. As we come to the end of Revelation, we see the answer key, the final, completed picture. By studying this and from the encouragement gained from it, we can better fill in the squares of our living for Christ now.

### Exposition

A preacher said about thirty years ago, "The earth in all its beauty God created in six days. And Jesus said to his disciples that he is going to prepare a place for them. And if God took six days to make the world, and he has been working 2000 years on the new place, imagine what it will be like!" The speaker was being a bit facetious, because we know that God could create in less than an instant whatever he wanted to create. But I think his point was that God is preparing something for us, and it will be beyond our imagination. That is why John has some trouble describing it in human terms. The sight of what he saw overwhelmed him.

Much of what John sees in Revelation 21 and 22 mirrors what Ezekiel saw in Ezekiel 4–48. There are two primary sections from 21:1–22:5. 21:1–8 has the dual purpose of concluding 19:11–21:8 and introducing 21:1–22:5. It acts as a bridge between the heavenly and earthly. Heaven comes down to earth; earth comes to Heaven. The two become one.[1]

In verse 1, we see a drastic contrast between the image of heaven and the image of judgment from the last four verses of chapter 20. John sees a new heaven and a new earth. There is no longer the old or first heaven and earth, since these had been cast from the presence of the Lamb. God is preparing something new. Isaiah 65:17 says, "For behold, I create new heavens and a new earth, and the former things shall not be remembered or come into mind." Contrasting this idea of not remembering the old is the sustaining reality of the new in Isaiah 66:22, "For as the new heavens and the new earth that I make shall remain before me, says the Lord, so shall your offspring and your name remain."

The old will be forgotten. The new will endure forever. Mounce notes that the idea of a renovated heaven and earth is common in apocalyptic literature. In 1 Enoch 45:4–5, the heavens and earth are transformed into a place reserved for the elect. In II Esdras 7:75, there is a future time when God shall "renew the creation." There is to be a physical transformation. As the new covenant is superior to and replaces the old, so the new heavens and the new earth are superior to and replace the old.[2] What makes the heavens and earth "new" is that now God is dwelling with men. The Greek word "new" (*kainos*) means new in quality, fresh, rather than recent, or new in time.[3]

The passing away of the world is also described in the statement "there was no longer any sea." Why is the sea among those parts of creation singled out as no longer a part of creation? Beale believes that a correct understanding of the identification of the sea helps in answering this question. There are five possible identifications: 1) The origin of cosmic evil (4:6; 12:18; 13:1; 15:2); 2) The unbelieving, rebellious nations that stood

---

1. See Osborne, *Revelation*, 728.
2. Mounce, *The Book of Revelation*, 369.
3. Johnson, *Hebrews through Revelation*, 592.

against God and God's people (12:18; 13:1; Isaiah 57:20); ) The place of the dead (20:13); 4) The main location of the world's idolatrous business and economic practices (18:10–19); 5) Literal body of water, often mentioned together with earth, to show that the sea is a symbol of the part of the old world that represents the whole (5:13; 7:1–3; 8:8–9; 10:2, 5–6, 8; 14:7). The meaning probably encompasses all five of these identifications. The sea is no more, because Satan and all his influence are no more. They have been cast from the presence of God.[4]

With the sea gone there is no longer a threat of evil or the power of evil. John sees the bride coming down from God. The bride beautifully adorned for her husband is the church. So here, the holy city, the new Jerusalem, is the church. This brings back the image of the bride in Revelation 19 and the wedding supper of the Lamb. Isaiah 52:1 says, "Awake, awake, put on your strength O Zion; put on your beautiful garments, O Jerusalem, the holy city; for there shall no more come into you the uncircumcised and the unclean." Johnson holds that a "bride-city" captures something of God's personal relationship to his people as well as something of their life of communion with him and one another.[5] And so, Osborne also believes that this New Jerusalem is both a people (the redeemed of the Lord), and a place, in contrast to the wicked city of Babylon, also both a people and a place.[6]

The comments in verse 2 concerning the bride beautifully dressed for her husband, does not mean that she prepared herself by her own efforts, just as 19:7, "made herself ready," did not mean that. The righteousness and beautiful garments of the bride are given to her by the Groom. She is "prepared" in verse 2, a divine passive, indicating God's role and not human effort.

Verse 3 is a fulfillment of Leviticus 26:11–12. If the Israelites were faithful in following God and not worshipping the idols of the nations, God promised to them, "I will make my dwelling among you, and my soul shall not abhor you. And I will walk among you and will be your God, and you shall be my people." The fellowship lost because of sin in the Garden of Eden will be restored. God would dwell with men and live with them. What began through the coming of the Immanuel, the birth, ministry, death, and resurrection of Christ, will be consummated at the end of all things. Speaking of the return of the glory of God to the temple, God said to Ezekiel in Ezekiel 43:7, "Son of man, this is the place of my throne and the place for the soles of my feet, where I will dwell in the midst of the people of Israel forever. And the house of Israel shall no more defile my holy name, neither they, nor their

---

4. See Beale, *The Book of Revelation*, 1042.

5. Johnson, *Hebrews through Revelation*, 593.

6. Osborne, *Revelation*, 733.

kings, by their whoring and by the dead bodies of their kings at their high places." God will "tent" with his people, *skenosei*, similar to the word used in John 1:14. The Word become flesh and "tented" with us. This dwelling will be completed with the New Jerusalem.

2 Corinthians 6:16 says, "We are the temple of the living God." Beale notes that all the Old Testament prophesies refer to a singular people (*laos*) which will be the dwelling place of God. Revelation 21:3 changes the singular into a plural (*laoi*) to make the clear point that the prophesies originally given to Israel and thought to apply only to Israel, is finally consummated by the salvation of every tribe, tongue, people and nation (5:9; 7:9). Zechariah 2:10–11 anticipates this consummation: "Sing and rejoice, O daughter of Zion, for behold, I come and I will dwell in your midst, declares the LORD. And many nations shall join themselves to the Lord in that day, and shall be my people. And I will dwell in your midst, and you shall know that the LORD of hosts has sent me to you."[7]

The images of joy and the end of death, mourning, crying, or pain were common images of the final state of peace. Isaiah 35:10 says, "and the ransomed of the Lord shall return and come to Zion with singing; everlasting joy shall be upon their heads; they shall obtain gladness and joy, and sorrow and sighing shall flee away." Isaiah 65:19 says, "I will rejoice in Jerusalem and be glad in my people; no more shall be heard in it the sound of weeping and the cry of distress." See also Isaiah 51:11. Isaiah 25:8 says as well, "The LORD God will wipe away the tears from all faces." John heard this sung in 7:17. Mounce writes, "The tears are not tears of remorse shed in heaven for failures on earth, but tears of suffering shed on earth as a result of faithfulness to Christ."[8]

In verse 5, the new creation is reiterated by the One speaking from the throne. All things will be made new. The emphasis in the Greek is on the newness of all things, literally translated, "new I am making all things." Isaiah 65:17 and 66:22 have already been alluded to in verse 1 and in verse 4, along with Isaiah 43:18. Isaiah 43:19 seems to be the background for verse 5, "See, I am doing a new thing." The "new thing" began with the new man in Christ (see 2 Corinthians 5:17) and is consummated in the end. Beale calls the present tense ("I am making") a prophetic present, like the Hebrew prophetic perfect, foreseeing the time when God will be

---

7. Beale, *The Book of Revelation*, 1047; see also Mounce, *The Book of Revelation*, 372. John modified the traditional concept of "people" from Jeremiah 7:23, 30:22, and Hosea 2:23 to indicate the many peoples of redeemed humanity.

8. Mounce, *The Book of Revelation*, 372; see also Ladd, 277. The tears represent all human sorrow, tragedy, and evil.

creating all things new, not referring to the present time of the church age. It emphasizes the certainty.[9]

The One speaking from the throne then speaks to John. "It is done" reminds the reader of 16:17, when the judgment was pronounced finished. Here it indicates a final fulfillment. What began "to be done" with the seventh bowl of wrath, is now fully and completely done with pronouncement from the throne. God is identified again as the Alpha and Omega, the Beginning and the End, just as in 1:8. God is speaking of the dissolution of the old order caused by the first sin in the beginning of time, and the restoration of that old order with the new in the new age. He is the beginning and the end.

And from him comes living water. As Jesus declared to the Samaritan woman in John 4, and on the day of the feast in John 7:37, "If anyone is thirsts, let him come to me and drink," so here God declares, "To the thirsty I will give from the spring of the water of life without payment." Both these encounters of Jesus and Isaiah 55 are probably in mind here as John reports what is said by God. In Isaiah 55 it is wine and milk that is offered without money and without cost. The idea is the same.[10]

All the gifts and joys of God are the inheritance of him who overcomes. Those who overcome are those who have remained faithful even unto death. These are those who have refused to worship the beast and the dragon, and, in so doing, have overcome them. They are victorious and they enter into the covenant relationship with God as his people. See Revelation 2 and 3 for the many exhortations and rewards for those who overcome.

Those who do not receive the gift of the water of life are those who have rejected God, whose place will be in the fiery lake of burning sulfur, the second death. The list in verse 8 is not a list of those people who were like that before Christ, but those who remained like that even after hearing the gospel, but rejecting it. These are those who worship the beast and his image. These are those who receive the mark. That is why they are the cowardly, the unbelieving, the vile, the murderers, the sexually immoral, those who practice magic arts, idolaters and liars.[11] These are character traits of the dragon, the beast, and the false prophet. The small Greek word meaning but, *de*, contrasts the cowardly with those who conquer. The conquerors did not bend to the pressures of the dragon. The cowardly did.[12]

9. Beale, *The Book of Revelation*, 1052.

10. Mounce, *The Book of Revelation*, 374, also see Jeremiah 2:13 and Psalm 36:9 to get helpful background. Both make reference to God as the fountain of living water.

11. Thomas (Thomas and Macchia, *Revelation*, 372) notes that there is a stark contrast between those who lie and the followers of the Lamb in whom no lies or deception are found (14:5).

12. See Beale, *The Book of Revelation*, 1059.

John is then shown the bride, the wife of the Lamb. We saw the bride, beautifully dressed, in chapter 19 and the beginning of this section. Here is a recapitulation of this, another picture, "from another angle" as it were. There is a very distinct parallel here with 17:1 to contrast the prostitute with the bride of the Lamb, a contrast that is hard to compare because it is so great. Beale notes that each of the two cities (Babylon and the New Jerusalem) are adorned with the same attire ("gold," "precious stones," and "pearls" (see 17:4; 18:12, 16; 21:18–21), which is symbolic of their works, though very different in character. The prostitute's adornment represents ungodly economic greed working in coordination with the wicked nations of the world. The bride's adornment represents her faithfulness to the Lamb and his righteousness given to her.[13]

Just as John was carried by the Spirit to see the great prostitute of Revelation 17:3, in verse 10 he is carried by the Spirit to see the bride on the mountain of God. Here we have introduced, like in Ezekiel 40:1–2, the vision of the future temple. Ezekiel saw a future vision, as did John, but John further interprets this vision, more fully interpreted by the identity of the New Jerusalem with the renewed and completed people of God. Why a mountain? Mounce provides a good answer. In Jewish thought, mountains always had a significant role. Moses' historical encounter with God on Mount Sinai (Exodus 19), and Ezekiel's great vision of the restored temple (Ezekiel 40:1–2). The holy city that John sees descending from God out of heaven is a "real event" within the visionary experience.[14] In other words, it is something that is going to take place sometime in the future, but is loaded with symbolism, for one, the mountain as a divine revelation.

The city of God, the bride of Christ, reflected the glory of God (*doxan tou theou*). The glory is her possession because she is forever now in his presence. The glory is like crystal. Here John uses symbolic language again (Gr. *hos*) to convey something that he most likely had never seen before. The goal of the church now is to "become blameless and pure, children of God without fault in a crooked and depraved generation, in which you shine like stars in the universe" (Philippians 2:15). Beale believes that the reference to the glory of God here must be taken from Isaiah 58:8 and 60:1–12, which

---

13. Beale, *The Book of Revelation*, 1064.

14. Mounce, *The Book of Revelation*, 378. Aune (Aune, *Revelation 17–22*, 1151) observes that the "proximity of high mountains to the celestial world makes them appropriate settings for revelations and visionary experiences." Thomas (Thomas and Macchia, *Revelation*, 374) believes that the description of the mountain as "high and great" may indicate a mountain of supernatural size, the vantage point from which to see the enormous city of God coming down from heaven.

portrays the "glory of God" as something that belong to those residing in "Jerusalem" at the end of time.[15]

The description of the temple in verse 12 is similar to what Ezekiel saw in Ezekiel 48:31–34. This is the church, the people of God, with the names of the twelve tribes of Israel and the names of the twelve apostles (see verse 14). The wall of the temple is described and "great and high." In Isaiah 26:1, the song sings of a "strong city," at the end time in Judah where "God makes salvation its walls and ramparts." The city wall is high and great because it cannot be broken. It is impenetrable. It is unscalable. It knows no enemy who can come against it. One feature not included in Ezekiel is the angel stationed at each gate. Beale compares these angels with the angels of the seven churches,[16] angels associated with the people of God. In Isaiah 62:6, we see the watchmen at the walls of Jerusalem, commissioned to pray and intercede for the people, and Ladd sees these angels as such.[17] But Osborne agrees with Beale. These angels are not guards or watchmen, but linked to the angels of the seven churches.[18]

Strengthening Osborne and Beale's concept of the angels of the seven churches as a parallel for these twelve angels at the gates of the new city is verse 14. Here we have the "churchifying" of the people of God, as the names of the twelve apostles are on the foundations.[19] The names of the twelve tribes combined with names of the twelve apostles gives the idea of completeness, representing God's people before God's presence in the temple. It is interesting to note, as Beale does, that the apostles are the foundation, and not the tribes of Israel. Chronologically one would expect the opposite. But this emphasizes the importance of the fulfillment of the promises in Christ as part of the foundation stone of God's people, the new temple, the church, the new Israel.[20] The identity of the apostles and their worthiness to be the foundation stones of the temple is linked intimately with their identity with the slain Lamb of God who purchased them.

15. Beale, *The Book of Revelation*, 1066.

16. Beale, *The Book of Revelation*, 1068.

17. Ladd, *A Commentary on the Revelation of John*, 281.

18. Osborne, *Revelation*, 751. The twelve gates, according to Mounce (Mounce, *The Book of Revelation*, 379), symbolize abundant entrance. But it could just as easily be tied to the vision of Ezekiel 48, where the three gates on all four sides represent the twelve tribes of Israel.

19. See Matthew 16:18, 1 Corinthians 3, and 1 Peter 2.

20. Beale, *The Book of Revelation*, 1070. Mounce (Mounce, *The Book of Revelation*, 379) writes, "The juxtaposition of the twelve tribes with the twelve apostles shows the unity of ancient Israel and the New Testament church."

John sees another angel with a measuring rod in his hand. This alludes both to the measuring rod of 11:1 and Ezekiel 40:3–5. Whereas in 11:1–2 only the inner court was measured, here both the outer and the inner court are measured with the measuring rod, indicating that God would protect his people in every way, both spiritually and physically. There is no more evil. There is no more threat.[21] Osborne notes that measuring rods at the time were only about ten feet, four inches long. This rod was too small to measure such a vast city.[22] But this emphasizes again the metaphorical or symbolic nature of the figures mentioned here, figures which astound the imagination (see verse 16–21).

The city was measured out like a square, just as the Most Holy Place of the temple was a cubic square.[23] But in this case, the numbers are vast. 12,000 stadia is 1,380 miles or 2,221km. The distance is not as important as the symbolic number (12 x 1,000), a large number showing the perfect dimensions of the holy city of the saints. Beale makes the interesting observation that the size of the city is apparently the approximate size of the then known Hellenistic world. This suggests further that the temple-city was not only for the Israelites but was expanded to include the redeemed the nations of the world.[24]

The walls of the city are even more amazing, and out of proportion with the size of the city. The 144 cubits is 12 squared, or a multiple of 12, another symbolic figure for perfection. This echoes the 144,000 of chapter 7, as does the 12,000 stadia. 12,000 x 12 is 144,000. John is going out of his way to show the perfection and completeness of the temple. But the fact that there will be no evil in the New Jerusalem begs the question as to why have a wall in the first place, since walls kept the enemy outside? But this misses the point and reminds us of John's symbolism here as well as the magnificence of the vision that he was seeing. And as Osborne notes, the purpose of the wall was not to keep people out. It is too small in comparison to the city. Its purpose is beauty. And it adds a further emphasis on the great size of the city.[25] The final parenthetical comment in verse 17 concerning the human measurement the angel was using emphasizes even more so the symbolic nature of this vision. This is human terms that are used for the size. But we cannot forget that an angel was measuring it. It has a heavenly quality.

21. See also Beale, *The Book of Revelation*, 1073.

22. Osborne, *Revelation*, 752.

23. See 1 Kings 6:20; Ezekiel 45:2–3.

24. Beale, *The Book of Revelation*, 1074.

25. Osborne, *Revelation*, 754.

The material of the city, more symbolism, is glorious and beyond compare. The twelve jewels may be a reference to the ephod with the twelve jewels of the people of Israel, redefined as the people of God in Christ. Isaiah 54:11–12 reads, "O afflicted one, storm-tossed and not comforted, behold, I will set your stones in antimony, and lay your foundations with sapphires. I will make your pinnacles of agate, your gates of carbuncles, and all your walls of precious stones." In Isaiah, the promise was to the afflicted. God would honor what the world despised. So, in Revelation, the promise to the church is that though there is great trial and sorrow in this life, we know that the final and greater reward is coming. For the sufferings of this life cannot compare to the glories that will follow (see Romans 8). The multicolored character of the city gives a brilliance and glory. It is not important what the stones stand for. What John sees is a city alight with brilliant colors reflecting the glory of God. This was a glory that was beyond description.[26]

After the mind-boggling description of the city, John notes that there was no temple. There is no need for a temple. The presence of God has been revealed and there need not be a restraining place for God's glory. In other words, the Most Holy Place was the place for the ark of the covenant. If one entered there un-permitted, one would die. Moses was only permitted to see the back side of God. The glory of God fully experienced would have killed him. In heaven, in God's presence, there need no longer be that kind of barrier. So, there is no need for a temple. Also, the Lord God Almighty and the Lamb himself are the temple. They are the glory, the presence, and the eternal sacrifice. This brief sentence summarizes all the detail of Ezekiel's prophesy in Ezekiel 40–43. Christ has already been portrayed as the cornerstone of the temple in Ephesians 2:20, which is the church in Paul's context. See also Romans 9:32–33; Matthew 21:42; Mark 12:10–12; Luke 20:17–18; and Acts 4:11.[27]

Just as there is no need for the temple, so there is no need for the sun and the moon. The glory of the Lord and of the Lamb is sufficient. Isaiah 60:19 says, "The sun will no more be your light by day, nor for brightness shall the moon give you light; but the Lord will be your everlasting light, and your God will be your glory." By this glory the nations would walk. Isaiah 60:3 says, "And nations shall come to your light, and kings to the brightness of your

---

26. Beale, (Beale, *The Book of Revelation*, 1083) sees a connection between these stones and the first creation. This is a reinstitution of another new creation like the first creation preceding the sin of humanity. The same stones were found in the garden of Eden.

27. Beale, *The Book of Revelation*, 1090–91. See also Jeremiah 3:16–17 and Isaiah 65:17. Mounce (Mounce, *The Book of Revelation*, 383, writes, "For John there is no temple because symbol has given way to reality."

rising." The wealth of the nations would be brought to the city of Zion, meaning the glories of man will be laid down before the Lamb in acknowledgement of his greater glory. See Isaiah 60: 5, 11 as well. We ought not be too stressed about where these Gentile nations are at the end. If they belong to Christ, they are of the temple. If they do not, they are in the lake of fire. The glories they bring are their lives and praises devoted to the Lamb.

The unclean, and the false are kept out of the city. No longer is their defilement and deception a part of the experience of the people of God. Only those who have been cleansed by the blood of the Lamb have access to the city. To these the gates are open. To the impure and shameful the gates are permanently closed. This does not mean that the wicked will be sitting outside the walls of Jerusalem. This is apocalyptic language that fulfills many of the prophetic images of Isaiah and Ezekiel. Beale explains, "It is better to see John's use of the Old Testament as emphasizing the consummated redemption of those from among the nations, which will happen simultaneously with the final redemption of Jewish Christians. Prophesy portrays the future with language that is understandable to the prophet's contemporary readership."[28]

## Conclusion

First John 3:2–3 says, "Beloved, we are God's children now, and what we will be has not yet appeared; but we know that when he appears we shall be like him, because we shall see him as he is. And everyone who thus hopes in him purifies himself as he is pure." The hope that we have in seeing Jesus, and the finalization of the wedding plans, spurs us on to live for Jesus in the here and now. We can be pure now just as he is pure, as we look toward the day when we shall see him as he is and be like him.

In a Jewish ceremony of the first century, the young man who wanted to marry the daughter of a certain man in the village, would need to seek his permission first. If he gave an affirmative reply, the young man was invited to the house for a cup of wine. With the daughter at one end of the table, and the young man at the other end, in front of the cup of wine, the man would pick up the cup and take a drink. If the young woman accepted this well-understood act of proposal, she would also drink from the cup. If so, the young man would say, most likely in excitement, "I will not drink from the fruit of this cup, until I drink it with you in my father's house," meaning after the wedding.

28. Beale, *The Book of Revelation*, 1098.

Jesus said the same thing to his disciples in John 14:1-3, words and phrases very familiar to the disciples as betrothal vocabulary. Jesus is preparing a place for his bride. He is preparing his bride, beautifully dressed. May the vision of this heavenly home, the New Jerusalem, the final and glorious picture of the church, spur us on now to love and good deeds, as we wait for his return!

# Revelation 22:1–21

We Want to See Jesus, the Lamb

## Introduction

Have you ever come to the end of a book and been absolutely disappointed by the ending? It maybe wasn't what you expected. Or maybe it was a boring and uninspiring ending. Or it simply didn't fit with the rest of the book. Part of what makes a good book good, is the ending. Lora and I read out loud together the trilogy by J.R.R. Tolkien, *The Lord of the Rings*. We have the trilogy together in one volume, over 1000 pages long. The story is about the struggle between evil and the dark lord's lust for dominance through the one ring of power; and the small band of hobbits, elves, dwarves and kings who seek to destroy evil. But in order to destroy evil they have to suffer much. The end is the climax not only of that suffering, but also of their final victory over evil. The end fits with the rest of the book.

With Revelation 22, we come to the last chapter of the book of last things. And this chapter is also a climax befitting the story, the end of the world created by God and stained with the sin of humanity, and the beginning of the rest of eternity, the unwritten story of future glory. But the book of Revelation is not just an ordinary book, not just a piece of literature about the struggle between good and evil. It is a book of hope, of promise, of life, of heaven, and of Jesus. The book of last things becomes for the church, a book of first priority. In other words, the church ought to hear the book of Revelation and the return of Jesus again, and make it a common theme in conversation, thoughts, longings, and hope.

## Exposition

Revelation 22:1–5 is a continuation of the description of the New Jerusalem, with 22:6–21 serving as the epilogue of the book, and the final vision of hope, the return of Jesus. In eight of the final fifteen verses there is an exhortation to obedient, holy living. This is one of the important themes of the

234

book, emphasized more clearly and strongly here in the final chapter. The people of God must remain faithful to his name and to his glory. The end of the story is meant to motivate the followers of the Lamb now, in the midst of the story.[1] This epilogue is meant to close the prologue. There are quite a few similarities: The book is a genuine prophesy (1:3; 22:6, 9–10, 18–19); 2) The prophet is commissioned (1:1, 9–10; 22:8–10); 3) The book is meant to be read in the churches (1:3, 11; 22:18); and 4) The book is to encourage the faithful (1:3; 22:7, 12, 14).[2]

The vision opens in verse 1 with another scene of the river of life (see 21:6 and the discussion there concerning Isaiah 55 and John 4). There is only one source for this river, the throne of God and the of the Lamb. There is no lake source, so we cannot get bogged down by geographical details. God himself is the source of the river of life, because God himself is the source of life. A river is often associated with the final temple/presence of God. See Ezekiel 47:1, and Zechariah 14:8. Joel 3:18 says, "And in that day the mountains shall drip with sweet wine, and the hills shall flow with milk, and all the streambeds of Judah shall flow with water; and a fountain shall come forth from the house of the Lord and water the valley of Shittim."

You may remember those rugged football practices, or cross country runs, or basketball practices, or whatever sport, where you were so thirsty, your throat felt like it was filled with cotton. You may also remember how refreshing the long drought of water felt when you finally got the chance to drink and quench your thirst. When we get to heaven, there will be the river of life, the most thirst-quenching, both physically and spiritually, drought of water ever tasted by humanity.

What is the symbolic meaning of the river? If the water refers to the Spirit, as in John 7:37–39, then the Spirit proceeds from the Father and the Son.[3] But if not a reference to the Spirit, then the water must primarily represent the waters of eternal life that flow from God's presence, from God himself, the source of life. Thomas points out that this is God's river and the Lamb's river. It is their gift of salvation to all who believe in them and offer faithful witness to them.[4]

The river flows down the middle of the New Jerusalem. On the banks of the river, on each side, stands the tree of life, yielding fruit each month.

1. See Beale, *The Book of Revelation*, 119, 122.

2. Mounce, *The Book of Revelation*, 390.

3. Osborne (Osborne, *Revelation*, 769) says that this is not the Holy Spirit, but merely is emphasizing the purity, holiness, and transcendence of the glory of God.

4. See Beale, *The Book of Revelation*, 1104; Thomas and Macchia, *Revelation*, 387. Ladd (Ladd, *A Commentary on the Revelation of John*, 286) believes the river is a promise of immortality.

The exact placement of the street, the river, and the tree is unclear, but is actually not important. It is the symbolism that is important here. Ladd notes that the placing of the river down the middle of the city emphasizes the centrality of eternal life in the New Jerusalem.[5] This is a strong reference to the restoration of the Garden of Eden. The tree of life was in the garden, but Adam and Eve were barred from the garden so they would not take from the tree. Beale makes an interesting and convincing argument for the temple standing as a model for the heavens and the earth, and for the Garden of Eden. The cherubim guarding the ark of the covenant represent the cherubim guarding the entrance of the Garden after the fall of Adam and Eve. And the decorations of Solomon's temple were filled with themes of leaves and flowers. The lampstand, as well, was maybe symbolic of the tree of life. The lampstand stood outside the Holy of Holies.[6]

There is much symbolism in this passage that is taken as well from the Old Testament prophets. Ezekiel 47:12 says, "On the banks, on both sides of the river, there will grow all kinds of trees for food. Their leaves will not wither, nor their fruit fail, but they will bear fresh fruit every month, because the water for them flows from the sanctuary. Their fruit will be for food, and their leaves for healing." Isaiah 35:6b says, "For waters break forth in the wilderness, and streams in the desert." The tree of life in Revelation 22:2 yields more fruit than the tree in Ezekiel 47:12. This may mean that the consummation is much completer and more significant than the inauguration. Another difference is that there are multiple trees in Ezekiel's vision. Here, John is collecting all those trees into one.[7]

The fruitfulness of the tree is unique. It yields a perfect and complete amount of fruit, twelve harvests of fruit for the twelve tribes of Israel and the foundation of the twelve apostles. Even the leaves can be used (see Ezekiel 47:12). The tree in its fullness is for the healing of the nations. The nations, and all the wickedness, rebellion, and sin that is in them, will be restored to the original purpose of creation. All this will take place in the New Jerusalem, the new city of God. Beale believes that the healing effect of the fruit is symbolic for the redemption won by Christ and consummated at his second coming.[8]

5. Ladd, *A Commentary on the Revelation of John*, 287.

6. Beale, *The Book of Revelation*, 1106.

7. See Aune, *Revelation 17–22*, 1178 and Johnson, *Hebrews through Revelation*, 599. Osborne (Osborne, *Revelation*, 771) also sees a possible connection with the "splendid cedar" of Ezekiel 17:22–24, and "tall tree" that is the "envy of all the trees in Eden" in Ezekiel 31:2–9, or the tree that touched the sky in Daniel 4:10–12.

8. Beale, *The Book of Revelation*, 1108.

As part of this healing of the nations, there will no longer be any curse. As there is no longer any curse, there is no longer any sin. Central in the city is the throne of God and the Lamb. And the servants of the Lamb will serve and worship him. Zechariah 14:9 prophesies the time when "The Lord will be king over the whole earth." At that time, verse 11, Jerusalem "shall be inhabited, for there shall never again be a decree of utter destruction." In light of the vision of Revelation 22, this can only refer to the New Jerusalem, not the physical city in the state of Israel. The curses of Deuteronomy 28:15-28 will no longer be a part of the experience of God's people. The curse will be removed not only for the Jewish nation, but for all nations. What Adam brought into the earth through his one sin, the curse of sin upon humanity, will be removed by the Lamb in the last garden. What Jesus did on the cross, to bear the curse on behalf of humanity (Galatians 3:13), will be fully completed at the consummation of all things. The curse of sin will be totally removed. "At the end of time, the redeemed will be ushered into the sanctuary again on the coattails of the Lamb's work."[9]

Whereas even Moses was not allowed to look at the face of God (see Exodus 28:36-38; 33:20), the redeemed will be able to look upon the face of God and the face of the Lamb. John says as well in 1 John 3:2b-3. Paul wrote in 1 Corinthians 13:12, "For now we see in a mirror dimly, but then face to face. Now I know in part; then I shall know fully, even as I have been fully known." Unlike those who hide from the presence of the wrath of the Lamb in Revelation 6, those who are redeemed and remain faithful to the Lamb will look upon his face.[10] There is no need to hide because there is no longer any shame. There is no longer any shame because there is no longer any curse. Not only is there no longer any curse, but also, the name of the Lamb will be on the foreheads of the redeemed. This signifies ownership. The saints will be in the presence of the One who paid the price for their souls (see discussion of this in 3:12).[11]

I know other saints will be in heaven, and I can't wait to see them. It will be a great family reunion. But when I see Moses, I'm going to say, "Moses, I would love to talk to you about how you parted the Red Sea and how tough it was to deal with those complaining Israelites, but not now. Now, I want to see Jesus." "David, I want to talk to you about your great love for God, what it was like to kill Goliath and lead the kingdom of Israel, but not now. Now, I want to see Jesus." "Abraham, I want to talk to you about what

9. Beale, *The Book of Revelation*, 1112.

10. Thomas and Macchia, *Revelation*, 391.

11. See the Aaronic blessing in Numbers 6:25-27. The shining of God's face upon a people is a sign of his continued blessing and peace upon them. The name of God would be upon the forehead of his people. See Beale, *The Book of Revelation*, 1116.

you felt when you were asked to sacrifice Isaac, and the meaning of being the father of many nations, but not now. Now, I want to see Jesus." "Daniel, I want to talk to you about your vision of the Ancient of Days, but not now. Now, I want to see the Ancient of Days." "Paul, I want to know about your vision of Jesus on the road to Damascus and how you carried the gospel all the way to Rome, but not now. Now, I want to see the Jesus you saw on your way to Damascus." "Peter, I want to talk to you about what it was like to be forgiven by Jesus after you denied him three times, but not now. Now, I want to see the One who forgave me." "Lottie Farquharson, I want to personally thank you for sharing the gospel with my mother in Lebanon all those years ago, but not now, Lottie. Now, I want to see Jesus." "Dad, I want to sit and talk to you about the rest of my life and how God was with me since you died, but not now, Dad. Now, I want to see Jesus." And each of these will say, "We understand. We want to see Jesus too!"

Verse 5 repeats the thoughts of 21:23. There will no longer be any night, because the night was associated with the darkness and the darkness with sin. Because sin will no longer be present, darkness will be no more. Zechariah 14:7 speaks of this day, "And there shall be a unique day, which is known to the Lord, neither day nor night, but at evening time there shall be light." The light of the glory of God will be enough, and the saints will reign with God forever and ever. This thought is repeated from Daniel 7:18, "But the saints of the Most High shall receive the kingdom and possess the kingdom forever and ever." Paul as well writes in Romans 5:17, "For if, because of one man's trespass, death reigned through that one man, much more will those who receive the abundance of grace and the free gift of righteousness reign in life through the one man Jesus Christ." And in 2 Timothy 2:12, Paul writes, "If we endure, we will also reign with him." Thomas notes the following comparisons: just as the thousand-year reign dwarfed the limited activity of the dragon and the beast, and the period of suffering for the church, so this reign forever and ever dwarfs the thousand-year reign.[12]

In verse 6, John reiterates the trustworthiness of the letter of the Revelation of these things. Just as God led the prophets through the Spirit, so has he led John. And the angels were messengers of these things. Daniel had said something similar after he interpreted King Nebuchadnezzar's dream for him in Daniel 2:45, "A great God has made known to the king what shall be after this. The dream is certain, and its interpretations are true." Given the context of Daniel 2, it seems that John is taking the same posture as a prophet, ascribing a high level of authority to this word from God.

---

12. Thomas and Macchia, *Revelation*, 390.

The phrase "the Lord, the God of the spirit of the prophets," is a little enigmatic. Some, like Aune, go as far to say that the spirits of the prophets may be referring to the psychic power of the prophets.[13] It seems, however, more likely that the phrase refers to the origin of the inspiration of the community of the prophets and the close connection this inspiration has with the throne of God, before whom the Seven-fold Spirit appears.[14] The phrase refers, then, to the office of the prophets in both the Old Testament and the New Testament. But that office, or ministry, can be extended to others in the church whom the Lord so chooses. 1 Corinthians 14:32 say, "The spirits of prophets are subject to the prophets." The plural for "spirits" then indicates that this is not referring to the Holy Spirit, but the spirit with the prophets (in other words, their human spirit) in communion with the Holy Spirit, the source of all divine inspiration.[15]

Another beatitude is uttered in verse 7 for those who hold to the prophesy of the book, in other words, to those who persevere until the end. This is either Jesus speaking directly, or an angel speaking proleptically. I think it is Jesus speaking directly just as he spoke directly in chapters 2–3. This ties the beginning of the book with this epilogue. Jesus counsels every generation to be alert, just as he did in Matthew 24:42–44. We are to watch and pray. And in doing so, we will continue to keep the words, or exhortation, of the prophetic words of Revelation.[16]

After John heard the things and seen the things the angel had revealed to him, he makes the same mistake he made before, that is, worshipping at the feet of the angel. But his phrase, "one who heard and seen these things," is reminiscent of what he had written in 1 John 1:1–2. Eye-witness testimony is important to the validity of a prophetic witness. And here John is testifying to the validity of this testimony, and in doing so, places himself in a long line of prophets who preached and pleaded with the people of God concerning God's covenant stipulations and the warnings and blessings accompanied with it.[17]

As in 19:10, the angel rebukes John (corrects him) for bowing down to worship. He is just a servant like the brothers of John and the prophets. John is exhorted with the imperatival verb, "worship!" And God is placed in the

13. Aune, *Revelation 17-22*, 1182.

14. So Thomas and Macchia, *Revelation*, 391.

15. See the discussion in Beale, *The Book of Revelation*, 1125; Mounce, *The Book of Revelation*, 390; Osborne, *Revelation*, 780.

16. See also Mounce, *The Book of Revelation*, 391; Ladd, *A Commentary on the Revelation of John*, 290.

17. See Beale (Beale, *The Book of Revelation*, 1127–28), who also refers to 2 Kings 17:7–23, 2 Chronicles 24:18–19, and Nehemiah 9:26–27a.

front of that phrase for emphasis, "It is GOD you must worship!" This stands as a warning to believers in whatever age. Whether it is Roman idols, charismatic political heroes, gods of paper money, or athletes of great prowess, our calling as followers of the Lamb is to worship God alone.

John is commanded by the angel not to seal up the words of the prophesy. Why? Because the time is near. Daniel could not reveal all that was revealed to him (see Daniel 12), but John's book remained unsealed. According to Ladd, John's prophesy was not meant for a generation to come, but for the first century church and the entire history of the church after that. For this reason, he was told not to seal the book.[18] What Daniel could not know has begun to be fulfilled by the cross and resurrection of Jesus. When Jesus came to the earth, died, and rose again, the end began to take place. That is why we can say, as the apostles said, and Jesus himself said, the end is at hand. We are in the days of the end. There is still the reality of conflict between the forces of evil against God's people. But the book can remain open, because the end is in sight. The end has been near since Christ's victory on the cross and out of the tomb.

Because the end is at hand, and particularly after Christ comes back and the final judgment commences, what side men and women choose will continue to dictate their character. Daniel 12:10 says, "Many shall purify themselves and make themselves white and be refined, but the wicked shall act wickedly. And none of the wicked shall understand, but those who are wise shall understand." John takes these words from Daniel as an exhortation to those who remain. The wise will heed the words of the prophesy and submit to the Lamb. The vile and the wicked will continue to be vile and wicked. The saying, then, should be taken idiomatically. In other words, evil will continue to be evil, the redeemed will continue to act like the redeemed. Paul perceived the same kind of attitude of the wicked in 2 Timothy 3:13, "While evil people and imposters will go from bad to worse, deceiving and being deceived." Those who have ears to hear will hear. Those who have shut their ears will continue to shut their ears.

In verse 12, we come back to the direct words of Jesus, just as in chapter 1–3. Jesus reiterates the imminence of his return. Beale comments that the saying, "I am coming soon" refers to the climactic coming. Quickly, ταχύ (*tachu*) refers to this imminence of that coming. We have seen this already in Daniel 2:28–29, 45, fulfillment in the near future.[19] Again, "soon," here should be understood from the perspective of God. In 2 Peter 3:8–10 we can read of this perspective. With God, a day is like a thousand years, and a

---

18. Ladd, *A Commentary on the Revelation of John*, 291.

19. Beale, *The Book of Revelation*, 1134.

thousand years are like a day. From the perspective of the passion of Christ, the cross was one big event, the resurrection the next, the ascension the next, Pentecost the next after that. The next big event is his return. So, this is why it is soon.

When Christ comes, he will come as the Judge. He is the Alpha and Omega, the Beginning and End (see also 1:8; 1:17; 21:6). In Isaiah 44:6 God says, "I am the first and I am the last, besides me there no god." This under-scores his deity and his control over all things, and his authority to judge "everyone according to what he has done." The ungodly have already been cast into the lake of fire, the second death. This judgment for everyone ac-cording to their deeds has to do with rewards given to the faithful.[20]

In verse 14, we meet the seventh and final blessing of Revelation. "Blessed are those who wash their robes." Osborne notes that all the bless-ings focus on the perseverance of the faithful: 1) 1:3—God's blessing is on those who "read" and "heed;" 2) 14:13—He blesses those who die "in the Lord;" 3) 16:15—The blessed are those who stay awake and guard their clothes; 4) 19:9—The blessed are those who are invited to the wedding sup-per of the Lamb; 5) 20:6—The blessed are those who have part in the first resurrection; 6) 22:7—The blessed are "those who keep the words of the prophesy of this book;" and 7) 22:14—"Those who wash their robes."[21]

The washing of robes is similar to the idea of 7:14. But, whereas the verb "washed" in 7:14 was aorist, indicating a particular event in the past, in 22:14, it is in the present tense, suggesting continual action, "being washed."[22] It is not the saints' worthiness or self-righteousness that makes them ready to enter the heavenly city, but the worthiness of Christ and his sacrifice on their behalf. This has been the theme in the entire book of Rev-elation: the Lamb that was slain before the foundations of the earth, who purchased men for God with his own blood. Those who wash their robes in the righteousness of Christ have access to the tree of life, as appeared in 22:2. They may enter the gates of the city. Psalm 118:20 reminds us, "This is the gate of the Lord, the righteous shall enter through it."

But outside this gate are the ungodly and wicked. Similar to the situa-tion in chapter 21, in contrast to the righteous in the city, the unrighteous, and those who did not persevere, are outside the city. One term that is not

---

20. See also 2 Corinthians 5:10.

21. Osborne, *Revelation*, 789.

22. See also Mounce, *The Book of Revelation*, 393 and Ladd, *A Commentary on the Revelation of John*, 293. Thomas (Thomas and Macchia, *Revelation*, 397), notes that the idea of ongoing cleansing is consistent with Johannine thought (1 John 1:5–2:2; 3:3–10, 19–24; 5:14–17). This is evidence of the saving and purifying impact of the blood of the Lamb.

found in the lists of 21:8 and 21:27 is the term "dogs." Dogs are a synonym in the first century for those who do not believe. Jesus used the term in Matthew 7:6 and 15:26, the latter in reference to those outside Israel, or the people of God. In early Christian literature, the term "dog" is applied to those who are unbaptized and unclean (*Didache*.9:5), as well as to heretics (Philippians 3:2; 2 Peter 2:22; Ignatius.Eph.7.1).[23]

Being outside the gate does not mean that the wicked are literally outside the gates of heaven, or the New Jerusalem, but that they are outside of the grace of God, and the joy of the eternal light of God's presence. Beale is right in suggesting that "outside" is the "lake of fire," since essentially the godless people listed in 21:8 are consigned to the "lake of fire." This is parallel to being cast outside the entrance to the Garden of Eden, except the consequences of rejecting the Lamb continue on into eternity.[24]

Jesus further identifies himself with two more meaningful titles in verse 16. He is first, the Root and Offspring of David. Isaiah 11:1 prophesy that "There shall come forth a shoot from the stump of Jesse, and a branch from his roots shall bear fruit." Matthew 1:1–17 is very precise in identifying Jesus as the son of David, the Messianic King. Second, Jesus identifies himself as the bright Morning Star. Balaam's prophesy concerning Israel in Numbers 24:17 says, "I see him, but not now; I behold him, but not near. A star shall come out of Jacob, and a scepter shall rise out of Israel." Isaiah 60:3 says, "And nations shall come to your light, and kings to the brightness of your dawn." Both of these prophesies were fulfilled when the star appeared over Bethlehem in Matthew, drawing the Magi from the east to worship the Christ child. Jesus is the morning star, the glory of the heavens.[25]

Verse 17 brings us again to what was spoken in 21:6, a fulfillment of Isaiah 55 as an invitation to all those who are thirsty. Here, the Spirit and the Bride, the church, are inviting those who are thirsty to come to the Lamb. That is the only place of security and salvation in light of all that is going to come to pass. Mounce writes, "It is the testimony of the church empowered by the Holy Spirit that constitutes the great evangelizing force of this age."[26]

---

23. See Aune, *Revelation 17–22*, 1223.

24. Beale, *The Book of Revelation*, 1142.

25. The "you" in verse 16 is plural. This probably means that Jesus meant the message to be to John, as well as the churches in Asia Minor, and, by extension, to all the churches who read this letter. John was the conduit for the general exhortation to all the churches.

26. Mounce, *The Book of Revelation*, 395. The speaker is not Jesus, but the church. The final church and the current church call for the reader to "come" to Christ. See Osborne, *Revelation*, 794.

A warning is then given not to add anything or take away anything from this prophesy John has seen. This is based maybe on Deuteronomy 4:12; 12:32; and Proverbs 30:6. John is equating his work on the same standard of authority as the Law of Moses and the writings. Deuteronomy 12:32 says, "Everything that I command you, you shall be careful to do. You shall not add to it or take from it." If there are those who take away from the words of this prophesy (v.19), they will be discounted from those who are of the elect. They will not eat of the tree of life and will not have a place in the city. Furthermore, adding and taking away from the prophesy is the equivalent of false teaching with the intent to deceive, and to idolatry. The link to Deuteronomy 12–13 and the false prophets is clear.

## Conclusion

Verse 20–22, the last verses of the Bible, appropriately give us a final appeal to Jesus to come back soon. The answer to the problems in this world, or in our own personal lives, do not lie in man's abilities to overcome, but in the promise of the return of Christ.[27] Verse 21 closes with a final word of blessing, common in epistles. How strong is this desire to see Jesus come back? Has this been lost in the church? The greater the attractiveness of this world, the less desirable the Lord's return. We are in danger, often, of wanting Jesus to return soon just so that he can pay back Hollywood, or the Media, or the evil tyrants of the world. But the desire should be much more than that—we should be yearning for Jesus to return so that we can see him face to face. That should be the cry of the church. When Jesus says, "Yes, I am coming soon," the church should respond with "Amen, come Lord Jesus."

We reach the end of a wonderful book, maybe not fully comprehending all of it, but hopefully at least hearing the heart of its message. Jesus is coming back! We must hold on, persevere, and live our lives in humble obedience to him until he does. The reality of life is that there still is the reality of life. We still have to live our Christian lives in our normal worlds, filled with its turns and twists and pains and pleasures. This is why we have the rest of the word of God. But let us continue to study the book of Revelation. The more we pour ourselves into its pages, the more expectant we will become for Jesus' return. And the more expectant we are of Jesus' return, the more compelled we will be to live for him.

*Marantha!*

---

27. Mounce, *The Book of Revelation*, 396.

# Bibliography

"Alert to Satan's Work." Christianity Today. https://www.preachingtoday.com/illustrations/2000/march/12357.html.

Arnold, Clinton. *Ephesians*. Zondervan Exegetical Commentary on the New Testament Series. Zondervan, 2011. Kindle edition.

Aune, David E. *Revelation 1–5*. Vol. 52a of *Word Biblical Commentary: Revelation*. Nashville, TN: Thomas Nelson, 1997.

———. *Revelation 6–16*. Vol. 52b of *Word Biblical Commentary: Revelation*. Nashville, TN: Thomas Nelson, 1997.

———. *Revelation 17–22*. Vol. 52c of *Word Biblical Commentary: Revelation*. Nashville, TN: Thomas Nelson, 1997.

Bauckham, Richard. *New Testament Theology: The Theology of the Book of Revelation*. Cambridge: Cambridge University Press, 1993.

Beale, G.K. *The Book of Revelation*. The New International Greek Testament Commentary Series. Grand Rapids, MI: Eerdmans, 1999.

———. *Revelation: A Shorter Commentary*. Grand Rapids, MI: Eerdmans, 2015.

Blomberg, Craig L. and Sung Wook Chung, eds. *A Case for Historic Premillennialism: An Alternative to "Left Behind" Eschatology*. Grand Rapids, MI: Baker, 2009.

Chapell, Bryan. *Holiness by Grace: Delighting in the Joy that is our Strength*. Wheaton, IL: Crossway, 2011.

Clouse, Robert G. *The Meaning of the Millennium: Five Views*. Downers Grove, IL: IVP, 1977.

Curtis, Rick. *Early Discovery: Growing in the Community of Believers*. Lulu.com, 2005.

Erickson, Millard J. *Pandangan Kontemporer Dalam Eskatologi (Contemporary Options in Eschatology: A Study of the Millennium.)* Grand Rapids, MI: Baker, 1977.

"The Eternality of Hell." Christianity Today. https://www.preachingtoday.com/illustrations/1997/december/2743.html.

Fernando, Ajith. *A Universal Homecoming?: An Examination of the Case for Universalism*. Evangelical Literature Service, 1983.

Flint, Annie Johnson. "I See Jesus." Homemaker's Corner. https://www.homemakers corner.com/ajf-seejesus.htm.

"Go Global: The Great Commission." My Bible. https://www.bible.net.nz/200810%20 Global_Missions_-_Great_Commission.pdf.

Hoehner, Harold W. *Ephesians: An Exegetical Commentary*. Baker, 2002. Kindle edition.

Hoekema, Anthony A. *The Bible and the Future*. Grand Rapids, MI: Eerdmans, 1994.

Ladd, George Eldon. *A Commentary on the Revelation of John*. Grand Rapids, MI: Eerdmans, 1972.

Lewis, C.S. *The Pilgrim's Regress*. Grand Rapids, MI: Eerdmans, 2014.

Johnson, Alan F. *Hebrews through Revelation*. Vol. 12 of *The Expositor's Bible Commentary*. Grand Rapids, MI: Zondervan, 1981.

Mounce, Robert H. *The Book of Revelation*. The New International Commentary on the New Testament Series. Rev. ed. Grand Rapids, MI: Eerdmans, 1997.

Noonan, Peggy. *A Heart, a Cross, and a Flag: America Today*. Wall Street Journal, 2003.

Osborne, Grant R. *Revelation*. The Baker Exegetical Commentary on the New Testament Series. Grand Rapids, MI: Baker, 2002.

Schaff, Philip, ed. *The Complete Ante-Nicene & Nicene and Post-Nicene Church Father's Collection*. Catholic Way Publishing, 2014. Kindle edition.

Thomas, John Christopher and Frank D. Macchia. *Revelation: The Two Horizons New Testament Commentary*. Grand Rapids, MI: Eerdmans, 2016.

Zacharias, Ravi. "Bound by the Spirit of the Age." Christianity Today. https://www.preachingtoday.com/illustrations/1996/december/2127.html.

# Subject Index

Aaron, 62
Abaddon, angel of the abyss, 117n5,
    118, 120
Abel, 144
Abraham, 144, 237–38
abyss
    holding those to be judged, 116
    judgment of, 117
    key to, 214
    as the source of the beast, 188
    as the source of the evil spirits and
        powers of judgment against the
        nations, 138
acts
    of judgment, 94
    of kindness or love, 48–49
Adam and Eve. *See also* Eve
    barred from the Garden of Eden, 37
    elevating knowledge above God, 122
    gave in to the temptation of the
        serpent, 143
    God's plan before, 159
    set into motion the destruction of
        the world, 94
Ahab and Jezebel, 203
"all nations," worshipping God, 176–77
"The Almighty," 204
Alpha and Omega, the Beginning and
    the End, 20, 227, 241
altar, as a witness of judgment, 180
"Amen," 65, 65n3, 105
"Amen, Hallelujah," 203
amillennial position, 8, 213, 216
anarchy and bloodshed, common in
    John's era, 93
*anastasis*, as physical resurrection, 216
Ancient of Days, 26, 48, 176, 191

angel. *See also* "another angel"
    announced "It is done," 182
    bound the dragon and threw him
        into the Abyss, 215
    calling on the birds to gather for the
        great supper of God, 210
    in charge of the waters, 179
    flying overhead, 168
    with the golden censer at the altar,
        110
    placing a seal on the foreheads of
        the servants of God, 102
    rebuking John for bowing down to
        worship, 239
    referred to as Yahweh himself, 125
    reflecting the glory of God, 194
    showing John the punishment of the
        great prostitute, called Babylon,
        185
    swinging his sickle on the earth, 172
    telling John he needs to have a mind
        of wisdom to understand, 189
    warning against those who join the
        beast and worship him, 169
angels
    as always angels in Revelation, 126
    carrying off the souls of the wicked,
        119
    carrying out God's judgment, 117
    cast into hell by God, 116
    in charge of the heavenly worship of
        God, 77
    commanded to pour out the bowls
        of wrath, 178
    elders viewed as, 76, 76n13
    four winds as, 101–2
    as the harvesters, 171

angels *(continued)*
> joining the four living creatures and the twenty-four elders in an ever louder crescendo of praise, 86
> must worship God and be faithful, 206
> of punishment "bound at the great river Euphrates," 121n18
> representing the early churches, 148
> seven standing before God holding the seven golden trumpets, 110
> "spirit" reference to, 17n20
> standing at the four corners of the earth, 101
> in the throne room reflecting the glory of God, 76
> two more appearing, 171–72
> voices of from heaven, 166

anguish state of existence, hell as, 212
annihilationism, defined, 212
"another angel." *See also* angel
> came down from heaven, 125–28
answer key, of Revelation, 223
Antichrist
> beast as, 188
> coming from Dan, 120
> imitating miracles, 160
> opposing and exalting himself against every so-called god, 158
> as a person, 157
> released upon the earth and deceived mankind, 124
> "resurrection" of, 157
> setting up his image in every city, 160n16
> standing against Christ, 156
> "victory" of as brief and insignificant, 139
> the woman's relationship to, 186
antichrist-type of figure, whose forces seek to conquer the followers of Christ, 92
Antietam, battle of, 153
Antiochus Epiphanes
> persecution under, 149n15
> time of, 135
> wife, Laodice, 65
Antipas, 43

apocalyptic holy war texts, types of, 191
apocalyptic imagery, of John in Revelation, 13
apocalyptic literature, idea of a renovated heaven and earth common in, 224
apocalyptic picture, of the victory won by the Lamb of God, 144
apocalyptic signs, of the coming of the Day of the Lord, 96
apocalyptic "soon." *See* "soon"
Apollo, 120n15, 146n6
Apollyon. *See* Abaddon
apostles, as the foundation, 229
*arche*, as "source" or "origin," 66n5
Areopagus, Dionysius, 200
ark of the covenant, 141–42
Armageddon, kings of the earth led to, 182
armies of heaven, riding white horses, 209
army
> church as, 137
> of locusts in Joel, 117
Artemis, 32, 36
Asia Minor, 5, 6
Assyria, 195
astrological figure, woman as Virgo, 145
"at that hour," referencing the day of the LORD and the final end, 140
Athens, Greece, 200
Augustus, temple to, in Pergamum, 43
Aune, David E.
> on the amount of wheat and barley, 94n14
> on "another angel" based on Colossus of Rhodes, 126n6
> on avoidance of the temptations of corrupt features of the Greco-Roman culture, 195n8
> on chapter 13 as a perverse reflection of the investiture of the Lamb, 156n2
> chart of the various possibilities for the seven kings, 189–90
> on the concept of seven churches, 16n16
> on the contents of the scroll, 82n4

on demons in the guise of locusts,
117–18

on discipleship that may result in
death, 167

dividing the text of chapter 5 into
three sub-units, 80

on "first-fruits," 167n10

on the form of the letters as a mixed
genre, 30

on the heavenly door, 73

on Hesiod's Theogony, 214n4

on the incense offering, 111n8

on Jeremiah's influence on chapter
18, 193–94

on John being on Patmos, 22

on John's divine name for God, 17

on John's marveling being an
indication of confusion, 188

on large sections of Revelation as
the work of an editor, 3

on long and disheveled hair in the
Old Testament, 119

on many waters reminding us of
Babylon, 185n3

on the New Testament wrath of
God, 175

on the 144,000, 165n3

on the open door referring to
"reserved seats" in the heavenly
kingdom, 59n5

on parallel between Revelation 12
and combat myths of the ancient
near east, 145n4

on the population of Sardis, 54

on proximity of high mountains to
the celestial world, 228n14

on Satan's throne, 43n2

on the second rider taking peace
from the earth as a universal
phenomenon, 93n12

on secret name of Rome as *Amor*
("love" in Latin) or Roma
spelled backwards, 187n11

on the seven angels sounding the
trumpet of judgment, 110

on the seven spirits as "the seven
principle angels of God," 17n20

on special effects equipment used to
produce speaking and moving
statues, 161

on "in the Spirit," 23

on the spirits of the prophets, 239

on the star as an angelic messenger,
117n5

on the switching of scenes between
earth and heaven, 74n5

on the threat to obliterate the
Ephesian congregation, 34

on the tribulations introducing the
end, 90

on "the twelve apostles," 6

viewing the desert negatively, 186

author, of Revelation, 3–4

authority
of the Dragon compared to Christ,
147
of God to judge, 241
of Jesus, 48
lack of, 47
needed by the world, 52
over the nations for the overcomer,
51

avenger, God as, 196


Baals, following, 113

Babylon
cast into the sea, 112
deceived the nations of the world,
195
destruction of, 213
fall of, 169, 193–200
imprisoned, 194n5
as political power that oppresses,
168
portrayed as a female, a prostitute,
168
pride of, 113
quickness of the judgment of, 197
referred to as dragon, 148
standing for the kingdoms of the
world, 183
as a symbol for the spirit of
godlessness, 168

Babylon *(continued)*
>    as symbol of all the wicked nations,
>        164, 168
>    as a symbol of the universal empires
>        opposing God, 181
>    theme in Revelation as another date
>        indicator, 6
bad news, sharing, 124
Balaam, 43, 44, 44n8, 51, 144
Balak, 43
baths, 200
battle
>    joining against Satan, 154
>    over before it started after the Lamb
>        arrives, 210
Bauckham, Richard
>    on the confrontation between the
>        serpent and the woman in the
>        garden of Eden, 144
>    on the devil given a last chance to
>        deceive the nations, 218
>    on the divine Spirit as "the agent of
>        visionary experience," 23
>    on John not wishing to represent
>        Jesus as an alternative object of
>        worship alongside God, 87
>    on the opening of the seals
>        preparing for the revelation of
>        the contents of the scroll, 90
>    on the people of God redeemed
>        from all the nations, 133
>    on two reapings, 171n24
>    on the witness of the two witnesses
>        (or the church), 140n23
Beale, G.K.
>    on the abyss, 116
>    on the altar incense, 110n6–11n6
>    on the angels associated with the
>        people of God, 229
>    on "another angel," 125
>    on the apocalyptic use of "half,"
>        110n4
>    arguing for a "recapitulation"
>        understanding of Revelation 20,
>        213, 213n1
>    on arguments for the rider of the
>        white horse being identified
>        with Christ, 91–92

on the author of Revelation, 4
on the beast rising out of the abyss,
>    138n16
on believers sealed to bear an
>    enduring and loyal witness,
>    125n1
on the binding of Satan, 214
on birth pains representing
>    persecution of the covenant
>    community, 146n8–47n8
on both scrolls, 126n7
on Christ ruling over such an
>    apparent chaotic world, 90
on a coin depicting the goddess
>    Roma sitting on the seven hills
>    of Rome, 185
on the combination of God or
>    "Lord" and "his Christ" found
>    only in Psalm 2:2, 151
on communication levels in
>    Revelation, 2
on comparing the scrolls, 126
on connecting the trumpets with the
>    prayer for judgment, 109n2
on the contents of the scroll eaten by
>    John, 129
corporate identification of the two
>    witnesses supported by six
>    considerations, 136
on the crystal sea, 77n16
on the darkness as not literal, 113
on dating of Revelation, 4, 6
on the death of Balaam, 44n8
on dissemination in Revelation, 15
on the elders, 76, 76n12
on an evil angel fallen from heaven,
>    117
on examples of Old Testament
>    desert experiences, 149
explanations of how Death and
>    Hades can be thrown into the
>    lake of fire, 221n32
on the ferocity of the demons,
>    121–22
on flood waters as symbols of
>    persecution and deception, 152
on the focus of Revelation, 7

on four beasts introduced in the second half of the book of Revelation, 145

on the healing effect of the fruit of the tree of life, 236

on "I am coming soon" as referring to the climactic coming, 240

on identification of the sea, 224–25

on interpretive suggestions for the identity of what is written in the scrool, 82

on John conveying the image of the glory of God and judgment, 178

on John emphasizing the consummated redemption, 232

on John using the Old Testament as his primary filter, 146n6

on John viewing Jesus as the ideal Davidic king, 18n21

on John's position in relation to the Old Testament, 2

on Judeans fleeing Jerusalem during persecution under Antiochus Epiphanes, 149n15

on judgment upon the economic systems of the world, 179

on lack of repentance, 181

on lament sections enforcing the curse involved in Babylon's coming judgment, 193

listing common interpretations of 11:1–2, 133–34

on "lost their first love," 33

on the mark of the beast, 161n19

on a multi-faceted dimension to the silence metaphor, 110

on the new song, 85

noting the expensive and attractive clothing of prostitutes, 187n9

on Old Testament prophesies of a singular people which will be the dwelling place of God, 226

on the phrase "Mount Zion," 166n6

on the prophetic present, 226–27

on the rainbow, 75n10

reasons why John's marvel for the woman should be understood as shock or fear, 188

on the reference to the glory of God, 228–29

on Revelation as a prophesy, 1

on "revelation of Jesus Christ," 14

on saints wearing white garments, 209

on Satan not released from his bondage to Christ, 215

on the sea of glass as a reminder of the Red Sea, 176

on the seal, 102n9

on the seven churches, 16n16

on the seven spirits, 17

on a similar structure between Revelation 4–5 and Daniel 7, 72–73

on similarities between the double-written scroll of John and the legal background of Roman wills, 83

on the size of the holy city, 230

on "soon" referring to the definite, imminent time of fulfillment, 14–15

on spirits becoming the agents of Christ throughout the world, 85n12

on spiritual intensity of the next woes, 113–14

on spiritual rapture in which the witnesses are restored, 140n22

suggesting that "outside" is the "lake of fire," 242

supporting the a-millennial view, 215

on symbols portraying a transcendent new creation, 3

on the temple as a model for the heavens and the earth, and for the Garden of Eden, 236

on ten of the tribes losing their national identity in the Assyrian exile, 104n13

on the thigh as the typical place of the warriors' sword, 210

on "Thus says the Lord," 32

on the triple repetition of sixes, 162

on the true church, 138

Beale, G.K. *(continued)*
on two cities adorned with the same
attire, 228
on the use of "The Lord, the
Almighty God," 180
on "What must take place after this,"
74n7
beast
acting in line with the deeper plans
of God, 192
angel describing, 188
came out of the sea in Daniel, 147n9
captured and thrown into the lake
of fire, 211
defeated by the deaths of the
faithful, 187–88
making war against the witnesses,
136
no re-run of the rule of, 218
not measuring up to the perfections
of Christ, 162
penalty for non-conformity to as
death, 160
as scarlet reflecting the red color of
the dragon, 186
speaking words against the Most
High in Daniel, 158
temporary victory of, 144
those following not written in the
book of life, 188–89
those who worship, 227
turning on the kings of the earth,
192
from a wicked foundation with a
sure destruction, 190
beast and the false prophet, destruction
of, 214
beast from the earth
forcing the inhabitants of the earth
to worship the beast from the
sea, 160
given power and authority from the
dragon, 160
performing miracles, 160
released upon the earth to deceive
mankind, 124
rising out of the abyss, 118, 138n16
beast from the sea
coming out of the sea, 156

continued revival of, 157
given power to make war against the
saints and to conquer them, 158
having ten horns, and seven heads,
and crowns on his horns, 156
as an individual representing all the
kingdoms opposed to God, 157
known for his proud and
blasphemous words, 158
offering a salvation of sorts to those
who follow him, 157n7
opposed to everything good and
holy, 156, 158
receiving power and authority from
the dragon, 156n2
recovering from a serious setback,
157
recovery from the fatal head wound,
160
released upon the earth to deceive
mankind, 124
representative of all earthly
kingdoms, 156
trying to usurp the authority of
Christ, 156
beasts
identity of two tied together, 189
introduced in the second half of the
book of Revelation, 145
beatitudes. *See also* blessing
in Revelation, 206n16, 218, 239
beauty, sense of, 75–76
"bed of suffering," 50
Behemoth, 145
belief systems, not giving room for
truth, 132
believers
activity during the judgments of the
seals and trumpets, 124
called to come out of Babylon, 195
enduring tribulation, 23
last generation of sealed, 100
losses faced by, 38
marked from the judgment to come,
102
not perceiving their growth, 48
remaining faithful to Christ, 111
suffering of, 151

surviving until the end as 144,000, 165n3

warning the church not to defend itself by the use of force, 159n13

Belshazzar, 122

Benjamin, survived the exile, 104n13

betrothed woman, prepares herself in her father's house, 204

binding
of Satan, 150n17
taking place at the end, 150n19

bitterness, rotten food of, 44

black plague, 94

black third horse, 93

blameless, the redeemed as, 167

blazing pitch and sulfur, shall not be quenched, 170

"Blessed are those who wash their robes," 241

blessing. *See also* beatitudes
as a direct result of reading Revelation, 12
promised to all who read, hear, and keep the words of the prophesy, 15
seventh and final of Revelation, 241
for those invited to the wedding supper of the Lamb, 206

blood
Christ's robe dipped in, 208
flowed for the length of Palestine, 172
of the lamb or goat sprinkled on the ark for atonement, 142
of the prophets and saints found in Babylon, 199

blood of the Lamb
cleansing us from all unrighteousness, 103
nations redeemed by, 128
saving and purifying impact of, 241n22
seal of that marked the doorposts of the children of Israel, 102
white robes washed in, 106

blue civil war ghost, legend of, 89

body of Christ, 96, 101

body of water, sea as, 225

book of deeds, 220

book of judgment, 57

book of life
names in, 43, 57, 159, 220, 221–22
opening, 220

book of redemption, scroll as, 82

book of remembrance, 221

book of Revelation. *See* Revelation

books
none more valuable to read than the Bible, 12
as we know them not yet invented, 81–82

bowls of the seven angels, 177

bowls of wrath, 124, 175, 178

Branch of Jesse, 28, 207

Bread of Life, 42, 45, 46

breastplates of iron, of the locusts, 120

breath of his lips, killing the wicked, 209

bride of Christ
adornment representing faithfulness to the Lamb, 228
as the church, 204
coming down from God, 225
contrasting with the prostitute, 228
given fine linen to wear, 205
loyalty to, 167n8
righteousness and beautiful garments of given to her by the Groom, 225
seen in all her beauty and true worth after the great harlot is exposed, 185–86
waiting in her home for the groom to come in a Jewish wedding, 201

bridegroom, approaching the bride in a Jewish wedding, 201–2

bridge, between the heavenly and earthly, 224

bright Morning Star, Jesus as, 242

business and economic practices, sea as the main location of the world's idolatrous, 225

Buzz Lightyear, in the movie *Toy Story*, 47

bystanders, not protected by the armor of the Lord, 154

Cain, 144
call of repentance, versus a call of
    judgment, 168n13
"camp of God's people," as the church,
    219
Canaan, enemy of Baal as a serpent, 147
"capturing Sardis," as doing the
    impossible, 54n1
carrion birds, feasting on the flesh of
    humanity, 210
carrying away in the Spirit, parallel in
    Ezekiel, 74n8
casting out of heaven, as a different
    event from the binding, 150n19
celestial beings, impacted by the
    judgments of God, 113
celestial world, proximity of high
    mountains to, 228n14
celibate people, 60
cemetery, free house in, 89
censer, 110, 111
Chapell, Bryan, 69–70
cherubim, 111, 236
Chicago Cubs, 38, 58
the child, symbolic identity of, 144
Christ. See also Jesus
    coming as a Judge, 9, 241
    coming in the clouds, 209
    coming of, taking place "without
        delay," 62
    mystery of the gospel made known
        in, 128
    portrayed as the cornerstone of the
        temple, 231
    reality of the coming of, 205n12
    reigning with on the earth when he
        returns, 86n17
    retribution on enemies of, 60n6
    snapshot of his life, 149
Christian remnant, of ethnic Jews, 104
Christianity, as a matter of the heart, 34
Christians, 34, 195
Christology, of Revelation, 1
Christophany, appearance of the angel
    as, 194n4
chronological accuracy or preciseness,
    as not important, 185

chronological framework, not
    interpreting Revelation through,
    165n1
Chrysostom, doubted John's authorship,
    4
church
    alert and prepared for battle, 56
    appearing defeated, 138
    being patient as a theme in
        Revelation, 9
    as the bride, 204
    calling for the reader to "come" to
        Christ, 242n26
    clothed in sackcloth as symbolic,
        137
    conflict with demonic evil, 145
    engaged in a spiritual war on the
        earth, 99
    flirting around with the night, 56
    goal of, 228
    having authority and reigning
        because of Jesus' death and
        resurrection, 86
    having to go through the great
        tribulation and be cleansed, 91
    as a healing station for the
        spiritually sick, 67
    inviting those who are thirsty to
        come to the Lamb, 242
    Jesus as Lord and King of, 50
    kept from the hour of trial, 61
    looking more like Jesus, the Groom,
        223
    ministering from the fulfilled power
        of Christ, 137
    needing to arise from sleep today,
        55–56
    as the new and true Israel, 18
    not to fight back with the sword, 162
    referenced as saints, apostles, and
        prophets, 85n14
    reigning in the present as, 86n17
    remaining faithful in its witness, 137
    righteous faith and deeds judged,
        205
    sharing in the eschatological reign
        of Christ, 86n17
    as "Sleeping Beauty," 57

suffering in the fire of tribulation, 40
testifying, 136, 137
in Thyatira tolerated Jezebel, 49
the two witnesses representing, 135
the woman representing, 145
church in Pergamum, commanded to
repent, 44
church in Philadelphia, 59, 61, 62
church in Sardis, 54, 55
church in Smyrna, 39
church in Thyatira, 48
church leaders, earliest testimonies
dating Revelation at the time of
Domitian, 6
church of Jesus, joining the battle
against Satan, 154
church universal, 24, 31
churches
current undergoing intense
persecution, 40
enemies entering into, 53
general exhortation to all, 242n25
seven churches as literal, 25
walking by sight claiming
sufficiency, 68
in the world very much like
Laodicea, 66
citrus wood, from Africa, 198
city of God (the bride of Christ),
reflected the glory of God, 228
civilians, none in the mind of terrorists,
53
classic premillennialism, 8
Clement, on calamitous events in 96
AD, 5
clothes, of the overcomer, 182
Colossae, cold, refreshing and pure
waters of, 66
Colossus of Rhodes, 126n6
command, to fear God and worship
him, 168
commandments, of vertical love for
God and horizontal love for one
another, 33
commitment, of the 144,000, 166–67
communication, four levels of in
Revelation, 2–3

community of faith, as congregations,
133
"completed" (*etlesthe*), aorist passive
of, 175
completeness, seven heads and ten
horns emphasizing, 147
compromise, 44, 52
congregations, 16, 35, 73
conquerors, contrasted with the
cowardly, 227
consequences, for being late, 174
cosmic sea dragon, abyss abode of, 116
covenant relationship, with God as his
people, 227
covetousness, not even be named
among you, 45
created order, creature with four sides
representing, 77n19
creation, 66, 90, 220
Creator, 78, 86
creature, with four sides in Ezekiel,
77n19
crime, paid back in full, 196
crowns
of the elders as symbols of authority,
76
elders laying before the throne, 78
given to the faithful, 41
as the reward for faithfulness, 62
showing the unlimited power and
authority of the Lamb, 207
crucifixion, 139, 151
crystal sea of glass, before the throne, 77
cup of wrath, poured out by God onto
the wicked, 196
curse, removed for all nations, 237
Cyril of Jerusalem, doubted John's
authorship, 4

Damascus Document, picturing a time
of a man of mockery, 152
Dan, not listed and associated with idol
worship, 103
danger, being oblivious to it, 143
Daniel
on King Nebuchadnezzar's dream,
238

Daniel *(continued)*
    saw "four winds of heaven stirring up the great sea," 101
    sealing up the book until a later time, 82
    ten days of testing of, 40
    understanding of "soon" as temporal fulfillment, 15
    wanting to talk to, 238
darkness, 113, 180, 238
dating, of the book of Revelation, 4–7
daughter of Babylon, attitude in the mouth of, 196–97
David
    and the Descendant of David, 103
    Jesus as the son of, 242
    a man after God's own heart, 144
    wanting to talk to, 237
day of judgment, 97–98
day of salvation, as now, 123
day of the Lord, coming like a thief, 183
days of the end, being in, 240
the dead
    in Christ, 140
    John seeing, 220
    sea as the place of, 225
    who have not followed the Lamb, 217
death, 18, 220–21
Death and Hades, 28, 94, 221n32. *See also* Hades
death and resurrection of Christ, providing the death stroke upon the beast, 157
debates, on whether the church goes through the tribulation or doesn't, 91
deceitful spirits and teachings of demons, 152
deception and lies, from the mouth of the dragon, 152
declarative purpose, of the judgments of the trumpets and the seals, 112
defeat, as ultimate victory, 158
*dei*, meaning "must" or "necessary," 14
demonic beings, released from the sixth trumpet, 121
demonic figures, locusts as, 119

demonic frogs, convincing the kings of the world to make war against God, 182
demonic horses and riders, as distortions of God's creation, 121
demonic host, coming out of the dried-up Euphrates, 181
demons
    cast into the abyss, 116
    direct involvement of, 114
    recognized Jesus but did not love him, 30
    seeing the supernatural Jesus, 29
depravity, of earth dwellers refusing to repent, 90
desert, as a place of spiritual refuge for John, 149
destroying angel, representative of the devil, 120
Devil. *See also* Satan
    complete cessation of his influence on earth, 215
    deceptive waters of, 152
    destroying angel representative of, 120
    Pharisees as children of, 40
    as a roaring lion, 153
    servants of heaven as tools of, 148
    seven-headed dragon as, 147
diary, requiring a key to open, 82
Dionysius, doubted John's authorship, 4
Dionysius (god)
    as an important deity for Philadelphia, 59
    ivy-leaf symbol of, 161n19
dirge, for Babylon, 197
discipline, from a parent as not really a sure thing, 115–16
dispensational interpretation, of the rapture, 73n4
dispensational views, 7, 61n8
dispensationalism, on seven dispensations, 8
dispensationalist future, 133
dissemination, defined order of in Revelation, 15
divine aura, around "another angel," 125

divine Judge, Jesus as, 26
divine judgment, 42, 141
divine passive, used frequently in
    Revelation, 9
doctrinal truth, importance of, 33
doctrine
    church in Ephesus remained faithful
        to sound, 33
    love legitimizing, 30
dogs, as a synonym for those who do
    not believe, 242
Domitian
    decree that half of the grape vines be
        cut down in Philadelphia, 59
    giving himself the title, "Our Lord
        and God," 204
    persecution motive, 5
    requiring worship of his image and
        his person, 161
door, open in heaven, 73, 74
double retaliation, emphasized by the
    prophets, 196
double the penalty, as a common theme
    in the Old Testament, 196
dragon
    bends to the mighty will of God, 215
    as the biggest enemy of God, 148
    continuing to attempt to deceive,
        155
    defeat of, 144
    final judgment of, 219
    forces of given power to make war
        against God's people and to
        conquer them, 155
    hurled down because of the blood of
        the Lamb and the testimony of
        God's people, 150
    intention of to devour the child, 148
    knowing his time is short, 151
    as Leviathan, 144–45
    lost his place in heaven, 150
    participating in the defeat of, 104
    pursued Jesus during his ministry
        and now pursues the church,
        144
    pursued/persecuted the woman, 151
    as Satan, the Devil, 215
    as the source of wickedness, 169

standing on the shore of the sea, 153
swept a third of the stars from the
    sky and flung them to the earth,
    148
trying to usurp the authority of
    God, 156
drakon, as a serpent or sea monster, 147
dreadful anticipation, silence of, 109
dried-up Euphrates, as a symbol of the
    judgment of God, 181
dried-up rivers, symbolized the
    spiritually dried and worthless,
    181
dry bones, rising up to testify and
    declare the word of God, 139
dying, to ourselves to truly live, 84
dying child, saying "The Lord is my
    shepherd" with his fingers, 88

eagle, calling out warning prior to
    trumpets 5–7, 113
earnestness, Jesus calling the Laodicean
    church to, 68
earth
    being silent before the final plunge,
        109
    coming to heaven, 224
    keeping silence before God, 109
    one third burned up by the trumpet
        of the first angel, 112
    radiant with the splendor of God's
        glory in Ezekiel, 194
    wearing out like a garment, 220
earthly gods, disproving, 112
earthquake
    final, 183
    judgment accompanied by, 111
    seven thousand killed in, 140
    as a sneak peek at the final end,
        111n9
east, angel coming from, 102
eclectic method, of interpretation, 8–9
economic oppression, 162
economic prosperity, 195, 197
economic systems of the world,
        judgment upon, 179

edict, from a king combined with a
    prophetic word, 31
Egyptian army, judged in the midst of
    the Red Sea, 181
eighth day, Christ rose on, 190
eighth king, 191, 191n24
elders
    falling on their faces before the
        throne, 141
    as not saints but angels, 85
    one telling John not to weep, 83
    response of worship falling before
        the throne of God, 78
    singing a new song, 85
    still before the throne, 203
    surrounding the throne of God, 76
elect
    gathering from the four winds, 101
    names of in the book of life, 221–22
Eliakim, 59, 62
Elijah, 136
emperor worship, 39, 43
emperors of Rome, worship of, 5,
    120n15
end, being at hand, 240
"end is near," interpreting, 15n9
end of all things, at hand, 182
ending, of a good book, 234
end-times tribulation, intensification
    of, 61
enemies of God
    blood of, 208
    coming against God's people, 162
    description of the different, 129
enemy, that you cannot see, 53
engagement period, looking forward to
    the Bridegroom, 223
engagement ring, as a symbol of being
    spoken for, 99
Ephesian church, 32, 33, 34
Ephesus, 5, 30–37
Ephraim, son of Joseph, 103
epi Greek pronoun, translation issue
    regarding, 130
epilogue, meant to close the prologue,
    235
"the eternal gospel," from the beginning
    of time, 168

eternal life
    internet search of, 184
    Jesus giving to his sheep, 62–63
    in the New Jerusalem, 236
ethical code, Christ inaugurated a new,
    16
ethical standards, of people inside the
    church, 35
Euphrates, four angels bound at, 121
Eusebius, 4, 5
Evangelical church, on unbelievers
    ceasing to exist, 212
evangelical churches, not living out
    what is taught, 35–36
evangelism, task of the church in, 214n3
Eve. See also Adam and Eve
    serpent deceived, 215
"everlasting torment," times Jesus
    referred to, 212–13
evil
    Abyss the source of, 214
    continuing to be evil, 240
    sea as the origin of cosmic, 224
    taking the beautiful of God and
        making it into garbage, 155
    threat or power of no longer a threat
        with the sea gone, 225
evil and sin, new song celebrating the
    defeat of the powers of, 86
evil forces of the world, 128, 129, 182
evil frogs, 181
evil kingdoms, future controlled by the
    beast, 191
evil of the nations, emphasized, 9
evil trinity, 175, 181
executor, putting a will into legal effect,
    83
exile, only nobility and priests given the
    luxury of, 22
exposition, of Revelation, 12–20
eyes, of Jesus as flames of fire, 50
eye-witness testimony, validating a
    prophetic witness, 239
Ezekiel
    heard the sound of many waters,
        166, 204n8
    influence on John's vision, 73

saw a measuring rod in the hand of the angel measuring the temple, 133

saw the Lord on the throne, 27

*ezesan*, using of physical resurrection, 216n13

face, of Jesus as the glory of God, 28

faith

bringing about the obedience of, 128

of the church in Thyatira, 49

enduring in trouble and hardship, 170n19

no evidence of a full in Sardis, 55

of the saints, 106

as true riches, 68

faithful

access to the tree of life, 37

becoming pillars in the house of God, 62

called to hold fast until the coming of Jesus, 51

continued in their faith despite the persecution, 95

established as morning stars, 51

place of honor reserved for, 58

as victims but in reality victors, 187

"faithful endurance," of the Ephesus congregation, 32

faithful witness(es)

Antipas as, 43

Jesus as, 17, 65

at the wedding supper of the Lamb, 218

fall, of Babylon, 168, 193–200

false christs, arising to lead astray even the elect, 160

"false Christs and false prophets," prophesy of, 92

false prophet(s), 32, 160, 211

famine, scales having to do with, 93

Farquharson, Lottie, 238

father of lies, Devil as, 152

fear, having to do with punishment, 98

feast, after western and Jewish weddings, 202

feet, of Jesus like burnished bronze, 27

"fellow servant," angel identified himself as, 206

fellowship of God, lost because of sin, 225

fiery furnace, making us truly rich, 68

fifth beatitude (statement of blessing), for those sharing in the first resurrection, 218

fifth bowl of wrath, bringing the world into a deep darkness, 180

fifth trumpet, introducing a star given the key to the shaft of the Abyss, 116

final judgment of God

announcement of, 132

completeness of, 175, 178

description of, 182

ending with the eternal lake of fire, 213

not strictly chronological, 113

final reaping, accomplished by harvesting angels, 172

final resurrection, prophesy of, 141

final wrath of God, falling upon the earth, 178

fire, devouring the wicked from heaven, 219

fires of the blazing nations, quenched by the judgment of God, 113

first, as last and the last first, 84

first angel, blew his trumpet with judgment on the land, the trees, and the grass, 112

first horseman, as different than the others, 92

first interlude, 99–107

first resurrection, those sharing, 218

"the firstborn of the dead," Jesus as, 18

first-fruits, 167, 167n10, 171n24

five, meaning a few, 118

five months, of suffering inflicted by the locusts, 118

flames of fire, Jesus's eyes as, 26

"flesh" (*sarkas*), occurrences of in Revelation, 210n28

followers of God, marked, or set apart, from the wrath of God, 161

followers of Jesus, having hope, 20

followers of the beast, receiving a mark
    on their forehead or hand, 161
followers of the Lamb
    giving up their lives, 160–61
    motivating now, 235
    as people of integrity, 167
food
    enduring to eternal life, 46
    sacrificed to idols and sexual
        immorality, 44
    of the world as spoiled and rotten,
        42
football game, silenced by a serious
    injury, 108
foreheads of the people of God, seal
    placed on, 102
"forever," as a successful marketing
    strategy, 184
forgiveness, now as the time to receive,
    123
fornications, association with idolatrous
    practices, 187
forty-two months, as 1,260 days, 135
foundation stones, apostles worthiness
    to be, 229
four, symbolizing the whole world, 2,
    101, 101n7
four angels, holding back the judgment
    of God, 101
four beasts, coming out of the sea in
    Daniel, 156
four horses, leading 200 million
    demonic forces, 121
four living creatures. See living creatures
four winds, 101, 102n8
fourth trumpet judgment, affecting the
    celestial world, 113
freed from sins, idea of being, 18
frogs, representing the demons of the
    nations, 182
fruitfulness, of the tree of life, 236
fulfillment, emphasizing the certainty
    of, 192
funeral homes, churches turned into, 67
fury (thumou), as a very passionate
    word for anger, 169
fury of God, drinking the wine of, 169
futurist method, of interpretation, 8

Galilee, judgment against the villages
    of, 138
Gandalf, hobbits afraid without, 47
garbage dump, smell of a, 42
Garden of Eden
    G.K. Beale on, 236
    restoration of, 236
    Richard Bauckham on, 144
    serpent deceived Eve in, 215
    tree in, 37
gardening, work involved with, 164
gehenna, 211
gematria, giving numerical value to
    letters, 6–7
genres, of Revelation, 1n1
gifts and joys of God, as inheritance, 227
glories of man, laid down before the
    Lamb, 232
glory
    associated in Revelation either with
        God or Christ, 194n4
    of the God of Israel coming from
        east, 194
    like crystal, 228
    that Babylon depended upon, 199
    transformed from one degree to
        another, 57
glory and power, images of, 75
glory of Christ, "another angel"
    reflecting, 126
glory of God
    belonging to those residing in
        "Jerusalem" at the end of time,
        229
    departing the temple in Jerusalem,
        178
    overwhelming brilliance of, 75
    prophets confronted with, 28
goats, not intimidating when small, 80
God
    allowing evil to operate, 90
    allowing the woman and the beast to
        exercise authority, 185
    as a consuming fire, 137
    in control, 73, 74, 81
    declared just (dikaiai) in his
        judgment of the great prostitute,
        203

discerning weeds and the wheat (ungodly and the godly), 164
dwelling with men, 224, 225
as the emphasis of worship, 206
as the eternal Creator and rightful Judge, 128
exalted in the song of the twenty-four elders, 78
giving authority to the Son to open the scroll, 83
giving each of us a place of honor, 58
as "him who is and was and who is to come," 16–17
holiness of, 71, 78
judging those who have slain the righteous, 95
as just and upright, 180
as king having the right to judge and the right to show mercy, 74
knew Pharaoh's heart, 181
led John through the Spirit, 238
not letting the guilty go unpunished, 195–96
not sparing angels when they sinned, 215
outside of time and holding time in his hands, 78
paid the cost of our guarantee with the life of his Son, 123
paying back the nations for the injustice inflicted upon the people of God, 199
pouring out his judgments, 122n23
preparing a place for us, 224
protecting the church from potential demise and deception, 152
right to judge as the Creator, 168
as righteous in his judgments, 179
seeking to bring the world to repentance, 4
as the source of the river of life, 235
sovereignty of, 14, 78, 81, 90, 127, 176
sparing his people from his wrath, 149
"tenting" with his people, 226
as a theme in Revelation, 9
of truth as God of the Amen, 65
will be your glory, 231
will keep his promise to judge and condemn, 116
wining victory alone with passive people, 191
worshipping, 240
as worthy of praise, 75, 176
God and the Lamb, thrones of, 72
God-initiated sign, for John, 145
God/Jesus, on the throne at the last judgment, 220
gods/goddesses, worshipped in Ephesus, 32
Gog, 112, 192
Gog and Magog, symbolic identity of, 218–19
golden cup, in the woman's hand, 187
golden lampstands, as the seven churches, 32
golden sashes, as the symbol of priesthood and the kingdom, 177
the good, harvest of, 171
good and evil, long struggle between, 143–44
good fish and the bad fish, parable of, 171
good news, 124, 128
good works, as a non-causal necessary condition, 204n11
gospel, 67, 146
gospel of John, writing different from Revelation, 3
grace and peace, offering as a greeting, 16
grain, harvest of as a positive harvest, 171
"grain, oil, and wine," representing the basic necessities of life, 94
grammar, in Revelation as unique, 3
grapes, 171, 172
gratitude, to Jesus, 107
the "great city," wherever God is opposed, 139
great commission, of Jesus to his disciples, 51
Great Doctor, Jesus diagnosis as, 54

"the great prostitute." *See* prostitute
"the great sword," as a tool of judgment
    on the nations, 93
great tribulation. *See also* tribulation
    background of, 105–6
    book containing events of the
        future, 82
    introducing the end, 109
Greco-Roman myths, New Testament
    demythologizing, 146
greed, rotten food of, 44
Ground Zero, relief effort at, 114
growth, not perceived by the ones
    growing, 48

Hades, 116, 220. *See also* Death and
    Hades
hail, 183, 183n30
hair, in Revelation, 119
"half," involving time of crisis and
    judgment, 110n4
Hallel Psalms, connection with, 202n3
"hallelujah"
    found only here in the New
        Testament, 202
    multitude repeating, 204
Hallelujah Chorus, of Handel's Messiah,
    78–79
harpists, singing a new song, 166
harvest
    called for from the throne of heaven,
        173
    of humanity, 164
    of judgment, 171n24
    types of, 172
    of the unrighteous and wicked or of
        the righteous, 171
"haunt," *phulakh*, Greek for meaning a
    place of judgment, 194n5
healing of the nations, tree of life for,
    236
heart
    of mankind, blackened before God
        in the end, 181
    spiritual hardening of, 115
heaven
    coming down to earth, 166, 224

eternality of, 170n18
no need for a temple, 231
uniting with earth, 207
as a wonderful scene, 107
heaven and earth, coming together, 165
heavenly bodies, burned up and
    dissolved, 183
heavenly city, established on the new
    earth, 165
heavens
    opened for Ezekiel and his visions,
        207
    passing away with a roar, 183
Hebrew *Tau*, people marked with in
    Ezekiel, 102
Helios, Phaethon the son of, 180n22
hell, 116n2, 212
Heqt (goddess) in Egypt, 182
"He's got the whole world in his hands"
    (song), 81
hidden manna, referenced by Jesus, 45
Hierapolis, 66
High Priest, Jesus as, 26
Hilkiah, palace administrator for David,
    59
historical approach, to the seven kings,
    189–90
historicist method, of interpretation,
    7–8
history
    God sovereign over, 20, 78
    included in the scroll, 83
holiness of God, 71, 78
holiness of worship, re-evaluating, 79
holy city
    descending from God out of heaven,
        228
    dimensions of, 230
    material of as glorious and beyond
        compare, 231
    unclean, and the false kept out of,
        232
Holy Spirit. *See also* Spirit
    as a dangerous power, 137
    human spirit in communion with,
        239
    Jesus threatening to remove, 34

as the obvious choice for the seven
spirits, 17
prophetic influence of, 74
role in John's visions, 23
seal of like an engagement ring, 103
as the sevenfold Spirit, 32
testimony of the church empowered
by, 242
"Holy to the Lord," 62, 102
honor, Jesus promising a restoration
of, 60
hope, in seeing Jesus, 232
horses
of judgment, 91
restrained before the sealing of the
saints, 121
hortatory subjunctives, intensifying joy,
204n10
Horus (sun god), 146
host of heaven, rotting away, 96
hour of trial, keeping the Philadelphia
church from, 61
"how long," as a common call for help,
95
human depravity, running its course, 92
human race, close to fulfilling the task
of the four horsemen, 94
human society, mourning the coming of
the wrath of the Lamb, 97
human spirit, in communion with the
Holy Spirit, 239
human trafficking, by the Roman
Empire, 198
humanity, scorched with fire by the sun,
180

idealist method, of interpretation, 8
identity marker, of those who belong to
God, 102
idol worship, 122
idolatrous feasts, participation in by
Sardis church friends, 56
idolatry
defined, 122
Ephraim associated with, 103
as folly, 113
as the root cause of every sin, 122
standing against, 52

image (eikona), set up to honor the
beast, 160
immanence, within God's control, 190
imminence, describing an event possible
any day and impossible no day,
14
imperial cult, rituals of, 5
impurity, 43, 45
"in the Spirit," John as, 23, 74
incense, offering the prayers of the
saints with, 110
Indonesia, technological growth not
improving economic conditions,
214n3
inhabitants of the earth, 159, 160
innumerable multitude, robes washed in
the blood of the Lamb, 100
intensity, of God's judgment continuing
to increase, 113
interludes
first, 99–107
none between the sixth and seventh
bowl, 175
second, 124–31
third, 132–42
internal enemies, slowly growing on the
inside, 53–54
interpretation, methods of, 7–9
investiture, of the Lamb, 80–81
Irenaeus, on John being released from
Patmos, 22
iron scepter, in the hand of the King,
210n26
Isaiah
calling Israel to come out of Assyria,
195
commanded to write, 24
on the day of the LORD, 113
prophesied the union of Christ and
the church, 205–6
seeing the "train of [the Lord's] robe
fill[ing] the temple," 25
Isis, woman as, 145–46
Israel. See also Jews; Judah
ark of the covenant symbolizing the
rebellion of, 141
holy to the Lord as firstfruits of his
harvest, 167

Israel *(continued)*
    made to be a kingdom and priests to
        serve God, 86
    people of as bright lights in the
        world, 51
    remnant come to believe in Christ
        during the tribulation period,
        103
    saints often portrayed as stars or
        angels, 148
    saved at Christ's second coming, 104
    shameful nakedness of in the
        context of idolatry, 68
"It is done," spoken from the throne, 227

Jehovah's Witnesses, 60
Jeremiah
    influence on chapter 18, 193–94
    told to write, 24
    took the pot of manna, 45
    on the word of God, 129
King Jeroboam, set up two golden calves
    with one in Dan, 103
Jerusalem
    called Sodom and Gomorrah, 138
    destroyed by Roman armies, 6
    measuring in Zechariah, 133
    Mount Zion as literal, 165
    nations coming to worship God in,
        177n9
    Revelation prophesying the fall of, 8
    siege of by the Romans, 149n15
Jesse. *See* Branch of Jesse
Jesus. *See also* Christ; the Lamb
    attributing worship to, 19
    as Bridegroom, 50, 99, 201, 202,
        205, 233
    called *logos* only in John and
        Revelation, 3–4
    calling John up to the next stage of
        his vision, 73
    caring enough to be with us, 26
    as the center of attention, 87
    center of importance of, 81
    coming back, 243
    commissioned his church to be
        harvesting now, 173

compared the kingdom of God to a
    man who is harvesting his grain,
    171
as a conquering King to the earth,
    214
in control with authority, 48
counseling every generation to be
    alert, 239
determining entrance requirements,
    60
at the door knocking, 68–69
as a faithful and true witness, 65
final appeal to come back soon, 243
as the "First and the Last who was
    dead and is now alive," 39
as firstborn in the sense of
    sovereignty, 18
as God of gods, 210
great multitude caught up in, 105
as the harvester of his people, 171
has already won the battle, 99
having keys to the palace of his
    Heavenly Father's home, 59
having the keys of death and Hades,
    116
holding the key of David, 59
holding the seven stars in his right
    hand, 32
identified with the seven-fold Spirit
    and the seven stars, 54
identifying himself, 242
as judge, 43
judgment of as final, 45
knocking and hoping we will
    answer, 70
knowing the situations we face, 39
living for, 64
as the Manna sent from God, 45
"in the midst of the lampstands," 25
need of an accurate picture of, 29
not ashamed of the faithful, 57
not fighting against Satan, 150
not overlooking acts of love, 49
observing what we do, 49
opening vision of, 21–29
power and authority of, 47
powerful description of, 207
preached on the topic of hell, 212

punished the false prophetess, 50
as real and present, 25–26
rebuked the Pharisees, 60
receiving worship along with God, 9
referring to the cessation of death,
    221
reiterating the imminence of his
    return, 240
represented humanity before God,
    84
requesting permission to enter and
    re-establish fellowship, 69
riding on a white horse to reveal
    all, 211
as the sacrificial sufferer, 84
saying what will happen, 65
seeing, 234–43
seeking, 46
setting all things straight, 182
sitting side-by-side with God, 9
speaking of a literal hell, 212
as a theme in Revelation, 9
thinking for the tomorrow that is to
    come, 107
threatening a coming and imminent
    judgment, 55n7
as the truth, 199
wanting to see, 237–38
as a warrior, 9
witnessing the sufferings of
    believers, 41
won the kingdoms of the earth
    through his death, 17
worthy of praise and devotion as the
    Lord of all, 19
yearning to see him face to face, 243
Jewish literature, 13, 110n6, 207n20
Jewish tradition, on the ten tribes,
    104n13
Jews. *See also* Israel; Judah
    Greek king registering among the
        common people, 161n19
    persecuting Christian believers, 40,
        59–60
Jezebel, 49, 49n3, 50, 51
Joachim of Fiore, 7
Job, 68

John (apostle of Jesus)
    appealing to the divine I am of
        Exodus, 17
    astonished at the image of the
        woman, 188
    attributing glory and worship to
        Jesus, 19
    calling for patient endurance, 159,
        162
    commanded not to seal up the
        words of the prophesy, 240
    commanded to write about what he
        has seen, 29
    creating a new kind of epistle, 31
    describing the locusts, 119
    equating his work to the Law of
        Moses, 243
    expecting obedience from believers,
        15
    face to face with the holy King in all
        his beauty, 75
    familiarity with *gematria*, 6–7
    fell down "as though dead," 28
    hearing a sound like the voice of
        many waters, 166
    hearing about a Lion of Judah but
        seeing a Lamb, 84
    hearing the number of those who
        were sealed, 103
    hearing the voice of Jesus and
        seeing images that bewilder and
        overpower him, 25
    identifying Jesus with several
        significant titles, 17
    as the most probable author of
        Revelation, 1, 3–4
    never using a plural verb or a plural
        pronoun to refer to both God
        and Jesus, 87n18
    noting that there was no temple, 231
    on Patmos "on account of the word
        of God and the testimony of
        Jesus," 22
    positive understanding of God's
        control, 13
    prophesy meant for the first century
        church, 240

John (apostle of Jesus) *(continued)*
  prophesying against nations
    as a means of warning and
    judgment, 130
  referring to Jesus as the Word,
    208–9
  seeing a city alight with brilliant
    colors, 231
  seeing a more detailed description
    of the woman, 186
  seeing a new heaven and a new
    earth, 224
  seeing a second angel in verse 8, 168
  seeing a throne in heaven and one
    sitting on the throne, 74
  seeing an angel coming down out of
    heaven with the key to the Abyss
    and a great chain, 214
  seeing an angel flying in midair and
    proclaiming the eternal gospel,
    167–68
  seeing an angel standing in the sun,
    210
  seeing an open door, 73
  seeing "another angel" so glorious
    that the earth was illuminated
    by his splendor, 194
  seeing another angel with a
    measuring rod in his hand, 230
  seeing another figure with the same
    traits as Jesus, 170
  seeing heaven similar with what
    Ezekiel and Daniel (and Isaiah)
    saw, 73
  seeing heaven standing open and a
    white horse, 207
  seeing Jesus' hair as "white, like
    white wool, like snow," 26
  seeing seven lampstands, one for
    each of the seven churches, 25
  seeing that the woman is drunk with
    persecution, 187
  seeing the same kind of vision that
    Isaiah and Ezekiel saw, 78
  seeing the seven angels with the
    seven plagues, 175
  seeing the tabernacle of the
    testimony in heaven opened to
    prepare for the final judgment,
    177
  seeing the woman fleeing into the
    desert, 149
  seeing visions of heaven and earth,
    74
  on the seven thunders, 127
  shown the bride, the wife of the
    Lamb, 228
  as "in the Spirit," 74
  story-line well known to his readers,
    146
  suggestions as to the identity of, 3
  taken to the desert or wilderness to
    see the woman sitting on many
    waters, 186
  tasting the bitterness of the message
    he is compelled to proclaim, 124
  themes similar to the myths of the
    pagan nations, 146
  told to measure the temple of God
    and the altar, 133
  unveiling evil forces behind the
    scenes of history, 129
  use of the number seven, 17
  wept because no one was worthy to
    open the scroll, 83
  witnessing the finalization of
    judgment, 186
  worshipping at the feet of the angel,
    239
John the Baptist, 136
Johnson, Alan F.
  on the announcement of divine
    judgment, 168n13
  on the blood on Jesus's robe, 208n24
  on a "bride-city," 225
  on Christ's threat of judgment, 55n7
  on the church's garments, 205
  on the contents of the scroll, 82
  on John seeing five places as one,
    139
  on Paul's use of the word for temple,
    134
  on the silence, 110n4
  on the sword of Jesus, 27–28
Johnson Flint, Annie, "I See Jesus"
    (poem), 200, 200n22

Jonah, 130
Jordan River, 181
Joseph, 103, 144
Joshua, the high priest of Zechariah, 144
Judah, 101, 103, 104n13. *See also* Israel;
    Jews
judge, Jesus as, 26–27
the judged, fleeing from the wrath of the
    Lamb, 106
judgment
    against all who have not turned to
      Christ, 131
    of the bowls of wrath, 124
    as eternal, 203
    in the fifth and sixth trumpet blast,
      116
    of the first horse, 91
    of God's wrath as complete, 172
    "hour of trial" as a technical phrase
      for, 61
    message of never bringing joy,
      130–31
    to the nation of Israel, 83
    not joyful to speak of, 130
    from a parent as not really a sure
      thing, 115–16
    with pestilence and bloodshed, 112
    progressive expansion of, 111,
      111n9
    pronounced finished, 227
    prophesied upon the daughter of
      Babylon, 197
    revealing God's righteous character,
      9
    revelation of, 89
    for the saints of the Most High, 191
    of the seven seals, 90
    against the unrighteous, 209
judgment and redemption, book
    containing God's plan of, 82
judgment seat of Christ, all appearing
    before, 220
justice
    angel in charge of the waters
      recognizing, 179
    Faithful and True rider making war
      with, 207

    prayers for now being set in motion,
      111
    seeking in light of the law, 162
    whiteness of the throne indicating,
      220
justification, necessary for entrance into
    the eternal kingdom, 204n11

keys, Jesus holding, 28
"keys of David," 59
"kill," used by John to refer to the death
    of Christ or his followers, 93
king
    of Babylon falling from his self-
      exaltation, 117n4
    doing what he pleases in Daniel, 158
King of Kings, 24, 210
kingdom and priests, from every tribe,
    tongue, people, and nation, 86
kingdom of God, as a fellowship of
    people from all nations, 177
kingdom of the earth, symbolic imagery
    of the vileness of, 184
kingdom of the end times, predicted in
    the Old Testament, 16
kingdoms, spanning many centuries in
    Daniel, 189
kingdoms of the world, 140–41, 183
kings, mourning the fall of Babylon, 197
kings and priests, believers as, 18
kings of the earth
    allying with the beast and war
      against God's people, 185
    led by the demonic frogs to a placed
      called Armageddon, 182
    mourning over the loss of Babylon,
      197
    taking their stand against God in the
      Old Testament, 211
knowledge, legitimized by love, 30

Ladd, George Eldon
    on apocalyptic language, 102
    on the breaking of the seals, 90
    on Christ's coming, 55n7
    comparing Revelation to Jewish
      apocalyptic literature, 13

Ladd, George Eldon *(continued)*
on the composition of the kingdom
of God, 177
on the elders as angels, 76n13
on the idea of people in the church
as priests, 18
on identifying the star with Satan or
an evil power, 117n5
on interpreting the scroll, 82
on John anticipating a localized
persecution in Smyrna of short
duration, 40n5
on John being no longer on Patmos
when he composed Revelation,
22
on John not sealing the book, 240
on the judgments of God, 122n23
on Mount Zion standing for
eschatological victory, 166
on nominal Christianity devoid of
spiritual life and power, 55n4
on placing of the river of life down
the middle of the city, 236
on the rebellion of mankind after
the millennium, 218n20
on Rome not sitting on many waters
as Babylon did, 185
on Satan never being loosed from
bondage to Christ, 215
seeing Jerusalem as standing for the
Jewish people, 135n8
on the series of destructions, 213
on the silence, 109
on suffering from the perspective of
heaven, 153
on the switching of scenes between
earth and heaven, 74n5
on tears representing all human
sorrow, tragedy, and evil, 226n8
on the two witnesses, 139n18
on warfare between God and Satan,
145
on the warning against hurting the
oil and the wine, 93
on the woman seated on many
waters, 186
lake of fire
background for, 211
godless people consigned to, 242
as real, 222
in the second death, 41
torment of as eternal, 219
the Lamb. *See also* Jesus
as Alpha and Omega, 20
authority of, 97, 105
coming of, 204
consummation of victory, 201–11
doing battle against, 218
as the focus of praise, 87
as Lord of lords and King of kings,
191
opening the seals, 91
owning and possessing the book of
life, 159
receiving the scroll from the One on
the throne, 85
riding with the armies of heaven,
209
as the shepherd leading the saints,
107
slain from the creation of the world,
159, 241
standing with the 144,000, 165
striking terror in the hearts of all
who have opposed him, 89
suffered the punishment of
separation from God, 221
worthy to open the scroll, 80–88
lambs, as not intimidating, 80
Lamb/servant, of the Lord, 85
Lamech, as seventh generation from
Cain, 144
lampstand, symbolic of the tree of life,
236
Laodicea, Jesus' message to the church
in, 64–70
Laodicean church, 6, 66, 68
large boulder, understood as the final
judgment of God, 199
last battle, Armageddon as a symbol
for, 182
lateness, various levels of, 174
later date, of the writing of Revelation, 7
law, God having the right to rule by his,
74–75

Law of Moses, standard of authority of, 243

leaders of the world, falling to the power of money and comfort, 186

Lee, Robert E, 153

Leto, mother of Apollo, attacked by the dragon, Python, 146n6

Leto and Zeus, Artemis the child of, 32

letter writers, common greeting of first-century, 16

letters to the churches, witnessing for Christ in a pagan culture, 31

Leviathan, 144–45, 147

Lewis, C.S., 155

light, at evening time, 238

linguistic level, of communication, 2

lion
    concurrent identity with the slaughtered Lamb, 84
    roaring, 153, 214
    shout of the angel like the roar of, 127
    as a symbol for the conquering Messiah, 84n7
    of the tribe of Judah, the root of David, 83

lion pen, boys in, 69–70

lions' teeth, of the locusts, 119

little scroll, 125, 126

"little time," as the three and a half year period, 151

living by, every word that comes from the mouth of God, 45

living creatures
    always giving praise to God, 78
    angels joining in praise, 86
    commanding horses to come, 91
    described as animals, in pure form, 77
    singing a new song, 85
    still before the throne, 203

Living One, Jesus as, 32

living water, 227, 227n10

locusts
    compared to horses and chariots, 119
    as creatures bent on war, 120

power given to for great suffering, 118

sent to judge the nations, 117

traveling as a column darkening the sun, 118n7

logos, Jesus as only in John and Revelation, 3–4

Lord, as your everlasting light, 231

Lord Almighty, title used for God, 9

Lord God Almighty, 204

Lord of Lords, Rider identified as, 210

The Lord of the Rings (Tolkien), 47, 234

"the Lord's day," as Sunday, 23–24

loss of love, caused by struggle with false teachers, 33

loud voice like a trumpet, heard by John, 24

love
    for Jesus, 34
    legitimizing knowledge, 30
    message acted out in, 36
    for one another, 33–34
    perfecting us, 97

Luke, seven woes of, 91n6

lukewarm water, filled with disease and bacteria, 66

Macchia, Frank D., 1

"make war," in Greek as "polemic," 44n8

male child, as the Messiah, 148–49

mankind
    elevating their own names over the name of God, 122
    plagues against, 118
    as the primary recipient of the judgment, 178
    unwilling to bend the heart while bending the knee, 218

man-made images, worshipping, 122

manna, contrasted with idolatrous food, 45, 46n10

Marcion, rejected John's authorship, 4

mariners, mourning the fall of Babylon, 197, 198–99

mark of the beast, 162, 187

mark of the Lamb, 165

marriage, of the author compared to the
        marriage of Jesus, 201–2
married couples, becoming more and
        more alike over time, 223
Mars Hill, Paul's famous religious debate
        on, 200
martyrs, 100, 217
Mary, as the woman, 145
material wealth, of the Laodicean
        church, 67
materialism, rotten food of, 44
McClellan, George, 153, 154
meal, sharing of a common, 69
measuring, representing the security of
        the city's inhabitants, 133
measuring rod, indicating God would
        protect his people, 230
mediator, Jesus as our, 26
meek, inheriting the earth, 84
Megiddo, lying on the north side of
        Carmel Ridge, 182
merchandise, listing of that going
        unsold, 198
merchants, mourning the loss of
        Babylon, 197–98, 199
Merrit, Barry, 143
message, from Jesus himself to the seven
        churches, 30
Messalina, wife of Claudius, 196n11
Messiah, "forced" worship of in
        Zechariah, 140
messianic promises, time of fulfillment
        of, 166
messianic woes, of the people of God
        throughout history, 146
Michael, representing Christ, 125
military service, getting married before,
        99
millennial reign, looking forward to,
        141
millennium, interpreter's position on,
        213
millstone, large boulder the size of, 199
ministering spirits, sent out to serve,
        206
miracles, beast from the earth
        performing, 160
Miriam, Moses' sister, 157–58

mission for the church, not changing,
        132
mission of Jesus, continuing by his
        authority, 51
modified futurist interpretation, 134
monsters, typical pair of, 145
Moody, D. L., 170
moon, turned to blood, 96
moral issue, in the Sardis church, 56
moral purity, of people inside the
        church, 35
morning star
        authority of, 51
        fallen from heaven in Isaiah, 113
        in Isaiah referring to the king of
                Babylon and not to Satan,
                113n13
        Jesus as, 242
        shining like, 52
Morris Antique Mall, in Hot Springs,
        Arkansas, 35
Moses
        on being silent, 109
        God answered him in thunder, 77
        God telling "I am who I am," 16–17
        on Mount Sinai, 24
        not allowed to look at the face of
                God, 237
        set the precedent for the church's
                prophetic witness to the world,
                136
        told to write and recite in the ears of
                Joshua, 24
        wanting to talk to, 237
        warned Pharaoh of the plagues, 115
Most Holy Place, as the place for the ark
        of the covenant, 231
mother, spreading out her arms to her
        boys, 70
mother of prostitutes, 185, 187
Mounce, Robert H.
        on Abaddon as prince of the
                underworld, 120
        on Babylon, 168
        on the burning judgment of the first
                trumpet, 112
        on Christ as the revealer, 13

on Christ never appearing as an angel in Revelation, 125
on the contents of scrolls, 82, 129
on the eighth king, 191n24
on the elders as twenty-four priestly and Levitical orders, 76n13
on the fate the witnessing church, 133
on fleeing unto God on the wings of faith, 195n8
on "the great tribulation," 106n18
on history as not a haphazard, 14
identifying the beast with the Roman Empire, 156n3
on Jesus receiving the scroll, 85
on John moving beyond the storm about to break, 165
on John portraying the collapse of an anti-Christian world order, 193
on John referring to a historical person, 162
on the judgment of God, 179
on juxtaposition of the twelve tribes with the twelve apostles, 229n20
on the kingdom as a period of future blessedness, 23
on the lake of burning brimstone, 211n30
on the laying on of the right hand, 28
on the letters to the churches, 31
on locusts traveling in a column darkening the sun, 118n7
on losing of their first love, 33
on the mark of the beast, 161n19
on meaning ascribed to gems, 75
on no doubt about righteous retribution, 207
on no temple, 231n27
on the oath, 125n4
on the 144,000 and the innumerable multitude, 100
on the outer court as the church, 135
on the primary reference for the forty-two months, 135

on the purpose of Revelation 4–5 as a vision, 73
quoting Tacitus, 187
on the recapitulation argument, 214–15
on the reign of God, 141
on the reign of the beast, 158
on Satan's release, 218
on scarlet used to display magnificence, 187n9
seeing the star as a divine agent, 117
on the sevenfold spirits, 17
on "showing yourself watchful" in Sardis, 55
on the sickness of the Laodicean church, 67
on the suicide of Nero and his rumored future return (*Nero Redividus*) from the Parthians, 157n7
on tears of suffering, 226
on the term "virgin," 167n8
on the testimony of the church, 242
on the time for intercession as past, 178
on torment, 169n18
on the twelve gates, 229n18
on visions meant to stir the imagination, 78
on the war in heaven, 149–50
on water considered critical, 179n16
on the wine poured out, 169n16
on Zion as a mother, 146
Mounce, William D., 4
Mount Sinai, 24, 76–77
Mount Zion, 165
mountains
    significant role in Jewish thought, 228
    symbolizing kingdoms, 112, 189n19
mountains and islands
    being removing from their place, 96
    fleeing, 183
mourning, hair as a sign of, 119
mouth, like a sharp sword, 28
multitude, of the group beyond count, 104, 105

Murray, Annie, 81
mystery of God, accomplished with
    the sounding of the seventh
    trumpet, 128

nakedness, references to, 192n28
name of Christ, no one knowing, 208
name of God, written on the one who is
    faithful to the end, 62
name of the Lamb, on the foreheads of
    the redeemed, 237
names
    not found in the book of life, 220
    of the twelve tribes combined with
        names of the twenty apostles,
        229
nation of Israel, virgin applied to in the
    Old Testament, 167n8
nations
    coming to worship God in
        Jerusalem, 177n9
    of the earth analogous to the nation
        of Israel in Zechariah, 2
    gathering for battle one last time,
        218
    outside of the city, 134
    as those who dwell on the land, 128
natural world, turned upside down by
    the plagues of the angels, 183
Nebuchadnezzar
    devoured Zion "like a dragon" or
        "serpent," 148
    dream of, 238
    giving glory without repenting,
        140n23
    ordered the execution of any who
        did not bow before the image of
        his glory, 161
Nero (Nero redivivus), myth of the
    reappearance of, 6
"new" (kainos), meaning new in quality,
    224
new covenant, established through the
    death of Christ, 86
new creation, 66, 226
new heaven and a new earth, 219–20,
    223–33

New Jerusalem
    as the church, 225
    coming down from heaven, 166
    continuation of the description of,
        234
    as the destination of the faithful, 62
    Mount Zion as, 165
    river flowing down the middle of,
        235–36
    throne of God and the Lamb central
        in, 237
    vision of a heavenly home, 233
new name, 46, 208
new song, 85–86, 166
New Testament, interpreting the Old, 2
New Yorkers, celebrities in a human
    drama at Ground Zero, 114
Niagara Falls, feeling the power of the
    water, 27
Nicolaitans, 35, 44
night, associated with the darkness, 238
Nineveh, dependence upon the idolatry
    of economic gain, 185n3
no more delay, after the sounding of the
    seventh trumpet, 127
Noonan, Peggy, 114
now and now yet eschatology, case of,
    86
numbers
    carrying symbolic meaning, 2
    figurative use of by John, 189

oath, of the "another angel," 125
office of the prophets, in both the
        Old Testament and the New
        Testament, 239
offspring of the woman, 144, 153
old heaven and earth, 219, 220
Old Testament
    announcements accompanied by the
        image of an eagle, 114
    background on the fall of Babylon,
        194
    cross and the resurrection key to
        understanding, 2
    earth opening up and swallowing
        God's enemies, 152

evidences of the dragon's representation of the evil enemies of God, 147–48

as God's work against the designs of the enemy, 144

interpreting the New, 2

making associations with texts of, 3

nations coming to worship God in Jerusalem, 177n9

picturing Israel as a mother who prostitutes herself, 187

redemptive works associated with drying up of water, 181

on a restoration of all the tribes of Israel in the latter days, 104n13

as a source text for Revelation, 2, 13

written on the scroll in Daniel, 82

Old Testament Israel, unifying the church with, 18

Old Testament prophets, 13, 236. *See also* prophets

one fourth of the population of the earth, killed because of the judgment of the fourth rider, 95

144,000

as the complete community of the redeemed, 165

explanations of the identity of, 100, 103–4, 165n3

further description of, 166–67

going to heaven, 60

have no deceit in their mouths, 181

as saints honest before God, 167

standing with the Lamb, 165

symbolizing the faithful, 165

"one like a son of man," Jesus as, 25

One on the throne, description of, 75

open door, into the palace of Heaven, 60

opinions, trusting, 64

oppressive power, completeness of, 147

oppressors, eating their own flesh and being drunk with their own blood, 179–80

Osborne, Grant R.

on angels linked to the angels of the seven churches, 229

on "another angel" as a special herald of Christ, 126

on anticipation of the "rapture" of the church, 140n22

on the author of Revelation, 4

on the beast as a person embodying every evil empire, 157

on the blessings of the faithful, 241

on (*dei*) referring to God's will and way, 14

on the final messianic banquet, 69

on God allowing things to happen, 156

on hearing and obeying as common themes in John's writing, 15–16

on historical methods of interpreting Revelation, 7–9

on interludes, 100

on manna, 46n10

on the nations of the earth, 2

on New Jerusalem, 225

on the one evangelistic victory in Revelation, 140n23

on the 144,000, 165n3

on the primordial fall of Satan, 150n17

on protection from the wrath of God, 61n10

on the purpose of the first four trumpets, 112

on the purpose of the wall as beauty, 230

on the river of life, 235n3

on the role of the elders, 76n13

on Roman treatment of Philadelphia, 59

on "in the Spirit," 23

on themes in the judgments of the seals, trumpets, and bowls, 89–90

on trees of the Old Testament, 236n7

on uses of the trumpet, 24

on the wind that brought the locusts and parted the Red Sea, 101n8

on the woman as Isis, 146

on the words "wrath of God is complete," 175

outer court, as the physical expression of the true, spiritual Israel, 134

outline, of the book of Revelation,
10–11
overcomers, 182, 191
overcoming Lamb, sitting on his throne,
72

pagan celebrations, compromise to by
the church in Thyatira, 49
pagan hostility, limitations placed upon,
135
painful sores, of the first plague, 179
pale or speckled fourth horse, 94
Palestine, length of, indicating judgment
on a world-wide scale, 172
palm branches, as tools for praise to the
Lamb on the throne, 105
"paradise," original meaning of, 36
parallelism, between the seals and the
trumpets, 109
"parenetic salvation-judgment oracle,"
30–31
parents
giving warnings to our children, 115
silence of, right before punishment,
108
Parousia, of the day of the LORD, 55
parousia, time of the tribulation
immediately preceding, 133
Parthenon, 200
Parthians, 92, 121n18
partner, John as, 22–23
Passover Lamb, of Exodus, 85
patient endurance
John calling for, 159, 162
necessary for the church universal,
31
needed since the time of the first
church, 159
reality of the coming judgment
calling for, 170
required in the interim period, 23
Patmos, like an island prison, 22
Paul
on answering back to God, 74
on the Antichrist, 157
on being encouraged by our right
love for others, 34–35

burdened about the future of Israel,
130–31
on the grace and the gift of
righteousness, 238
planted the church in Ephesus, 31
on preaching the gospel, 71
on spiritual separation, 195
wanting to talk to, 238
Pax Romana (the peace of Rome),
93n12, 177
peace, 93, 218, 226
pearls, highly prized, 198
people of God
bringing terror to the people of the
earth, 139
called to disassociate with the
wickedness of the world
systems, 195
"churchifying" of, 229
dwelling place of, 158n10
enemy of continuing to pursue
God's people, 153
as first the nation of Israel and then
the nations of the world, 104
gathering of the deceived marching
against, 219
marked or sealed by the mark of the
blood of Jesus, 103
mounting up with wings like eagles,
152
must remain faithful, 235
never be deprived again, 106
not deceived by the beast, 160
as one throughout all redemptive
history, 146
power of the wicked beast against,
138
redeemed from all the nations, 133
sealed and protected from the
pursuits of the dragon for a
limited time, 152
"sealed" by God, 104
segment of in the outer court, that
are not measured, 134
subject to ridicule and shame in the
world, 138

submitted to persecution after a
specified and limited period of
time (1260 days), 133
understanding what is required of,
189
winning the battle spiritually, 155
within the temple, 134
worldwide celebration over the
demise of, 139
people of the earth
under the authority of the great
prostitute and the beast, 192
following the beast, 157
gloating over the broken church for
three and a half days, 139
led astray into false worship of an
idol, 160
set in their stubborn rejection of
God, 180
tormented by the truth of God's
word, 139
underestimated the power of God
and the power of God's church,
139
verse of praise for the wicked beast
of the sea, 158
perfect love, casting our fear, 98
Pergamum, Jesus' message to the church
in, 42–46
persecution
of all desiring to live a godly life, 138
of Christians for resisting imperial
worship, 5
church undergoing a period of, 135
as a common theme in the history of
the church, 95, 142
John writing in the midst of, 22
mandating passivity and
dependence upon God, 159n13
patient endurance and, 23
as a perceived crisis rather than a
real one, 8
perseverance in the midst of, 61
reality of believers going through,
61n8
saints made white through the fires
of, 56
as world-wide and universal, 188

perseverance, 68, 241
Peter, wanting to talk to, 238
Phaethon, drove the chariot of the sun
too close to the earth, 180n22
Pharaoh, 115, 144, 147, 181
Pharisees, 40
Philadelphia, Jesus' message to the
church in, 58–63
physical resurrection, 216, 217
physical suffering, 61n8, 118
picture puzzle books, 223
pillars, God preparing us as, 62–63
place of honor, having, 58
plague against the Nile, compared to the
second trumpet, 112
plagues
from the bowls of wrath, 178–79
continuing to come, 180
against mankind, 116, 118
parallel with the plagues of Egypt,
122
plan of God, 71, 159
Pliny, 5
Polycarp, burned alive, 39
polytheistic, John avoiding sounding,
87n18
postmillennial position, on the
millennial reign, 213
postmillennial view, as not a viable
option, 214
poverty, of the church in Smyrna, 39–40
power, of Jesus's voice, 27
praise
from all who serve God and fear
him, 203
final elevation of the crescendo of,
87
to God and to the Lamb, 72
thanksgiving and, 163
prayers, of "all" the saints, 111, 120
pregnant woman, Israel like, 147
premillennial position, on the
millennium, 213
premillennial view, of this commentary,
214
premillennialists, believing that the
thrones are on the earth, 216

presence of God, shining as a
     lampstand, 29
preservation, of believers from the
     wrath of God, 134
preterist interpretation, 8, 134
pride, 44, 197n12
prison, church in Smyrna tested in, 40
professing but apostate church, joining
     together with the persecutors,
     134
promise, of God spreading his tent over
     the faithful, 106
prophesies, 15, 226
prophesy, adding and taking away as
     false teaching, 243
prophesy movement, seeing every detail
     of Revelation fulfilled, 7
prophetic experience, of John compared
     to Old Testament prophets, 73
prophetic proclamation, 206
prophetic speech, 30
prophetic task, John recommissioned to,
     129–30
prophets, 15n9, 24. See also false
     prophet(s); Old Testament
     prophets
proposal ceremony, of the first century,
     232
prostitute
     adornment representing ungodly
          economic greed, 228
     Babylon portrayed as, 168
     becoming food for the birds and a
          home for demons, 194
     called great only in terms of her
          influence in corrupting the
          earth, 203
     defeated by the deaths of the
          faithful, 187–88
     destruction of the great, 203
     G.K. Beale on, 187n9
     as if she is known to the readers, 185
     leading astray the kings of the earth,
          186
     people of the earth under, 192
     purple linen of, 205
     queen acting the part of, 196n11

united with the beast with seven
     heads and ten horns, 186
prostitute/city, treated as she treated
     others, 196
protection, from the wrath of God,
     61n10
protector, Jesus as, 27
punishment, 89, 179, 196
purity, of our lives proving our message
     true, 36
purity and holiness, as the result of
     being justified by Jesus, 56
purple dye, as extremely expensive, 198
Python (dragon), attacked Leto, 146n6

queen, acting the part of the prostitute,
     196n11

race, running with perseverance, 49
rainbow, 75n10, 125
rapture, 73n4, 91
Reason Alone, rescuing from the Spirit
     of the Age, 155
reassurance, of Jesus, 28
rebellious nations, identified with the
     sea, 224–25
recapitulation theory, 219
"recapitulation" understanding, of
     Revelation 20, 213, 213n1
reception of the judged, bitter nature
     of, 130
red dragon, Isis pursued by, 146
red or fiery second horse, 92–93
Red Sea, collapsed upon the armies of
     Egypt, 152
redeemed
     able to look upon the face of God
          and the face of the Lamb, 237
     continuing to act like the redeemed,
          240
     harvest of, 171
     144,000 as, 165n3
redeemed army of the Lord, 144,000
     as, 104
redeemed humanity, many peoples of,
     226n7
Redeemer, Jesus exalted as, 86

redemption, 77, 83, 86n16

redemptive victory of the Lamb, blood reminding us of, 208

referential level, of communication, 2

Reformers, on the Pope as the antichrist, 7–8

reign, of Jesus as King, 208

religious people, having no relationship with Jesus, 36

remembrance, Ephesian church commanded to, 34

repentance
    commanded for the church in Sardis, 55
    Jesus calling the Laodicean church to, 68
    lack of "irremediable," 181
    required for the Ephesian church, 34
    as sending in our warranty, 123
    of the two thirds of mankind not killed, 122

reputation, of a church of being a great place to belong, 54–55

resurrection
    physical, 216, 217
    reference to, 149
    of the saints at the coming of Christ, 139

return, of Jesus "with the clouds," 19

"revelation," coming from the Greek word apokalupsis, transliterated "apocalypse" in English, 12–13

Revelation
    as applicable at all times and focused on Jesus Christ, 14
    as a both/and kind of book, 23
    as a call to moral and ethical faithfulness, 15
    claiming the promise of blessings for those who read it, 12
    continuing to study, 243
    describing the seventh age, 8
    meant to be read and then circulated to each of seven churches, 7
    as a message of worship, 19
    outline of, 10–11
    as a prophesy cast in an apocalyptic mold, 1
    as a sensual document meant to be heard, 1
    sent to the seven churches of Asia Minor, 24
    similarities with Daniel, 72–73
    as a theological work addressing churches in their present contexts, 1n1
    written in a definite context to seven specific churches while looking ahead to the future final conflict, 8–9

"revelation of Jesus Christ," as subjective or an objective genitive, 13–14

revenge, rotten food of, 44

reversal, on the day of the LORD, 114

reward, to those who refused false teaching, 51

"riches and splendor," suggesting replacement of false glitter and glory, 198

rider
    of the fourth horse is Death with Hades as his companion, 94
    of the red horse given power to take peace away from the earth, 93
    of the white horse, 92, 207, 208

righteous acts of the saints, as linen, 205

righteous deeds, of the bride, 205

righteousness, 68, 69, 207

ripe, translating as "overripe" or "withered," 172

river of life, 235–36, 235n4

roaring lion. See lion

robe and a sash, as a part of priestly attire, 25

robes, washing of, 241

Rock, that struck the statue in Daniel as Christ, 150

rod of his mouth, striking the earth with, 209

rod of iron, as an image of the Messiah, 51

Roma eaterna (eternal Rome), 203

Roman armies, 6, 149n15

Roman Empire, 8, 59, 84

Roman government, not using economic sanctions against Christians, 162

Roman wills, contents of, 83

Rome

    as Babylon for John, 168

    beast from the sea identified with, 156

    dominion epitomized by the power of, 138–39

    measures of wealth of, 198

    one more short reign of the oppressive dominance of, 190

    persecution of the Christians not affecting other Christians, 5

Root and Offspring of David, Jesus as, 242

root of David, referring to a prophesy of Isaiah, 84

rotten food of the world, ridding our lives of, 45

royal or imperial edict, genre of, 30

ruler of God's creation, Jesus as, 65

rushing waters, roar of as the sound of praise and shouting, 204

Russia, losses during WWII, 94

sackcloth, two witnesses clothed in, 136

sacrifice, 24, 84

saints

    under the altar, 95, 95n17, 177

    as anyone knowing Jesus, The Lamb of God, 111

    in the armies of heaven, 209

    "defeat" of, 144

    following the Lamb wherever he goes, 167

    as God's people on earth, 85

    having harps in their hands, 175–76

    as the multitudes, 202

    possessing the kingdom forever and ever, 238

    praising God for his great and marvelous deeds, 176

    prayers accepted by God, 111

    protected from the wrath of God but not protected from the wrath of the beast, 101, 158

    serving God day and night in his temple and dwelling in his presence, 106

    singing the song of Moses and the song of the Lamb before the throne, 176

    standing by the sea of glass, 176

    suffering of, 15, 128

    testifying to defy the sin of the world, 163

    testimony of condemning the oppressors, 209

    wearing white robes and holding palm branches, 105

    will be victorious, 165

saints, apostles, and prophets, as a reference to the church, 85n14

salt waters, becoming blood, 179

salvation, 105, 123, 202n2

*samek*, referring to an awful smell, 45

Sardis, Jesus' message to the church in, 53–57

Satan. *See also* Devil

    ability to accuse as severely curtailed, 150

    active in the world since he was cast out of heaven, 214

    battling with, 99

    binding and destruction of, 214

    deceiving by imitating Christ's appearance, 92

    defeat of as a theme in Revelation, 9

    dragon as, 215

    expulsion of, 150

    falling like a star from heaven, 117

    gathering the nations of the earth, 218

    hair of, 119

    having power to deceive, 161

    necessary to release for a short time, 216

    not specifically confined to the underworld, 117n5

    offspring of, 144

    released from his prison, 218

"so-called deep secrets" of, 51
as the source of all evil authority,
156
strategies of, 154
throne, meanings for, 43n2
throne located in Pergamum, 43
thrown into the lake of fire, 219
trying to turn the hearts of God's
people, 106
ultimate end of, 144
satanic forces, under the governance of
the throne, 94
scales, in the hand of the rider of the
third horse, 93
scepter, rising out of Israel, 51
scholars, starting with a human
understanding of God, 213
scroll
background on in Daniel, 82
of chapter 5, 126
containing judgments that will be
revealed, 82–83
contents of eaten by John, 129
of destiny, 13
in the right hand of the One on the
throne, 81
sweet to the taste but sour in the
stomach, 129
scrolls
concerning the destiny of "peoples,
nations, tongues, and tribes/
kings," 126
only opened by the owner himself,
82
of papyrus written on one side, 82
sea
becoming a source of death, 179
chaotic powers of calmed, 176
as a source of wickedness, 77n16,
179
as the traditional source of evil, 127,
153, 156, 220
understanding of the identification
of, 224–25
sea monster, combined with monster of
the earth, 145
sea of glass, as a symbol of purity and
judgment, 176

sealed by God, marked with his name,
18
seals
on the foreheads of the servants of
God, 102
opening of 1–6, 89–98
second beast, coming out of the earth
having horns like a lamb but
speaking like a dragon, 159–60
second death, 218, 221
second interlude (the little scroll),
124–31
second plague, turning the sea into
blood, 179
"second resurrection," John never
mentioning, 218
second trumpet judgment, on the sea,
112–13
seeking, Jesus, 46
self, idolatry of, 197
selfishness, rotten food of, 44
Seneca, called Rome "a filthy sewer," 187
September 11, 2001 attack, on the
World Trade Towers, 114
sequential pattern, used by John, 31
serpent, 144, 215
servants of heaven, portion of became
tools of the Devil, the Great
Dragon, 148
servants of the King, rights of, 75
service, church in Thyatira commended
for, 49
service contract, on our lives, 123
Set or Typhon, Isis pursued by, 146
seven
as a symbol of completion or
perfection, 25, 83, 189
symbolic for the power of the
Roman Empire, 189n19
as a symbolic number, 2
seven angels, 175, 177
seven bowls of wrath, 90, 174–83
"seven golden lampstands," John seeing,
25
seven heads and ten horns, of the beast
from the sea, 156
seven hills (or kings), as rulers allied
with the beast, 189

seven horns and seven eyes, of Jesus, 85
seven kings, symbolic and historical
    approach to, 189–90
seven lamps, describing the Spirit of
    God, 76
seven seals
    each opened by the Lamb of God, 90
    as introductory judgments to the
        seven trumpets and the seven
        bowls of wrath, 89
    scroll sealed with, 81, 83
seven spirits, referring to the fullness of
    the Holy Spirit, 17
seven stars, in Jesus's right hand, 27
seven thunders, voices of, 127
seven trumpets, 90, 108, 109
sevenfold retaliation, called for in
    Psalms, 196
seven-headed dragon, as Satan or the
    Devil, 147
seventh angel, pouring out his bowl of
    wrath, 182
seventh bowl, announced the beginning
    of the end, 185
seventh seal, opening of, 108
seventh trumpet, 132, 140
sexual immorality, 43, 44, 45
sexual perversion, rotten food of, 44
shame, no longer any, 237
shekinah glory, 106
shepherds, marked the ears of their
    sheep, 102–3
shining, of God's face upon a people,
    237n11
"shown," Greek word for (esemanen), 15
sick churches, signs of, 67
silence, 108, 109, 110, 110n4
silk, from China to Rome, 198
silver, highly valued in Rome, 198
sin, 237, 238
sins
    associated with acts of idolatry, 122
    of the woman clearly on display, 187
six seals, relating the forces leading up
    to the end, 109
sixth and seventh bowl, no hesitation
    between, 178

sixth bowl of wrath, poured out upon
    the river Euphrates (a traditional
    source of evil), 181
sixth seal, 96, 97
sixth trumpet (second woe),
    announcement of, 120–21
skies, rolling up like a scroll, 96
"slaughtered Lamb," Jesus continuing to
    exist as, 85
slave and free, no difference between, 97
slaves, in the Roman Empire, 198
Sleeping Beauty Disney movie, 57
sleeping habits, of depressed people, 56
smoke
    from the abyss darkening the sun
        and sky, 117
    analogy with prayer, 111n8
    as an image for terrible suffering,
        170
    from Mount Sinai, 77
    rising as an occasion of rejoicing,
        203
    temple filled with from the glory of
        God, 177
Smyrna, Jesus' message to the church
    in, 38–41
"Sodom and Egypt," John referring to
    Jerusalem as, 138
Sodom and Gomorrah, the LORD
    rained sulfur and fire out of
    heaven, 122
solecisms, appearing deliberate in
    Revelation, 3
Son of God, 48, 80
Son of Man
    coming on the clouds of heaven,
        19, 96
    in Daniel 7, 48, 85
    as the sower, 171
song of Moses, 77, 176
song of the Lamb, song of Moses
    fulfilled in, 176
song of "worship," of the peoples of the
    nations, 176
sons and daughters of the King, new
    identity in Christ as, 75
sons of Korah, earth opened up and
    swallowed, 152

sons of Zeus, worshipped in Thyatira, 48
"soon," 14–15, 61, 240
souls, of those who had been beheaded
        for the cause of Christ, 216
souls under the altar. *See* saints, under
        the altar
source of life, God as, 235
sovereignty
        of God, 14, 78, 81, 90, 127, 176
        of Jesus, 18, 27
sower, parable of, 130
Spirit, 23, 25, 242. *See also* Holy Spirit
Spirit of Christ, interpreting the voice of
        Christ, 37
Spirit of God, hovering before the
        throne, 76
Spirit of prophesy, going out into all the
        world, 206
spirit of the prophets, 239
spirits of the prophets, as subject to the
        prophets, 239
spiritual blindness, Laodicean church
        exhorted to buy salve for, 68
spiritual hardening of the heart, disease
        of, 115
spiritual healing, not found among the
        sick, 67
spiritual lives, entrusting to a reliable
        pilot, 21
spiritual resurrection, 216, 217
sports, comeback wins in the world of,
        38
spouse, taking a test on knowledge of,
        30
stamp of approval, of the beast, 161
star
        as an angel or a demon fallen from
            heaven, 117
        appeared over Bethlehem drawing
            the Magi, 242
        coming out of Jacob, 51
stars
        as the angels of the seven churches,
            32
        falling from the sky, 96
        identity of, 148
        shining like, 52
        symbolizing angels, 148

statues, ventriloquism and other magic
        tricks involving common in the
        Roman world, 161
Stephen, Greek word crown the same
        as, 41
"The Street of God," curved around
        Mount Pagus, 39
"strong city," at the end time in Judah,
        229
struggle, of the church between good
        and evil, 143
stuff, Roman lust for, 198
stump of Jesse, Branch coming from, 28
suffering
        and apparent defeat of followers
            of Christ turned into ultimate
            victory, 95
        bed of, 50
        of believers, 41, 74, 151
        of the church, 96
        as a common theme in the history of
            the church, 142
        definite clock/calendar time-limit
            to, 95
        as part of God's greater plan, 151
        from the perspective of heaven, 153
        physical, 61n8, 118
        of the saints as limited, 15
        smoke as an image of terrible, 170
        tears of, 226
        of those who do not know Jesus, 91
        of the ungodly as eternal, 169
        as a victory for the saints of God,
            128
        of the wealthy, 40
suffering (*basanismos*), connoting a
        spiritual and psychological
        suffering, 118
Sumerian myth, of a seven-headed
        dragon, 147
summons, to fear, honor, and worship
        the Creator, 168
sun
        impacted by the fourth bowl
            of wrath so that it becomes
            scorching hot, 180
        as no longer necessary, 106, 231
        turned to darkness, and the moon to
            blood, 96

sun and the moon, no need for, 231
sun and the sky, darkened by smoke
        from the abyss, 117
Sunday, as "the Lord's day," 23–24
Sustainer, God having authority as, 78
swimming, in shark-infested area, 143
sword
        coming out of Jesus' mouth, 42
        of Jesus, 27–28
        from the mouth of the Rider of the
            white horse, 209
        used in contexts of persecution, 93
symbolic level, of communication, 3
symbolism, apocalyptic vision, filled
        with, 73
symbols, 2, 8
synagogue, in Philadelphia shut to
        people of the church, 59–60
synagogue of Satan, 40, 59
synecdoche, cases of, 16n16

tabernacle, lampstands of, 25
"tabernacling," with the people of Israel
        in the wilderness, 106
Tacitus, on Rome, 187
Tartarus, as the word for "hell," 116n2
tears, of suffering shed on earth, 226
temple
        description of, 229
        filled with smoke from the glory of
            God, 177
        as no longer necessary, 158n10
        opening to prepare for the
            unleashing of the seven bowls of
            wrath, 177
        perfection and completeness of the
            new, 230
        return of the glory of God, 225–26
        vision of the future, 228
temple community, God's presence
        guaranteed to be with, 133
temple-city, expanded to include the
        redeemed nations of the world,
        230
temples
        ancient, 200
        in Pergamum, 43

in Sardis, 54
in Smyrna, 39
templum Iani (the temple of Janus),
        opened as a prelude to war, 177
temptations, lulling us to complacency
        and apathy, 153
ten horns, of the beast as also ten kings,
        191
ten kings, submitting to the authority of
        the beast, 191
terrified, being, 89
terror, not needing to face, 97
terrorists, on September 11 struck from
        the inside, 53
testator and executor, Jesus as, 83
testimony of Jesus, 136, 151, 206
thanksgiving, for God's work in
        creation, 166
themes, in the book of Revelation, 9
theodicy, as a theme in Revelation, 9
thief, Jesus promised to come to Sardis
        like a, 55
third plague, turning fresh waters into
        blood, 179
third trumpet judgment, turning waters
        bitter, 113
third woe, 116, 140
thirst, chance to drink and quench, 235
Thomas, John Christopher
        on "another angel," 125–26
        on the blood on Jesus's robe, 208n24
        on both scrolls, 126n7–27n7
        comparing the 144,000 to the evil
            trinity, 181
        contrasting those who lie with
            followers of the Lamb, 227n11
        on the idea of ongoing cleansing,
            241n22
        on John concealing the date he was
            writing, 7
        on John's "in the Spirit" state, 74n8
        on Judah and Benjamin, 104n13
        on the Lamb slaughtered from
            before the foundations of the
            world, 159n12
        on "lost their first love," 33
        on the mountain as "high and great,"
            228n14

noting that *naos*, temple, referring
   to Jesus' body, 134
on the 144,000, 165n3
on a progression of Satan's
   limitations in Revelation,
   215n11
on the reign forever dwarfing the
   thousand-year reign, 238
on repentance in Sardis, 55
on Revelation as a sensual
   document, 1
on the river as a promise of
   immortality, 235n4
on the river of life, 235
on Satan being bound for 1000
   years, 215
on those invited to the wedding
   feast, 206
on the witness of Jesus and the Spirit
   of prophesy, 206
those still alive in Christ, meeting the
   Lord in the air, 217
those who die in the Lord, promised the
   Sabbath rest, 170
those who have been sealed, able to
   stand before God, 100
those who have died in Christ, coming
   with him in triumphal process,
   217
those who have rejected the Lamb of
   God, receiving the mark of the
   beast, 188
thousand years, as a day for God, 183,
   240, 241
three and a half, as the conventional
   apocalyptic number, 139
three and a half years (forty-two
   months)
   authority of the beast limited to, 158
   corresponding to the length of
      Christ's ministry and to Elijah's
      ministry of judgment, 137n15
   as half of seven years, 135
   as 1,260 days, 149
three woes, listing of, 116
throne mysticism (*merkabah*
   mysticism), 75n10
throne of God

elders falling before in worship, 76,
   78, 203
enveloped in praise and glory, 77
Ezekiel saw the Lord on, 27
of God, 71–79
of God and the Lamb in New
   Jerusalem, 237
God/Jesus on at the last judgment,
   220
harvest called for from, 173
"It is done" spoken from, 227
Jesus' worthiness to occupy, 84
John (apostle of Jesus) seeing in
   heaven, 74
John seeing a white, 219
of the Lamb, 192
saints singing songs before, 176
satanic forces under the governance
   of, 94
Spirit of God hovering before, 76
of those given authority from Jesus,
   216
white indicating judgment, 219
whiteness of indicating purity and
   justice, 220
word for occurs seventeen times in
   Revelation 4–5, 74
wrath from, 97
throne of Satan, 43, 43n2
throne of the beast, 180
thunder, 76, 204
thunder and earthquake, judgment
   accompanied by, 111
thunder and lightning, important events
   accompanied by, 77n15
thunder and loud rushing waters,
   describing the voice of God, 76
thunders, associated with the seven
   trumpet plagues and with the
   final bowl of God's wrath, 127
"Thus says the Lord," 32
Thyatira, Jesus' message to the church
   in, 47–52
time (*kronos*), will be no more, 127
time of tribulation, as against the
   community, 136
time of trouble, such as never has been,
   as foretold in Daniel, 127

time period, of Christ in the tomb, 139
Titans, conquest by Zeus, 214n4
"to kill with death," meaning "to slay utterly," 50n5
Tolkien, J. R. R., trilogy by, 234
too late, 174, 183
torment (*basanismou*), idea of annihilation and, 169
torment of hell, common portraits reducing, 212
total destruction, references to, 192n28
tragedies, causing many to question God, 81
transfiguration, Jesus during, 28
tree of life, 36, 37, 235–36, 241
trees, of the Old Testament, 236n7
trial
    endured by believers around the world, 38
    going through the refining fires of, 68
    life filled with, 41
    three and a half years of, 61
tribe of Judah, lion from, 83–84
tribes, listing of, 103, 104
tribulation. *See also* great tribulation
    believers enduring, 23
    church going through, 91
    church suffering, 40
    introducing the end, 90
    John calling himself a partner in, 22
    as the punishment of the ungodly, 61
Trinity, Jesus as part of, 19
true church, seeming defeated and appearing small and insignificant in the eyes of the world, 138
true riches, seeking, 68
trumpet blast, heard by Moses, 24
trumpet woes, depicting trials, 109n2
trumpets
    first four as plagues against the natural world, 116
    for the first two woes, 115–23
    as a partial judgment upon the earth, 178
    purpose of, 112

sounding of indicating a period of time, 128
truth
    found in Jesus, 65
    of God's word as sometimes difficult to proclaim, 124
    holding on to and looking to Jesus, 163
    as the irresistible power of divine judgment, 27
    Jesus identified as, 65
    knowing or holding to, 132
    that will be forever, 199
twelve crowns, referencing the twelve tribes of Israel, 145
twelve harvests of fruit, for the twelve tribes of Israel, 236
twelve squared and multiplied by a thousand, as a two-fold way of emphasizing completeness, 103n11
12 tribes
    of 12,000 each symbolizing completion, 103
    multiplied by the 12 apostles, times 1000, 104
twenty-four elders. *See* elders
two beasts, opposing the servants of the Lamb, 155–63
two horns, used to mimic the two witnesses, 160
200 million, symbolic significance of, 121
"two lampstands," witnesses as, 136
two olive trees, anointed to serve the Lord of all the earth, 137
two witnesses
    called to witness and suffer, 124–25
    empowered to prophesy for 1,260 days, clothed in sackcloth, 135
    as historical figures, 139n18
    prophesying for three and a half years, 136
    representing the church in its prophetic witness, 136n14
    visible throughout the earth, 136
Tyre

compared to harlots because of their dependence upon the idolatry of economic gain, 185n3
groups expressing sorrow over the demise of, 197n13
intense grief of the mariners over the judgment of, 198
silenced by the judgment of God in Ezekiel, 110

unceasing worship, contrasting with unceasing torment, 169
uncleanness, hair as, 119
unfaithfulness, bringing a great famine, 93
ungodly, 119, 169
unholy trinity, appearing as, 155
Union soldiers, found a copy of Lee's battle plans, 153
united front, against God's purposes and his people, 182
universal church, seven churches representing, 16n16
universal redemption, for people of all kinds, 86
unknown name, of the Rider, 208
unrighteous, as outside the city of God, 172, 241
urgency, of John's writing, 14
"utopia," Jesus' second coming after, 213

vast number, symbolic number for, 121
vengeance, of the Lord promised to come upon Babylon, 185
verdict, in the letter to the churches, 31
Caesar Vespasian Augustus, image of, 187n11
veterans of wars, victories and losses, 38
victorious followers of Christ, as both the 144,000 "Israelites" and the innumerable multitude, 100
victory, 38, 84
video camera, having a service contract, 122–23
virgins (parthenoi), 167, 167n8, 183
Virgo, woman as, 145
visionary level, of communication, 2

visions
confronting man with vivid portrayals of eschatological truth, 175
of Jesus, John's reaction to, 28
of John, 109
Revelation as, 24
of the woman and the dragon, 143–54
voice
of God, 76
like a trumpet heard by John, 24
telling John to take the scroll from the angel and eat it, 129

walls, of the holy city, 230
wanderings of Israel, desert as a reference to, 149
war
bringing much famine and plague, 94
between the forces of evil against the forces of God, 182
in heaven, 149
in the twentieth century, 94
warfare, 24, 145
warning, given not to add anything or take away anything from this prophesy, 243
washing, of robes, 241
water of life, those not receiving the gift of, 227
wealth, not the goal of God's people, 195
wedding, between the King of kings and his bride, the church, 202
wedding banquet, parable of, 206
wedding day, waiting for, 99
wedding grown, of noisy material, 211
weeds, differentiating from plants, 164
Western Europe, now spiritually dead, 66–67
wheat and barley, 93, 94n14
wheat and the weeds, parable of, 171
white, 56, 92
white (first) horse, 91, 92, 202
white clothes, 56, 57

white garments, Laodicean church
    exhorted to seek after, 68
white hair, as a reference to the Ancient
    of Days, 26
"white hot" anger of God, 169
white linen, describing the church's
    garments, 205
white robes
    associated with military victory, 105
    given to the saints, 95–96
    given to those who have been
        faithful, 106
    more background to, 106n19
    as a symbol of blessedness and rest,
        96n20
    those in coming out of the great
        tribulation, 105
white stones, given to those who
    especially invited to a feast, 46
white throne
    indicating purity and justice and
        vindication, 220
    John seeing, 219
whole earth, judgment from God upon,
    102
the wicked
    acting wickedly according to Daniel,
        240
    defeat of, 210
    defeating God's people, 138
    harvest of, 171
    having the mark of the beast written
        on their foreheads (or hands),
        165
    marching against the saints at the
        central city of the millennial
        reign, 219
    outside of the grace of God, and the
        joy of the eternal light of God's
        presence, 242
    partial conversion of, 140, 140n23
    perishing from the earth, 199
    will be judged, 165
wicked abyss, as the source of the evil
    spirits and powers of judgment
    against the nations, 138
wicked beast, making war against the
    saints, 184

wicked nations, "making war with the
    saints," 138
wicked servant, parable of, 56
wicked trinity, the woman sold her soul
    and her eternity to, 186
wilderness, viewing positively as a place
    to meet with God, 186n6
will, witnessed and sealed by seven
    witnesses, 83
willingness, of commitment to idolatry,
    195
"winds," as demonic powers or angels,
    101–2
wine of the wrath of God, as a common
    theme in the Old Testament, 172n2
winepress, gathering the grapes outside
    the city of God, 172
wings, living creatures having six similar
    to the seraphim in Isaiah, 77
wisdom, required for understanding,
    189
wisdom and purity, Jesus's head
    representing, 26
wise, heeding the words of the prophesy
    and submitting to the Lamb, 240
witness of God, Jesus as, 17
witnesses, continuing in the powerful
    ministry of the Spirit, 137
woes, listing of three, 116
woman
    adorned with the signs of wealth
        and prosperity, 187
    as Babylon the Great, or Rome, and
        symbolic of all the cities of the
        earth that persecute the church,
        187
    as both Israel and the church, 146
    demise of, 193–200
    fleeing into the desert, 149
    given two wings of an eagle, 151–52
    identity of in Revelation 12, 145
    as Mary, Eve, Israel, and the church,
        148
    as not only Eve but also Zion, 144
    pregnant with a child, 146
    representing the persecuted people
        of God, 145
    symbolic identity of, 144

wondrous sign, showing a vision is
    apocalyptic, 145
word
    of Christ, ultimately prevailing, 28
    of God, as bitter, 130–31
    of God, like a fire inside, 71
    of God, Rider on the white horse
        identified as, 208–9
    of Jesus as his sword, 28
    of the Lord, two lampstands
        identified as, 136–37
    sword standing for, 209
    treading the winepress of the fury of
        the wrath of God Almighty, 210
words of the prophesy, John
    commanded not to seal up, 240
work of God, believing in him whom he
    has sent, 46
world, 183, 184
"wormwood," star named for bitterness,
    113
worship
    of the beast from the sea and the
        dragon, 157

of God alone, 240
none addressed to "another angel,"
    126
place in the book of Revelation, 19
re-evaluating the holiness of, 79
worthiness, of the Lamb, 87
worthiness of Christ, of Christ, 241
wound of the beast, source of, 157
wrath of God
    overcoming the wrath of the
        nations, 141
    poured out in power and in final
        judgment on "Babylon," 164
    redemptive purpose of, 90
    from the throne, 97

Yahweh, Jesus assuming the role of, 32
young people, lost sense of respect
    among, 71

Zechariah, 91, 101
Zeus, 32, 48, 146n6, 214n4
Zion, 146, 232

# Scripture Index

## Old Testament

### Genesis

| | |
|---|---|
| 3:15 | 144, 157 |
| 13:16 | 104 |
| 16:10 | 125 |
| 17:4–6 | 104 |
| 18:20–21 | 196 |
| 19:24 | 122 |
| 19:28 | 122, 196 |
| 22:11–18 | 125 |
| 24:2, 9 | 210 |
| 24:7 | 125 |
| 31:11–13 | 125 |
| 35:11 | 104 |
| 47:29 | 210 |
| 48:19 | 104 |
| 49:8–12 | 83 |

### Exodus

| | |
|---|---|
| | 115, 133 |
| 3:2–12 | 125 |
| 3:14 | 16, 17, 28 |
| 4:17, 30 | 160 |
| 7:14–27 | 179 |
| 7:20 | 112 |
| 8:2–11 | 181 |
| 9:10 | 179 |
| 9:22–26 | 112 |
| 9:23 | 183n30 |
| 10:2 | 160 |
| 10:12–15 | 117 |
| 10:13, 19 | 101n8 |
| 10:21 | 113, 180 |
| 11:10 | 160 |
| 12:23 | 120 |
| 13:21–22 | 106 |
| 14:13–14 | 191 |
| 14:14 | 109 |
| 14:19 | 125 |
| 14:21 | 101n8, 181 |
| 15 | 152, 157 |
| 15:1–18 | 176 |
| 15:3–4 | 207n20 |
| 15:5 | 116 |
| 15:11 | 157–58 |
| 16:32 | 149 |
| 17:14 | 24 |
| 19 | 77, 228 |
| 19:4 | 152 |
| 19:6 | 18, 86 |
| 19:16 | 24 |
| 19:16–18 | 111n9 |
| 19:18–19 | 77 |
| 22:4, 7, 9 | 196 |
| 24:1 | 76n13 |
| 24:10 | 76n12 |
| 25 | 25 |
| 25:31–40 | 25 |
| 28:4 | 25 |
| 28:31 | 25 |
| 28:36–38 | 62, 237 |
| 29:5 | 25 |
| 30:1 | 110 |
| 32:27 | 210 |
| 33:19 | 74 |
| 33:20 | 237 |
| 34:29–35 | 194 |
| 35:8 | 25 |
| 40:34–35 | 178n15 |
| 40:34–38 | 106 |

## Leviticus

| | |
|---|---|
| 10:6 | 119 |
| 13:45 | 119 |
| 16:4, 23 | 177 |
| 21:10 | 119 |
| 26 | 106, 127 |
| 26:11–12 | 225 |
| 26:26 | 93 |

## Numbers

| | |
|---|---|
| 6:25–27 | 237n11 |
| 16:12–14 | 152 |
| 22:5—25:3 | 44 |
| 22:23, 31 | 44n8 |
| 24:14–20 | 51 |
| 24:17 | 51, 242 |
| 25:2–3 | 44 |
| 31:8, 16 | 44 |

## Deuteronomy

| | |
|---|---|
| 1:31–33 | 152n24 |
| 2:7 | 149 |
| 3:24 | 158 |
| 4:12 | 243 |
| 7:13 | 94 |
| 8:3, 15–16 | 149 |
| 10:17 | 210 |
| 11:14 | 94 |
| 12–13 | 243 |
| 12:32 | 243 |
| 28:15–28 | 237 |
| 28:28–29, 34, 65, 66–67 | |
| | 118 |
| 28:49 | 114 |
| 28:51 | 94 |
| 29:5–32:10 | 149 |
| 31:30 | 176 |
| 32 | 176 |
| 32:4 | 180 |
| 32:10–12 | 152n24 |
| 32:43 | 199n20 |

## Joshua

| | |
|---|---|
| 5:14 | 28 |
| 24:7 | 149 |

## Judges

| | |
|---|---|
| 2:1 | 125 |
| 3:16, 21 | 210 |
| 3:27 | 24 |
| 6:22 | 125 |
| 6:34 | 24 |
| 13:20–22 | 125 |
| 18:16–19 | 103 |

## 1 Samuel

| | |
|---|---|
| 2:8 | 177 |
| 2:9 | 180 |
| 12:16 | 110 |

## 2 Samuel

| | |
|---|---|
| 6:15 | 24 |

## 1 Kings

| | |
|---|---|
| | 133 |
| 6:20 | 230n23 |
| 8:10, 11 | 178n15 |
| 12:28–30 | 103 |
| 17 | 149 |
| 17:7–23 | 239n17 |
| 19:3–8 | 149 |

## 2 Kings

| | |
|---|---|
| 1:10–14 | 219 |
| 7:1 | 93 |
| 9:7 | 203 |
| 19:21 | 167n8 |
| 19:31 | 166n6 |
| 19:32–35 | 191 |

## 1 Chronicles

| | |
|---|---|
| 24:4 | 76n13 |
| 29:9–13 | 76n13 |

## 2 Chronicles

| | |
|---|---|
| 5:13–14 | 178n15 |
| 20 | 191 |
| 24:18–19 | 239n17 |

| | |
|---|---|
| 29:27, 28 | 24 |
| 32:28 | 94 |

## Nehemiah

| | |
|---|---|
| 5:11 | 94 |
| 9:19, 21 | 149 |
| 9:26–27a | 239n17 |
| 12:35–36 | 24 |

## Job

| | |
|---|---|
| 1–2 | 150 |
| 11:9 | 127n8 |
| 23:10 | 68 |
| 37:5 | 176 |
| 38:16 | 116 |
| 40:17 | 116 |
| 40:25 | 116 |
| 41:10 | 116 |

## Psalms

| | |
|---|---|
| 2 | 48, 51, 51n7 |
| 2:2 | 151, 211 |
| 2:5 | 141n26 |
| 2:6 | 166 |
| 2:9 | 148, 166, 210n26 |
| 6:4 | 95 |
| 9:8 | 207 |
| 12:2 | 95 |
| 23 | 107n22 |
| 29:3 | 127n9 |
| 29:3–4 | 76 |
| 33:3 | 166 |
| 35:10 | 158 |
| 36:9 | 227n10 |
| 40:3 | 166 |
| 45:3 | 210 |
| 45:3–5 | 91 |
| 46:10 | 109, 112 |
| 48:2, 10–11 | 166n6 |
| 60:3 | 169 |
| 68:8 | 111n9 |
| 70:20 | 116 |
| 71:19 | 158 |

| | |
|---|---|
| 72:2 | 207 |
| 73:10 | 95 |
| 73:12–13 | 116 |
| 74:2, 7 | 166n6 |
| 74:12–14 | 147 |
| 74:13 | 157 |
| 75:8 | 169 |
| 77:18 | 77n15, 111n9 |
| 78:5 | 95 |
| 78:5, 15, 19 | 149 |
| 78:44 | 179 |
| 79:1–13 | 139n21 |
| 79:12 | 196 |
| 82:5 | 180 |
| 86:8 | 158 |
| 87:2–3 | 219n25 |
| 88:47 | 95 |
| 89:27 | 18 |
| 93:1 | 204 |
| 93:3 | 95 |
| 96:1 | 166 |
| 96:12b–13 | 207 |
| 97:1 | 204n8 |
| 98:9 | 207 |
| 99:1 | 204n8 |
| 104:2 | 194 |
| 104:4 | 206 |
| 104:30 | 182 |
| 106 | 203 |
| 106:48 | 203 |
| 110:5 | 141n26 |
| 111:2 | 176 |
| 113:5 | 158 |
| 113–118 | 202n3 |
| 115:13 | 141n26 |
| 118:20 | 241 |
| 119:37 | 179n18 |
| 136:15 | 149 |
| 137:8 | 196 |
| 139:14 | 176 |
| 141:2 | 111 |
| 143:3 | 180 |
| 144:9 | 166 |
| 145:17 | 176 |
| 146:6 | 127n8 |
| 149:1 | 166 |

## Proverbs

| | |
|---|---|
| 2:13 | 180 |
| 6:9–11 | 55 |
| 8:17 | 29 |
| 8:29 | 127n8 |
| 16:21–24 | 129n15 |
| 24:13–14 | 129n15 |
| 27:21 | 68n10 |
| 29:23 | 197n12 |
| 30:6 | 243 |

## Ecclesiastes

| | |
|---|---|
| 2:14 | 180 |

## Isaiah

| | |
|---|---|
| | 2 |
| 1:10 | 138 |
| 1:18 | 106 |
| 2:2 | 189n19 |
| 2:2–4 | 177n9 |
| 2:19 | 97 |
| 3:16–17 | 197n12 |
| 4:2–3 | 166n6 |
| 4:4–6 | 106n19 |
| 6 | 25, 73, 77, 77n16, 83, 178 |
| 6:1 | 25 |
| 6:4 | 178n15 |
| 10:12, 20 | 166n6 |
| 11:1 | 84 |
| 11:4 | 28, 137, 207, 209, 211n31 |
| 11:10–13 | 104n13 |
| 11:10–16 | 217n16 |
| 11:12 | 101, 218n21 |
| 13:9–10 | 113 |
| 13:10–13 | 96 |
| 13:21 | 194 |
| 14 | 113, 113n13, 117, 117n4 |
| 14:1–2 | 177n9 |
| 14:12–15 | 113 |
| 14:15 | 113 |
| 20:17–18 | 231 |
| 21:1 | 186 |
| 21:9 | 169, 186, 193, 194 |
| 22 | 62 |
| 22:22 | 59 |
| 23:17 | 185n3, 186 |
| 24:1–6, 19–23 | 96 |
| 24:8 | 199 |
| 24:23 | 76n12 |
| 25:8 | 107n22, 226 |
| 26:1 | 229 |
| 26:17–19a | 147 |
| 27 | 157 |
| 27:1 | 93, 116, 144, 147 |
| 27:12–13 | 104n13 |
| 30:8 | 24 |
| 34:4 | 96 |
| 34:10 | 170, 203 |
| 34:11, 14 | 194 |
| 35:6b | 236 |
| 35:10 | 226 |
| 37:22 | 167n8 |
| 37:30–32 | 166n6 |
| 37:33–36 | 191 |
| 40:2 | 18, 196 |
| 40:9 | 168n13 |
| 40:18 | 78 |
| 40:18, 25 | 158 |
| 40:31 | 152 |
| 42:10 | 86, 127n8, 166 |
| 43:3 | 68 |
| 43:10–12 | 43, 65n3 |
| 43:13 | 43 |
| 43:18 | 226 |
| 43:19 | 226 |
| 44:6 | 241 |
| 44:7 | 158 |
| 45:14 | 60, 177n9 |
| 46:5 | 158 |
| 47:5 | 109 |
| 47:7–9 | 196 |
| 48:20 | 195 |
| 49:2 | 28, 209, 211n31 |
| 49:10 | 106 |
| 49:23 | 60 |
| 49:26 | 179 |
| 50:1 | 187 |
| 51:6 | 220 |
| 51:10 | 116 |
| 51:11 | 226 |

| | | | |
|---|---|---|---|
| 51:17 | 177 | 5:14 | 137 |
| 51:17, 21–23 | 169 | 7:23 | 226n7 |
| 51:22 | 177 | 7:30 | 118 |
| 52:1 | 225 | 7:34 | 193, 199 |
| 52:7 | 168n13 | 8 | 120 |
| 52:11 | 195 | 8:3 | 118, 119 |
| 53:7 | 85 | 8:16–17a | 120 |
| 53:9 | 167 | 8:16–18 | 120 |
| 54:11–12 | 231 | 9:13–16 | 113 |
| 55 | 227, 235, 242 | 10:25 | 178 |
| 55:1–4 | 106 | 13:16 | 180 |
| 57:20 | 225 | 13:27 | 187n10 |
| 58:8 | 228 | 14:13 (Septuagint) | 17 |
| 60:1–3 | 177n9 | 14:17 | 167n8 |
| 60:1–12 | 228 | 15:16 | 129 |
| 60:3 | 231, 242 | 16:9 | 193 |
| 60:5, 11 | 232 | 16:18 | 193, 196 |
| 60:14 | 60 | 16:19 | 177n9 |
| 61:1 | 168n13 | 17:10 | 50 |
| 61:6 | 18n26 | 17:18 | 196 |
| 61:10 | 205 | 18:13 | 167n8 |
| 62:1–5 | 205 | 25:10 | 193, 199 |
| 62:2 | 46 | 25:15–18 | 169 |
| 62:2–3 | 208 | 30:22 | 226n7 |
| 63:1–6 | 167 | 31:4, 13, 21 | 167n8 |
| 63:2 | 172 | 31:7–9 | 104n13 |
| 63:3 | 116, 172, 208, 209 | 32:24 | 93 |
| 63:6 | 169 | 33:11 | 193 |
| 63:8 | 167 | 36:2 | 24n16 |
| 65:16 | 65, 65n3 | 39:17 (Septuagint) | 17 |
| 65:17 | 224, 226, 231n27 | 46 | 121n18 |
| 65:20–25 | 217n16 | 48:40 | 114 |
| 66:7–9 | 144 | 49 | 101 |
| 66:10 | 219n25 | 49:22 | 114 |
| 66:18 | 177n9 | 49:36 | 101 |
| 66:22 | 224, 226 | 50:8 | 195 |
| | | 50:28 | 193 |
| | | 50:29b | 196 |

**Jeremiah**

| | | | |
|---|---|---|---|
| | | 50:32, 34 | 193 |
| 1:6 (Septuagint) | 17 | 50:39 | 194 |
| 2:2 | 33n11 | 51 | 185 |
| 2:3 | 167 | 51:5 | 185 |
| 2:13 | 227n10 | 51:6 | 193 |
| 3:16–17 | 231n27 | 51:6, 45 | 195 |
| 4:10 (Septuagint) | 17 | 51:7 | 185, 186, 193 |
| 4:13 | 114 | 51:8 | 193, 194 |
| 4:30 | 187n9 | 51:8–9 | 196 |
| | | 51:9 | 193 |

### Jeremiah (continued)

| | |
|---|---|
| 51:13 | 185 |
| 51:14, 27 | 120 |
| 51:25 | 112, 189n19 |
| 51:27 | 112–13, 120 |
| 51:30, 32, 58 | 193 |
| 51:33 | 171 |
| 51:34 | 148 |
| 51:37 | 193 |
| 51:48 | 193, 199n20 |
| 51:49 | 193 |
| 51:64 | 193 |

### Lamentations

| | |
|---|---|
| 1:15 | 167n8 |
| 2:13 | 167n8 |
| 4:19 | 114 |

### Ezekiel

| | |
|---|---|
| | 2, 133 |
| 1 | 27, 77n19 |
| 1:1 | 207 |
| 1–2 | 81 |
| 1:22 | 77 |
| 1:24 | 166, 204n8 |
| 1:26, 28 | 75 |
| 1:26–28 | 125, 220n29 |
| 1:28 | 28 |
| 2 | 24 |
| 2:9–3:3 | 126 |
| 3 | 112 |
| 3:12, 14 | 23 |
| 3:12, 14, 24 | 186 |
| 3:27 | 37 |
| 4:10, 16 | 93 |
| 4–48 | 224 |
| 6:9, 11 | 187n10 |
| 7:2 | 218n21 |
| 7:14 | 24 |
| 8:3 | 23 |
| 9:2 | 75 |
| 9:2–3 | 177 |
| 9:4 | 102, 118 |
| 10 | 178 |
| 10:1–8 | 111 |
| 10:2–4 | 178 |
| 11:1 | 186 |
| 11:1, 5 | 74n8 |
| 11:1, 24 | 23 |
| 12:2 | 37 |
| 14:19 | 178 |
| 14:21 | 94 |
| 16:7–14 | 205n15 |
| 16:36 | 68 |
| 17:3 | 114 |
| 17:22–24 | 236n7 |
| 20:28–30 | 187n10 |
| 21:14 | 93 |
| 23:25–29 | 192 |
| 23:28–29 | 192 |
| 23:29 | 68 |
| 24:10 | 75 |
| 26:13 | 199 |
| 26:16–17, 29–30, 35–36 | 197n13 |
| 27 | 196, 198 |
| 27:7–25 | 198 |
| 27:30 | 198 |
| 27:31, 36 | 198 |
| 27:32 | 110 |
| 28:13 | 198 |
| 28:13, 17–20 | 75 |
| 29:3 | 147 |
| 31:2–9 | 236n7 |
| 31:15 | 116 |
| 32:2–3 | 147 |
| 32:6–8 | 96 |
| 32:7–8 | 113n14 |
| 33 | 50n5 |
| 33:27 | 50 |
| 33:27–31 | 50 |
| 34 | 107 |
| 34:23 | 103 |
| 35:3 | 189n19 |
| 37 | 106n19 |
| 37:1 | 23 |
| 37:9 | 218n21 |
| 37:15–23 | 104n13 |
| 38 | 218 |
| 38:2–9 | 211 |
| 38:17–23 | 112 |
| 38:18–22 | 183n30 |
| 38:19–20 | 140n22 |

| | |
|---|---|
| 38:21 | 192 |
| 38:22 | 211n30, 219n26 |
| 38:22–23 | 112 |
| 38–39 | 219 |
| 39:2 | 211 |
| 39:6 | 219n26 |
| 39:17–18 | 210 |
| 39:17–20 | 210 |
| 40:1–2 | 228 |
| 40:1–4 | 133 |
| 40:3–5 | 230 |
| 40–43 | 231 |
| 40–48 | 6 |
| 43:2 | 27, 194 |
| 43:5 | 23 |
| 43:7 | 225 |
| 45:2–3 | 230n23 |
| 47:1 | 235 |
| 47:12 | 236 |
| 48 | 229n18 |
| 48:31–34 | 229 |

## Daniel

| | |
|---|---|
| | 2, 16, 133 |
| 1:12–15 | 40 |
| 2 | 238 |
| 2:18–19, 37, 44 | 140n23 |
| 2:28–29, 45 | 240 |
| 2:35 | 150, 189n19 |
| 2:45 | 238 |
| 3 | 161 |
| 4:2 | 188 |
| 4:10–12 | 236n7 |
| 4:19 | 188 |
| 4:27, 30 | 187 |
| 7 | 26, 48, 72, 80, 81, 85, 101, 170, 189, 213n1 |
| 7:2 | 101, 218n21 |
| 7:2–3 | 73 |
| 7:2–8 | 144 |
| 7:3–7 | 189 |
| 7:4–6 | 156 |
| 7:6, 8, 11, 20, 25 | 158 |
| 7:7 | 188 |
| 7:7, 24 | 147n9 |

| | |
|---|---|
| 7:7—8:24 | 85n12 |
| 7:9 | 72 |
| 7:9a | 72 |
| 7:9b | 72 |
| 7:9c | 72 |
| 7:9d–10a | 72 |
| 7:10 | 82, 159, 220n29 |
| 7:10–11 | 176 |
| 7:10b | 72 |
| 7:10c | 72 |
| 7:10ff | 57 |
| 7:11 | 211 |
| 7:13 | 19, 25, 125, 171 |
| 7:13–14a | 72 |
| 7:14 | 19, 86 |
| 7:14, 27 | 217n16 |
| 7:14a | 72 |
| 7:15 | 72 |
| 7:16 | 72 |
| 7:18 | 238 |
| 7:18, 22, 27a | 73, 217n14 |
| 7:21 | 136, 138, 158 |
| 7:21–22 | 191 |
| 7:24 | 191 |
| 7:25 | 110n4, 135, 136, 158 |
| 7:27b | 73 |
| 8 | 160 |
| 8:8 | 101n7 |
| 8:9–14 | 134 |
| 8:10 | 148 |
| 8:13 | 95 |
| 8:17 | 28 |
| 8:25 | 160 |
| 9:27 | 110n4, 135 |
| 10 | 27 |
| 10:5 | 177 |
| 10:6 | 26, 48, 207 |
| 10:13, 20–21 | 121n18 |
| 10:15 | 28 |
| 10:20–21 | 148 |
| 11:4 | 101n7 |
| 11:35 | 56 |
| 11:36 | 158 |
| 12 | 127, 128, 240 |
| 12:1 | 105, 183 |
| 12:1, 3 | 148 |
| 12:1–2 | 57, 159 |

### Daniel *(continued)*

| | |
|---|---|
| 12:2 | 61, 141 |
| 12:3 | 51 |
| 12:5–10 | 127 |
| 12:6–7 | 177 |
| 12:7 | 110n4 |
| 12:7, 11–12 | 135 |
| 12:8–9 | 82 |
| 12:10 | 56, 240 |

### Hosea

| | |
|---|---|
| 2:2–7 | 187 |
| 2:8, 22 | 94 |
| 2:14 | 149 |
| 2:14–20 | 205n15 |
| 2:23 | 226n7 |
| 4:17—14:8 | 103 |
| 8:1 | 114 |
| 13:5 | 149 |
| 13:8 | 94 |
| 14:9 | 176 |

### Joel

| | |
|---|---|
| 1:6 | 119 |
| 2, 3 | 113n14 |
| 2:2 | 180 |
| 2:4–9 | 120 |
| 2:5 | 119 |
| 2:10 | 117 |
| 2:19 | 94 |
| 2:30–31 | 96 |
| 2:31 | 117 |
| 2:32 | 166n6 |
| 3:11b | 191 |
| 3:13 | 171, 209 |
| 3:15 | 117 |
| 3:18 | 235 |

### Amos

| | |
|---|---|
| 3:4–8 | 128 |
| 3:7 | 127n9 |
| 5:2 | 167n8 |
| 6:20 | 180 |
| 9:3 | 116 |

### Obadiah

| | |
|---|---|
| 16 | 169 |
| 17, 21 | 166n6 |

### Jonah

| | |
|---|---|
| 1:9 | 127n8 |
| 2:6 | 116 |

### Micah

| | |
|---|---|
| 4:5–8 | 166n6 |
| 7:16–17 | 140 |
| 7:18 | 158 |

### Nahum

| | |
|---|---|
| 1:6 | 97 |
| 2:3 | 187n9 |
| 3:1, 5 | 199 |
| 3:4 | 185n3 |
| 3:5 | 68 |

### Habakkuk

| | |
|---|---|
| 1:6 | 219n26 |
| 1:8 | 114 |
| 2:16 | 196 |
| 2:20 | 109 |
| 3:6–11 | 96 |

### Zephaniah

| | |
|---|---|
| 1:14–18 | 97 |
| 1:15 | 180 |
| 3 | 211 |
| 3:8 | 178 |
| 3:13 | 167 |
| 3:14–17 | 219n25 |
| 4:4 | 119 |

### Haggai

| | |
|---|---|
| 1:11 | 94 |
| 2:6 | 219 |
| 2:7 | 178n15, 183 |

## Zechariah

|  |  |
|---|---|
|  | 2 |
| 1:8–15 | 92 |
| 1:12 | 95 |
| 2:1–5 | 133 |
| 2:6 | 101 |
| 2:10–11 | 226 |
| 3 | 150 |
| 3, 4 | 85n12 |
| 3:1–3 | 125 |
| 3:5 | 25 |
| 4:1–6 | 25 |
| 4:3, 11–14 | 136 |
| 4:6 | 25, 136–37 |
| 4:7 | 189n19 |
| 4:14 | 137 |
| 6:1–8 | 91, 92, 101 |
| 6:5 | 101 |
| 8:20–23 | 177n9 |
| 12:10 | 4, 19 |
| 12–14 | 211 |
| 13:9 | 68n10 |
| 14 | 140, 216 |
| 14:3 | 172 |
| 14:5 | 209n25 |
| 14:5b | 191 |
| 14:7 | 238 |
| 14:8 | 235 |
| 14:9 | 237 |
| 14:15 | 140n22 |

## Malachi

|  |  |
|---|---|
| 3:2 | 97 |
| 3:2–3 | 68n10 |
| 3:16–18 | 221 |

# Deuterocanonical Books

## 2 Maccabees

|  |  |
|---|---|
| 2:4–7 | 45 |
| 11:8 | 105 |
| 13:51 | 105 |

## 3 Maccabees

|  |  |
|---|---|
| 2:28–32 | 161n19 |

## II Esdras

|  |  |
|---|---|
| 7:28 | 217n16 |
| 7:75 | 224 |

## Wisdom

|  |  |
|---|---|
| 18:15 | 207n20 |

# Pseudepigrapha

## I Enoch

|  |  |
|---|---|
| 20:1–8 | 17 |
| 20:2 | 116n2 |
| 20:2–8 | 110n6 |
| 45:4–5 | 224 |
| 56:5—57:3 | 121n18 |

## II Enoch

|  |  |
|---|---|
| 32:2—33:2 | 217n16 |

## IV Ezra

|  |  |
|---|---|
| 11:37 | 84n7 |
| 12:31 | 84n7 |

## Apocalypse of Zephaniah

|  |  |
|---|---|
| 6:8 | 119 |

## Ascension of Isaiah

|  |  |
|---|---|
| 4:11 | 160n16 |

# Dead Sea Scrolls

## CD (Damascus Document)

|  |  |
|---|---|
| 1:14–15 | 152 |

# Rabbinic Works

## Babylonian Talmud

### b. Sanhedrin

| | |
|---|---|
| 110b | 104n13 |

## Jerusalem Targum

### On Genesis 30:2

| | |
|---|---|
| Sanh. 113a | 29n22 |

# New Testament

## Matthew

| | |
|---|---|
| 1:1–17 | 242 |
| 2 | 149 |
| 4:8–10 | 17 |
| 4:24 | 169 |
| 6:33 | 45 |
| 7:6 | 242 |
| 7:7–8 | 45 |
| 7:15 | 33n9 |
| 8:6, 29 | 147n8, 169 |
| 9:36 | 171 |
| 10:28 | 41n6 |
| 10:34 | 93 |
| 12:29 | 214 |
| 13:9–17, 43 | 37 |
| 13:24–30, 47–50 | 171 |
| 14:24 | 147n8 |
| 16:18 | 229n19 |
| 16:18–20 | 86n17 |
| 16:27 | 220n31 |
| 17:6 | 28 |
| 18:34 | 169 |
| 19:28 | 217n14 |
| 20:21 | 217n14 |
| 21 | 105 |
| 21:42 | 231 |
| 22:1–14 | 206 |
| 23:13 | 60 |
| 24 | 56, 94 |
| 24:4–5 | 92 |
| 24:5 | 160 |
| 24:9–22 | 138 |
| 24:12–14 | 33n10 |
| 24:21 | 105 |
| 24:24 | 160, 160n15 |
| 24:30 | 96, 170 |
| 24:31 | 101 |
| 24:35 | 12 |
| 24:42–44 | 55, 239 |
| 25 | 201 |
| 25:1–10 | 183 |
| 28:18–19 | 51 |
| 28:19–20 | 86n17 |

## Mark

| | |
|---|---|
| 1:24 | 59n3 |
| 3:27 | 214 |
| 4:29 | 171 |
| 5:7 | 169 |
| 6:48 | 147n8, 169 |
| 8:38 | 209n25 |
| 12:10–12 | 231 |
| 13:5–6 | 92 |
| 13:19 | 61 |
| 13:26 | 170 |
| 13:27 | 101n7 |

## Luke

| | |
|---|---|
| 2:34 | 216 |
| 3:7 | 175 |
| 4 | 30 |
| 4:25 | 137n15 |
| 4:34 | 29, 59n3 |
| 5:31 | 67n8 |
| 8:28 | 147n8, 169 |
| 8:31 | 116 |
| 9:36 | 209n25 |
| 10 | 117n4 |
| 10:2 | 171 |
| 10:17–19 | 214 |
| 10:17–20 | 117 |
| 12:4–5 | 41n6 |
| 12:39–40 | 182 |
| 13:29 | 69 |
| 15:24, 32 | 221 |
| 16:23 | 169 |
| 20:17–18 | 231 |

| | | | |
|---|---|---|---|
| 20:36 | 221 | 14:23–24 | 16 |
| 21 | 91n6 | 16:5, 28 | 149 |
| 21:8 | 92 | 16:21–22 | 147 |
| 21:24 | 135 | 17:15 | 61 |
| 21:27 | 170 | 17:24 | 159n12 |
| 22:29–30 | 69 | 19:37 | 4 |
| | | 20, 21 | 217 |
| | | 21:8 | 148 |

**John**

| | | | |
|---|---|---|---|
| 1:1 | 208 | | |
| 1:14 | 208, 226 | | |
| 1:23 | 186n6 | **Acts** | |
| 1:37, 40 | 16 | 4:11 | 231 |
| 3:13 | 149 | 8:3 | 148 |
| 3:14–17 | 181 | 13:6–8 | 161 |
| 3:15 | 186n6 | 13:33 | 51n7 |
| 3:17–18 | 116 | 15:29 | 35 |
| 3:30 | 14 | 17 | 200 |
| 4 | 227, 235 | 17:3 | 220n31 |
| 4:20, 24 | 14 | 19 | 31, 197n14 |
| 4:35–38 | 171 | 20:29 | 32n9 |
| 4:42 | 16 | 26:14 | 28 |
| 5–7 | 9 | | |
| 5:25, 28–29 | 16 | **Romans** | |
| 5:28–29 | 220 | 1:3–4 | 149 |
| 6 | 42, 45 | 1:4 | 51n7 |
| 6:27 | 46 | 1:18 | 175 |
| 6:31, 49 | 186n6 | 2:5, 8 | 175 |
| 6:37 | 206 | 2:6–11 | 220n30 |
| 6:68 | 59n3 | 3:5 | 175 |
| 7:37 | 227 | 5:3–5 | 101 |
| 7:37–39 | 235 | 5:9 | 175 |
| 8:14 | 149 | 5:17 | 238 |
| 8:38, 47 | 16 | 8 | 231 |
| 8:44 | 152 | 8:1, 33–37 | 151 |
| 10 | 60 | 8:12–39 | 101 |
| 10:3–4, 27 | 16 | 8:35 | 93 |
| 10:10 | 151 | 8:35–39 | 61n8 |
| 11:35 | 216n13 | 9 | 131 |
| 12:2, 26 | 49 | 9–11 | 40, 115 |
| 12:31–33 | 151 | 9:20 | 74 |
| 12:47 | 16 | 9:32–33 | 231 |
| 13:3 | 149 | 11:24–26 | 103–4 |
| 13:34–35 | 33 | 12:1 | 79 |
| 14:1 | 201 | 13:14 | 57 |
| 14:1–3 | 233 | 14:9 | 216n13 |
| 14:6 | 65 | 16:25–26 | 128 |

## 1 Corinthians

| | |
|---|---|
| 3 | 229n19 |
| 4:8–13 | 101 |
| 8–10 | 122 |
| 12 | 73 |
| 13:12 | 237 |
| 14:19 | 118 |
| 14:32 | 239 |
| 15 | 18n24 |
| 15:25 | 207 |
| 15:26 | 221 |

## 2 Corinthians

| | |
|---|---|
| 1:20 | 207 |
| 1:22 | 103 |
| 3:18 | 56 |
| 4:3–4 | 214 |
| 4:16—5:10 | 61n8 |
| 5:7 | 68 |
| 5:10 | 220 |
| 5:14 | 36 |
| 5:17 | 226 |
| 6:2 | 123 |
| 6:4–10 | 61n8 |
| 6:16 | 226 |
| 6:17 | 195 |
| 7:1 | 205n12 |
| 11:13–15 | 32 |
| 11:15 | 214 |
| 12:1–4 | 23 |

## Galatians

| | |
|---|---|
| 3:13 | 237 |
| 4:26 | 146 |

## Ephesians

| | |
|---|---|
| 2:1 | 221 |
| 2:2 | 117n5, 214 |
| 2:20 | 231 |
| 3 | 128n12 |
| 5:3 | 45 |
| 5:6 | 175 |
| 5:25–27 | 205 |
| 6:12 | 117n5 |

## Philippians

| | |
|---|---|
| 1:23 | 119 |
| 2:5–11 | 17 |
| 2:7–8 | 26 |
| 2:9 | 208 |
| 2:10–11 | 210 |
| 2:15 | 51n8, 228 |
| 3:2 | 242 |
| 3:10–11 | 61n8 |
| 3:20 | 62 |

## Colossians

| | |
|---|---|
| 1:15 | 18, 65 |
| 1:24 | 61n8 |
| 2 | 128n12, 150 |
| 2:13 | 221 |
| 3:6 | 175 |

## 1 Thessalonians

| | |
|---|---|
| 3:13 | 209n25 |
| 4 | 18n24 |
| 4, 5 | 217 |
| 4:4–7 | 101 |
| 4:17 | 86n17, 209 |
| 5:2 | 55n7, 182 |
| 5:19–21 | 32n9 |

## 2 Thessalonians

| | |
|---|---|
| | 44 |
| 1:7 | 209n25 |
| 1:7–10 | 207 |
| 2 | 157 |
| 2:1–12 | 61, 157 |
| 2:4 | 138, 158 |
| 2:8 | 182, 207, 209 |
| 2:9 | 160n15 |
| 2:12–17 | 162 |
| 2:14–15 | 163 |

## 1 Timothy

| | |
|---|---|
| 2:5 | 26 |
| 3:16 | 149 |
| 4:1 | 152 |

| | |
|---|---|
| 4:12–16 | 36 |
| 6:16 | 75n10, 194 |

## 2 Timothy

| | |
|---|---|
| 2:11–12 | 217n14 |
| 2:12 | 238 |
| 2:26 | 152, 214 |
| 3:12 | 40, 138 |
| 3:13 | 240 |

## Philemon

| | |
|---|---|
| | 34 |
| 4–6 | 35 |

## Hebrews

| | |
|---|---|
| 1:2 | 91 |
| 1:2, 5 | 51n7 |
| 1:6 | 18 |
| 1:7 | 206 |
| 1:8 | 91 |
| 3:5 | 176 |
| 4 | 106 |
| 4:9–11 | 170 |
| 5:5 | 51n7 |
| 7:28 | 51n7 |
| 9 | 177 |
| 11 | 144 |
| 11:34 | 93 |
| 12 | 17 |
| 12:1–2 | 49 |
| 12:4–11 | 101 |
| 12:22 | 166 |
| 12:26–28 | 219 |
| 12:29 | 137 |

## James

| | |
|---|---|
| 1:2–4 | 101 |
| 1:5 | 26 |
| 1:18 | 167n10 |
| 5:17 | 137n15 |

## 1 Peter

| | |
|---|---|
| 1:6–7 | 101 |
| 1:10–11 | 13 |
| 1:13 | 154 |
| 2 | 229n19 |
| 2:5–11 | 18 |
| 2:9–10 | 86n17 |
| 2:21 | 39 |
| 3:8 | 150n19 |
| 3:13—4:19 | 101 |
| 5:7 | 26 |
| 5:8 | 214 |

## 2 Peter

| | |
|---|---|
| 2:1–3 | 160n15 |
| 2:4 | 116, 116n2, 215 |
| 2:8 | 147n8, 169 |
| 2:22 | 242 |
| 3:8–9 | 183 |
| 3:8–10 | 240 |
| 3:10 | 55n7, 183 |
| 3:10–12 | 220 |
| 3:11–12 | 183 |

## 1 John

| | |
|---|---|
| | 33, 44n6 |
| 1:1–2 | 239 |
| 1:5—2:2 | 241n22 |
| 1:9 | 57 |
| 2:20 | 59n3 |
| 3:2 | 217–18 |
| 3:2–3 | 205n12, 232 |
| 3:2b–3 | 237 |
| 3:3–10, 19–24 | 241n22 |
| 4:1–3 | 32n9 |
| 4:16–18 | 97 |
| 5:14–17 | 241n22 |

## 1 John–2 John

| | |
|---|---|
| | 157 |

## Jude

| | |
|---|---|
| 6 | 116 |
| 9 | 125 |

## Revelation

| | |
|---|---|
| | 231 |
| 1 | 15, 31, 54, 83, 86, 125, 170, 186, 207, 209 |
| 1, 2 | 136 |
| 1:1 | 3, 13 |
| 1:1, 9–10 | 235 |
| 1:1–3 | 4, 10 |
| 1:1–8 | 10, 12–20 |
| 1:2, 9 | 16 |
| 1:3 | 3, 25, 206n16, 235 |
| 1–3 | 240 |
| 1:3 | 241 |
| 1:3, 11 | 235 |
| 1:4 | 3, 10, 16, 16n16, 29 |
| 1:4, 8 | 9, 141 |
| 1:5 | 17, 97 |
| 1:5–6 | 17, 18 |
| 1:5–8 | 10 |
| 1:5a | 23 |
| 1:5b | 18n21 |
| 1:6 | 18, 18n21, 19, 194n4, 218 |
| 1:7 | 4, 19 |
| 1:8 | 9, 28, 179, 227, 241 |
| 1:9 | 3, 22, 32 |
| 1:9–20 | 9, 10, 21–29, 36 |
| 1:10 | 23, 74 |
| 1:10–11 | 73 |
| 1:12 | 25 |
| 1:14 | 26 |
| 1:15 | 27, 166 |
| 1:16 | 9 |
| 1:16, 20 | 148 |
| 1:17 | 9, 28, 241 |
| 1:18 | 97, 116, 214, 216n13 |
| 1:20 | 32, 187 |
| 2 | 30, 40 |
| 2, 3 | 31, 227 |
| 2:1 | 31, 32 |
| 2:1—3:20 | 10 |
| 2:1–5 | 10 |
| 2:1–7 | 30–37 |
| 2:2 | 31 |
| 2–3 | 7, 9, 76, 239 |
| 2:4 | 31 |
| 2:6 | 35 |
| 2:6–11 | 10 |
| 2:7 | 31 |
| 2:8 | 216n13 |
| 2:8–11 | 38–41 |
| 2:9 | 6 |
| 2:10 | 151 |
| 2:11 | 39 |
| 2:12, 16 | 9 |
| 2:12–17 | 10, 42–46 |
| 2:18–29 | 10, 47–52 |
| 2:19–21 | 134 |
| 2:20–23 | 185 |
| 2:20ff | 203 |
| 2:26–27 | 191 |
| 2:27–28 | 51 |
| 3:1 | 55 |
| 3:1–6 | 10, 53–57 |
| 3:1–10 | 11 |
| 3:2 | 55 |
| 3:3 | 182 |
| 3:4 | 56 |
| 3:4–5, 18 | 209 |
| 3:7–13 | 10, 58–63 |
| 3:9 | 6 |
| 3:10 | 61 |
| 3:12 | 237 |
| 3:14 | 65, 65n3 |
| 3:14–20 | 10 |
| 3:14–22 | 64–70 |
| 3:15 | 26 |
| 3:21 | 92, 97 |
| 4 | 78, 81, 85 |
| 4, 5 | 72 |
| 4:1 | 72, 73n4, 74 |
| 4:1–2 | 4 |
| 4:1—5:14 | 10 |
| 4:1–8 | 10 |
| 4:1–11 | 71–79 |
| 4:2 | 74 |

| | | | |
|---|---|---|---|
| 4:2a | 72 | 5:12–13 | 194n4 |
| 4:2b | 72 | 5:13 | 194n4, 225 |
| 4:3 | 125n2 | 5:13–14 | 10, 73 |
| 4:3a | 72 | 5:14 | 77 |
| 4:4 | 209, 209n25 | 6 | 9, 89, 92, 100, |
| 4:4b | 72 | | 109, 110, 120, |
| 4–5 | 72 | | 127, 177, 237 |
| 4:5 | 72 | 6:1 | 91 |
| 4–5 | 73, 74 | 6:1–8 | 90, 92, 100 |
| 4:5 | 76 | 6:1–17 | 10, 89–98 |
| 4–5 | 203 | 6:1—22:9 | 82n4 |
| 4:6 | 73, 77, 224 | 6:2, 4, 8, 11 | 9 |
| 4:8 | 9, 59n3, 77, 141, | 6:3, 5, 7, 9, 12 | 13–14 |
| | 169 | 6:8 | 95 |
| 4:9, 11 | 194n4 | 6:9 | 16, 93, 95, 110n7, |
| 4:9–10 | 2 | | 121, 136, 151, 195 |
| 4:9–11 | 10 | 6:9, 11 | 138 |
| 4:10 | 76 | 6:9–10 | 133 |
| 4–22 | 8, 74 | 6:9–11 | 85, 109n2 |
| 5 | 78, 80, 81, 91, | 6:10 | 9, 59n3, 61, 111, |
| | 126, 126n5, | | 202, 203, 220 |
| | 126n7, 156n2, | 6:11 | 105, 209 |
| | 157n7, 202, 204 | 6:13, 14 | 96 |
| 5:1–5 | 10, 72, 80 | 6:15 | 97 |
| 5:1–8 | 11 | 6:16 | 106 |
| 5:1–14 | 80–88 | 6:16–17 | 9, 106 |
| 5:2 | 126, 175 | 6:17 | 100, 109 |
| 5:2–5, 9 | 72 | 6b–10 | 72 |
| 5:4 | 72 | 7 | 9, 77, 99, 100, |
| 5:5 | 92 | | 109, 121, 134, |
| 5:5, 7 | 13 | | 149, 158, 165n3, |
| 5:5–6 | 97, 100 | | 192 |
| 5:5a | 72 | 7:1 | 2, 112 |
| 5:5b–7, 9a, 12–13 | 72 | 7:1–3 | 225 |
| 5:6 | 160 | 7:1–4 | 118 |
| 5:6, 9, 12 | 93 | 7:1–8 | 100, 101 |
| 5:6–6:17 | 9 | 7:1–17 | 10, 99–107, 100 |
| 5:6–10 | 10, 80 | 7:2 | 9 |
| 5:8 | 76n13 | 7:3–8 | 103, 133n3 |
| 5:8, 11, 14 | 72 | 7:4 | 103 |
| 5:9 | 100, 133, 226 | 7:8 | 103 |
| 5:9–10 | 82 | 7:9 | 104, 226 |
| 5:9b | 72 | 7:9, 13–14 | 56, 209 |
| 5:10 | 73, 86 | 7:9–11 | 76n13 |
| 5:11 | 86 | 7:9–17 | 10, 100, 101 |
| 5:11–12 | 10 | 7:12 | 194n4 |
| 5:11–14 | 80 | 7:13–14 | 76n13 |
| 5:12 | 82, 105 | 7:14 | 61n8, 241 |

## Revelation (*continued*)

| | |
|---|---|
| 7:17 | 226 |
| 8 | 100, 108, 116, 117n4 |
| 8:1 | 14, 109 |
| 8:1–5 | 10 |
| 8:1–13 | 108–14 |
| 8:2 | 110 |
| 8:2, 3 | 9 |
| 8:3 | 110n7 |
| 8:3–4 | 111 |
| 8:4 | 85 |
| 8:5 | 77n15, 111, 141, 182 |
| 8:6–13 | 10 |
| 8:7–8 | 2 |
| 8:8–9 | 225 |
| 8:12 | 117 |
| 8:13 | 61, 113, 116, 168 |
| 9 | 2, 112, 115, 120 |
| 9:1, 3, 5 | 9 |
| 9:1–10 | 215 |
| 9:1–21 | 10, 115–23 |
| 9:5 | 169 |
| 9:7 | 92, 119 |
| 9:10 | 120 |
| 9:11 | 117n5 |
| 9:20 | 122 |
| 9:21 | 122 |
| 10 | 74, 124, 126n5, 126n7, 133 |
| 10, 11 | 124 |
| 10:1 | 125, 194n4 |
| 10:1–11 | 10, 124–31 |
| 10:1—11:13 | 100 |
| 10:2, 5–6, 8 | 225 |
| 10:4 | 129 |
| 10:6 | 125, 127, 133 |
| 10:7 | 187 |
| 10:8 | 129 |
| 10:11 | 125, 129 |
| 10:19 | 4 |
| 11 | 6, 22, 74, 124, 132, 133, 134, 140, 142, 144, 195 |
| 11:1 | 133, 230 |
| 11:1, 2 | 9 |
| 11:1–2 | 6, 133, 230 |
| 11:1–13 | 129 |
| 11:1–14 | 10 |
| 11:1–19 | 132–42 |
| 11:2 | 136 |
| 11:2–3 | 149, 151 |
| 11:3 | 135 |
| 11:3, 9 | 110n4 |
| 11:3–13 | 133 |
| 11:6 | 137 |
| 11:7 | 118, 136, 138 |
| 11:7–10 | 195 |
| 11:9 | 138, 177 |
| 11:9–13 | 136 |
| 11:10 | 61, 118, 169 |
| 11–12 | 150n17 |
| 11:13 | 140, 194n4 |
| 11:13, 19 | 182 |
| 11:15 | 109, 132 |
| 11:15–19 | 10 |
| 11–16 | 129 |
| 11:17 | 9 |
| 11:18 | 9, 76n13, 82, 85n14 |
| 11–18 | 129 |
| 11:18 | 141 |
| 11:19 | 77n15, 111, 127, 141 |
| 12 | 9, 74n7, 120, 135, 143, 144, 145n4, 146, 150n17, 150n19, 155, 156, 215n11 |
| 12, 13 | 141 |
| 12:1—13:18 | 100 |
| 12:1–17 | 10 |
| 12:1–18 | 143–54 |
| 12:2 | 146, 169 |
| 12:3 | 147, 189 |
| 12:3–4 | 120 |
| 12:5 | 166 |
| 12:6 | 149 |
| 12:6, 14 | 136, 151, 186n6 |
| 12:6–9 | 110n4 |
| 12:7 | 136, 149 |
| 12:7–9 | 125 |
| 12:9 | 9, 117n5, 147, 150 |
| 12:10, 17 | 195 |

| | |
|---|---|
| 12:10–12 | 150 |
| 12:11 | 151 |
| 12:11, 17 | 136 |
| 12:11a | 104 |
| 12:11b | 104 |
| 12:12 | 61 |
| 12–13 | 92 |
| 12:13–16 | 153 |
| 12:14 | 9 |
| 12:15–16 | 186 |
| 12:17 | 153, 157 |
| 12–18 | 139 |
| 12:18 | 153, 224, 225 |
| 12–20 | 145 |
| 13 | 7, 9, 102n9, 138, 154, 155, 156, 156n2, 162, 184, 186, 188, 189, 214 |
| 13, 14 | 144 |
| 13:1 | 224, 225 |
| 13:1, 11 | 145 |
| 13:1–2 | 189 |
| 13:1–8 | 101 |
| 13:1–18 | 10, 155–63 |
| 13:1ff | 120 |
| 13:2 | 156 |
| 13:3 | 186 |
| 13:3–4 | 6 |
| 13:4–8, 15–16 | 5 |
| 13:5 | 110n4, 151 |
| 13:5, 7, 14, 15 | 205n12 |
| 13:5–6 | 158 |
| 13:5–7 | 159 |
| 13:5–10 | 61 |
| 13:6 | 136 |
| 13:7 | 158 |
| 13:7, 14, 15 | 9 |
| 13:8 | 57, 93, 149, 187, 189, 222 |
| 13:8, 12, 14 | 61 |
| 13:10 | 93, 170 |
| 13:11–18 | 11 |
| 13:13 | 160 |
| 13:14 | 216n13 |
| 13:15 | 5 |
| 13:16 | 161 |
| 13:16–17 | 9 |
| 13:18 | 6, 170 |
| 13:36–43 | 171 |
| 14 | 141, 164, 171, 177, 209n25 |
| 14, 16 | 210 |
| 14:1 | 165 |
| 14:1–2 | 165n1 |
| 14:1–5 | 11 |
| 14:1–20 | 11, 164–73 |
| 14:3 | 76n13 |
| 14:4 | 167, 167n8 |
| 14:4, 6–9 | 56 |
| 14:4–5 | 166 |
| 14:5 | 227n11 |
| 14:6 | 61 |
| 14:6–7 | 11 |
| 14:7 | 2, 168, 194n4, 225 |
| 14:8 | 11, 168 |
| 14:9 | 169 |
| 14:9–11 | 5 |
| 14:9–16 | 11 |
| 14:10, 19 | 9 |
| 14:10–11 | 118 |
| 14:11 | 169 |
| 14:12–13 | 195 |
| 14:13 | 206n16, 241 |
| 14:14 | 91, 170, 171 |
| 14:14–15 | 125 |
| 14:14–20 | 175 |
| 14:17, 18 | 171 |
| 14–18 | 207 |
| 14:18–19 | 111 |
| 14:19 | 172 |
| 15 | 109, 140n23, 175, 178 |
| 15, 16 | 183 |
| 15:1 | 175 |
| 15:1, 7 | 9 |
| 15:1–4 | 175 |
| 15:1—16:21 | 174–83 |
| 15:2 | 5, 9, 77, 176, 224 |
| 15:2–4 | 165n1 |
| 15:3 | 9 |
| 15:4 | 176, 205 |
| 15:5–6 | 128 |
| 15:5–8 | 11, 178 |
| 15:6 | 209 |
| 15:7 | 2 |
| 15:8 | 178, 194n4 |

Revelation (*continued*)

| | |
|---|---|
| 15–16 | 174 |
| 15–19 | 141 |
| 15:26 | 242 |
| 16 | 112, 175, 178 |
| 16, 19 | 213, 219 |
| 16:1, 19 | 9 |
| 16:1–21 | 11 |
| 16:2 | 5 |
| 16:2–3 | 2 |
| 16:5 | 9, 179 |
| 16:5–7 | 180 |
| 16:6 | 85n14, 195 |
| 16:7, 14 | 9 |
| 16:8 | 9 |
| 16:9 | 140n23, 194n4 |
| 16:12–16 | 219n23 |
| 16:13–16 | 219 |
| 16:13ff | 181 |
| 16:15 | 182, 195, 206n16, 241 |
| 16:17 | 227 |
| 16:18 | 77n15, 111, 127 |
| 16:18, 21 | 141 |
| 16:19 | 169 |
| 17 | 6, 167n8, 184, 185, 189, 193, 194, 196 |
| 17, 18 | 182, 202 |
| 17:1 | 185, 228 |
| 17:1–3 | 4, 129 |
| 17:1–8 | 104 |
| 17:1–18 | 11, 184–92, 184n1 |
| 17:1—18:24 | 202 |
| 17:1—19:5 | 184n1 |
| 17:2, 8 | 61 |
| 17:3 | 228 |
| 17:4 | 198, 228 |
| 17:6 | 180n19, 185, 187, 195 |
| 17:8 | 6, 57, 118, 159, 188 |
| 17:9–10 | 6 |
| 17:9–17 | 104 |
| 17:11 | 6, 190 |
| 17:12 | 196 |

| | |
|---|---|
| 17:14 | 9, 92, 104, 191, 209 |
| 17:15 | 191 |
| 17:16 | 197n13, 210n28 |
| 17:17 | 16, 198 |
| 17–18 | 9, 175 |
| 17:18 | 185 |
| 17–22 | 129 |
| 18 | 49n3, 168, 179, 184, 193, 194, 202, 203, 213 |
| 18:1 | 194, 194n4 |
| 18:1—19:5 | 184n1 |
| 18:1–24 | 193–200 |
| 18:2a | 193 |
| 18:2b | 193 |
| 18:3 | 193 |
| 18:4 | 193 |
| 18:5 | 193 |
| 18:6 | 193 |
| 18:7, 10, 15 | 118, 169 |
| 18:8 | 193 |
| 18:9–19 | 193 |
| 18:10, 17, 19 | 191 |
| 18:10–19 | 225 |
| 18:12 | 198 |
| 18:12, 16 | 228 |
| 18:12–13 | 198 |
| 18:18 | 170 |
| 18:18–19 | 198 |
| 18:20 | 193 |
| 18–20 | 213 |
| 18:21 | 112, 193 |
| 18:22c–23b | 193 |
| 18:23c | 193 |
| 18:24 | 9, 85n14, 93, 180n19, 193, 195, 199 |
| 19 | 9, 46, 50n5, 91, 141, 171, 182, 199, 202, 205, 208, 213, 216, 225, 228 |
| 19:1 | 194n4, 202 |
| 19:1–5 | 202 |
| 19:1–8 | 11, 202 |
| 19:1–21 | 11, 201–11 |
| 19:1–24 | 11 |

| | | | |
|---|---|---|---|
| 19:2 | 180n19, 203 | 20:8 | 2 |
| 19:3 | 170 | 20:9 | 219 |
| 19:4 | 76n13, 203 | 20:10 | 118, 169 |
| 19:6 | 2, 141, 166, 204, 204n9 | 20:11 | 219 |
| 19:6, 15 | 9 | 20:11–15 | 11, 43 |
| 19:6–9 | 69 | 20:12, 15 | 57, 159 |
| 19:7 | 204, 225 | 20:12–15 | 224 |
| 19:7–8 | 145 | 20:13 | 225 |
| 19:8 | 209 | 20:13–14 | 94 |
| 19:8, 14 | 209n25 | 21 | 241 |
| 19:9 | 206, 206n16, 241 | 21, 22 | 224 |
| 19:9, 13 | 16 | 21:1 | 220, 224 |
| 19:9–10 | 202 | 21:1, 4 | 226 |
| 19:9–21 | 11 | 21:1–8 | 11, 224 |
| 19:10 | 136, 188, 239 | 21:1–17 | 223–33 |
| 19:11 | 207, 208 | 21:1—22:5 | 11, 36, 202, 224 |
| 19:11–16 | 91, 207n20 | 21:2 | 166, 225 |
| 19:11—20:6 | 213n1 | 21:3 | 158n10, 225, 226 |
| 19:11—21:8 | 224 | 21:5 | 226 |
| 19:12 | 207 | 21:6 | 9, 235, 241, 242 |
| 19:13–20 | 213n1 | 21:8 | 221, 227, 242 |
| 19:14 | 191, 206, 209 | 21:9–10 | 4, 145 |
| 19:15 | 9, 97, 211n31 | 21:9–27 | 11 |
| 19:15, 21 | 9 | 21:10 | 228 |
| 19:17–21 | 219 | 21:11, 23 | 194n4 |
| 19:18 | 210n28 | 21:11, 23–24 | 198 |
| 19:20 | 5 | 21:12 | 229 |
| 19–20 | 9 | 21:14 | 6, 229 |
| 19–21 | 9, 211 | 21:15–17 | 133n3 |
| 19–22 | 219 | 21:16–21 | 230 |
| 20 | 41, 141, 150n19, 213, 215n11, 221 | 21:17 | 230 |
| | | 21:18, 21 | 205 |
| 20:1 | 214 | 21:18–21 | 228 |
| 20:1–2 | 214 | 21:22 | 9 |
| 20:1–3 | 11, 215 | 21–22 | 219 |
| 20:1–15 | 11, 212–22 | 21:23 | 238 |
| 20:2 | 215 | 21:27 | 57, 159, 242 |
| 20:2, 8, 10 | 9 | 22 | 9, 15, 106, 165, 234, 237 |
| 20:3 | 213n1 | 22:1 | 235 |
| 20:4 | 5, 9, 16, 136, 216, 216n13, 217, 218 | 22:1–5 | 11, 234 |
| | | 22:1–21 | 234–43 |
| 20:4–6 | 11 | 22:2 | 236, 241 |
| 20:5 | 216, 216n13 | 22:4 | 165 |
| 20:6 | 206n16, 218, 241 | 22:5 | 238 |
| 20:7 | 218 | 22:6 | 238 |
| 20:7–9 | 214 | 22:6, 9–10, 18–19 | 235 |
| 20:7–10 | 11 | 22:6–7 | 4 |

Revelation *(continued)*

| 22:6–21 | 11, 234 |
| 22:7 | 239, 241 |
| 22:7, 12, 14 | 235 |
| 22:7, 14 | 206n16 |
| 22:8 | 3, 188 |
| 22:8–10 | 235 |
| 22:9 | 3 |
| 22:11 | 237 |
| 22:12 | 240 |
| 22:13 | 9 |
| 22:14 | 106, 241 |
| 22:14–15 | 172 |
| 22:15 | 221 |
| 22:16 | 242, 242n25 |
| 22:17 | 242 |
| 22:18 | 235 |
| 22:19 | 243 |
| 22:20–22 | 243 |
| 22:21 | 243 |

## Apocrypha

*Didache*

| 9:5 | 242 |

## Early Christian Writings

Augustine

*City of God*

| xviii.18 | 195n8 |

Clement of Alexandria

*1st Ep. of Clement to the Corinth.*

| 1.1 | 5n19 |

*Paedagogus*

| 2.108 | 4 |

Eusebius

*History of Eusebius*

| 3.20 | 5n18 |

Ignatius

*Epistle to the Ephesians*

| 7.1 | 242 |

Irenaeus

*Against Heresies*

| 2.22.5 | 22 |
| 4.20.11 | 4 |

Martyr, Justin

*Dialogue with Trypho*

| 81.4 | 4 |

Origen

*De Principalis*

| 1.2.10 | 4 |

Tertullian

*Against Marcion*

| 3.14.3 | 4 |

## Greco-Roman Literature

Pliny the Younger

*Epistles*

| 10.96–97 | 5n17 |